UNIVERSITY
AND RESEARCH
LIBRARIES
IN JAPAN AND
THE UNITED
STATES

Proceedings of the First
Japan-United States Conference
on Libraries and Information
Science in Higher Education , 1st, Tokyo, 1969
Tokyo, 15–19 May 1969

Edited by
Thomas R. Buckman
University Librarian
Northwestern University

Yukihisa Suzuki
Head, Asia Library
University of Michigan

Warren M. Tsuneishi
Chief of the Orientalia
Division, Library of Congress

AMERICAN
LIBRARY
ASSOCIATION

Chicago 1972

Library of Congress Cataloging in Publication Data

Japan-U.S. Conference on Libraries and Information
  Science in Higher Education, 1st, Tokyo, 1969.
    University and research libraries in Japan and the
United States.

    Includes bibliographical references.
    1. Libraries, University and college—Japan—
Congresses. 2. Libraries, University and college—
United States—Congresses. 3. Research libraries—
Japan—Congresses. 4. Research libraries—United
States—Congresses. I. Buckman, Thomas R., ed.
II. Tsuneishi, Warren Michio, 1921-   ed.
III. Suzuki, Yukihisa, ed. IV. American Library
Association. V. Title.
Z675.U5J35   1969   027.752   76-178155
ISBN 0–8389–3111–1 (1972)

International Standard Book
Number 0–8389–3111–1 (1972)

Library of Congress Catalog Card
Number 76–178155
Copyright © 1972 by the
American Library Association

Printed in the United States of America

Contents

iv – Contents

Preface

This volume contains forty-seven contributions by American and Japanese librarians, educators, and scholars which seek to define issues in library and information science as they relate to higher education and research in both countries.

They range over a diversity of subjects and yet each of the general and specific topics has its important place in efforts to enhance the flow of information across national borders.

Maintaining the interchange of information between countries presupposes and requires strong national and local information delivery systems. At every major point along an international network, there must be a setting of institutional vitality and support within which libraries and information centers may work, as well as the professional competence to operate them, if they are to be responsive to international needs. Accordingly, the writers whose papers follow have addressed themselves not only to the international aspects of library and information science, but also to the national and local characteristics of their work, all of which may ultimately have an effect on the user's access to information.

In the relatively brief span since these papers were delivered there have been some rather decided changes within the information professions and in the conditions determining their development. Nonetheless, there is in these pages a valuable summation of views by qualified practitioners and users at the close of a decade of important advances in the library and information fields. It is a valid surveyor's benchmark against which may be measured attempts to achieve many of the goals still ahead of us.

Thus we are hopeful that the essays gathered here will be of continuing interest not only to those concerned with books and libraries in Japan and the United States, but also to librarians and information scientists in many other countries.

As Chairman of the U.S. Planning Committee, I am pleased to record my warm thanks to the Japanese Organizing Committee for its generous arrangements, and to the Council on Library Resources, Inc., and the Ford Foundation for their financial support of the Conference. I am especially indebted to my coeditors, Yukihisa Suzuki and Warren Tsuneishi, who shared responsibility for preparing the manuscripts for publication, and to Richard Gray of A.L.A. Publishing Services.

THOMAS R. BUCKMAN

Explanatory Note
on the Romanization of
Names and Titles

Romanization. In the representation of Japanese names, book and periodical titles, etc., in roman letters the modified Hepburn system is employed. However, the wishes of an author who uses another system of romanization in the spelling of his name have been respected; and Tokyo, Osaka, and Kyoto are given in their conventional anglicized forms.

Names of persons. The names of Japanese authors and participants are generally recorded in the order given name–family name.

Names of corporate bodies. The names of corporate bodies are generally given in their English form followed, when deemed necessary, by the name in roman letters, e.g., Imperial Library (Teikoku Toshokan). In the case of well-known bodies, only the English form of the name is given, e.g., Tokyo University, National Diet Library. In the case of lesser-known bodies, some of which are not known to have English names, the Japanese romanized name is given, followed in brackets by a supplied English name, e.g., Nippon Shin'yō Chōsa Kabushiki Kaisha [Nippon Credit Research Company].

Titles of books, periodicals, laws. In general the romanized Japanese title is given first, with the English title in parentheses if it is known to appear in the piece. If the book, periodical, or law has no English title, a translation is supplied in brackets:

Toshokan Zasshi (*Library Journal*)

Kokuritsu Kokkai Toshokan Hō (*National Diet Library Law*)

Seifu Kankōbutsu Geppō [*Monthly Report of Government Publications*].

Part 1

BACKGROUND: U.S.–JAPAN CULTURAL INTERACTIONS

A Progress Report

Thomas R. Buckman
*University Librarian,
Northwestern University*

Although relationships between Japanese and American libraries can be traced back more than a hundred years, they have been particularly significant since the end of World War II. Both before and after World War II, the Rockefeller Foundation aided in the reconstruction of the Tokyo University Library building, and later in the development of services. A number of American advisers were invited to Japan to assist in these projects, as well as for the purpose of establishing the National Diet Library and the Japan Library School at Keiō University.

In the postwar years there have been many contacts between public and special librarians of the two countries. Intermittently, a number of Japanese librarians and students of library science have come to the United States for training and observation of American library practice. In the medical library field the interchange of professional people and information has been very active; in cooperation with the Keio Medical School Library, the National Library of Medicine established a center in Tokyo for the indexing of Japanese medical literature. Through the years the U.S. Department of State and the American Embassy have taken an informed interest in Japanese library development and have aided in sending Japanese librarians to the United States. The directors of the International Relations Office of the American Library Association have visited Japan from time to time, calling at libraries in many parts of the country, participating in seminars, and making themselves available for consultation.

In 1963 Douglas W. Bryant, the university librarian of Harvard University, spent two months in Japan visiting and lecturing at Japanese universities. His seminar discussions on university library problems, arranged by Professor Hideo Kishimoto, then director of the University of Tokyo Library, were attended by hundreds of people at most of the major universities in Japan and at other centers. His mission was well received and encouraged Professor

1

Kishimoto's initiatives looking toward the further modernization of Japanese university libraries. On his return Mr. Bryant recommended to the American Library Association an ongoing American program of liaison with Japanese libraries to build further on the enthusiasm and momentum that had been generated in Japan by his tour and by the leadership and reform measures proposed by Professor Kishimoto. Professor Kishimoto's death in 1964 brought these plans temporarily to a halt.

In 1966 the Third Japan–U.S. Conference on Cultural and Educational Interchange, meeting in Tokyo, issued a statement in its final communiqué calling on the American Library Association to aid in the development of a program of cooperation between American and Japanese libraries. Exchanges of personnel, mutual help in their training, and help in the selection and acquisition of materials were mentioned specifically.

During the following year Mr. Bryant and Dr. Lester Asheim, who was then director of the ALA International Relations Office, began to explore possibilities. Early in 1967 Mr. Bryant and Dr. Asheim asked me as the new director of the International Relations Office to visit Japan to reassess the situation and to determine what steps might be taken toward a program of development and cooperation.

My visit revealed an interest on the part of many Japanese librarians in a binational conference and in the regular interchange of people. On my return I recommended the formation of a permanent American group to be concerned with professional relationships with Japanese libraries, and shortly thereafter there was appointed an ALA Advisory Committee for Liaison with Japanese Libraries, all of whose members had visited Japan in a professional capacity on one or more occasions and had developed a growing knowledge of the Japanese library world.

In April 1967 a conference plan was discussed with the American committee of scholars and specialists responsible for the general Japan–U.S. Conference on Cultural and Educational Interchange. It was recommended that there be further visits on both sides prior to a conference. In the next two years, nine prominent Japanese library leaders visited the United States to observe American libraries and to meet with their U.S. colleagues. These were individually patterned study tours, funded partly from U.S. and partly from Japanese sources. The representatives from Japan included the director and a senior officer of the Tokyo University Library; the director and two senior officials of the National Diet Library; an official from the Ministry of Education concerned with university libraries; the director of the Osaka University Library; the director of a private research institute library; and a special librarian from Osaka.

In February 1967 Mr. John Lorenz, Deputy Librarian of Congress, visited Tokyo to discuss with officials of the National Diet Library possible Japanese participation in the U.S. National Program for Acquisitions and Cataloging. This program was later successfully implemented.

Concurrently with these efforts, two American scholarly organizations continued to pursue their interest in Japanese librarianship and publication, particularly with reference to the development of American resources (both staff and collections) supporting Japanese studies in the United States. These were the former American Committee on U.S.–Japan Educational and Cultural Cooperation and the permanent Committee on East Asian Libraries (CEAL) of the Association of Asian Studies, Inc. Both were informed of the plan of the American Library Association for a program of liaison and were in agreement with its general aims. The Committee on U.S.–Japan Educational and Cultural Cooperation endorsed support of a second ALA mission to Japan in late 1967. Two members of the ALA Advisory Committee, incidentally, are members of CEAL and represent other units concerned with Japanese resources in the United States, e.g., the Foreign Acquisitions Subcommittee on the Far East of the Association of Research Libraries. Thus, all of the major American organizations concerned were involved directly or indirectly in the planning for further Japan–U.S. library cooperation.

In April 1967 two Japanese library leaders were invited to the library divisional meeting of the 27th International Congress of Orientalists in Ann Arbor, Michigan, in August 1967, convened by Mr. Yukihisa Suzuki, a member of the ALA Advisory Committee and then Head, Asia Library, University of Michigan. Discussions with several Japanese representatives were held in Ann Arbor to discuss forms of binational library cooperation.

In November 1967 a three-man ALA mission was sent to Japan for further exploration of possible cooperative and developmental activities. The members of the party included Mr. Suzuki; Dr. Warren M. Tsuneishi, Chief, Orientalia Division, Library of Congress; and myself. This group attended the Japan Library Association (JLA) conference in Kanazawa and met with the council of directors of the National University Libraries Association. The responses continued to be favorable, and therefore it was decided that the present binational Conference be held. Planning was started immediately and has continued to the present. Mr. Suzuki and Mr. Foster E. Mohrhardt attended the next JLA conference in Sapporo in September 1968 and also met with the Japanese organizing committee of this Conference.

In the United States the ALA Advisory Committee constituted itself as the U.S. organizing group responsible for selection of the American delegates, securing of funds for their expenses, and mutual planning with the Japanese organizers. Support was generously provided by the Ford Foundation and the Council on Library Resources. The Xerox Corporation supported a part of the cost of the Conference site through its library service companies, R. R. Bowker and University Microfilms.

The 1969 binational Conference is but one element in a wider program of liaison and interchange which has these principal aims:

To provide *continuity* of leadership; exchange of professional information; and liaison, through frequent correspondence and personal contacts between the Japanese and U.S. committees which are designated to be channels of communication, in the field of library and information science in the two countries

To assure a sense of *equal partnership* in pursuit of solutions to library problems which both countries share, but which may be different in degree and emphasis in each country

To *involve those who make policy decisions* affecting university libraries, i.e., government officials, university presidents, deans, senior professors, and others; and to urge their support of strong library systems

To provide *opportunities for the further professional growth* of capable practicing librarians in both countries through an interchange of personnel

To provide, on request, *consultants and advisers* to libraries in both countries for specific tasks in areas such as library automation, processing, development of Japanese collections in the United States, establishment of professional schools, etc.

To develop *cooperative projects* in libraries and information centers where circumstances are favorable

To widen the scope of the liaison program to include *public and school libraries*

To *maintain the momentum* generated by the recent interchanges between the two countries and to turn to mutual advantage the present cordial relationships and community of interest existing among American and Japanese librarians.

We feel that significant progress has been made in the past five years, and that this Conference is the beginning—the gateway to more specific accomplishment of great potential benefit to libraries in Japan and the U.S. We look upon it as a means not only of exchanging ideas but also of discovering and developing practical and workable forms of library cooperation.

Japanese University Libraries Today

Yosoji Itō
President, Shizuoka College of Pharmacy

I should like to touch briefly on some of the problem areas in Japanese higher education, especially with reference to the university libraries existing in the country. In spite of the fact that the library is a nucleus and an indispensable functional unit of the university, it is legally excluded from the administrative organization of the university; it also is not considered a constituent element of the university. In the School Education Law there are provisions with regard to research institutes attached to universities, as well as with regard to lectures open to the public. Yet there is no mention at all of the library. Accordingly, even in the University Chartering Standards of the Ministry of Education, the provisions for libraries are very limited. It is regrettable that there is this lack of basic understanding in the law and in these chartering standards supposedly established to provide realistic objectives for education and research. Further, the chartering standards of the university are consistent in their emphasis on departments of instruction. In these circumstances, it is quite impossible to carry out the aims of comprehensive education required in the new university system.

In today's university, which consists of rather isolated departments, the effect or value of comprehensive education can be actualized *only* through the work of libraries. Yet the library is itself regarded as an isolated facility and its role and function are given little attention. This relative neglect is well expressed in the National School Charter. Here the idea is that the library, rather than being an inte-gral part of the university, is nothing more than a unit attached to the university. This idea also is apparent in the administration of the university.

In the rules regarding the Council of Public Universities, there is no provision that academic librarians be given academic recognition. It is stated that, if necessary, the director of the library may be added to the membership of the Council, as may the director of the hospital attached to the university. There is something wrong with the idea that the director of the university library, who is directly concerned with the education and research of the university as a whole, should be treated in this context in the same way as the director of the university hospital, which is in fact nothing more than a part of the department of medicine of the university.

A new school law was enacted in 1947. In the older university system an ordinance provided that the purpose of the university was to teach the theory and application of the academic disciplines. Its chief function, therefore, was to train researchers. But in the new school system the university was to be transformed. Its new purpose was to teach and carry on research in the theory and application of academic disciplines in order to contribute to the development of culture. It was further stated that the new universities would be established to teach extensive knowledge in academic disciplines and to contribute to the development of intellectual and moral capacities. However, at the time of the school reform in 1949 the universities of the older system were not transformed as intended, nor was the substance of study modified to conform to the purpose of new universities. Instead, the traditional ideas were carried to the new systems intact. Greater priority was thus given to professional education than to comprehensive education. It appears that the university in the new system is far from that provided by the school law, in which professional education was subordinate to general education.

I understand that in the United States the system of higher education has always placed great importance on the role and function of the library. Because we adopted the American system in our new universities, we should also have followed the American system in placing greater emphasis on the library as the foundation of education. Only by this means could we realize the ideal of general and comprehensive education. The administration of the new university should likewise have been planned so that the library might contribute effectively to the stated ideal of education. The reality is quite different. The construction and consolidation of equipment and facilities, of classrooms, gymnasia, and buildings of universities were given priority, and only after this work was completed were the conceptual problems of the universities taken up. This applies to both public and private universities in Japan.

I think the responsibility for such wrong directions and faulty guidelines lies with us, the teachers. It is needless to repeat that the mission of a university, under the old form, was carried out through continuing and ceaseless research by the faculty. In the older system, education was identical with the research of the faculty. Accordingly, the faculty member did not have to be interested in teaching so long as he devoted himself to research. In the new system this idea must be amended a little. The faculty is expected to exert as much energy and to spend as much time in the instruction of students as in research. I think it is also within the responsibility of the faculty in concert with the administration, to take measures for the improvement of university governance and management.

This is an urgent matter that faces us at the time of the centenary of modern Japan. There are many ways of making basic improvements. Above all we must first consolidate the facilities of the libraries so that they can function fully and efficiently. We have to correct the patterns of instruction in which classroom work is given almost exclusive priority. These changes will make the library a more important functional unit and enable students and faculty to cooperate better in achieving their common aims.

The locus of education is not only the classrooms or the laboratories. The library should also be regarded by faculty, librar-

ians, and administrators as one of the chief places for study and investigation, and should be utilized to this end. Those of us who hold office in the universities, whether they are public, private, or national, have the ongoing task of persuading the administration that the library is indeed vital to the educational process. Through this effort, I think that the understanding of the role of libraries on the part of the administration and faculty has increased in the past decade. However, it is regrettable that we still have not reached a complete understanding. We need a closer and more detailed view of how libraries aid and support the education of students in the United States, and therefore, as opportunities permit, we attempt to study the American system through visits to libraries in the United States.

Now I wish to turn to the background and development of plans for this Conference. Mr. Thomas R. Buckman, who was then director of the International Relations Office of the American Library Association, came to Japan in February 1967 to observe the state of the libraries. He discussed with Japanese librarians the possibility of greater cooperation between the libraries of the two nations. As a consequence of his mission, it was decided to set up a Japanese committee for this purpose. It was later decided to hold a conference on matters of interest to university and research librarians in the two countries. At the time I was director of the Tokyo University Library and chairman of the Council of National University Libraries of Japan, and thus I was keenly interested in this work.

In April 1967 the ALA Subcommittee for Liaison with Japanese Libraries was organized with Mr. Douglas Bryant, University Librarian, Harvard University, as chairman. Members included Dean Raynard Swank, University of California; Thomas R. Buckman, University Librarian, Northwestern University; Dr. Warren Tsuneishi, Chief, Orientalia Division, Library of Congress; and Mr. Yukihisa Suzuki, Head, Asia Library, University of Michigan. Subsequently Mr. Buckman became chairman. Recently this subcommittee was renamed the ALA Advisory Committee for Liaison with Japanese Libraries. The committee has served as the U.S. organizing committee for this conference.

At about the same time, on 25 April 1967, a Japanese planning group met at the University of Tokyo. The Council of Public University Libraries expressed its wish to cooperate actively in the planning of the conference. Thereafter I attended the ALA conference in San Francisco and took part in a meeting of the ALA Advisory Committee on June 28. Three points were discussed: the intention to promote cooperation among all types of libraries in both countries; the desirability of commencing the program with cooperation among university libraries; and the establishment of a Japanese organizing committee as soon as possible.

When I returned home I discussed the establishment of the counterpart liaison committee with my colleagues and concluded that at this point it would be best to organize it within the Japan Library Association. I requested that JLA proceed with the matter. However, progress was slow. Mr. Buckman later sent Mr. Satoshi Saitō a letter of formal opinion with regard to the plan of cooperation. In November 1967 an ALA mission came to Japan to attend the All-Japan Library Conference at Kanazawa. The ALA mission, headed by Mr. Buckman and including Mr. Suzuki and Dr. Tsuneishi, met with the directors of the two national councils for national and public university libraries and of the Association of Private University Libraries on 22 November at Tokyo University Library and discussed the projected Japan-U.S. conference on university libraries to be held in 1968. We exchanged candid views and came to the following conclusions: first, that it would be desirable to have regularly recurring conferences; second, that Japan would ask for financial assistance from the government and for recognition from the Japan Science Council and the Ministry of Education counterpart committee of the Japan-U.S. Conference on Cultural and Educational Interchange.

It was ultimately agreed to hold the first conference in 1969. The U.S. delegates at this time suggested several topics for discussion, and the Japanese side commented on them. Initially it was intended that the conference be deliberative, with a small number of people attending, including a few observers. However, final details were to be determined through consultation between representatives of the two countries and, in Japan, through joint meetings not only of the directors of libraries or librarians but also of presidents, department or division chiefs, or university administrators or those responsible for the university chartering for the national universities (i.e., the directors of schools or officials of the Ministry of Education), and, for the private universities, those representing local government.

To prepare for the conference, one delegate from each of the national, public, and private universities was appointed to the planning body, and the national universities nominated me as the chairman. Those attending the meeting on 22 November were Messrs. Kanaya, Itō, Tomonari, Shishido, Miyaji and Kitagawa from the national universities; from the public universities, Mr. Kitajima; and from the private universities, Messrs. Okumura, Sasaki, Takai, Itō, and Daidō.

University libraries in Japan are members of one of three separate and independent organizations, according to their status. Thus, for national university libraries there is the Council of National University Libraries; for public (i.e., municipal and prefectural) and private university libraries there are the Council of Public University Libraries and the Association of Private University Libraries, respectively. Unfortunately, in the past each association has carried out its own independent activities, with no coordination or cooperation among the three. For purposes of organizing the present binational Conference involving university libraries of all types, cooperation among the three Japanese associations was a prime requisite, and it was decided therefore that the participation of all would be sought. However, because of the timing of the meetings of the three associations—the resolutions of each organization through general meetings being required for participation—it was necessary to begin planning within the Council of National University Libraries, and this group therefore provided the initial impetus for the binational Conference.

We drafted a plan as follows: the name of the Conference, in Japanese, was to be Nichi-Bei Daigaku Toshokan Kaigi; the conference period was originally to be the latter part of November 1968, in Tokyo; there would be a planning committee under the Council of National University Libraries; and this planning committee would prepare detailed plans. Because at this time we could not expect any financial assistance from the government, it would be necessary to solicit donations from private sources. A secretariat would be established, attached to the Tokyo University Library. This was the outline made at the first meeting.

The opinion of the Council of Public University Libraries was sought, and in May the Council decided to cooperate with the other associations and participate in the conference. The same resolution was subsequently adopted by the Council of National University Libraries, and as a consequence the two councils formally shook hands. As for the Association of Private University Libraries, the board had decided to participate, but since its general meeting was not expected to convene until 30 August 1968, the Association sent temporary delegates to the committee. The planning committee, which thus included representatives of all of the national, public, and private university libraries, started to work in June. A member of the board of each association was appointed as a committee member. The planning committee formed a general affairs subcommittee, and planning and fund-raising subcommittees were established.

The secretariat, established in the Tokyo University Library, was headed by Mr. Daitsu Satake. The first meeting of the organizing committee was held on 20 October and many decisions were made. The time of the Conference would be May 1969, and the place, the Tokyo Prince Hotel. Funds would have to be raised as soon as possible to make this conference a reality. As many observers as possible would be permitted to attend. All these matters, which were generally agreed upon by the U.S. planning committee, were confirmed officially. The goal for funds was set, and the expenditures outlined. Also, assisting organizations and advisors were recommended by the organizing committee and formal requests to them were made. Thus, some eight months before the Conference, the organizing committee began its work. Subsequently we met with Foster E. Mohrhardt, the former president of the American Library Association, and Mr. Yukihisa Suzuki, then director of the Asia Library at the University of Michigan, both of whom attended the Japan Library Association Conference in September 1968. We took advantage of this opportunity to discuss problems and to exchange views with regard to Conference plans.

In November the unrest among Tokyo University students became more and more severe, and the main university library was blockaded by the students. Thus very little progress in preparing for the Conference was made before 20 January, when the blockade was lifted. At this time student rebellion spread to other universities, including Mr. Itagaki's university and Mr. Miyaji's university.* But, in spite of the troubles at these universities, these two subcommittee chairman continued their efforts in preparation for this conference.

Though it is regrettable that the first Conference should be held in such unsettled circumstances, the attendance by more than 300 participants is indicative of how interested we are. Expectations for the success of the Conference are high. We hope there will be, as a result, progress toward greater educational and cultural exchange based upon cooperation between Japan and the United States.

---

*Yoichi Itagaki, Director, Hitotsubashi University Library; Tōru Miyaji, Director, Osaka University Library.

The Shape of International Cooperation

Yoshikatsu Kōno
Director, National Diet Library

It is an impressive sight to see the highest authorities of American university and research libraries meeting here in Japan. I confess that I was greatly surprised when looking at the list of American participants, and even feared that with this galaxy of eminent people coming to Japan, the functions of the American libraries might be paralyzed. As everyone is well aware, an enormous effort was made by librarians and library organizations of the United States to assist the recovery and development of Japanese libraries during the postwar period. You are, of course, well aware that the establishment of the National Diet Library (NDL) was directly planned on the recommendation of the U.S. Library Mission consisting of two eminent American librarians, Mr. Verner W. Clapp and the late Dr. Charles Brown. To express our gratitude, we invited Mr. and Mrs. Clapp in the fall of last year to the ceremony in which we celebrated the completion of the National Diet Library building and the twentieth anniversary of the opening of the library.

Shortly after the establishment of NDL, Dr. Robert B. Downs of the University of Illinois Library came to Japan to give detailed recommendations on technical services; he made invaluable contributions to the development of the library. This kind of help was not confined to NDL alone. For example, the cooperation of the American Library Association was largely instrumental in the establishment of the library science department at Keiō University and its subsequent enlargement to include a graduate program. And I must not fail to mention the liberal assistance extended by the Rockefeller Foundation and the Ford Foundation for the reorganization and enlargement of university libraries in Japan, including the Tokyo University Library. I know well that highly competent advice and guidance were given in particular for the modernization of the Tokyo University Library by Dr. Keyes D. Metcalf, former University Librarian of Harvard University, and by Mr. Douglas Bryant, the present librarian, who is in attendance today. These are only a few of the numerous instances which might be mentioned.

It is well known that Japanese libraries are in many ways indebted to those of the United States. It is gratifying to note that in recent years cooperation between the libraries of the two nations has become more and more extensive. NDL is exchanging full sets of official publications with the Library of Congress and the University of California at Berkeley. It is worth remembering, however, that the Japanese effort for international exchange of official publications dates back to the year 1875, when such exchanges were first conducted between the Smithsonian Institution and the Foreign Ministry of Japan. If we reflect that nearly a century has elapsed since that time, perhaps we must say that the present state of exchanges is still not wholly satisfactory. Be that as it may, there are now 104 U.S. institutions with which NDL has exchange relations for selected official and nonofficial publications.

It is a great pleasure for me that we are engaged in close and conscientious cooperation with the Library of Congress in the project known as Shared Cataloging, a plan of global proportions for the acquisition of books and their central cataloging. The Tokyo Office of the Library of Congress, established exactly a year ago to further this project, is functioning well. In February 1967, when I was told of this ambitious project by Mr. John Lorenz, Deputy Librarian of Congress, I felt that this was precisely the work in which a dream of all librarians throughout the world would be realized. My feeling was confirmed in discussion with Quincy Mumford, Librarian of Congress, in August 1968 when I visited the United States.

I remember at Christmastime of 1968 watching the flight of the spaceship *Apollo VIII* being televised. We Japanese were as much excited and impressed as the Americans. I was particularly struck at that time by the words of the space pilot—that the sight of the earth viewed from the moon, seen as a luminous ball, inspired with fresh realization the idea that on earth there is just one world.

Returning to our subject of librarianship, we might say that the Shared Cataloging Program is our nearest approach to the pilot's feeling. All international cooperation ought to be supported by this idea of the oneness of humanity. At the same time, obviously enough, the multiplicity of the differences of nations must be fully recognized. Proper respect for individual dignity and the appreciation of personality are indispensable conditions for the progress of free societies. In the same way, proper respect for the traditions and civilizations of all nations is the first prerequisite for the development of a better international society.

Those of you from the United States, I am sure, would enjoy the beauty of the Imperial Palace. I hope that when you visit there you will look closely at the walls. The walls are made of rock of widely different sizes and shapes, piled one on top of another. They form a remarkable contrast with the practice of Western architecture, which would generally employ a straight line of bricks, uniform either in size or in shape. Castles are found in many localities of Japan, and most of them are more than 300 years old. The stone walls have survived to this day in their elegant form despite the frequent earthquakes for which Japan is so famous. This is because proper respect has been paid to the individual peculiarities of the rocks that, in their turn, have served to strengthen the wall as a whole. To me the rocks and the Imperial Palace itself seem to suggest the ideal pattern for our international cooperation.

Japan–U.S. Cultural and Educational Interchange

Tatsuo Morito
President, Japan Library Association

In April 1968 the Fourth Japan–U.S. Conference on Cultural and Educational Interchange was held in Washington. The theme was "Education and Development in Advanced Societies." On that occasion, it was hoped that both our nations, which represent the modern societies on either side of the Pacific Ocean, would do their utmost for the furtherance of friendly relations between us and for the establishment of peace in Asia within the framework of education and culture. Nevertheless, we discovered that some discrepancies and difficulties in realizing these objectives existed, particularly among university professors in both countries.

The final communiqué adopted by the Third Japan–U.S. Conference, held in Tokyo, noted the presence of "a number of obstacles that hinder full and accurate understanding of the cultures of Japan and the United States on the part of the scholarly communities, such as the different university traditions, differences in scholarly methodology and learning techniques, and in the subtleties of political outlook that may modify or color joint scholarly objectives and influence or even inhibit their accomplishment."

Personally, as the president of the Japan Library Association, I believe we owe a great deal to the suggestions and assistance extended by the United States in fostering the remarkable progress in the organization of Japanese libraries after World War II; the growth and arrangement of university libraries, public libraries, school libraries, and special libraries; the progress of library science and the establishment of training schools for librarians; and, more significantly, the foundation of the National Diet Library and institutionalization of legislation concerning libraries. I should like to express my feeling of deep appreciation for this valuable assistance. Nearly a quarter of a century has passed since the end of World War II, and Japanese libraries are now facing a period in which they are called upon to make further progress to answer the increased demands of a continually developing society. Therefore I believe closer collaboration with the United States is needed more than ever before.

As regards university libraries, the first U.S. Education Mission to Japan, which was sent to Japan in 1946, stated in its *Report*[1] that university libraries are "essential for research and for the development of the individual student on all levels of higher education," and made several concrete proposals which called upon these libraries to carry out their functions more effectively, as follows:

> To make available to all students the resources of the country, we suggest that each university consider unifying and consolidating its collections, preparing a single union catalog. These, together with similar catalogs of collections of learned societies, might be incorporated in a master catalog to be maintained at some central agency. Thus might be achieved the basis of a national bibliography that would be of inestimable value to scholars in locating the books they want.
>
> A system of interlibrary loans should be instituted within Japan, and as soon as possible, the system of international exchange which prevailed before the war should be resumed.
>
> It would be useful, we think, for the university libraries of Japan to organize a professional association. A library school might also well be established preferably affiliated with a university that has good library facilities, in order to train professional personnel.

In 1947 I myself, as Minister of Education, was engaged in carrying out the so-called new university scheme. The principal character of this new scheme was a change from the German style formerly used in Japanese universities to the American style,

in compliance with which the credit system and general education curriculum were introduced. As a result of this basic reform, the importance and responsibility of libraries in research and education in universities were highlighted, and the fundamental reform of libraries also became an urgent matter in that period. In this field, along with the creative efforts of Japanese libraries, assistance from the United States was greatly needed. To this end, four Japan–U.S. Conferences on Cultural and Educational Interchange have been held. In each conference the problems of library administration and the exchange of staffs, materials, and technique have been discussed. It has been our sincere hope that by these means we could contribute to the advancement and growth of culture and education in both countries.

At the first Japan–U.S. Conference in 1962 the general problems of Japanese libraries were taken up, and it was recommended that library catalogs be more completely prepared, that interlibrary loan be encouraged, and that other library services be reorganized so that utilization of books and materials would be further facilitated.

The Third Conference in 1966, which concerned itself with the role of the universities in developing mutual understanding between the two countries, noted in its final communiqué in connection with university libraries:

> Both Japanese and American libraries encounter serious difficulties in dealing with materials from the other country. While their difficulties are different, both library systems could benefit through a program of exchanges of library personnel and mutual help in their training, and in the selection and acquisition of materials. The help of the American Library Association in the development of such cooperation would be welcome.
>
> Further study is also needed on the feasibility of a central collection of research material on America which could serve scholars throughout Japan as well as of improvements which can be made in the access which American scholars have to Japanese materials. Furthermore, in America the collection of Japanese mate-

rials must be expanded as rapidly as possible. In both cases, modern techniques of microfilming and reproduction deserve consideration.

Furthermore, the communiqué of the Fourth Conference in 1968 recommended the establishment of a permanent joint committee as one of the specific needs which were singled out for priority consideration. It stated these goals in connection with university libraries:

> In the field of library development and the exchange of published materials, the desirability in each country to work toward the establishment of one or more comprehensive libraries of materials published in the other country, to enrich a number of smaller collections primarily for undergraduate study, to establish an effective clearinghouse to assist libraries in both countries with bibliographic information and with acquisitions problems, particularly of official publications and other materials not available in regular commercial channels, to advance cooperative cataloging, to exchange library consultants and in-service trainees.

To be sure, the Japan–U.S. Conference on Cultural and Educational Interchange is not a special organ dealing solely with the problems of university libraries. However, I believe the conferences have so far made a considerable contribution to emphasizing the importance of university libraries in both countries and, although in very general terms, have paved the way toward desired improvements.

As an example of the effort for improvement of Japanese university libraries, I should like to mention the achievements of the late Professor Hideo Kishimoto of the University of Tokyo. He was one of my good friends and also one of the Japanese delegates to the conference. As a director of the University of Tokyo Library for five years, until he passed away in 1964, he literally devoted his life to modernizing his library as well as all university libraries in Japan, and achieved an epoch-making reform in this field. According to Dr. Kishimoto, "The university library is not a warehouse of books and old documents. Its mission lies not simply in the preservation of books, but rather in their active utilization. The ultimate goal of the reform, therefore, should be the reorganization of a university library along lines of scholarly utility." However, the fact that his effort for the reform of the university library should have begun from this basic modern concept, instead of aiming at it, clearly indicates the backwardness of Japanese university libraries at that time.

Among Americans who have helped us, we cannot forget the earnest cooperation of Dr. Keyes D. Metcalf, former librarian of the Harvard University Library, and Douglas W. Bryant, the present librarian of Harvard, who helped Dr. Kishimoto in his work of reform. In addition to them, we should note the names of Dr. Charles H. Brown, Chairman of the National Committee on Oriental Collections in the USA and Abroad, American Library Association; Dr. Verner Clapp, Chief Assistant Librarian of the Library of Congress; Dr. Robert Downs, Dean of Library Administration at the University of Illinois; Dr. Philip Keeney; and Dr. Robert Gitler, Director of the Japan Library School,* Faculty of Letters, Keiō University, in connection with the establishment of the National Diet Library, the creation of the library science program at Keiō University, and help with other problems of Japanese university libraries. Also I should mention the name of Dr. Charles Fahs, who was a director of the Rockefeller Foundation and later minister-counselor at the United States Embassy in Tokyo. His advice and cooperation were of great value to Japanese libraries.

As will be evident from what I have said so far, in spite of abundant advice and assistance from many people, Japanese university libraries cannot yet be said to have been satisfactorily modernized. Of course, individual universities, libraries, and library associations are constantly making important efforts for the reorganization of libraries. Also, the Ministry of Education, which is responsible for educational and cultural affairs, has instituted policies and

---

*Now called School of Library and Information Science.

has provided assistance through the creation of a special department in the Ministry which deals with the problems of university libraries and with such other matters as enactment of provisions for the modernization of university libraries; establishment of a junior college for the training of librarians; fundamental revision of the comprehensive catalog of academic journals; establishment of a document center in the field of humanities and social sciences; subsidizing of private university libraries; and so forth.

I should now like to mention five of the important items which need reform in our university libraries:

1. Generally speaking, there are many universities in which administrative policy recognizing the basic mission of university libraries is not yet firmly established. Consequently, research and teaching are not well balanced, and services to the undergraduate students who are the major users are often neglected. It would appear that this is one of the reasons for the radical student movements we see today.
2. The system of usage in common of library materials in a university is not well established, and the understanding that library materials are the common possession of the entire university is lacking even among faculty members.
3. Systematic access to basic reference books and books indispensable for library administration is lacking.
4. The system of library operation is neither rationalized, standardized, nor mechanized to a sufficient degree to meet the tremendous increase in the number of students and in the amount of scientific information.
5. The training of library personnel is insufficient.

It is my sincere hope that discussions during the Conference will contribute toward finding solutions to these problems with which our university libraries are confronted at this moment.

In connection with university libraries, I would like to inform you of my personal experience in Hiroshima. As you know, Hiroshima, along with Okinawa, is one of the most delicate spots in the U.S.–Japan relationship. I served as president of the University there for thirteen years after the war. At that time, it was my wish to see the city of Hiroshima changed from a city of the atomic bomb, with all the accompanying feelings of hostility and revenge, into a city of peace symbolic of reconciliation and friendship. I wanted to make Hiroshima University, as its spiritual core, the symbol of a peaceful school in a peaceful city. With this in mind, I sent letters to different universities of the world asking them to send books for the rehabilitation of the university library. I stated in the letter that we were planning to create an "International Peace Bibliotheca" in the Hiroshima University Library to serve as the basis of spiritual rehabilitation of the peaceful city of Hiroshima. I was thankful that my appeal was answered by many universities abroad. We have since received many books, with the largest contribution coming from American universities. Among others, the most substantial contributions were 8,000 volumes from the Library of Congress through the courtesy of Dr. Luther Evans, then the Librarian of Congress, who later became general secretary of UNESCO; 256 volumes from Columbia University; and 56 volumes from the American Library Association. On this occasion of the Japan–U.S. Conference, my thoughts go back to the warm hand of assistance extended to us in the rehabilitation of the Hiroshima University Library by the United States, and I should like to express my deep appreciation in this connection.

Finally, I would like at this point to refer to a report entitled *Policy Recommendation on Measures to Meet Problems Facing University Education,** which was recently sub-

*Editor's note: A tentative English translation of the document bearing this title and dated 30 April 1969 was attached as an appendix to the paper by Dr. Morito, but it is not included here. The Japanese text was published as a report of the Chūō Kyōiku Shingikai under title: *Tōmensuru daigaku kyōiku no kadai ni taiō suru tame no hōsaku ni tsuite* (Tokyo: Monbusho, 1969). 88p.

mitted to the Minister of Education by the Central Council for Education (Chūō Kyōiku Shingikai), of which I am presently serving as president.

The new university scheme which started as an integral part of postwar educational reform in Japan was an imported one, borrowed from the model of American universities. Ironically, for the last two or three years, radical student movements accompanied by squatting, blockading, and violence have been exported from Japan to American universities. Yasuda Hall of the University of Tokyo, which has long played an eminent role in the academic life of Japanese universities, has been transformed for several months from an ivory tower to a citadel of violence. This symbolizes only too clearly the nature of the crisis in Japanese universities. Similar events have spread in leading American universities, such as Harvard, Columbia, and California. The freedom and autonomy of universities are thus being threatened, not from the outside, but by violence from within.

The *Policy Recommendation on Measures to Meet Problems Facing University Education*, which was drafted with such national and international developments in mind, consists of the five following chapters:

1. Causes of the present disturbances in universities and the themes for this report
2. Expectations for parties concerned in settling university problems
3. Decision-making and executive procedures in universities
4. The status and role of students in universities
5. Responsibilities of universities and of the government for the termination of the present disturbance.

This report, dealing with university problems and countermeasures for them, has been very well received by the general public as the most timely and concrete document on the subject. Although the universities of the United States and Japan differ in their substance, tradition, and social conditions, this report may also be of some interest to your university people. I commend it to you in the hope that it may come to the attention of universities in the United States through the good offices of the American Library Association.

NOTE

[1]U.S. Education Mission to Japan, *Report of the United States Education Mission to Japan*; submitted to the Supreme Commander for the Allied Powers, Tokyo, 30 March 1946 (Washington, D.C.: Govt. Print. Off., 1946). A second report was issued in 1950.

Part 2

ROLE OF UNIVERSITY LIBRARIES IN HIGHER EDUCATION

Library Roles in American Higher Education

Logan Wilson
President, American Council on Education

In considering the relations between libraries and educational institutions, it may be useful to review briefly the changing functions of libraries and librarians. In America the first libraries were rather limited book collections for even more limited circles of readers. Perhaps inevitably, the early librarian was thought of primarily as a guardian or human watchdog. One of his first duties was to preserve from harm the scarce and valuable commodities in his custody. Instead of trying to put books and periodicals into as many hands as possible, the librarian's main task apparently was to keep them out of the wrong hands.

An amusing account of the role of the early American librarian is to be found in *The Old Librarian's Almanack*, alleged to have been written in 1773 by one Jared

Bean. Some of his admonitions are as follows:

> Keep your Books behind stout Gratings, and in no wise let any Person come at them to take them from the Shelf except yourself.

> It were better that no Person enter the Library (save the Librarian Himself) and that the Books Be kept in Safety, than that one Book be lost, or others Misplac'd. Guard well your Books—this is always your foremost Duty.

> Question each Applicant closely. See that he be a Person of good Reputation, scholarly Habits, sober and courteous Demeanour. Any mere Trifler, a Person that would Dally with Books, or seek in them shallow Amusement, may be Dismiss'd without delay.

Our old librarian goes on to caution against admitting to the library anyone younger than 20 years, advises strong suspicions of all women, and the complete exclusion of politicians, astrologers, teachers of false knowledge, fanatic preachers, and refugees. He further counsels the true librarian to cast out and destroy all books merely frivolous and empty of serious meaning. Finally, he praises the librarian as one who "lives protected, avaricious neither of money nor of worldly fame, and happy in the goodliest of all occupations—the pursuit of wisdom."

With the expansion of education and the growth of knowledge, the librarian emerged from his initial role as guardian of carefully culled knowledge for the select few into a second, predominant role. In this second stage he may be described as the omnivorous collector of practically anything in print. This period saw the rise of American public, college, and university libraries from the base of the subscription library. All over the United States libraries were established as rather indiscriminate repositories of miscellaneous information. The growth was often an unplanned, mushroom development, and librarians were for the most part essentially amateur rather than professional workers. The collector-librarian was (and to some extent still is) in his heyday. Too frequently little attention was paid to real needs, and even in college and university libraries quantities of books were gathered and housed with a cavalier disregard for the comfort, convenience, or requirements of those to be served. The number of titles steadily mounted, cataloging grew progressively more complex and expensive, and the omnivorous collector-librarian was as happy as a miser who gathers unto himself a large hoard.

American librarians are quite familiar with the assertion that if this tendency continues unchecked, university campuses will be as filled with libraries as the landscape of China is with cemeteries. Several decades ago somebody pointed out that the then current rate of growth of the Yale University Library would in the year 2040 result in a book collection numbering more than 200,000,000 volumes, occupying 6,000 miles of shelves, and requiring 6,000 librarians merely to do the cataloging.

The present-day librarian is neither a mere custodian of books nor an omnivorous collector of miscellaneous printed works. On the campus he must and does work closely with subject-matter specialists in teaching and in research. If his library is modern and well designed, it is a convenient and inviting place for students, as well as for more advanced scholars and researchers, to work with and enjoy books. Moreover, the confines of the library contain not only books, manuscripts, and periodicals, but also slides, films, recordings, various microforms, and the facilities for using them. With the growing emphasis on independent student learning and the declining stress on classroom lecturing and textbook memorization, the modern college or university library is no less important than the classroom and the laboratory as a place where learning is disseminated and advanced.

All these developments mean, of course, that a new breed of librarian is emerging to meet changed and more complex demands for services. In addition to being able to communicate effectively with advanced scholars and beginning undergraduates, he and his colleagues in the library must know a great deal about data-processing technology. Not only must he be able to analyze and manage the knowledge system over which he presides, but also he must be able to relate it effectively to national and international networks of information.

This international Conference in Tokyo signifies very concretely the widened horizons of library leaders and their enlarged roles in contemporary society. As librarians in various countries look to one another for new and better ideas about how to conduct their increasingly complex enterprises, I would emphasize that institutions of higher education throughout the civilized world also look to them for ways to enhance teaching, learning, and research.

In an era of strident mass communication, it seems to me that librarians and other educators have a particular obligation to promote the wider and better use of one of man's greatest inventions, the book. I do not minimize the importance of other communications devices, including the latest gadgets of the new learning technology, but their spectacular features are likely to cause us—indeed are causing us—to overlook many of the advantages residing in the book as a superb device for human communication and understanding.

Because of the time-honored relationship between books and learning, we need to remind ourselves that the relationship is still viable. The world about us has grown so complex and the accumulated knowledge about it so vast, and often abstract, that book learning and its practitioners are essential elements to social survival. What other device enables a wide range of thinkers of the past and the present to speak to us so readily? Despite progress in making mechanical communications devices inexpensive and portable, I still know of none that can be purchased in paper covers for less than a dollar, borrowed without cost from a library, carried in one's pocket, used anywhere without plugging in, and then placed back on a shelf to be always ready for later use. Great teachers are not always accessible in person, but the wisdom of all the ages, including our own, is distilled for us on every conceivable subject in book form. No admission is charged for those who wish to read for enjoyment, and no station interruptions puff the virtues of cosmetics, breakfast foods, or cigarettes. Moreover, the reader as learner can set his own pace, and as enjoyer does not have to fit his taste to that of thousands or millions of other people.

Many years ago Francis Bacon noted that reading makes the full man. Librarians and other educators need to join efforts everywhere, it seems to me, in doing all in their power to further the use of that familiar but often neglected object, the book. For those who want knowledge or inspiration, there is no handier place to get it. For the worried or weary, there is no better tranquilizer. For the bored or the adventurous, there is no easier mode of flight to other times and places. For those who want to promote a better understanding of other cultures, readily available books in translation afford inexpensive means of bringing diverse peoples into closer association with one another's ideas and aspirations.

In colleges and universities, especially, the library constitutes the keystone of teaching and learning. Paul Buck, Harvard historian and librarian, once noted that "a quality education is impossible without a quality library," and compared "the student in many college courses to a traveler abroad who keeps his nose in the guidebook and never looks at the life around him. Teaching with textbooks means offering the student body only a guidebook instead of the variations and depth of experience to be found in living books." His book on *Libraries and Universities* also notes that, in the United States, a superior library is an important element in attracting a superior faculty to an institution of higher education.

Although many American collegiate libraries fall below the standards set by Dr. Buck, I certainly agree with him that "the library is the heart of education." In an era when students in many countries, including Japan and the United States, are protesting the kind of classroom instruction they are getting, I wonder why more of them do not spend more time in the library freely pursuing their own intellectual interests and less time milling about on the campus demanding pedagogical reforms. Some of their professors may indeed be stodgy and limited in their points of view, but there is nothing limited about the range of ideas or perspectives to be had in a well-stocked library. Nowhere else on the campus—or away from it, for that matter—is there more freedom to run the whole gamut of what men of all times and places have thought and said.

Furthermore, a good library can never be accused of spoon-feeding those who use it. The student who can use the library as an intellectual resource is not a passive recipient of information and ideas obtained from lectures and textbooks. By searching out the answers to his own questions, he engages actively in self-education. A common task of teachers and librarians, therefore, is to stir the curiosity of young people and to show them how to satisfy that curiosity. In short, I believe that student activists who really want to change the world would be well advised to "invade" the library instead of the office of the president.

I am not familiar with practices in Japan, but in the United States a good many colleges and universities make an honest effort to acquaint beginning students with the rudimentary uses of the library. Freshman orientation week often includes a tour of the library, with some instruction about how books are classified and shelved, what the rules and regulations are for borrowing and returning books, where different kinds of materials may be found, and so on. Further instruction may be given during the opening semester as part of one or more courses of study, such as the introductory course in English. A national survey published a few months ago indicated that such teaching is increasingly common, although American librarians agree that more is needed.

The growing vogue among many American colleges and universities of independent study for advanced students has given rise to programs that may require few, if any, regular class meetings. The student has periodic conferences with his professor— in effect, he teaches himself. In the humanities and social sciences, his most important aid to learning necessarily is the library. Independent study cannot be recommended as superior to all other modes of learning, to be sure. It can, however, as one critique has mentioned, have a "liberating effect on the student, who becomes freer to exercise his choice of discrimination, and on the instructor, who becomes less involved in the purveyance of information and more concerned with the development of curiosity and judgment."

To make libraries more physically and intellectually inviting to their undergraduates, some of our most comprehensive universities have established separate buildings for them. In these buildings bookshelves are typically open to browsers, and reading rooms are often furnished with comfortable chairs and even ashtrays for those who wish to smoke. For example, the Harvard University Library, with its 8,000,000 or so volumes, has adjacent to its large main building a much smaller one for undergraduates with only 150,000 volumes, all readily accessible. The University of Michigan has twelve residence hall libraries, the largest offering approximately 2,500 books, 1,100 phonograph records, and 70 periodicals and newspapers. When I was at the University of Texas, we followed the Harvard example and built a library primarily for undergraduates next to the much larger main library. The response of students to our emphasis on "access and exposure," I might add, was most gratifying.

At a time when higher education in most countries is beset with the twin problems of growing numbers of "consumers" and soaring costs, perhaps we can find solutions through a better utilization of our libraries. In my country, more and more institutions are willing to grant credits to students who can pass examinations covering the subject matter of scheduled courses in which they have not been registered. It is also becoming increasingly common to give advanced standing by examination—that is, to allow a student to take a sequential course on a higher level than that to which his completed course work would entitle him. I suggest also that colleges and universities give more attention to the continuing education of mature persons who may not be formally classified as students. They, too, require aid in the process of self-education and in the use of libraries as indispensable adjuncts to the achievement of learning.

As all of you well know, the quality of library holdings does relate to the quality of formal education. To identify quality in advanced education and to find out what factors are associated with it, the American Council on Education made a comparative study several years ago, *An Assessment of Quality in Graduate Education*, of graduate departments in 29 academic disciplines among the 106 American universities offering appreciable work at the doctoral level. In commenting on the relation between academic quality and library recources, the author, Allan M. Cartter, noted:

> The library is the heart of the university; no other single nonhuman factor is as closely related to the quality of graduate education. A few universities with poor library resources have achieved considerable strength in several departments, in some cases because laboratory facilities may be more important in a particular field than the library, and in other cases because the universities are located close to other great library collections such as the Library

of Congress and the New York Public Library. But institutions that are strong in all areas invariably have major national libraries. The 17 universities among the first 20 institutions in our study (omitting the three leading institutions of science or technology) had total library holdings ranging from 1.3 million to nearly 8 million volumes; the average holding was 2.7 million volumes. The bottom 20 institutions among the 106 in the survey had libraries ranging from 125,000 to 1 million volumes, averaging 465,000.

The monograph goes on to point out that the size of a library does not necessarily measure its adequacy for scholarly purposes. During the study an index was devised, accordingly, for total volumes, for volumes added, for periodicals, and for an overall library indicator. In the computation the figure 1.00 was chosen to indicate the average number of volumes or periodicals for all universities in the survey. When this base figure was applied in each of the four comparisons, Harvard was found to have a higher index standing than any other American university library, except on the periodicals index, where it was exceeded by the University of California at Berkeley.

The other top-ranking university libraries in the United States, in respective order, were at Yale, the University of California at Los Angeles, Cornell, Illinois, Stanford, Michigan, Columbia, and Chicago. The next nine, listed alphabetically, were those at Johns Hopkins, Minnesota, Northwestern, Ohio State, Pennsylvania, Princeton, Texas, Washington, and Wisconsin. The overall library resources index for the first group of institutions ranged from 2.44 to 5.29, and for the second group, from 1.50 to 1.99.

The study observed that all universities having overall faculty ratings of "strong" or "distinguished" also had library resources scores above 1.4. It is true that library resources hold somewhat less importance at such specialized and distinguished institutions as the Massachusetts Institute of Technology and the California Institute of Technology. Even in these instances, however, a significant relationship obtains between the strength of the library and the academic standing of the institution.

Turning now in the last part of my remarks from the academic scene to a broader consideration of what might be called "the power of books," I want to relate library resources more broadly to national resources. As a strong believer in the generally beneficial influence of books on human beings, I am somewhat dismayed to acknowledge for my own country the inordinate amount of time people of virtually all age groups spend watching television. In reading about Japan, I noted that here, also, more than 80 percent of the households own television sets, and the per capita ownership of books is low. In these respects the masses of people in both nations apparently make somewhat similar use of their leisure time. I found encouragement, however, in learning that both nations rank among the leading five publishing countries in the world.

As an American with a warm feeling of friendliness toward Japan, I was pleased to observe that you import more books from the United States than from any other country. Unfortunately for us Americans, there are more Japanese who read English than persons in my country who read Japanese, and thus the flow of books is not equal in both directions; I can assure you, though, that our interest in your people and culture is growing continuously. To my way of thinking, the interchange of books and ideas, of scholars and students, is even more important than diplomacy in the furtherance of international understanding and world peace. Librarians, no less than diplomats, need to communicate with one another, and in so doing everyone benefits.

Furthermore, I think it could be demonstrated that there is a fairly close relationship between the prosperity and strength of a nation and the values it attaches to the kinds of knowledge found in libraries. The recent *Report of the President* of the Carnegie Institution of Washington, commenting on some findings by an American scholar, Derek Price, notes:

In a series of penetrating studies, he [Mr. Price] has been able to show that the contribution of the various nations of the globe to the world's store of scientific information *per se,* as measured by the share of the world's scientific papers in various fields annually issuing from them, is remarkably coordinate, not with their total populations, not with their own estimates of the funds which their governments expend in research and development—which may vary from less than 1 percent of their annual budgets to the high of approximately 3.5 percent of the gross national product reckoned for our own country—but, remarkably enough, with their overall national wealth. That proportion turns out to be extraordinarily uniform among all nations which are making significant contributions to the global accumulation of scientific knowledge.

In the unremitting competition of our planet, it is crystal clear that any nation which permits its scientific resources to wither, or even to diminish, over any considerable period of time is *ipso facto* gravely compromising its position in the world. And the greatest of these resources, of course, is the human one.

This citation speaks only of scientific knowledge and resources, of course, but I suspect that a comparable inquiry into library resources and their utilization would yield similar findings and conclusions. Japan and the United States are both prosperous, strong nations. To maintain their prosperity and strength, however, both nations must be willing to ensure adequate support for their libraries and educational institutions. We librarians and educators therefore have an obligation not only to render the best services we can but also to impress upon our patrons the indispensability of sufficient material support and public understanding for a continuous enlargement and improvement of these services.

In closing, let me say that mankind owes a debt of gratitude to libraries and librarians for services to the advancement of higher learning and of civilization. Although libraries already are estimable social agencies, the presence at the Conference of leading Japanese and American librarians signifies a desire on your part to improve their efficiency and effectiveness further. Your effort to enhance the increase of knowledge and its better utilization not only strengthens nations but also promotes the rule of reason and mutual understanding throughout the world. Far from being mere custodians of accumulated knowledge, you play vital roles in raising the quality of human life.

The Role of University Libraries in Higher Education

Douglas W. Bryant
University Librarian,
Harvard University

At this opening session of the Japan–U.S. Conference on Libraries and Information Science in Higher Education, I am profoundly aware of a sense of return and recognition, and yet I am also struck by signs of tremendous change. So much is familiar, but so much at the same time is new and different. Six years ago, when my wife and I spent many weeks of personal pleasure and professional satisfaction in Japan among friends and colleagues from Kyūshū to Hokkaidō, such a Conference seemed a distant ideal. The great program for modernization of Japanese research libraries that was the imaginative concept of the late Professor Hideo Kishimoto was only just getting under way. My own visit at that time was intended as a small contribution to the beginning of that large enterprise. Professor Kishimoto and I traveled the length and breadth of Japan, meeting and talking with librarians, university presidents and deans, professors, officials from the Ministry of Education, and many others—all with the aim of organizing support for this plan to increase the usefulness of libraries to their universities and to Japanese higher education as a whole.

Professor Kishimoto dreamed, among his many dreams, of just such a Conference as this, and before going on I should like to pay tribute to the man who contributed so much not only to the intellectual life of his own country but also to the cause of intercultural understanding between Japan and the United States. When Professor Kishimoto became director of the University of Tokyo Library, he was determined to make the very most of his tenure in that post. He dedicated his efforts to a broad improvement and modernization of Japanese university libraries generally, in the firm conviction that ultimately the strength of any university depends on the strength of its library. During the early period of his directorship, he reorganized the administrative structure of the library at the University of Tokyo to make it more efficient and flexible and to take fuller advantage of the talents of its staff. He planned the renovation of the central library, which has increased the efficiency of the building and made it a more agreeable place for research by students and professors. Within a very short time after he took office, Professor Kishimoto enthusiastically embarked on the project that was to culminate in the miracle of a Union Catalog for the vast Tōdai library system—a miracle in the eyes of librarians everywhere because of the short time in which it was accomplished.

Professor Kishimoto then undertook to organize university library directors and librarians throughout Japan in his ceaseless effort to make more effective their contribution to the life of the universities in this country. His untimely death in 1964, before much of what he had hoped to see achieved could be accomplished, was a cruel loss to Japan and to America as well, for he was influential and respected there, too. But in reviewing Professor Kishimoto's library career from this vantage point, the wonder is that he was able to accomplish so much in the short time he had. Hideo Kishimoto was one of the preeminent figures of modern Japanese scholarship and of contemporary Japanese librarianship; he was the man whose vision, untiring efforts, and broad planning opened the way for this historic Conference.

Academic librarians in Japan—and most particularly Professor Kishimoto's distinguished successor, Professor Itō—have moved steadily along the path toward closer collaboration between Japanese and American university libraries. In the six years since my last visit to Japan there have been many notable advances in the university libraries of both countries. In a lecture I prepared in 1963, I suggested a number of developments which I thought would take place, at least in the libraries of my own country, within the next several years. It is interesting and instructive now to observe that some of the advances I then thought most promising have either proved to be of only secondary value or have not materialized. On the other hand, we have advanced considerably farther in other directions than I had thought possible in so short a period. The principal point, of course, is that while progress may have been along different lines than one had foreseen in some cases, and sometimes faster and sometimes slower, there have been real advances of considerable significance to libraries and to the students and scholars whom they serve.

If there is one predominant characteristic of this period—both the past few years and those just ahead—it is *growth*. There is explosive growth in the number and variety of publications, both those that are printed and those reproduced by other methods, that are appearing all over the world, many of them in areas where very little had been published until the last few years. At the same time there is a great increase in the number of fields in which serious research is taking place, and there is a rapid development of interdisciplinary research. There is also a ceaseless increase in the number of students in our universities, students at all levels, from matriculating undergraduates to the most advanced postdoctoral scholars. Constant growth thus seems to be a factor in all aspects of a university's life and work. When change comes to a university or to its library, it is usually a reflection of growth of one kind or another, and this must be kept in mind as we consider the part that university libraries play in higher education.

I should like first to remark on the relationship between the library of a university and the processes of teaching within that university. It is obvious that there is a reciprocal relationship here—that the methods used in teaching will affect the nature of the library, while the kind and quality of library resources and services will profoundly affect teaching methods themselves. In many countries, perhaps particularly in the United States, libraries have come increasingly to play a central role in the instructional process. Instead, for example, of restricting students to one or two standard textbooks for each course of study, reading in a broad range of books, journals, government documents, and other materials in the library is encouraged. In a growing number of colleges and universities, also, certain periods of time are designated each term during which no lectures or other formal instruction are given, but under the general guidance of professors and librarians, students are free to read independently on the subjects they are studying during the term. In other programs, now quite common, students spend a very considerable portion of their time in research work and in writing papers which are expected to reflect individual research and original thought. Seminar courses, as distinct from large lecture courses, are becoming more widespread in undergraduate instruction, and in a number of colleges and universities there are now seminars established specifically for first-year students. All these trends inevitably bind the instructional programs more closely to the library.

To illustrate the pervasive and extremely effective influence that the use of good libraries has on students, let me cite a phenomenon that has appeared repeatedly in the United States. In the last twenty years a number of universities have established special libraries for undergraduates. On the theory that these students can best use a library of moderate size, whole collections have been designed especially to meet most of the library requirements of undergraduates. In every university where such a library has been established, undergraduate students, in addition to their use of the new library, have almost immediately made strikingly greater use of the research collections within their university libraries. This phenomenon surely illustrates the point that serious students are capable of using libraries effectively and, given good library resources and services, will require more research materials and more sophisticated services.

It should perhaps also be noted that in many cases students entering universities nowadays come with far wider library experience than their counterparts a generation ago. Trained in their precollege years to regard libraries as indispensable means of study, such students are quite naturally able to use libraries more effectively throughout the whole of their university careers and understandably make much greater demands on their libraries than was the case even a few student generations ago.

How are university libraries adapting themselves to meet these challenging possibilities for contributing to the enrichment of higher education? Let me point to several innovations, in addition to undergraduate libraries, that have become fairly standard in the past few years. University libraries have introduced various kinds of specialized reference services and counseling designed to assist students, both undergraduate and graduate, in the use of large and complex library systems and in the efficient use of an ever-increasing number of bibliographies, catalogs, indexes, and other bibliographic instruments. Many libraries have established orientation programs for new students to acquaint them with the collections and the services of the libraries they will be using in their study and research. Similarly, many libraries conduct formal courses of instruction in the use of libraries. Handbooks and descriptive guides to library resources provide a most useful aid to students, and such publications are issued quite routinely by most libraries. Another medium for informing readers of the resources at their disposal is the exhibition in which books and many other kinds of library materials are placed on display to suggest a range and depth of resources which might be overlooked by the casual reader.

For fifty years and more, college and university libraries in the United States have employed students to perform a variety of library tasks. At Harvard University, for example, the library regularly employs about 350 students and pays them a total of $275,000 a year. Many students work in the library stacks, finding books that are requested, replacing returned books, and keeping the shelves in correct order. Students also perform very successfully many kinds of bibliographic work, such as searching for titles in catalogs, filing cards, doing preliminary cataloging, and arranging books to be included on reading lists compiled by professors. This kind of employment has many advantages. It provides a kind of working scholarship arrangement for students who need to supplement their incomes; it provides the library with a group of employees who often have unusual language or subject competence and who are essentially interested in the world of learning; and over the years it has proved to be one of the most effective devices for recruiting to the profession of librarianship able young men and women who decide, on the basis of their work in the library, to make that their career.

Finally, I must point to what is perhaps the most important single contribution that libraries make to the total educational experience of college and university students. This, of course, is the thrill of discovery to be found in the ability to range freely through the rich mines of informational, instructional, cultural, and aesthetic treasure that comprise the holdings of a fine library.

We come now to the collections that form our academic libraries. Where once such collections included traditional printed books and a few manuscripts, they now have an enormous variety of printed works and what are curiously called "near-print" publications, scientific and technical research reports by the tens of thousands; ancient manuscripts and the personal archives of influential literary, cultural, or political figures; maps, drawings, architec-

tural plans, and photographs; sound recordings of all kinds, both in language and in music; and increasingly in the years to come, they will be sure to have extensive collections of information on every conceivable subject stored in some kind of computer form. As scholarship and research reach farther and farther outward, pushing the frontiers of knowledge forward, and as they increasingly involve interdisciplinary work in ever-changing combinations, the demands for materials to support research of all kinds become correspondingly greater. And yet, for all the new kinds of material we are collecting and for all the libraries whose holdings number in the millions of volumes, no single library can hope to fill all the needs of its scholarly community. Librarians have long realized this and have accordingly over the years devised various means for interlibrary cooperation, in order that scholars may discover what materials exist in other institutions as well as their own and may then gain access to these materials for their research.

The National Union Catalog at the Library of Congress has long been a major instrument for location of research materials, and we have long dreamed of multiplying its usefulness by providing copies of it in research libraries throughout the world. Publication in book form has begun at last, and the first of the 600 volumes is at hand. This has been described as the largest publishing project ever undertaken, and it is clearly a major landmark in the history of bibliography, libraries, and scholarship.

Another cooperative venture that has grown out of our attempt to cope with the problems of growth is the Center for Research Libraries, through which participating libraries have developed cooperative collecting programs for little-used materials that are of importance to scholarship but which are not required in many individual libraries so long as they are available from a central depository. Clearly, there will have to be even more cultivation of this kind of joint activity, and it is fortunate that the advent of the computer, with its immense potential value in the whole realm of catalogs and bibliography, has come at just this time.

In considering the relationship of academic libraries to higher education, let me mention one feature that is sometimes overlooked but is too important to be omitted here. This is the close relationship between research library collections and trends in scholarship. The existence in a university library of a major collection in a special field of learning will often cause a scholar to begin exploration in a direction that would not otherwise have attracted him. This, in turn, may give rise to the emergence of a whole group of young scholars to work the freshly discovered field. Not only, then, do research library collections reflect the requirements of scholarship, but also very frequently they anticipate new directions and make possible progress along lines not otherwise feasible.

In many American colleges and universities with substantial collections of rare books and manuscripts, another new trend in the use of the collections is becoming apparent. Such materials are now more heavily used by students than ever was the case. The effect of this is greatly to enrich the quality of education and research. Furthermore, as historians of every period and every human activity are drawn more and more to the use of personal archival collections made by individuals of significance, libraries are acquiring more collections of this sort. In this period, during which many new universities are being established and many small colleges are becoming research institutions, there is the concomitant necessity for existing libraries greatly to expand their research holdings and for completely new libraries to be developed. Whereas one of the serious problems facing these new and expanding libraries is the unavailability of major and sometimes standard publications of the past, the acquisition of archival collections is quite feasible and provides new libraries with bodies of original research material for the use of both students and faculty members.

Students and professors are not the sole population of a university; inevitably there are also administrators, and something should be said of the role of university libraries in higher education from the point of view of university administration. It is axiomatic that great libraries attract and hold great scholars, who in their turn attract the most promising young students. Because of this essential dependence of serious scholarship on strong libraries, university presidents and deans, ministers of education, and others responsible for the smooth functioning of universities are understandably eager to foster and maintain strong and healthy libraries. It is also axiomatic that such libraries cost a great deal of money to maintain and to keep strong; moreover, their costs inescapably rise year by year. Thus it is incumbent upon university librarians to ensure that their libraries are organized and operated in such a way as to realize maximum efficiency and economy.

Among a host of means for achieving these ends, a few particularly effective methods come readily to mind. First, it is essential that academic libraries, which may have inadvertently indulged for many years in the luxury of leisurely inefficiency, be brought into line with modern administrative and management practices. Much economic and substantive gain can result from the adoption of modern business procedures. In view of the ever-rising costs of research libraries and the pressure for additional money to support them, it seems to me quite clear, for example, that unnecessary duplication of materials within a single university—and even among universities—must be eliminated. I speak here particularly of collections which in many universities have developed within the research institutes that have formed around the work of one professor or one small group. In the interests of university-wide library development and with a view to making the broadest possible resources available to the whole university community, it is inevitable, I believe, that there must be great reliance on central library collections that are regularly and freely available to all members of the university, students and professors alike.

24 – Role of University Libraries in Higher Education

I have mentioned earlier the creation of many interlibrary programs for joint or cooperative collection building, and these quite obviously must continue and expand. Organizations such as the Center for Research Libraries and the newly established University Information Technology Corporation, founded jointly by the Massachusetts Institute of Technology and Harvard University, will play increasingly important parts in searching for greater economies in total library operation while at the same time endeavoring to provide greater total resources for research.

Ceaseless effort must be devoted to ensuring the most efficient use of professional library personnel, for if academic libraries are to thrive, we must have highly qualified and proudly professional librarians whose energies must be channeled entirely in professional activities.

Much has been done in recent years to improve the architectural design and methods of construction for library buildings. This has resulted in ingenious renovation of existing library structures, which has made many old buildings more efficient and more attractive. At the same time, we must continue to improve the designing and construction of libraries, as universities are going to continue to require major library buildings. It is important, therefore, to continue to devote considerable thought to library architecture as such, so that we can produce buildings which are attractive and efficient to operate and yet as economical as possible to build and to maintain.

From the general administrative point of view, one of the potentially most promising developments in libraries is the feasibility, after many decades of striving, of creating schemes for collaborative cataloging among a number of major libraries. If such schemes can be developed, individual libraries will not have to catalog separately, and thus duplicate, so many tens of thousands of titles each year. Any such plan for simplifying the total cataloging effort by academic libraries must rely on two basic propositions: computer technology and centralized bibliographic control in each country through the facilities, presumably, of the national library. Thus, in Japan I

should venture to suppose that the National Diet Library, so dramatically come of age in two short decades, will play an increasingly greater part in the whole bibliographic economy of the country. On the American side, the Library of Congress since the beginning of this century has been the keystone of the bibliographic structure of the United States. As the national library, it can be expected to be an ever more important participant in the day-to-day bibliographic operations of individual research libraries in America and, so far as United States publications are concerned, presumably in libraries of other countries as well.

Finally, we can hardly consider the place of universities or their libraries in higher education without taking into account the fact that higher education is no longer by any means the only purpose these libraries serve. The universities, in other words, do not merely produce trained men who then leave the academic world to engage in research elsewhere, to practice their professions, or to enter business or politics. The universities are major centers of research, much of which is done under contract for the government. Men go back and forth between university faculties and the world of government and business. University libraries serve as information centers; in medicine, for example, medical-school libraries have become national centers for information in designated fields, and are also providing regional services to physicians.

Research has become a major factor in the national economy; knowledge is a leading industry. University libraries share with the great national libraries responsibility for the organization and dissemination of information and for its preservation. To meet the needs of numerous new colleges and universities, publishers are issuing a rapidly increasing number of facsimile reprints and microform editions, and the originals on which this industry depends are supplied for the most part by the old established university libraries. At the same time, these libraries are confronted with the need to preserve hundreds of thousands of volumes on rapidly deteriorating paper; the task appears to be far too large to be handled unless there is a national plan and financial support from the national government.

National support and national systems have been emphasized, but scholarship is a human rather than a nationalistic undertaking, and strong national library systems must be linked together. Indeed, as computer technology is refined and comes to have more importance in the day-to-day operation of every major research library anywhere in the world, I would expect that a common bibliographic language to be used by all libraries will be developed. This is one reason for my conviction that librarians of Japan and the United States —as two of the major technological nations in the world—will have more and more in common, and that conferences such as this will become regular occurrences of our professional lives.

University Libraries and Their Role

Satoshi Saitō
Professor Emeritus,
Nihon University
Former Chief Librarian,
Nihon University Library

Professor Harold J. Laski of the University of London has asserted that World War II might have been prevented if Great Britain and Soviet Russia had had information readily accessible and reference services sufficiently available in libraries and other public agencies. These peoples then would have had a more adequate grasp of their situation, and the step toward open conflict might have been avoided. This is a notable example of the role which libraries can play if they have reached an effective state of development.

Naturally, university libraries are charged with the task of meeting the demands of the essential mission of universities, education and research, and thus they ultimately contribute to world peace. Therefore, they bear a very important responsibility.

Let me briefly sketch in the recent history of Japanese university libraries. After the war, the Japanese educational system underwent a sweeping reform, and universities were recast as so-called "new universities." Their libraries, as well, have undergone various changes, especially in the establishment of standards and in training. In July 1947 a democratic University Accreditation Association (Daigaku Kijun Kyōkai) was established, and some years later, in 1952, standards for university libraries were set up. Later the work of the association was shifted to the Ministry of Education, which enacted and put into effect the present standards in 1956. The National Junior College for Librarianship (Toshokan Tanki Daigaku) was founded in 1964, and in 1965 a Library Information Section was established under the Bureau of Higher Education and Science in the Ministry of Education. Now courses in library science are offered in 130 universities, and the graduate School of Library and Information Science at Keiō University offers a full professional curriculum.

With the appearance of reformed universities, high schools and technical schools all over the country sought the title "university." Yet these schools could not be accredited without meeting university standards, and problems arose due to their efforts to attain these standards. For instance, some universities were formed by combining schools on different campuses. Consequently, there were some 339 libraries in the 72 national universities, in a decentralized pattern. This was true not only of national universities, but also of private universities. Units of the university were often scattered in both types of institution. At that time, the fundamental library problem was the acquisition of materials. This resulted in a highly competitive search for books for the purpose of increasing library collections. Today, twenty years later, the pace has slackened somewhat, but many universities still face a serious shortage of library books.

Unification of scattered campuses has often been impossible, but at least library collections can be centralized. This was a goal of the university library standards. For the effectiveness of the whole library program, it was felt to be highly important to adopt a system centered around a general library, uniquely responsible for acquisition of books, uniform procedures, and general cataloging. Further, it was deemed necessary to establish a system of inter-branch borrowing and lending. Thus the reformed university libraries have attempted to evolve toward simpler and more efficient organizational patterns.

The concept of a library consisting only of collections of books, a building, and librarians has remained unchanged since the war, but this is merely a formal way of thinking. A library, in its true sense, should not remain a matter of form, but should possess the real resources required to accomplish the university's mission. In order that a library may thoroughly fulfill its purpose, there must be a corps of professional librarians, charged with the task of bringing students and faculty together in the use of library collections. Therefore, librarians must receive specialized technical education and, at the same time, they should strive to keep pace with the advancement of knowledge and should have a broad background in the arts and sciences. Only when librarians of such competence are active in the organization does a library in name only become a library in the real sense of the word.

Quite frankly, conventional, and especially prewar, university libraries did not accomplish what they should have. Consequently, the librarians' role was not assigned great importance. In extreme cases the universities regarded their libraries as a trivial part of the institution, a junkyard for personnel assignments or a convenient marginal area for adjustment of overall budgetary allocations. To some degree, this is still true today.

Also, a university library used to be merely an organization for preserving books. Each university seemed intent on showing off its voluminous collection of books and on building an ivory-tower atmosphere. Use was a rare and well-guarded privilege. Librarians were watchmen over a storehouse, uselessly bent on preserving and safeguarding books, and were in constant fear of loss of or damage to books. In spite of such an undesirable situation, prewar libraries did satisfy the reading needs of students to a considerable degree.

In the personnel system of prewar national universities, there existed an expert staff of "librarians." After the war, despite the fact that such laws as the Library Law for public libraries, enacted in April 1950, and the School Library Law for primary, junior high, and senior high schools, enacted in August 1953, provided for "librarians" and "teacher-librarians," the profession of "librarian" came to be less well-defined in university libraries.

After the war, the introduction of the American library system stimulated Japanese university librarians to reflect profoundly upon their role. Notwithstanding the dire circumstances of the times, Japanese librarians made steady efforts to improve, modify, and expand their libraries, and finally they began to make noteworthy progress. But when we turn our view toward the instructors and teachers and their concept of libraries in education, there still remains cause for anxiety.

Teachers seem to regard libraries as no more than a place to store documents. They tend to collect any documents relevant to their studies, but they are bitterly criticized for their inclination to keep source books for their lectures out of the sight of other readers. Their attention is directed only to books in their own field of interest, and the task of guiding students' research and reading is naturally overlooked and neglected. However, it is a fundamental principle of the reformed universities that teachers guide and advise students on reading for their courses. That is to say, teachers should actively cooperate with librarians in enriching the collection of books by suggesting books necessary for students, thus giving students the widest possible opportunities for study. In short, teachers should correct their view of the library and cooperate with librarians to let students make the best use of the book collection. This, I think, is a most important factor in the proper functioning of a university library.

The reformed universities originally adopted a policy of allotting time for preparation and review before and after lectures. If that policy were actually carried out to the fullest extent, use of libraries by students would be indispensable, and the value of libraries would be entirely different. Nevertheless, this may be only an impractical dream in the modern production-line universities.

Statistics show that as of November 1968 there were 75 national universities (292 libraries), 35 public universities (47 libraries), and 267 private universities (332 libraries), or 671 libraries for a total of 377 universities. The total student population is 1,410,000, an average of more than 3,800 students per university. However, there are all kinds of universities, ranging in scale from small to gigantic. Furthermore, there are innumerable differences in organization among the various universities. Under these conditions, averages and standards become meaningless.

In any case, universities with a large student population are approved without due consideration for provision of adequate library service. Therefore, if any teacher attempts conscientiously to follow the fundamental principle of the university, many of the present university libraries become unserviceable.

Actually, libraries are often not in great demand, inasmuch as many Japanese university students complete a course for credit solely on the basis of reading one or two specified textbooks. Although a reserved-book system is provided for by the Standards for University Library Establishment, one or two reserved books are of no use to students in a "mass-production university." It might be said that the present library system totally neglects students. There must be quite a large percentage of students who have never been in a library. Some students do not even know that the library exists. However true this may be of

undergraduates, a library is generally indispensable to the studies of graduate students.

One may justifiably say that Japanese university libraries today serve mainly graduate students and scholars in specialized studies and research, while undergraduate students receive secondary attention. In a sense, Japanese university libraries have a strong tendency to be research libraries. In order for university libraries to fulfill their functions as information and documentation centers, it is desirable that smaller libraries be consolidated into larger units. Furthermore, this must be accomplished on the basis of nationwide integrated efforts to establish a powerful academic information and documentation center, which is the ideal of library administration.

The above-mentioned ideal is no longer an unlikely possibility, what with the development and progress of computers. I understand that the United States is now taking the lead in this field through the establishment, for example, of the MARC II system. In Japan the National Diet Library has already made a budget appropriation of 6,800,000 yen for installation of a computer. The application of computers for library use shows great promise in Japan. Leaving aside the subject of social revolution through computerization, one wonders why there have as yet been no decisive plans for the achievement of something like an academic information and documentation center, commensurate with wide demand.

In the first place, keeping a general catalog up to date requires manual revision of the card catalog, thus making catalog maintenance very difficult. In the second place, large numbers of personnel are necessary for communication among university libraries, in part because of the formidable task of coordinating cataloging systems, which presently vary in technique from library to library. In the third place, specialized knowledge, often in short supply, such as a fairly good knowledge of foreign languages and of other disciplines, must be duplicated, in so far as possible, in many libraries at high cost. However, if a general catalog for all academic publications belonging to each university were created, it would undoubtedly contribute much not only to Japan but also to worldwide handling of information.

Education is an ongoing business. University libraries with small collections may come to have millions of books in the future, and documents other than library books may become too voluminous to handle properly. If so, it is urgently necessary to establish and foster a system based on predictable growth and on techniques of logical arrangement before the volume of materials gets out of hand. A system of preparing a card catalog which permits error or much variation in the form of entries may result in extreme difficulty in finding the publication wanted, or in failure to find it. Therefore, it is quite naturally desirable that the form and compilation of cards be unified and standardized on a nationwide basis. A library is, after all, not merely a storehouse of thousands of books and documents. A library is essentially an organized system of knowledge, where every piece of information is processed with utmost care and each kept in its proper place with respect to every other.

Everyone realizes that a book is the result of an author's painstaking toil, but are the efforts of librarians to preserve and make accessible that result equally well understood? There is at present little chance for recognition of the efforts and contributions of librarians in Japan, and this may well be in part due to the nature of their task. Librarians are the media for linking users with books and other publications, and ideally the media should not be interposed. Perhaps users can best make use of books when they are not unduly conscious of the librarian's existence and when they feel no hesitance in using libraries. The more efficiently a library functions, the more inconspicuous librarians become, excepting as their specialized bibliographic knowledge is called into play.

The work of the librarian consists essentially of service to others. I believe that serving others is most desirable in maintaining a peaceful society. If such service is necessary in preserving social organization, librarians are truly entrusted with a valuable mission. If librarians fully understand and fulfill their mission, they will undoubtedly be appreciated and respected by students and faculty. The library itself will then be regarded as a vital part of the university.

Part 3

LIBRARY RESOURCES AND QUALITY IN HIGHER EDUCATION

Teaching Methods and the Use of Libraries

William S. Dix
University Librarian,
Princeton University

Two anecdotes may help introduce our discussion of the relationship between the library and the teaching program of the university. About a dozen years ago I spent some time observing education and libraries in another country—not Japan or the United States. During this time I often compared notes with another foreign observer, a visiting professor in the medical school of the university. One day when he showed up at an unaccustomed hour, I asked why he was not teaching. He replied that classes had been suspended by order of the Minister of Education. The professor, it developed, had given his first examination, one so shocking to the students and so different from the educational methods to which they were accustomed that they had in protest demonstrated violently

at the office of the Minister. This being a rather volatile country, the Minister had been actually afraid that the students might bring down the government and had suspended classes. What my friend had done was to prepare an examination that required *thought* as well as *memory*—which demanded that the students solve the equation A + B = C. They had memorized A and B and all the other letters of the alphabet, but never before had they been required to put A and B together and produce that new and startling quantity, C. They were outraged at the unfairness of asking them to produce on an examination something which they had not been given.

The other incident, I regret to say, happened at an American institution of higher education. Having heard the officials expound with enthusiasm the quality of their educational process, their small classes, and the fact that every student participated every day, I asked to visit a class. What actually happened was something like this: The instructor, class roll in hand, called on each student in turn: "Mr. A, at what temperature does water boil?" or "Mr. B, what was the date of the fall of Constantinople?" (I even forget the subject of the

29

course at this point!) Mr. A or Mr. B stood at attention, said "100 Centigrade" or "1453," just as the textbook had told him, sat down, and received a grade in the little book.

Now in neither of these institutions, it seems to me, was much real education going on. Education involves dialogue, the interplay of mind with mind, the development of an intellectual instrument so tempered that it can cut through sham and nonsense and reveal at least an approximation of truth. It involves not merely memorizing the words of Plato or Jefferson or Ogyū Sorai but an understanding of the thought behind the words, an appreciation of the nobility of those ideas which can stimulate new ideas, hopefully just as noble. It involves learning not only to think but also to feel, the development of a passion for justice and beauty and understanding.

There is no space here for an extended discussion of educational philosophy. What I have just said is obviously oversimplified. But it seems to me essential at the beginning for us to understand what we mean by the word *education*, for that word is critical to our discussion. It may be used, I suppose, for a process by which predigested pellets of information are dropped by the professor into the minds of passive and hopefully receptive students. This process may be useful in training students to perform specific routine tasks, although I have some reservations even about this. But it has little to do with real education.

The kind of education which I have in mind has as its objective the preparation of students in both the ability and the desire to live lives which are both productive for society and satisfying to themselves as individuals. This kind of education involves the whetting of the intellect and the stimulation of understanding and imagination. It proceeds by dialogue, as I have said, not aimless conversation, but the orderly examination of information and opinion, the eliciting of response, and the refining of this response by a continuation of the same process. The role of the student is active, not passive. The role of the teacher is not to be dogmatic, but to guide the whole process. He is a wise moderator,

not an oracle, stimulating, clarifying, and focusing the continuing dialogue through his own broader knowledge and what can only be described as his mastery of the art of teaching.

Now what does all this have to do with libraries? Not very much, in the case of the educational process illustrated by my two anecdotes. Those institutions, if these episodes are typical, do not really need libraries to carry out that sort of teaching process.

On the other hand, libraries are intimately involved in the kind of education which I have attempted roughly to define. In the first place, the educational dialogue cannot be carried on without information. Even if it were to take place entirely in the formal classroom or seminar (and in a moment I shall attempt to show that it cannot take place there alone), its participants must bring with them as a part of their intellectual luggage a substantial amount of information accumulated in a variety of ways. The library is the principal central repository of recorded information on the university campus. The growth of the total body of recorded information in the last few decades and the consequent cost of these records make it doubtful that any wide-ranging educational dialogue can be supported entirely by the books owned by individual students. Furthermore, books and other records of human thought and creativity are themselves the objects of examination in many aspects of this discourse. One cannot talk intelligently about the modern novel without reading modern novels or examine critically the statistical procedures used in assessing economic development in an African nation without access to the reports of that development. Only the library can supply these books and other records in sufficient depth, and only the library can supply the bibliographic and other tools with which to use them effectively.

But I would submit that a considerable part of the educational dialogue can take place outside the classroom. It would have been magnificent to sit across a seminar table from Plato or Einstein and engage in intellectual discourse. It is still possible to carry on a considerable amount of this discourse through books. Reading is by no means necessarily passive, and under the skillful guidance of a good teacher the student can respond actively to seminal thinkers and broaden the discourse to include in the give-and-take of ideas a host of other students and scholars who have reacted in print to nature and the mind of man. And a considerable part of the role of guide and teacher can be played by the librarian.

In other words, it is my opinion that we can safely encourage more independent study by our students. With the proper stimulation and guidance this independent study can be both exciting and vigorous, can become, in fact, the most effective kind of true education. At my own institution, where there is a substantial amount of independent study, students after graduation almost uniformly report this to have been the most exciting and productive part of their educational experience.

Let us therefore reflect in quite specific terms upon some of the factors which affect this relationship between the library and the teaching process. None of what I am saying is dogma. It is merely a statement of some of the opinions formed by one individual on the basis of thirty-five years of experience as a teacher and as a librarian.

Let us look first at the collections themselves. What sort of collections does a university library require? The obvious answer is to say that it should have all those books, journals, and other forms of recorded communication necessary to support the teaching and research program of the university. But this truism requires some further investigation. If the teaching program of the university requires only that each student in each course memorize the contents of a single textbook, then a library is hardly a necessity for that university. But that university is clearly not engaged in education, for surely education proceeds by and in turn nourishes the spirit of free inquiry. It is not enough for a college student to accept ex cathedra one author's opinion about the nature of the world or society or art. He must surely be led to

ask questions, to disagree, to explore the facts for himself, to seek the differing interpretations of those facts expressed by others, and in the process develop the ability and the habit of thinking for himself. This kind of teaching program requires many books, more than the student can normally afford to purchase individually. Thus a library becomes essential as a common pool upon which all may draw.

The size of this collection depends, of course, upon the nature of the curriculum and the methods of instruction. It is commonly said in the United States that a collection of 80,000 to 100,000 *titles* may support a major portion of the work in a general liberal arts undergraduate program, meeting perhaps 80 percent of each student's needs. Note that these estimates, which may not have much solid evidence to support them, refer to *titles*, not *volumes*. To make this library effective for a large student body, there must be as many copies of each title as are required to make that volume reasonably available when it is needed. Furthermore, this library covers only a general program. Any strong infusion of preprofessional work into the undergraduate curriculum or any special subject content will obviously require a broader collection. For example, if each student is required to do a reasonable amount of work on some culture completely different from his own, as many think desirable, the collection must be expanded accordingly.

Furthermore, even if these rather modest estimates of adequacy are accepted, they meet, as I have said, only 80 percent of the needs of each student. None of us wants to produce students who are only 80 percent educated. The remaining 20 percent of needs obviously cannot be met by merely adding another 20,000 titles, for the additional 20 percent required by each individual student will hopefully be different from those needed by many other students. These are often the books the student wants or should have when intellectual curiosity has taken over and he is running free, motivated by his own desire to learn for himself.

Where is the student to get these essential additional books? Here is where there seems to be some advantage in pursuing undergraduate education within the context of a university, rather than in a small independent college. I hasten to say that the small college may have other, but different, advantages. A university presumably exists to develop new knowledge as well as to teach. The presumption is that it will include a community of scholars engaged in research. I think that we may take it for granted that research and advanced teaching require larger library collections than undergraduate teaching alone. Some samples in American universities suggest that the average graduate student uses three to five times as many books as the average undergraduate.

In other words, the research activities of a university require research collections. It is these collections which can support and reinforce the limited undergraduate collection of which I have spoken. They can do this, however, only if they are available to the undergraduate. If they are held by some special interest group or by many such groups, available only to a single faculty or a few advanced students, they are not serving the general instructional purposes of the university. These purposes must then be met by duplicating in the central library a very large number of expensive books, journals, and other library materials. There are not many universities in the world which can afford this luxury.

The alternative is to make all of the books owned by the university freely available to all the members of the university. The most certain way to ensure this availability is to place the management of all the libraries of the university in the hands of a competent director, responsible to the highest officer of the university. These libraries are not really in his hands unless he has control of the total library budget of the university.

In brief, excellence in education seems to me to require inevitably those kinds of teaching processes in which the student, under the guidance and inspiration (to use an old-fashioned word) of the instructor, spends a very large proportion of his working time in relatively independent study.

These teaching methods require that the student have easy access to quite a large number of books, journals, and other forms of recorded communication.

Other things being equal, the larger a library is, the better it is. But in measuring this size and consequent quality, one cannot include books which cannot be used, which are not accessible to all. Expediency thus suggests that the best way to make large numbers of books accessible to all, avoiding wasteful duplication and expense, is to give management of the total book collections of the university to an administratively centralized university library. The universe of recorded knowledge is so large that no library in the world can hope to have enough money to buy all of it. Therefore, the money which is available should be used as efficiently as possible to give maximum support to the teaching and research program of the university.

It is not enough that an adequate number of books be owned by the university, theoretically accessible to all students and faculty members. They must obviously be brought under some system of bibliographic control so that the user may learn easily which books may be useful to him as he pursues his own inquiries, whether the university owns these books, and finally where the full text is located within the library. It may safely be taken as axiomatic, I believe, that the easier this whole process is made, the more effective the library becomes as an active educational instrument.

We have built up over the past seventy-five years or so a vast and sometimes self-defeating international apparatus to help us identify and locate the published, and indeed often the unpublished, texts appropriate to particular lines of inquiry. There is neither the space nor the necessity to discuss abstracts and indexes and all the other varieties of general bibliographic control. Many of these essential tools are managed by professional societies or governmental agencies, and the university library must simply make as many of them available as possible. More locally, most of us have developed some form of subject cataloging, in card or book form, designed to give the users of our own libraries who are looking for material on a particular subject information about the books we have relevant to this subject. Marvelous instruments though the best of these systems are, they are gross tools which cannot take us far beyond the covers of a volume into its substance. We all await the day, perhaps rather remote, when the computer will enable us to open up the contents of our libraries on a more effective subject basis. That topic will appear in another part of our discussions.

Access to the text itself is a matter which I do want to discuss briefly, for it seems to me to have received too little attention at the level of elementary principle. The deployment of the books themselves, the vehicles of the text, is a matter of some importance in enabling the library to perform as a teaching instrument of quality. Where shall we put the books?

The benefits of centralized administration of the whole university library seem to me inescapable, but this does not mean that all the books need to be housed in a single building. The obvious guiding principle is that the books should be as close as possible to the people who use them. The interpretation of this principle will depend upon a number of local factors. In a relatively small university, compactly housed, a single central library building is probably the best solution, for a probable corollary of our principle is that as many books as possible should be in one place, for both convenience and economy. On the other hand, if the collections, the student body, and the physical area of the university are all very large, some dispersal of the collections may offer educational advantages. For example, if a highly specialized portion of the collections is used almost exclusively by an identifiable segment of students and scholars whose offices and classrooms are in a building remote from the central library, the advantages of a separate specialized library might be considered. For us in the United States, an East Asian language library might present such a situation. Or in certain situations the misnamed "undergraduate library"

currently in vogue in our larger universities might be desirable.

In other words, I for one do not find all of the arguments on the side of centralization and against dispersion. There are many factors to consider. A relatively small, specialized collection located near the majority of its users and managed by a skilled professional librarian with specialized knowledge on the subject can offer extraordinary support of a teaching and research program and may be worth a short walk for the student in a different discipline who has a temporary need for material generally unfamiliar to him. On the other hand, there are seldom sharp boundaries between areas of knowledge, and too much dispersal of libraries is a disaster. A Scottish librarian once told me in despair that his university had something like thirty libraries in its medical school, four in anatomy alone. The result was either no real library at all or a most un-Scots extravagance in duplication.

How should we arrange the books on the shelves within the units of the library? They can be shelved by order of acquisition, by date of publication, by size, and in other ways, but I think that most of us, in Japan or in the United States, would agree that some arrangement by subject, which associates on the shelves books of related content, is the best system for a general university library.

There will be, of course, some form of catalog, whether on cards, in books, or in a computer, which will direct the reader looking for a particular section of the shelves by means of a number assigned uniquely to each volume. I avoid all discussion of the philosophical merits of various systems of classification. For purposes of education the important thing is some system which will bring related books together, recognizing that no classification system can satisfy both the sociologist and the classicist in locating on the shelves a book with the title *Slavery in the Roman Empire*. But a good system of subject classification seems to me terribly important in the kind of education we are discussing, for it makes possible what we call "browsing."

To stand before a shelf of related books, once having found a starting point, to let one's eye run over the titles, to pull volume after volume off the shelves and leaf through them, skimming the prefaces until one finds just what he wants, lies close to the heart of independent study, and indeed of some kinds of research. The student needs the formal and methodical apparatus of bibliography, abstract, and library catalog, but he also needs the excitement of handling books themselves, of almost accidental discovery. He is denied this unless he is permitted direct and open access to as many books as possible among the library's shelves, not access to books one by one as they are brought to him from some locked area after he has laboriously filled out call slips and endured a tedious wait. How can he ask for what he did not know existed? I plead, in other words, for what we call "open stacks."

This brings us to library architecture, which has the most direct relation to quality in education. We seem not to have given much thought to the function of academic library buildings until the time of World War II; at least, at about that time we seem to have reappraised the functions of libraries as teaching instruments. Examine the college and university library buildings built in the United States in the 1920s and 30s. One intention of their builders strikes one immediately: They set out to glorify the library as a symbol of the continuity of learning. To do this, they made the library an imitation of the Cathedral of Chartres, or the Baths of Caracalla, or some other imposing monument; the names of philosophers, poets, and scientists were carved upon its facade; and it was located prominently, but not always functionally, on the campus.

The library as a symbol needs glorification, even though one questions some of the aesthetics used in these buildings. But basically the designers of these libraries seem to have recognized only two major elements: a handsome, monumental (but poorly lighted) reading room, and a large, locked warehouse for the storage of books. These two were linked in a most tenuous way by only the call desk. This sort of library seems designed to separate books from those who would use them. Only since the war have we begun to build academic library buildings specifically designed to do just the opposite, to bring books and readers together. The forbidding reading room and the closed stack are not really necessary in most situations. The library can become a series of pleasant and human spaces, comfortable areas for both books and people, flowing into one another with an easily understood logic of their own. I have not yet seen it achieved adequately, but it should be possible to bring together all three elements of superior education— not only books and students but teachers as well. In this mode the library building would not so much *serve* the university as *become* the university, the center of the essential dialogues between student and teacher and student and book, the true laboratory of the humanities, surrounded by the other laboratories, where nature is studied, and by the large lecture halls, which will play a minor role in this sort of education.

We do not have this sort of library-university in America. Perhaps it will be developed in Japan, whose lovely traditions of domestic and temple architecture might be adapted by an architect of genius into totally new forms. I would find a library floored with *tatami* mats delightful, if only one could push book carts over them!

The final and the most important element in this integration of the library with the teaching program of the university is the staff. The kind of library which I have been attempting to envision cannot exist without a good staff. The professional members of this staff should have essentially the same skill in teaching and the same scholarly training as the teacher-scholars who comprise the conventional teaching faculty. For their essential role is teaching, although of a somewhat different sort. The good cataloger may have somewhat more bibliographic skill than the classroom lecturer and somewhat less oral facility, but he will be a better cataloger if he has that inborn ability of the real teacher to put himself in the place of the student and from minute to minute feel how well he is reaching the student. The cataloger must be able to perceive the relationship of what he is doing to the learning process of the student. The reference librarian facing a student in need of assistance is in an admirable teaching situation.

If all the members of the professional staff think of themselves as teachers, partners with the classroom teachers, much of the sense of inferiority which librarians sometimes seem to have in our universities should disappear—unless the librarian really is inferior. University libraries now need, I believe, a number of people of scholarly attainments comparable to those of the teaching faculty. When librarians have these attainments, their status and their pay should be equal. Ralph Ellsworth, director of libraries at the University of Colorado, states the situation well in his most recent annual report:

> The effects of granting teaching titles to the librarians who had academic status are beginning to show through the enthusiasm with which the staff members are expanding their activities far beyond the normal call of duty. This enthusiasm has taken several forms—sponsoring workshops and institutes, initiating sponsored research projects, publishing articles in journals, editing professional journals, teaching in formal classes, cooperating with the Boulder school system on a research project, initiating new and interesting kinds of service, and reorganizing departments to increase efficiency.

> The point of view the staff takes is important. If a library staff is encouraged to think of itself as academic it will act the way academicians act. If, on the other hand, it is encouraged to think of itself as technical, then it will act the way technicians do. It is obvious that in a university library everyone, students and faculty, will benefit by having librarians on their side of the academic fence. The record proves the point.

Of course, about two-thirds of all library work is essentially repetitive and clerical. To permit professional librarians to do clerical work is to downgrade the whole library operation, and at the same time increase its cost.

I repeat: The kind of library which I have been describing probably does not quite exist anywhere, in Japan or in the United States. But it almost does in many places, with a working partnership between the library and the faculty which ensures the library a major role in creating a superb environment for learning. This kind of a library will not be a dead warehouse of books; it will be reaching out with eagerness and imagination.

Even though the library which I have been describing does not exist in its perfect form, there is nothing very new about it. It has been described for at least twenty years in the library literature. Yet artificial barriers between student and book persist. It is my plea, therefore, that all of us begin to make the kind of libraries we already know how to make by concentrating on removing these barriers. As we examine administrative structure, collections, bibliographic controls, the deployment of the books, the buildings, and the staff and its attitudes, we might try applying one simple test to each: Does this really help the student get closer to the book and to what is in the book? If not, why not?

The Scholar and the Library

P. M. Mitchell
Professor of Germanic Languages, University of Illinois, Urbana

The function of the scholar in a large company of librarians is presumably to speak for the host of library users for whom the library, in the last analysis, exists. In this day and age where groups of people, be they students, taxpayers, or railroad patrons, who traditionally have accepted the wisdom and experience of specialists and administrators, formulate their own ideas in terms of demands, not infrequently identified as nonnegotiable demands, librarians demonstrate considerable tolerance but perhaps also cautious foresight in expressing a willingness to take into consideration the observations of a library user, be he a scholar or no.

My responsibility is heavy for the simple reason that the number of library users many times exceeds the number of librarians. Since there probably is no typical library user, my remarks will be valid with regard to some users in some situations in some libraries, but not valid for all readers in all situations in all libraries. Perhaps I should state my own limitations so that my remarks may create a minimum of distortion and be understood in the context and spirit in which they are made. I hold a chair in Germanic languages and literatures at one of the large state universities in the midwestern part of the United States. My research work is concentrated on Scandinavian literature and on bibliography. I also edit a learned journal, or, more specifically, the "Germanic" part of the *Journal of English and Germanic Philology*. In my research I have had occasion to use fairly intensely and for long periods of time several libraries, both in the United States and Western Europe—chiefly three libraries in the United States and the Royal Library, i.e., the national library, in Denmark. I can state without exaggeration that my relations with the libraries which I have used have been remarkably agreeable and profitable. Only rarely have rules and regulations seemed in any way to hinder my work. On the contrary, I have found librarians, whether in Denmark, Germany, Sweden, Algeria, or my native United States, invariably to be helpful when they have comprehended that my bibliothecal interests were of a serious nature and when they were apprised of my research. As a matter of fact, practically all my scholarly work done in the past twenty-five years has been carried out in libraries. In short, as a scholar, I am totally dependent on libraries and can only subscribe to the truism that the library is the humanist's laboratory and workshop.

The scholar is almost always also a teacher (and I am no exception). Here again he is dependent on the library, in this case, however, specifically the library or libraries of his own university. For all but elementary courses at the university, students must use the library in a number of ways, for two general reasons: to obtain from books and periodicals the knowledge of facts and of texts which they seek when taking certain courses; and—albeit for a smaller number of students—to familiarize themselves with the library as the laboratory and with books as the tools of scholarship so that they themselves may become the teachers and scholars of the future and both pass on traditional knowledge and seek to increase the sum of what already is known. Since the theme of the library as an adjunct to teaching is simpler, but by no means ultimately less important, than the theme of the library as the temple of research, let us consider it first. Perhaps the differences between library practices in Japan and the United States are more noticeable at this level than on the level of scholarly research.

When American—or German or Danish —students arrive at the university, they are ordinarily bibliographically naïve. Most have had experience with card catalogs in school and public libraries, but they are unaware of the ramifications of a large research library, and they are unable to use such bibliographic tools as indices of periodicals to locate books and articles pertaining to special problems about which they may be asked to read or to prepare written reports. At the very start of their education at the university, an effort is usually made to acquaint them with the general working of the library, so that they can order the right book, locate a better-known periodical, find their way to departmental libraries, and—above all—make use of the reference desk, which so often is the salvation of all of us after we have looked in vain for a book the author of which escapes us or for an article on a subject tangential to our own major interest. This kind of hasty library orientation suffices for the younger students, but is not adequate for the older students (the so-called graduate students), who already have acquired their baccalaureate degrees after four years of study, and who now wish to address themselves with greater commitment to a special facet of learning, their intent being to achieve an advanced degree, either the master's or doctor's degree, and to make some independent contribution to knowledge.

In the United States it has become necessary to give some special instruction, generally a one-semester course, in the bibliography of almost every discipline, so that the graduate students may be equipped to keep abreast of what is being done on any given topic and be in a position to decide judiciously which book or which edition of a writer's works is indeed most useful. Such bibliographic courses are often taught in the library building, if there is some classroom facility there. In many cases the teacher accompanies the students to a part of the library, perhaps to the reference room or the bibliographic shelves, to help them make physical acquaintance with unwieldy reference works, such as the several national bibliographies or the *Bibliographie der deutschsprachigen* (or *fremdsprachigen*) *Zeitschriftenliteratur*. Or perhaps the teacher and students go to the rare book collection to examine especially valuable items which do not circulate.

After such an introduction to the literature of a certain discipline under the tutelage of an experienced scholar, the graduate students are expected to be able to work on their own, with occasional guidance from their teachers, and to exploit the holdings of the university library—and perhaps other libraries as well—fairly thoroughly. From now on the problem is really whether the repositories to which the student has access do indeed possess the necessary book or periodical. Unlike the situation at, say, German universities, where one needs a special pass or key to gain access to a seminar library, the holdings of which are only in part duplicated in the main library, the American university library tends to be integrated, with a central catalog and with easy access to departmental or special collections. Despite very liberal rules about the circulation of books, many items must be used in special collections, but they are nevertheless readily available. On occasion, but fortunately infrequently, there may be a clash of interest between the serious-minded student and the recalcitrant professor, who does not heed the pleas of the loan desk to return a book which is needed by another reader. Alas, it has been my observation that the uncooperative professor fails to return the book through thoughtlessness; he is not actually using the book the few days that it might be wrested from him (especially if he already has had it checked out for six months). This is not peculiar to the American scene; it is part of the international academic obstacle course.

There are, to be sure, research libraries which restrict the use of some books to certain types of readers. Thus the Royal Library in Copenhagen will not ordinarily lend belles-lettres to general readers, even in the reading room. The library requires some assurance that the books are indeed being put to scholarly use. The principle here is that the Royal Library as the national library of Denmark is the permanent repository of Danish literature—so to speak, the court of last resort—where the preservation of the book for the scholars of future generations is as important as the use the book may have currently. Patrons are referred to the public library system if they wish to read novels, short stories, and poetry for their own edification. Such restrictions serve to help rather than to hinder scholarship in the field of literature, however. Similarly, restrictions on the use of certain kinds of material often can be advantageous to the scholar, albeit a source of irritation to the general reader and perhaps the student, who is neither an acknowledged scholar nor merely a general reader.

This suggests the classical and semi-humorous librarian's pronouncement that the proper place of the book is on the shelf. Such a philosophy, if indeed it really ever existed in its pure form, is certainly less and less prevalent, because libraries, especially in state institutions of all the countries which I am familiar with, base their requests for funds to legislative and other money-granting bodies on the irrefutable basis of circulation statistics. A corollary of the new argument for more funds is, therefore, the encouragement of prospective readers to use books. There is a danger in this new trend, however. Librarians have become more logisticians and less lovers of books in recent decades. The scholar's heart is not warmed by the librarian who is efficient in the techniques of circulation or cataloging and is not primarily concerned with the *contents* of books and the aims of research. For this reason the scholar is pleased when librarians who also are scholars are at the helm in a university library, despite the anguished cries from some quarters that the competent scholar is incompatible with the competent administrator. Perhaps this anguish is not without foundation, but the ideal synthesis of the scholar and the librarian is always worth striving for, and there are enough examples of living scholar-librarians who evoke admiration from their peers in both categories to prove that the ideal is not totally unrealistic.

Let me now discuss the relation of the scholar and the library somewhat more concretely and aside from the scholar's role as a teacher. I may be forgiven for espousing the scholar's point of view and probably pontificating without sufficient consideration for the problems of library administration. As every experienced librarian knows, the scholar tends to be intolerant and impatient. He is intolerant of the procedures which are necessary to preserve order and avoid chaos in the flood of printed matter which threatens to engulf the research library daily. He is impatient to get the book or the periodical which he wants, if only to assure himself that that book or periodical is in fact of negative value to him in his research. When a scholar needs to examine a book or article at 9 A.M., he does not want to wait until 3 P.M. for it, not to mention the next day (if it has to be fetched from a closed stack area or an outlying deposit library) or three weeks (if it has to be ordered through an interlibrary loan system or be microfilmed). I shall blithely assume that all librarians will agree that I should not have to wait until 3 P.M. for any publication which I want to examine at 9 A.M. I proceed to make a series of observations

which are loosely connected with this admirable hypothesis.

The library-oriented scholar's first basic concern is with the size and quality of the collection of books and periodicals with which he works. A historian whom I know once said that he could not work in a library with fewer than a million books. This is a fairly good if snobbish rule of thumb. The individual scholar does not need a million books; he may never use more than a thousand of them, but in a smaller library he will not find the large reference collection which is important for research, especially in the humanities, if trivial matters are to be taken care of expeditiously, so that all the tangential questions pertaining to his research can be readily answered without any significant loss of time. The smaller library simply will not come near to owning all the national bibliographies, all the major encyclopedias, all the biographical dictionaries, and the standard histories, sets, grammars, and statistical tables in both major and minor languages. The large library will at least approach a more comprehensive collection, not merely because of the size of the collections but because of the larger number of library users with varying interests who have some say about book purchasing. There is, of course, a correlation between material means necessary for continued acquisition and the size, and more particularly, the growth of a library. Fortunately I have not been asked to address myself to the problem of a source of constantly increasing funds. I note only that the number of books which I need in 1969 is larger than the number of books I needed in 1959, and that the funds required to procure the books which I need are relatively greater, too.

I stated that the scholar's first basic concern was not only with size but with size and quality. Duplication versus breadth can be a contentious issue. It probably is not an entirely soluble issue because of various human factors involved, from tired feet to empire building. Teachers in American (but not European) universities frequently want their libraries to acquire multiple copies of the textbooks which are used by large numbers of students. Students want standard reference works—expensive dictionaries and encyclopedias—available in every working area, i.e., in every reading room and special or seminar library. Scholars want duplicate or multiple copies of certain works which they use regularly to be easily accessible, and, quite understandably, they also want the library to acquire revised editions, even if the revision consists only of a brief foreword or afterword by another scholar. This type of purchasing, in which to a greater or lesser extent all libraries seem to be engaged, does help statistically to swell collections, but it militates toward a rather static collection, and at the same time reduces the quantity of other items which the library might be purchasing and therewith the quality of the collection's texture. The advent of the Xerox machine has alleviated this situation slightly, but even it is not the answer to the need for four or five copies of the standard Danish-English dictionary and innumerable sets of the *Encyclopaedia Britannica* in the University of Illinois library.

Size, then, must be tempered by quality, if the scholar really is to be best served. It is against his own interest to insist that collections of little used, if intrinsically valuable, material be found both in the main university library and the seminar or departmental library which lies nearer his study or over which he has more control. In part, this problem, which represents a serious conflict of interest not only between the faculty and the administration of a library but within the scholar himself, has been solved at many institutions in a very subtle way by establishing the scholar in the library and perhaps even moving his own special collection into the main library building. The newer university libraries in the United States usually have studies built adjacent to the stacks of the libraries or in connection with special libraries which are housed in the same building as the main collection. With such an arrangement, the apparent need for duplication is to a large extent alleviated.

The quality—or what I have called the texture—of the library is determined by a combination of factors working in time. While money to purchase books is perhaps the single most important factor determining the nature of a research library, the criterion for the selection of books is certainly the second most important factor. Assembling a very large number of different titles more or less at random will ultimately serve scholarly purposes, if only by means of an interlibrary loan system, but it will not produce a satisfactory working library for any given group of scholars. Since the universal library is no longer a goal which can be achieved, any all-around reduction of this goal so that all fields are well represented in the library is essentially unsatisfactory. Scholars are aware of, and reconciled to, the fact that only certain libraries will serve their purposes unless they are given a strong voice in the acquisitions policy of a library to which they are bound accidentally. The libraries which already serve the purpose of, say, the historian of Japan in America, are monuments to the special interests of either scholars or collectors whose great interest has been Japan. He who would work with the history of Japan had best try to use these libraries. If, however, he is not attached to an institution of higher learning that already owns a good collection in Japanese history and he does not have easy and continual access to such a collection, his only hope is having enough funds at his disposal to be able to build up a collection which will serve his purposes in the course of a few years. In so doing he will be only one of many scholars affiliated with the same institution who are using library funds to build up collections in their own fields of research.

While there are critics who feel that this way of acquiring books leads to a checkerboard of imperfect special collections, especially when the faculty member with a vested interest in library acquisitions in his field elects to move to another institution and is not replaced by a scholar with equivalent interests, I am convinced that the scholar with the vested interest is indeed the best agent for building a strong research library. During the years that he is responsible for purchases, he is working methodically and carefully so that the books which he has ordered, taken in the aggregate, represent an ideal realized and constitute a closely knit fabric of research material. In many cases, but not in all, to be sure, another scholar will come along who can make good use of such research material and add to it methodically. In some cases the collection may become outstanding enough to attract scholars from far and near and therewith both add to the general prestige of the university and encourage public and private sources of funds to support a library which is eminent in one or more fields.

The Cornell University Library provides us with a good example. The Icelandic Collection bequeathed to the library by Willard Fiske is unequaled in the United States and, until recently, its holdings have compared favorably with those of the National Library of Iceland and the Royal Library in Copenhagen. Willard Fiske also gathered significant Dante and Petrarch collections which also are widely known. The eminence of these collections, which were the work of a single scholar and bibliophile, have, through their printed catalogs, certainly contributed to giving the Cornell University Library the name which it enjoys, encouraged building up other facets of the Cornell Library, such as its books in Germanic philology and Scandinavian literature, and doubtless helped attract other donations to an already distinguished library.

When I speak of collections built up by individual scholars, I am not referring primarily to collections which are kept separate and perhaps cataloged separately from the main collection of the university library (as indeed is the case with the Fiske Icelandic Collection), but merely to that group of books for the acquisition of which a certain faculty member (or even group of faculty members) bore the responsibility. I am aware of the various arguments pro and con regarding separate special collections. On the whole I favor them, because they achieve an identity which the same number of books scattered throughout a larger library would not have, and they do save an enormous amount of time

for the scholar who works almost entirely within the field covered by the collection. Printed catalogs of special collections are much more often published than the catalogs of large libraries and are very useful to scholars everywhere, not only for the location of books but also for the identification and description of the books listed. To be of optimum use, however, special collections must exist in conjunction with a general library that can furnish at once the standard reference works which are not to be found in a separate collection. From the standpoint of the general reader who may have occasion to refer once or twice to a book in such a separate collection and from the standpoint of everyday efficiency, one could make a case for their not existing at all.

While I have used the pejorative term "vested interest" in mentioning the efforts of scholars to have the libraries with which they are affiliated acquire large numbers of books in their fields of endeavor, such efforts spring from a feeling of obligation and represent a very large investment of time. In the first instance, the scholar who wants to increase acquisitions in his field must determine what the library does and does not have in that field. In the second instance, he must make a concentrated effort to locate books which are of importance to the field. This he does primarily by reading booksellers' catalogs and on occasion by visiting secondhand bookshops (usually abroad, if his regular station is in the United States).

I have never tried to establish how many hours a year I spend reading booksellers' catalogs, but I do know that I read several every week, probably on the average of one a day. The catalogs are themselves informative and sometimes bibliographically enlightening, even though 99 percent of the time spent reading them is without any positive result. Once the catalog is read, there should be some efficient way to check it against library holdings before recommending that certain books be ordered, but in my experience the efficient and dependable method has yet to be found, if we except the wasteful practice of using trained librarians to check titles against catalogs of both processed and un-processed books. Assuming good communication between the interested scholar and the acquisitions department of a library, an order can be sent off within two or three days of the receipt of the catalog, although for a number of reasons, there are more frequently some delays along the way.

The participation of the scholar in the acquisitions process may end at this juncture. He may now wait until the book appears on the shelf. If, however, the book is of immediate interest to him, he will arrange for some sort of notification so that the book is made available to him as early as possible. There are cases where notification of the book's arrival prior to its being cataloged can serve a good scholarly purpose (as, for example, in the preparation of annual bibliographies), and in such cases the personal relations between the acquisitions department and the scholar are of primary importance. It is a disservice to scholarship to insist (as some librarians unfortunately do) that no book be available until it has been cataloged—not to mention bound, if the book has been received unbound.

Just as the scholar should feel an obligation to read booksellers' catalogs, he should be ready to give advice where needed when material of a highly specialized nature in his field is being classified. This is a facet of the relationship between scholars and libraries which probably receives the least attention at most American university libraries. The compensation which the scholar receives for such cooperation is a large amount of goodwill generated in the library and the willingness of librarians to tolerate his foibles and to give him speedy service and bibliographic help when he especially needs them.

While it is important that the book-buying scholar enjoy such a relationship with the acquisitions department of a library that there is a minimum of delay in ordering books, it is even more important that the necessary funds for both regular and extraordinary purchases be available when needed. Some reasonable annual budget for each discipline or subdiscipline is a sensible arrangement, but there must

be a relatively large contingency fund administered intelligently so that unusual opportunities may not be passed by or special block purchases be impossible. Since no library has unlimited funds, encumbering available funds requires wisdom and diplomatic skill on the part of some authority—a committee of librarians and faculty members who determine library policy, the head librarian alone, or the head librarian acting in concert with certain specialists in the library.

The second major concern of the scholar is having access to the books which are in fact in the library, or, in the case of a university, in any of the departmental, divisional, or institute libraries which belong to the university. Essential to this concern is some kind of central library catalog—ideally a single catalog arranged according to a single system, but in any case some comprehensive catalog of holdings which will ensure that, once the scholar has examined the catalog or catalogs, there will be no hidden collections which he has overlooked.

The single catalog covering all the books owned by a university consisting of many faculties is perhaps an impossible goal, but if there are several catalogs which must be examined each time one is searching for a title, they should at least be available in the same building and should be of such a nature that even the uninitiated can use them. While I enjoy leafing through the antiquated catalogs of the Royal Library in Copenhagen, catalogs which are almost the antithesis of the ideal I have just established, they are not for the uninitiated; they are, as far as the Danish collection is concerned, systematic and not alphabetical, and they are handwritten, partly in Gothic script, in folio volumes. The classification dates back to the eighteenth century, so that a fairly good knowledge of history is required even to imagine how books might have been classified at some earlier time. There are separate catalogs both in folio volumes and on handwritten cards of the Foreign Division of the Royal Library. In addition, there are special catalogs of dissertations, serial publications, and books which fall into certain other special categories. The casual user of the library cannot hope to penetrate the system unaided and has no recourse but to appeal to a reference librarian for help merely in using the catalogs.

Similar situations obtain at many other old libraries, where the principles of classification have been changed in the course of time and where old systems have been superseded by new systems, and the books classified under the old system have never been reclassified. As a consequence the scholar must spend a very large percentage of his time working through catalogs in an essentially inefficient way, and frequently with the disturbing suspicion that he probably has overlooked something. Reclassification of large older collections is probably almost out of the question, because of the large amount of time and money which would be required. The method employed in classifying books is not of signal importance for the scholar, providing it is consistent and thorough, and preferably with cross-references which will alert the scholar to possibilities that he might not think of himself. Too many entries are here a vice to be preferred above too few entries, as, for example, the bewildering mass of academy publications and certain serials, individual parts of which may or may not be considered to be separate publications.

Access to recent acquisitions is a different matter from the location of books classified under an antiquated system. We all know of cases where books have been acquired but have not been cataloged for months, and, sad to say, even years. The great delays are not usual in the case of newly published books, but rather with older books which present more problems in classification and analysis and which may be part of a large collection for which there seems to be no time or personnel available for immediate cataloging. This is a deplorable situation, for the very item which a scholar is seeking may indeed be in the library building awaiting the attentions of a cataloger who is busy with some other equally important matter. The use of an order catalog, if there by good fortune is a single such catalog, or access to the lists of books which have been ordered

or are being processed, is much better than nothing but is bound to cause some disruption in the ordering and processing departments. The way out of this dilemma seems to be a quick temporary classification, perhaps by acquisition number. Again, the method of classification, even though it is completely arbitrary, is secondary to the principle of making the book available. Some libraries have tried to make a division between books that will be much used and little used, but the reason for a judgment invariably turns out to be illusory, since one man's meat is another man's poison.

Subordinate to the matter of locating books by the use of catalogs is the matter of gaining physical access to the book where it is kept. Whereas the European university and research libraries traditionally deliver to the scholar in a reading room only those books which he has specifically ordered, the American university library invariably gives the scholar (and graduate student) free access to the stacks, where he can fetch a desired book himself and, much more important, where he can orient himself on the holdings of books cataloged in the vicinity of the book which he originally set out to locate. Access to stacks is an education in itself. Here the reader can examine twenty books quickly in the time it would take him to get a single volume in the reading room. He can compare issues and editions without further ado. He can even make a selection among duplicate copies of the same book.

Especially for a bibliographer like myself, who often has to have recourse to the same book more than once but for only a few minutes each time, access to the stacks is a particular blessing, and a great relief to library personnel as well. The bibliographer may easily need to refer to a hundred books in the course of a working day. I recall some years ago that I ordered sixty items in one day at the Royal Library in Copenhagen. Instead of a cart full of books in response to my many order slips, there appeared a worried librarian who told me that the library simply did not have the personnel to locate sixty items for a single patron in the course of one day—especially since the books in the stacks of the Royal Library bear no classification marks on their spines. Such a situation, were there not a solution through the expedient of breaking the rules of the library regarding access to the stacks, would have been a serious bibliographic stumbling block. It is really not difficult to imagine some rather easy solution to the difficulties of furnishing the voracious bibliographer with large numbers of books from the stacks in a short time. Service in the main library of an American university is rapid. Despite the unavoidable complaints of some users about slowness, books are ordinarily delivered within ten minutes of their having been ordered in the American libraries I have used, although the scholar ordinarily does not order books at all if he has access to the stacks—unless the book he wants cannot be located, must be recalled, or is in a restricted area of the building.

Because the privilege of entering the stacks is shared by a very large number of people (at the University of Illinois, the number must run to more than 8,000), and because the shelving of books is the responsibility of students who are temporarily employed, there is at any given time a relatively large number of books out of place on the shelf or removed from the shelf and left on desks or sorting shelves. In a collection as large as that of the University of Illinois, one finds one or more books out of place every time one has occasion to look through a few shelves of books for any purpose. The scholar is sometimes nonplussed because books which are not charged out are not on the shelves, especially when he considers that the number of misplaced books in a library with closed stacks (such as the Royal Library in Copenhagen) is infinitesimally small. The disadvantages of many displaced books must be weighed against the principle of open stacks, however. On the whole, I opt for open stacks, although I fully realize that certain research libraries, especially those which are national repositories and which do not separate more from less valuable books, or old from new books, and do not use a perfectly lucid cataloging system, would do humanistic research a disservice by opening the stacks to any but

trained personnel. What the individual scholar probably envisages as an ideal solution to his own personal needs is access to closed stacks, a self-contradiction which does indeed sometimes come to pass.

Access to the stacks has increased as the function of the main reading room in American university libraries has changed. Whereas some European reading rooms are, on the whole, still the province of researchers and scholars, the reading room of an American university library is simply a study area for students. The students in the reading rooms are only to a small degree actually using library materials. In part for this reason, it has seemed necessary and desirable to create special "undergraduate libraries," with smaller collections of books and large reading areas. Such arrangements serve the scholar only indirectly, by decreasing the pressure on the main library collection and on the reading room or rooms in the research library.

The pleasant atmosphere of a group of scholars working in concord in a single reading room, such as the reading room of the Royal Library in Copenhagen, where patrons not infrequently call upon one another to answer questions in special fields and benefit mutually from such an arrangement, is not easily achieved. No American —or German or Danish—university library has such a reading room, but certain special research libraries, such as the Folger Library in Washington and (I am told) the Huntington Library in California, do preserve something of a temporary community of scholars who know one another and who have an opportunity to discuss various matters with one another in the halls or canteens of the library itself. The main reading rooms of the library of the British Museum and the Library of Congress still suggest such a self-contained reading room, but they are too large and house too heterogeneous a population to resemble strongly the scholars' reading room of a Scandinavian research library. The library of the future cannot be expected to reproduce any aspect of the medieval community of scholars; the individual scholar must necessarily retire to a desk in the stacks or to a study. Although the scholar can reasonably expect to have all the reference books to which he regularly may refer in a single library building, he should not expect to have all such works at arm's length. Reading rooms still function as general reference rooms, so the scholar must be peripatetic, if he has frequently to use national bibliographies, periodical indices, foreign bibliographic dictionaries, and lexica.

Perhaps I should state at this juncture that I have consciously referred to university libraries and to research libraries, but not to public (communal) libraries. In the United States and in Western Europe, their functions are pretty much separate; as a consequence the scholar rarely has occasion to use public libraries. The New York Public Library in New York City is only a nominal exception, for it is not really a public library in the usual sense of the term. It is a privately supported metropolitan research library.

The third major concern of the scholar is periodicals. Here he has two overwhelming needs: first, that his library subscribe to all the important periodicals in his field, and second, that the current numbers of a given periodical be immediately available. Now the scholar himself probably subscribes to several learned journals, notably those published by societies of which he is a member. Ironically enough, these are usually among the journals which he can be certain his library also will have, whereas he has to depend (if only for economic reasons) on his institutional library for a score or more of other periodicals which he should follow regularly. Few libraries can afford to subscribe to every periodical in any large field of learning, especially because of the proliferation of journals in recent decades and the ephemeral nature of many publications. Even if a scholar's institutional library is so fortunate as to be able to subscribe to every periodical that he suggests, there is still a mighty moment of irritation when the periodicals either fail to arrive or take many days to be processed and to reach their place in the proper reading room or on the proper shelf. Since periodicals from abroad are ordinarily received by surface mail, the delay between their being published and their being re-ceived can be great. Moreover, for reasons of ostensible efficiency, some libraries concentrate their orders with a few dealers, perhaps even dealers outside the country where a journal is published. And for ostensible reasons of efficiency, these same dealers may not send on periodicals immediately. Such delays are exasperating and decrease the value, especially to a bibliographer, of the periodical in question.

It is a matter of fact that people in various parts of the world concentrate on similar problems at about the same time. There is nothing psychic about this example of *Zeitgeist*; comparable conditions produce comparable results in Japan, the United States, or Denmark. For this reason it is essential that scholars in one part of the globe be informed as quickly as possible about the work of scholars in the same discipline in another part of the globe, so that there will not be duplication of effort and so that the one researcher can build on the contributions made by the other. Librarians, faced with an influx of periodicals which cover the entire spectrum of human endeavor, do not and cannot always place each number of each periodical in the right spot with the minimum of delay. In part, their inability to do so after the periodical has been received is to be ascribed to the narrow attitude of some scholars. The very simple question of the ideal location for the periodicals to which any given university research library subscribes has never been answered to the general satisfaction. Many researchers make a strong case for having the periodicals in their own disciplines in their departmental libraries. They plead that their use of the periodicals is so closely tied to their own research that the periodicals must be, so to speak, ever present. Unfortunately, several disciplines in several locations regularly make the same plea, and the only solution is multiple subscriptions—which are or can be exceedingly costly, particularly in the physical sciences. Moreover, the general rule is that the current numbers and unbound numbers of a periodical may not circulate, so that a scholar from one departmental library cannot borrow a current periodical from another.

Even if the principle is accepted that the main repository of periodicals should be the departmental library, there are many periodicals left over of general or tangential interest to the scholar (and not only the general reader) which should not be deposited in departmental libraries. All this means is that the researcher who feels obliged to follow forty or fifty periodicals must use several, even as many as eight or ten, separate libraries more than once during the year, to fulfill his bibliographic obligations. This arrangement is wasteful in terms of time and motion, for the periodicals do not arrive according to a schedule, and one never sees all the current numbers of the periodicals one is interested in a single visit to any of the several repositories for such periodicals.

There have been simple and sophisticated plans worked out to alleviate this problem. One of the simplest is to have the current numbers of the leading periodicals circulate among all interested persons in a certain discipline. While there is some virtue to this as a private arrangement among scholars, a library would be ill-advised to let its current periodicals circulate in such a fashion. One of the most sophisticated plans is the MEDLARS system of information retrieval for medical scholars. The methods of information retrieval are certainly going to be applied to many more disciplines in the near future. As a consequence, some aspects of research will be made more efficient, but no system of information retrieval can ever be exhaustive retrospectively. While abstracting and information retrieval will produce all the current contributions on a given subject immediately, it leaves unanswered the question of what else is being or has been recently published. The scholar must still scan journals himself.

The best solution I have experienced is at the University of Wisconsin, where a single large periodical room tries to make available the vast majority of periodicals to which the library subscribes. This may mean that a good many toes have been stepped on at Wisconsin, for the scholars in many disciplines may feel themselves imposed upon to have to go to the period-

ical room in the main library rather than the periodical section of their departmental libraries. This slight inconvenience for all connotes a great advantage for all; one has to use only a single repository to keep up with the journals one is interested in. Whether this arrangement, in my opinion admirable, has in actuality meant that departmental libraries have insisted on multiple subscriptions to many journals, I do not know. In any case, all journals are available in one place, whether or not specialists have additional copies of certain journals essentially for their own use in some other part of the university.

Since the arrival of the copying machine we are much better off in regard to periodicals in many libraries. By having such a machine in the proximity of periodicals, it is possible to reproduce a single article for a small sum and to avoid the aggravation caused by a current journal's being non-circulating. For one reason or another, not all libraries have strategically placed machines; some still have none at all. Such machines are so incredibly useful, however, that it certainly will only be a matter of time before they are installed everywhere.

The fourth major concern of the scholar is the material he requires which is *not* to be found in the library where he regularly works. While I have implied above that research libraries should have minimum holdings of a million volumes, it would be arrogant to assume that they all do. The number of very large libraries which are capable of satisfying most of the immediate needs of scholars in a variety of fields is very small. By no means all scholars are working or want to work in these libraries. Therefore, the number of titles that any scholar will seek in a given library is necessarily a good deal larger than the number of items he will find. To a greater or lesser extent he must depend on some other source of supply than his library. Moreover, even in the largest libraries in the United States, the outgoing demands of an interlibrary loan system are very heavy.

The large library is convenient because of its stock of reference works. It may have very few holdings in a certain field, however. I have recently completed a bibliography of certain imprints from the seventeenth century. Although I ordinarily work in the third largest university library in the United States, my library does not have more than half a dozen of the 3,000 items which are recorded in my bibliography. In fact, perhaps only two libraries in the United States have any more than that, a fact which I was able to determine only by assiduous use of the American interlibrary loan system and the National Union Catalog in Washington. While the interlibrary loan system and the National Union Catalog could not produce books not already in the libraries in the United States, the negative information which they provided was very useful and demonstrated clearly that I had to look elsewhere for the material which I needed—as it turned out, principally in Copenhagen, Denmark, and Kiel, Germany.

An interlibrary loan system, even though it may be somewhat slow and not entirely dependable, is invaluable. The concept of a national union catalog is brilliant; one can only hope that at some future date it will indeed be possible to check the holdings of all libraries, or at least all research libraries, in a single country by the use of a single catalog.

Actually, much of my work was done with the help not of the American interlibrary loan system but with that of a superior service in Germany, the Auskunftsstelle der deutschen Bibliotheken in Berlin. The Auskunftsstelle combines the virtues of a union catalog with those of an interlibrary loan system. If it cannot locate a book in its own union catalog (which goes back to the beginnings of the incomplete *Deutscher Gesamtkatalog*), the Auskunftsstelle sends postal cards for each title being searched to every library which cooperates with it, both in West Germany and in the German Democratic Republic. All these libraries are obliged to check all titles and to report on the cards furnished them by the Auskunftsstelle. Positive information is then sent to the library from which the original enquiry has been made, and the item which has been located can then be ordered directly from one library to another. If the results of this search are negative, one can be fairly sure that at least no research library

of any size in Germany possesses the desired item. This system seems to function more efficiently and rapidly than the American system of sending out printed lists of unlocated books occasionally. Moreover, there are several bibliographic centers in Germany where it is possible to check the holdings of libraries in a given area—including libraries which are not part of the research library complex covered by the Auskunftsstelle, such as the monastery libraries in Bavaria, which have their holdings recorded in the regional bibliographic center at the Staatsbibliothek in Munich.

Although the United States may not have perfected its interlibrary loan system or have adequate national or regional bibliographic centers, it does have an extraordinarily useful tool in the *Union List of Serials*, which is (in its current third edition) very nearly up to date and which locates the holdings of all periodicals owned by the libraries (including many more than the university, college, and research libraries) of the United States. At any library it is possible to determine with a very high degree of certainty not only which libraries own which periodicals, but even which years are held by specific libraries.

Having determined where a desired periodical is to be found, the scholar ideally has it ordered through the interlibrary loan system. In actual practice, however, libraries are tending to restrict the shipment of periodicals through the mails and instead furnish microfilm or Xerox copies of the article wanted by a reader in another library. In most cases this is satisfactory, but for a scholar who wants to study the entire contents of several volumes of a periodical, the inability to obtain certain volumes can be frustrating. If his library will agree to purchase an entire run of a periodical on microfilm, he is fortunate in a sense, but having to examine such a large amount of material on microfilm is never an entirely practical or happy arrangement.

In recent years many reprints of older journals have appeared. Generally they are rather expensive, since the reprint company feels it must amortize its investment by the sale of only a few copies of a single item. Such reprints are naturally much more welcome than microfilm. The many new reprints are also of utmost importance for the growth of new scholarly libraries, since many of the reprinted items do not appear on the market in the original editions. Given the funds, one can assemble a very creditable scholarly library entirely of reprints today.

Any interlibrary loan system can be expected to furnish only a small number of books to any scholar. Where there is a concentration of books on a special subject in a certain library elsewhere, it is more sensible to move the scholar to the library rather than the library, or large parts of it, to the scholar. This is a matter which is ordinarily beyond the control of a library, and the scholar must look to other sources than the library for funds to proceed to a distant or perhaps even a foreign library, unless he can meet the expenses from his own pocket. There are a few privately endowed research libraries in the United States—I know of none elsewhere—that do have funds which enable them to award grants and fellowships to scholars who need to use those libraries. Perhaps the best known of such libraries is the Folger Shakespeare Library in Washington, D.C., which has made grants to scholars of many nationalities.

The conditions under which one works are something out of the ordinary when one is a visiting scholar at a strange library or the library of an institution of which one is not a part. The problem is not so much of gaining admission to another library; merely because of a prevailing sense of reciprocity, the visiting scholar usually finds himself well received. The problem is rather getting to know and use a different catalog, perhaps a different system of classification, locating reference works in new places, accommodating oneself to different hours and different rules for library use, and, of course, sometimes trying to overcome a language barrier. None of these matters is ever insuperable, but they may use up precious hours. I recall, for example, my dismay when I was ejected from the Herzog August Bibliothek in Wolfenbüttel, Germany, a few years ago for an unwanted two-hour break for lunch. My dismay was,

however, only partially justified, for I was, after all, a guest. I was enjoying privileges and not rights as a foreigner and a visitor—a fact which a scholar sometimes forgets in his devotion to the subject of his research. Actually I enjoyed the cooperation of the librarians and had their sympathetic ear. I had been taken in without credentials or a letter of introduction and was permitted to use all the facilities of the library during the regular library hours.

The established scholar has easier access than the embryonic scholar—by which I mean the candidate for an advanced degree in the United States or Western Europe—to strange libraries. In part this is because it is easier to recognize (and harder to turn away) a researcher who has a title, but in part it is for reasons of security and because of previous observation that the fledgling scholar is less certain what he wants to look at and how he should determine just what to do. The candidate for a degree would do well to have a definite plan in mind when he goes to a strange library, and should have either a letter of introduction with him or the name of some person who knows his professors or with whom he already has corresponded. These suggestions are so simple and straightforward that they probably sound quite superfluous, but the fact is that they are often more apparent to the older scholar who does not need to follow them than to the younger scholar who does.

Most library users feel that there should be few restrictions on libraries which are in the public domain or which are supported by the state. In point of fact, there are very few restrictions either in America or Europe compared to conditions which obtained only a few decades ago, not to mention a century ago. This attitude on the part of library users is, however, also carried over to private collections, at least those private libraries which regularly admit large numbers of users. There is a possibility of some conflict here, where grievances conceivably are justified on the part of the scholar as well as that of the administration of private libraries. The sort of private collection which is in effect a personal library and is never open to the public is quite a different matter; yet there is a key which opens the door to almost all of even such collections: sympathetic interest shared by the scholar and the owners of the private collection. The scholar wishing to examine such a private collection does not simply beat on the door and expect to be admitted. He either seeks admittance by correspondence or through the good offices of another scholar or librarian who is acquainted with the owner of the private collection. Here, as elsewhere, the importance of personal relations cannot be underestimated. I do not mean knowing influential persons but establishing a bond of understanding between scholar and bibliophile.

Since libraries are often the repositories of manuscript material as well as books, a certain library which may possess unpublished material can become of the greatest importance for a scholar whose interest may focus on that material. Here the questions of restricted usage are readily understandable. The person who wants to use the manuscripts is probably best aware of their unique quality and value and is therefore not taken aback by many special security regulations which are set up to preserve the very material in which he has a vested interest. Moreover, the relatively easy ways to copy manuscript material now mean that a single visit to a library may suffice, since most scholarly work, if we except such unusual disciplines as the study of paper and watermarks, can be done on the basis of reproductions.

The scholar's fifth basic concern should be—but is not always—the nature of the reference service available in his library. The difference between adequate and inadequate reference service is frequently brought home dramatically to the American scholar on weekends and holidays (when he may have the most free time at his disposal) when the library in which he works may have a skeleton staff on duty—or, still worse, may be mainly in the hands of untrained student assistants who may be unfamiliar with the reference collection, ill-equipped in foreign languages, bewildered by the maze of government documents, and uninformed about the authority to whom a patron in distress can turn for information after a vain struggle to solve an apparently

soluble problem. Such a situation does not obtain in European libraries, which are given to closing when their regular staff is not functioning. This is something of a dilemma to the scholar and, of course, a cause of vexation to the outside visitor who is not fully cognizant of the vagaries of the library's hours.

My debt to well-informed librarians who man their posts, if not on Sunday evenings, then during the regular working hours of the week, is too great to be delineated adequately here. They have saved me hours and days of work; they have saved me from making inexcusable blunders; they have brought me up to date on publications tangential to my own field, and they have initiated me into bibliographic shortcuts which have then become a regular part of my own routine. Fortunately, not a few of them are charming ladies whom I can admire unabashed. The life of a good reference librarian is one of service and dedication. It has been my observation that they receive little recognition for their services simply because they help a very large number of people, each for a short time, and rarely become collaborators in scholarly efforts.

Subordinate to these major concerns of the scholar in a library, and more particularly in a university library, are several lesser concerns which from time to time loom very large in his eyes, since they may interfere with his routine or his rhythm of work and actually erode some of the precious time which he has to spend in the library. I refer to such matters as the number of hours that a library is open, the nature of the working areas—studies or carrels—which are available in the library, the unexplained loss of a book or periodical, distractions in the vicinity of the area where the scholar is working, the fact that the book or periodical must sometimes be at the bindery, not to mention occasional arbitrary and sometimes ossified regulations which do not seem to be supported by the justification of common sense.

Two further points should be made regarding the scholar and his relation to the modern library. First, only certain kinds of scholarship are as dependent on a library as

I have indicated here. As a consequence, only certain kinds of scholars are the regular patrons and habitués of research libraries. These are chiefly humanistic scholars with an historical bent, if we disregard the bibliographers, who are in a sense mobile extensions of the libraries' holdings. Some of my colleagues who are among the most productive and prestigious of scholars in their fields are scarcely ever seen in the library, since they work either in a laboratory, or with abstract problems, or are dependent on a rather limited amount of current periodical literature. Neither the mathematicians nor the natural scientists, for example, are assiduous library users, whereas the literary historian has his spiritual home among books.

Second, many modern libraries are not only places where books may be used but also institutions which actively encourage research and themselves publish the results of work done in conjunction with their holdings. Here again there is a fruitful interplay between librarian and scholar. The scholar may depend on the librarian not only to provide him with the raw material of his studies but sometimes even to publish the results of those studies. This state of affairs has greatly encouraged research oriented on libraries and research concerning the history of books and bibliothecal problems in general. As a result, the many-faceted functions of libraries have been more adequately delineated and the quality of library service improved, while the extent and nature of books and manuscripts preserved in a library have been described so that they can be more fully exploited in the constant struggle to push back the borders of the unknown, to contribute to a better understanding of the past, and at the same time to cast light on what the German poet Schiller once identified as the dark land of the future.

Hobbledehoy: Japanese Collections in American Libraries

James William Morley
*Professor of Government,
Columbia University*

American specialists on Japan depend beyond measure on American collections of Japanese-language materials and, when we are fortunate enough to be able to visit Japan, on the libraries there as well. We are still a relatively small group. Japanese studies, after all, are a recent innovation in America. Although introduced at a few universities more than thirty or forty years ago, it is only over the past twenty years or so that the study of Japan has become a serious part of the curriculum of American higher education. But we are growing rapidly. During the past twenty years Japanese language courses have been instituted in 55 colleges and universities. The total number of student enrollments in these language courses is today close to 4,000— still far too few for the national need, but nevertheless exercising a significant influence, for around these language students are being organized a number of courses of study relating to Japan in the humanities and social sciences for undergraduates, and from them are rising the graduate students interested in more specialized study. In this same period, some 500 doctoral dissertations relating to Japan have been accepted by approximately 70 American graduate schools. All of these were not based on vernacular sources, but the number that are so based is growing as significant comprehensive programs of graduate study on Japan are now being offered at a number of American universities.

This growth owes much to the efforts of the pioneer scholars in this field, the encouragement of university administrators, and the financial support of private foundations and government agencies. But it also owes a great debt to our friends in Japan, and I should like to acknowledge that debt here. It would take too long to cite all of the ways that the Japanese people have helped us in our study of Japan, but a few examples will illustrate the significance and breadth of that help. It is, after all, to a small number of distinguished visiting or émigré Japanese scholars that we owe the introduction of Japanese studies into a number of our universities. Many are still there, helping us to this day. Many other Japanese scholars in Japan have set up special classes in English to help our non-Japanese-speaking undergraduates who visit to learn, while other Japanese specialists have given freely of their time and knowledge to help our visiting graduate students and research scholars, anxious to work in Japanese-language materials but needing the advice and help of specialists. And for those who are qualified, Japan's universities have opened their doors to their regular lecture courses and seminars. We owe a very special debt to the librarians: to librarians in Japan, who have always so hospitably opened their collections to our use, and to American librarians, on whom our entire educational and research effort in America most fundamentally rests.

Having acknowledged these debts, I hope I may be permitted to go on to say that, in all honesty, our Japanese-language collections in America are not what they ought to be. They have not kept pace with our scholarly needs.

I am reminded of a little rhyme taught me by my English grandmother. It goes:

Hobbledehoy
Hobbledehoy
Not yet a man
Nor yet a boy.

A "hobbledehoy," I believe, was originally a horse which had been hobbled so that it could move only with a very restricted and graceless gait. In the rhyme the word refers to a teen-age youth, who is just gaining a man's physique, but, being unused to his new strength and size, uses it in an ungainly way. Not yet a man and no longer a boy, he moves about awkwardly like a hobbledehoy. And that, I think, might be a fair description of the immature state of most of our American collections of Japanese-language materials.

A simple count of holdings will indicate one dimension of their inadequacy. I do not have a completely up-to-date count, but as of 1965, if one added together all the Japanese-language holdings in America, one would get only 1,358,821 volumes, and these were scattered in 52 different libraries all over the country, with many duplications. The Library of Congress had the largest collection, and at that time, with one exception, no major university center of Japanese studies was supported by a library collection with as many as 100,000 volumes. Most collections were far smaller; the fifth largest had only 70,000, and the tenth largest had only 25,000. And this, it should be remembered, was at a time when more than 50 universities were accepting doctoral dissertations on subjects relating to Japan.

Overall size is not the only deficiency. Even these small collections are in many cases inadequately serviced, there being both a shortage of budget and a shortage of trained personnel available to do the work. A few are relatively strong in one field or another because of special bequests of the personal interest of one or more librarians or faculty members who introduced Japanese studies there; but nearly all are weak in other areas, especially in the social sciences, and none is a well-rounded collection which could support serious research in all fields of our expanding interest.

These remarks are not made to disparage the tireless efforts of the librarians of these collections, but rather to call attention to the seriousness of their problem, and also to their need and the needs of their clients, the American specialists on Japan, for help. The situation would seem to call for an overall strategy of development. First of all, the goal needs to be identified; then the practical steps to achieve that goal need to be analyzed and undertaken.

The Goal

What, first of all, should the goal be? What kinds of Japanese-language collections does American higher education require? I should suggest three:

1. Comprehensive collections. When two countries mean as much to each other as Japan and the United States do, it is really insupportable that neither country has even one truly comprehensive collection of the publications of the other, available for the use of government officials, scholars, businessmen, writers, and all others of our citizens. It would seem to me that one pressing goal which should be set before each government should be to establish in each country at least one, but preferably three or more, regionally located libraries which have a truly comprehensive collection of the other's publications. These holdings should, of course, be available on interlibrary loan, in the original or in facsimile, to all other libraries in each country requiring them.

2. Basic research collections. Each of the major university centers having comprehensive doctoral programs relating to Japan in the various humanities and social science disciplines should be equipped with a library containing the basic standard works required by any Japanese scholar working in such fields. For unique materials the specialist should be expected to refer to the regional comprehensive collections suggested above and, in the last analysis, to rely on the libraries in Japan, but he should be able to expect to meet his usual needs and those of his students at his own research center.

3. General education collections. With the extension of Japanese studies into undergraduate education throughout the United States, more and more university libraries need to build collections of materials relating to Japan for the use of such college students. Language competence cannot be expected, so the emphasis will need to be on Western-language works, but small collections of Japanese-language works will be

needed to support the research of the specialist faculty members who may be in residence.

Practical Steps

The achievement of such goals will require considerable time, effort, and money by many Americans in addition to librarians, but it will also require—or at least it would be greatly aided by—the continued and increased cooperation of our Japanese friends. What practical kinds of cooperation might be envisaged? Let me suggest seven:

1. Enlarged government-sponsored materials exchange. For any study of contemporary society, whether it be political, economic, social, or other, government reports are essential sources of information. Particularly as American scholarship has turned to the social sciences and as American professionals, whether businessmen, lawyers, government officials, or other, have developed close ties with their Japanese counterparts, these publications have become more and more vital to American universities.

A few years ago an agreement was worked out under which a fairly full run of Japanese government publications would be sent to two repositories, the Library of Congress on the east coast and the University of California Library at Berkeley on the west coast, and a much smaller run to a restricted number of centers elsewhere. This has not proved entirely satisfactory for a number of reasons. One is that these collections are not well enough serviced, so that irregularities in supply go unnoticed for long periods of time. A second is that the selection of materials to be acquired has not been kept under constant review on both sides to make sure that the materials that are being sent are really the materials needed by American users. A third is that the publications from which these exchange materials are selected generally do not include items known in the Japanese trade as *hibaihin*, that is, "materials not for sale." This is not because such materials are necessarily classified; most are simply produced for free or private distribution rather than for sale through commercial channels. Since such government publications are voluminous and often of high value for research, their general exclusion from the official exchange arrangement is a serious defect. Finally, even if these problems were solved, it must be recognized that the United States is simply too large and the important centers of research are simply too scattered geographically for only two relatively comprehensive collections to be sufficient.

It would seem to me very likely that Japanese scholars face a number of problems also, possibly similar, possibly different, in getting adequate access to American government publications. If that is true, is it not time to conduct a serious, high-level re-examination of this exchange arrangement, aiming at increasing the number of comprehensive repositories of Japanese government documents in the United States and, if desired, of American government documents in Japan, keeping under constant review the particular materials which are desired on both sides, and guaranteeing their constant servicing?

In addition to government publications, if the goal of several comprehensive collections of Japanese publications is ever to be reached, a reasonable percentage of total Japanese publications, not just of government publications, ought also to be exchanged. Such an enlarged exchange obviously would require heavy subsidy such as only governments could be expected to extend, so that ultimately a re-examination of the official exchange program should consider making this new request of the two governments: The Japanese government might be asked to supply a certain percentage of the total Japanese publishing output to several regional libraries in the United States, and the American government might be asked to reciprocate by supplying a similar percentage of the total American publishing output to several regional libraries in Japan.

2. *Enlarged Japanese Government Publications Service Center.* The present Service Center for Japanese Government Publications in Kasumigaseki has proved to be indispensable to American and Japanese scholars alike for buying Japanese govern-

ment publications currently on sale. But it would be even more useful if the Center could secure materials no longer current and if it could respond to mail orders from overseas. Since presumably such orders would pay for themselves, it is not immediately apparent why sales need to be limited to "cash-and-carry." My impression is that Japanese scholars and libraries have no difficulty in ordering any American government publications they may want directly from the Government Printing Office in Washington, but if there are any particular problems, they should be set forth and steps taken to solve them as soon as possible.

3. *Hibaihin Service Center.* The Japanese government is not the only publisher of "materials not for sale" in Japan. Many other Japanese materials also fall into this category, just as in America do many publications of business houses, political organizations, and the like. As already suggested, for scholars concerned with the study of contemporary society in all its ramifications, these *hibaihin*, whether books of poems published for self-gratification, biographies written for praising one's friends, working papers, propaganda pamphlets, or government reports, are essential for research. To the best of my knowledge, there is no systematic bibliographic control of this output, and many of the materials are not collected by university libraries even in Japan. It would be enormously useful if some kind of *hibaihin* service center could be established there which would attempt to compile bibliographies of these materials, locate sources of supply, and offer for a suitable fee to secure such of these materials as libraries or individual scholars may be interested in.

4. *Documentation centers.* I imagine no one will deny that librarians love books— the older, the rarer, the more substantial the binding, the better. It has been my experience that a librarian rarely objects, if he has the money, to acquiring a book by a well-known author, on good paper, put out by a reputable publishing house. But ask him to buy for his collection, save on his shelves, or catalog in his files such things as organ papers of trade organiza-

tions, pamphlets issued by political parties, mimeographed reports of investigatory committees or scholarly seminars, and he is apt to throw up his hands. "Ephemera," he calls them. "They're not available through the regular distribution outlets," he explains. "Not worth the cost of cataloging," he says. "We have no adequate way to handle them." And so on.

The truth is, however, that these materials, although they may not be written in graceful prose or printed on durable material or available through commercial channels, are what might be called society's working papers, and as such are indispensable for any study of society. The collection of such materials is a problem in every country, but I should like to illustrate what I mean by pointing out that, for example, the student of political science, whether he be American or Japanese, cannot at this moment go anywhere in either country and find a truly comprehensive collection, reaching back into history, of the publications of any single political party. It is time, I submit, that librarians begin to take such problems seriously and devise imaginative new documentation centers where the working papers of society will be collected and preserved.

5. Librarian exchange. It is indeed a rare Japanese collection in America that has an adequate staff. The difficulty, to be sure, is in part budgetary. Most universities have not yet given adequate recognition to the complexity of the problems of building and maintaining these collections and have therefore not provided adequate financial resources. Regrettably, since library expenses are both constant and increasing, philanthropic foundations and the government have been even more reluctant to shoulder the necessary burden. But the difficulty stems also from a lack of adequately trained personnel. We have too few trained librarians in America who know the Japanese language and are familiar with Japanese scholarship. Too often, particularly in the newer libraries, we have librarians who cannot read Japanese, or Japanese staff members who are not librarians. Recently special programs have been organized by various American schools of library science to

try to train the personnel needed. Another trend is for various American libraries to send representatives to Japan to try to recruit, on at least a temporary basis, trained librarians with experience in Japanese libraries.

Although I hesitate to say this, since I am not a librarian myself, it would seem to me eminently useful if a project could be devised which would permit some kind of systematic interchange of library personnel between the two countries. A select number of Japanese librarians might go to America for a year or two to work, perhaps part-time, in American collections of Japanese materials, helping to get them better organized and particularly helping to clear up the backlogs of cataloging which plague a number of them, while sharing, also part-time, in the work of the regular Western-language sections to improve their skills in handling such materials. Reciprocally, a select number of American librarians might come to Japan for a year or two to work, perhaps part-time, in Western-language collections to render whatever service they can there, while sharing, also part-time, in the work of the regular Japanese-language sections to learn their operations. Elements of language or library instruction might be included if they were found to be desirable. Such an exchange would not immediately solve the staffing problems of American libraries, but it might go a long way toward increasing the pool of talented persons available for the very skilled work these libraries require.

6. Acquisitions guides. We have already noted that most American collections of Japanese materials are not well balanced. They may be strong in one field, weak in another. If the basic research libraries at the major centers of study are to be made to support serious research in each of the fields scholars are now interested in, that is, across the board in the social sciences and the humanities, advice is seriously needed as to what to acquire. What are the standard works, say, in the field of politics or of economics or of sociology, which a Japanese specialist in such fields needs to be familiar with and to have close by for reference? This is a question often put to

Japanese professors or librarians who visit our collections, and many such visitors have given generously of their time and knowledge. Our own specialists, returning from periods of study in Japan, make their own recommendations. And at most centers of advanced study, faculty members, like the librarians, regularly pore over the book lists of Japanese publishers and secondhand bookstores for items of interest.

But I think any objective person will have to admit that the results are spotty. We are not usually in a situation of adding new materials to collections which already include what might be thought to be the standard works published over many past years. Many such previous works are out of print and no longer available in the market. Others, because of the narrowness of any specialist's attention, whether he be librarian or professor, simply have not been recognized to be sufficiently important. If Japanese specialists were willing to work with us to draw up specialized bibliographies of basic works needed in specialized research collections in each of a number of fields, these would, I should think, be immensely useful as guides for the acquisitions policies of our libraries.

I do not feel qualified to say whether Japanese scholars of Western subjects feel similar lacks in their own libraries, but my impression from visiting a number of Japanese universities with courses in one or more phases of American studies is that similar acquisitions guides in various fields of American studies prepared with the help of American professors and librarians might be useful to Japanese libraries, so that possibilities for a mutually helpful Japanese-American interchange project are present here, too.

7. Duplicate purchasing. Another device that might be explored for helping to improve the acquisitions policies of libraries on both sides of the Pacific might be a bilateral agreement between two institutions by which, in certain agreed-upon fields, each library might, when it orders books for itself, order second copies to be sent to the other library across the sea, up to whatever amounts are agreed upon and subject, of course, to an annual account

balancing. Thus a Japanese research library of American economics or politics or history might arrange with a sister American research library knowledgeable in that field to have the American library do its buying of American books for it up to a fixed amount, by simply having the American library buy a second copy for the Japanese library every time it buys one for its own collection. A Japanese library buying Japanese books in certain fields of Japanese studies might reciprocate by similar duplicate buying for an American library anxious to collect in that field but not possessing the competence or confidence to make its own choices.

Are these suggestions really practical? I do not know for sure. I speak only from an American user's point of view, with inadequate knowledge of the reciprocal needs my Japanese colleagues may have in working in their English-language collections and with no knowledge at all of the librarian's profession. But I should like to suggest that it would seem eminently suitable for a binational gathering of professionals to take up, as a matter of some priority, the devising of ways to cooperate in the improvement of Japanese-language libraries in America and English-language libraries in Japan.

As one concrete step the sponsors of this Conference might appoint a joint Japan–U.S. committee, with small national panels consisting of librarians and scholars on each side, who would conduct a serious survey of the needs in each country and the kinds of cooperation that might be offered, looking toward the presentation of a report to the next Conference, if one is planned, to each of the governments, and to such other bodies as might be in a position to act. The new Joint Japan–U.S. Committee for Cultural and Educational Exchanges, now being organized in accord with the recommendation of the Fourth Cultural Conference held in Washington in April 1968, would certainly be interested. If such a report included an identification of priorities and a recommendation for concrete action on one or more of these priorities, that would certainly move us forward. In addition, it may be that one or more of the specific proposals I have made above, or some other proposal which may come up, may recommend itself as so obviously desirable and so immediately practical that a special binational project committee could be appointed immediately to follow up on it. That would be even more desirable.

Conferences are judged by the beauty of their sites, the efficiency of their planning, the graciousness of the hosts, the distinction of the participants, the importance of the theme, and the interest of the discussion. In all these points, this first Japan–U.S. library Conference ranks high indeed. But conferences are also judged by whether or not they give rise to new, concrete developments of importance. If those who attend the Conference were to inaugurate a co-operative program for improving the English-language libraries in Japan and the Japanese-language libraries in America along some such lines as suggested here, they would have begun a work of truly seminal character, deserving of the gratitude not only of the librarians of both countries, but of the two nations as well, for it is fundamentally on these libraries that the advancement of knowledge of each other and the improvement of understanding between the two peoples rests.

Our Shared Concerns

Eileen Thornton
Librarian, Oberlin College

There is a popular saying that claims an expert is any ordinary person fifty miles away from home. This should make me 130 times an expert. To talk as though the libraries I know best are exemplary or as though I know the best practices of each of the libraries I shall try to represent is obviously arrogant. No one college or college library can, I believe, be held up as a complete model of academic virtue. However, examination of teaching methods, for instance, from college to college and discipline to discipline and even faculty member to faculty member often identifies excellence. The same is true, in large measure, with regard to the achievements of libraries as they follow or lead in the educational process.

All I can hope to do is to identify scattered policies and practices which I find illuminating, hoping they will be illuminating to others. All of us look with admiration and envy at colleagues around the world who seem to be doing their work effectively, and each of us tries, I think, as best he can, to learn from his counterpart elsewhere. I am sure the American contingent present at this conference is eager to hear about and learn from successes in Japanese academic librarianship.

Let me try to draw another sort of picture. Three persons—a university administrator, a university teacher, and a university librarian—consider a local problem. They face one another, looking toward the middle of a triangle, and their differences may be far greater than their similarities. Let the three face some major external problem, and they may line up shoulder to shoulder, facing essentially in the same direction. In this case, they are far more alike and united, drawn together by common concerns when facing a situation in which all three have a serious interest.

I trust that we are shoulder to shoulder rather than at odd angles to one another. It will be mutually helpful to stand together in the wide arena of higher education, for we must understand and support one another to achieve a total program that serves our times, our societies, and our students. We also know that each of us must be humble enough to learn from the other, whether that other be the different elements that go to make up a single higher institution or to make up one phase of higher education, such as library service.

Many things draw Japan and the United States together. Both are competitive societies, with ingenious and ambitious peoples, with high economic potential, with concern about our future leadership, and with critical problems in relating to our young people. Both countries know that the moral and cultural mold of the students with whom we deal is of vital importance today and tomorrow. Both of us feel an obligation to preserve our cultural heritage, to create and propagate new knowledge, and to respond to the exigencies of the contemporary world.

In both countries, we are experiencing severe growing pains in higher education. This growth is not simply one of population but of the increasing proportion of youth who aspire to advanced education. Grappling with the sheer numbers of students has left us little time and energy to consider the quality of higher education, but there are strong signs in both Japan and the United States that we are now turning our attention to questions of excellence. This can be a challenging and exciting time for academic libraries.

The Structure of Higher Education in the United States

Some generalizations about the structure of American higher education may provide us with a helpful base. We, like you, are experiencing great changes in academic life, and the statistics of higher education alter rapidly. The figures that follow are rather rough but provide an approximation of the quantitative scene.

There are 2,550 higher institutions of all kinds in the United States, enrolling more than 7,000,000 students. About 160 classify as complex universities. In them are enrolled about two-thirds of the million graduate students and about 45 percent of the students who seek the bachelor's degree. Nearly 900 institutions classify as junior colleges, and many of their students later enter the universities or the colleges to complete the baccalaureate programs. This leaves approximately 1,500 four-year institutions whose programs are essentially undergraduate, terminating in the bachelor's degree. In them are enrolled about 55 percent of all baccalaureate students and one-third of all graduate students. Typically, these colleges are what we call single-purpose institutions, offering minimal graduate work. They tend to be small in terms of

enrollment and staff, and their libraries range all the way from exceedingly weak to surprisingly strong. Three-quarters of these institutions are privately controlled and one-quarter are publicly controlled. The publicly controlled institutions are usually larger and are growing much more rapidly than the private colleges.

Libraries to Support the Educational Program

At the college level, the basic assumption is that the education of students is our main business. A corollary to that, of course, is that the teacher must continue to be competent to lead the educational process, and to do so he must constantly engage in further study, whether that be formal research and publication of findings, involvement in related activities such as government service, creation of new works of art, or other pursuits aimed at enriching and extending his capacities. The emphasis is on becoming a better teacher, rather than on research for its own sake.

College libraries reflect the aims of the colleges. Their first obligation is the support of the teaching program, and support that is as lavish as the institution can afford. This goes far beyond the selection of specific books for specific courses. It means the building up of highly selected collections of all pertinent forms of materials—books, serials, manuscripts, government documents, microreproductions, pamphlets, maps, audiovisual adjuncts and other graphic media—materials that form a strong net under all aspects of the curriculum and permit individual exploration by both faculty and students of a great diversity of possible interests. It also means the building up of a library staff that is knowledgeable about educational developments and competent to turn the library's holdings from a static stockpile into a lively contributor to quality education.

In the massive research-oriented universities, as you will hear from other members of this group, there must be concern for both the undergraduate student and the world of advanced scholarship. Though I shall not attempt to expand on the nature of the library problems the universities face in meeting the needs of undergraduate users, it is perhaps wise to point out that various approaches to their solution are possible. There is no universal agreement on one solution, but no university can afford to ignore these responsibilities. Whether the best way to serve both the undergraduate and the scholar is by means of separate library facilities or through other schemes, the choice has to be made in each large institution against a body of policy, practicality, campus geography, and long-term planning. The design of library services in the autonomous colleges is obviously a far less complex matter.

My particular concern in this presentation is the library service available to faculty members and students in undergraduate programs. I shall dwell mainly on the 1,500 four-year colleges and their libraries, though much will be, I hope, pertinent also to the undergraduate programs in the large universities.

To what extent can academic libraries really affect higher education? Should they be simply like tails on dogs, following where the dogs lead? To what extent are they—can they be—essential organs in the body of higher education? To carry the metaphor still farther, could they become the sensitive eye and ear and nose of the academic beast, sensing what is coming, what is somewhat hidden, what is worth strong library support?

Universally, the U.S. academic libraries are conceived of as libraries for students, first and foremost. This does not mean that they do not support the interests of the teaching and research staffs; even small college libraries, no matter how meager their holdings and their budgets, make some effort to supply their scholars with library materials. Among the 1,500 libraries in colleges which do not offer work at the doctoral level, many have library resources capable of sustaining considerable advanced scholarship in a variety of fields. But there is no U.S. library that does not feel bound to supply the needs of its undergraduate population. When there has to be a choice

between this and the support of faculty scholars, the student interests win.

Library Collections

The presses of the world are, as we are painfully aware, pouring forth a geometrically increasing mass of books. Periodicals, journals, and newspapers that can be considered pertinent to the academic world seem to double in number at every successive count. Other forms of materials, to which most of us paid relatively little attention a generation ago, have become vital to our interests, including our interests on the undergraduate level. These include governmental publications from around the world; technical and other reports of a bibliographically fugitive nature; and the films, tapes, recordings and other audiovisual aids which can enrich library resources. The availability of otherwise scarce and rare items through reprint and microform media give us, at least in theory, a new scope of accessible materials to consider.

As collegiate educational programs grow ever more sophisticated, the line between service to the scholar-teacher and service to the undergraduate blurs. What the scholar wants and what is needed for undergraduate instruction of a high quality frequently overlap. What satisfies the scholar soon comes to be of value to the undergraduate, provided the teaching is of a high order.

The book-selection process itself has undergone considerable change, in part because of changing curricula and teaching methods, in part because of the proliferation of new institutions, in part because of improved bibliographic apparatus and the increased availability of materials, and in part because of the improved ability of librarians and teaching staff to work together on the selection process.

It seems almost too obvious to say that when the teaching faculty and the library staff see eye to eye about basic objectives and ways to achieve those objectives, the library situation is the most satisfactory. It cannot be a high-class educational program in most subject areas without high-class library support. Much of the support depends on the skill and knowledge of librarians. Where teachers and librarians, for instance, collaborate to develop a collection, the collection is likely to be responsive to the needs of the institution, and a small amount of money can often be made to go a long way. Increasingly, librarians are taking the initiative in the selection of materials but always depend on the scholar for his recommendations and advice.

Educational Change

Curriculum and methodology

In the United States, coincident with this rising tide of potential library stock, has come a revamping of the educational programs offered in colleges and universities. What are the changes that are significant? Quite apart from sheer numbers, are there real changes in the nature of higher education, in its methodology and in the motivation of its participants?

Let us look first at the curriculum and teaching methods in the four-year institution. It is a safe guess to say that curricular reform, revolutionary or evolutionary, is taking place in almost every institution. For instance, we are at last awakening from provincialism. In many colleges new programs deal with those parts of the world where most of mankind lives—Asia, India, Africa, Latin America—cultures heretofore too largely ignored in curricula. The scope of such studies continues to widen; there is much more concern to teach the languages and to develop studies that deal in some depth with the history, the arts, and the social sciences of these areas. Thus, even for libraries that have had fairly strong collections in traditional subject matter, there is an urgency to build holdings of all sorts that will meet these greatly expanded demands.

Colleges are engaged in much self-study concerning the scope of the curriculum and the methods of presenting that curriculum to the student. In recent years, much greater emphasis has been placed on independent work, honors work, and outside preparation than on the lecture course. The day of the textbook is drawing to a close, and, as the book market and the academic library become more and more capable of meeting the demand, students are expected to exhaust a variety of resources in their pursuit of learning rather than to depend on a few books or the notes from a professor's lecture.

In what we like to think of as the best educational situations, students do not indicate their mastery of a subject by parroting factual information or by answering final examinations with memorized details. Instead they are expected to be able to reason from the information and insight gained during a period of study. As upperclassmen, they are more and more involved in special kinds of work that make them very largely responsible for their own progress under the guidance of a professor. All these trends make both faculty member and student increasingly dependent on library materials and library assistance from skilled librarians.

Students

Let us look next at the students themselves, especially the undergraduates. What characterizes and motivates those who constitute the justification for all higher educational enterprises? Students now come to us better prepared, in almost every way, than they did a generation ago. The competition to get into college is stiffer now, and this may be weeding out the students who are not really able to benefit from the experience. But, broadly speaking, there can be no question that secondary school graduates have had better teaching by way of preparation for collegiate study, they are better able to act independently, they are more critical in a good sense, they know a great deal more about using libraries profitably, and they expect a great deal more in the way of intellectual stimulation and hard work during the university years. Once admitted to the university, they know that the competition to retain a place will continue to be severe, so there can be no reduction of effort during the college years. Many students hope to go on to advanced study of one sort or another and know that successful collegiate records are essential if they are to be admitted to graduate schools.

Student unrest, with which we are all uncomfortably familiar, has its roots in both external and internal causes. It is becoming more clearly evident, however, that a part of this unrest springs from student dissatisfaction with old curricular boundaries and old teaching orthodoxies. For good or ill, some educational changes are arising from student demands for relevance, for social reform, for invigorating teaching, and for a greater share in the designing of the whole pattern of learning.

Students themselves ask "Why?" much more often than they used to. This query is applied not only to the nature of the curriculum and its fragments but to teaching techniques. This kind of questioning attitude can be fruitfully exploited in the kind of teaching that demands that students shall reason from what they learn, assemble evidence before making judgments, and really read widely and deeply before they generalize. Where this climate of learning exists, the effect on library use is dramatic. In economics, for instance, the study of the tax structure of the United States cannot be said to be covered by a textbook or two. Instead, such a study may send a student into government documents, doctoral dissertations, newspapers and journals, financial reports of corporations, background books in history and other fields. A thorough study of this one problem not only familiarizes the student with a wide range of possible kinds of graphic records, but teaches him, en route, how to use library resources to the limit. Ideally, his curiosity is aroused, he learns how to satisfy it, and he carries this kind of skill with him throughout his life. Hopefully, he is more to be trusted as a leader of tomorrow than the student who is content with the answer from a few textbooks.

Centralization and Access

All these changes in educational patterns have direct effects on library planning, administration, and operations. In institutions with massive library collections and diverse programs, there may come a point of diminishing returns if library resources are wholly centralized. But in by far the largest number of institutions, the library resources —human and material—have not reached the stage of being unmanageable unless divided.

To stretch limited resources of dollars, space, books, and library staff, there are strong pressures for centralization. In the colleges, student and faculty populations tend to be small, the campus is physically compact, and the curricular offerings are interlocking. Although there is almost always some centrifugal force at work, pleading for fragmentation of the library, centralization is becoming a commonly accepted good. Centralization includes administration, services, collection, and quarters.

To construct one central library building, planned for modern library use and large enough to house the whole collection and seat enough readers, and to have it house a strong staff, is increasingly regarded as a wiser investment than the creation of departmental libraries. The aims, of course, are to make as much as possible available to all members of the institution, to keep duplication of materials to a reasonable minimum to permit the acquisition of a wider range of stock, and to make more effective use of scarce library staff.

The changes in the content of higher education and in the ways in which higher education is made available to students argue for centralization and open-shelf arrangements, if such arrangements do not already exist. The reader exploring a field not neatly encased in an old, traditional discipline must roam through a great deal of literature. Some of this exploration is identified first through normal bibliographic channels. This will involve recommendations of starting points from the professor, the examination of the card catalog, perusal of basic and special bibliographic tools, consultation of documents and periodical indices and the like. But continuing from these procedures means the actual examination of many publications, and in this level of exploration, though basically systematic, serendipity can also play a part. We have all of us, as readers, experienced the discouragement that lack of direct access to materials produces; our exasperation should make us sympathetic to the student's wish to move freely through the entire collection. As teaching methods rely less and less on the rigidity of textbooks and more and more on source materials, the experience of finding one's way through the contents of a library becomes in itself an educational process of lasting value. One avowed aim of undergraduate education is to teach the student to go on teaching himself after graduation, and ease of access to a well-ordered collection furthers this aim.

Other factors, too, point to centralization and ease of access. Lines between traditional disciplines are breaking down or are being torn down. The physicist now turns to books in philosophy, the linguist to books in psychology, the historian collaborates with the sociologist and the economist in area study programs, the musician turns to the computer, and the artist and the biologist may cross over into one another's territory. Interdisciplinary studies are the order of the day. Tutorials, seminars, and all forms of independent study, plus a rising recognition of the capacity of the undergraduate to conduct real research projects, send both students and teachers into a library collection as a whole, not as a congeries of academic empires.

This expansion of the curricular universe poses problems. The pressures on libraries, especially on smaller libraries, to be all things to all users is enormous, and it is the rare college library that can afford to have all the materials that might be useful to meet this ever-widening kind of intellectual curiosity. Thus it becomes increasingly important for librarians to share in curriculum development and to work with their colleagues of the teaching faculty in order to understand teaching aims. Unless there is close cooperation, students may be urged by their professors to undertake work which simply cannot be done with the library resources available; this type of disappointment, if common, can kill all intellectual drive.

To rely extensively on borrowing books from other libraries for undergraduate use is also proving to be impractical. There must be joint planning, librarians with faculty members, to develop collections which will provide the best publications in many fields, and the hard realities of limitations and of painstaking book selection must be faced.

An American device on which there is divided opinion is worth mentioning as a sort of halfway house between the single textbook and the open library. This is the reserved-book concept. In theory, when many students are expected to read part or all of a publication in a brief time, and when the students cannot be expected to own all such items, the book should be handled by the library in a way that will permit fair use by all who must use it. The reserved-book collection or center grows out of this need. In it are placed, hopefully for only as long as the need exists, those books which are under pressure. Badly used, this device can create a little library within a library and can constitute spoon-feeding. It can blind the student to the existence of hundreds of other excellent and pertinent books. It can tie up with needless red tape (for reserved books are usually segregated and loaned for very brief periods of time) books that end by being little read after all, but that might have been read if freed of red tape and placed on open shelves with other books on the same general topic. It can create a new kind of textbook, in that if all students in a class are required to read a specific book and are not required to read other books, that book serves as a textbook for at least a segment of a course. On the good side, the reserved-book device may well be inevitable since it does make it possible for large numbers of students to read many significant books, under conditions that are equitable for all users, in a brief time, and without having to purchase all such books for themselves. If not treated as reserved books, these items would be available to only one or two users in the short period of need, and the rest of the group would be deprived of access.

Library Staff

In the collegiate library, there has been

a considerable change in the role of professional library staff members. The day is past when an academic library can be directed by the chief librarian alone. Today, because of the changed curricular concepts, variations in teaching methodology, exploitation of the library's resources by all users, and the drive of students, the library must be manned with persons who understand these factors and who can work together to make the library responsive to them all.

Librarians who are primarily active in the area of collection development must command a great knowledge of the world of materials, in both traditional and contemporary format. They must understand, new disciplines and be farseeing when old disciplines fade away without leaving in their stead clear indications of new subject matters that will be drawn into the educational offerings of the institution. They must be expert in the rapidly growing field of international and national bibliography and in the book market. They must make themselves competent to work hand in hand with faculty experts, so that faculty and librarians between them build library resources qualified to sustain the educational process.

Librarians who interpret the collection through such means as cataloging and classification also must be scholars of their own complex field and of the many fields represented by the materials they manipulate. To whatever extent it is necessary, they must create out of thousands of disparate items a whole that is coherent and orderly. The records they create are the keys to collection exploration for long years to come.

Librarians whose specialty lies in the field of modern technology as a tool for library operation and scholarly assistance must keep libraries abreast of pertinent developments and assist libraries to use the new technology economically, efficiently, and in a way that will eventuate in inter-institutional networks profitable to all libraries and all library users.

Librarians whose art and science lie in joining the user with the materials that will serve him best, whether they be reference librarians, documents librarians, archivists, subject specialists, interlibrary loan librarians, circulation librarians, or any of the other skilled staff members in person-to-person contact with users, have a special responsibility that extends beyond their obvious charges. They are in a position, as a rule, to sense the library's success or failure and to create a climate in which learning and scholarship flourish and in which the natural alliance between the library and its community grows constantly stronger.

Reference librarians in particular have a teaching role to perform. In every contact they make, their aim is to assist the student to master the tools of the learning trade rather than to do his work for him. They may also teach in the formal sense, through classroom participation or through meeting classes on the library premises. When libraries offer orientation programs for new students, it is generally the reference librarians who plan and carry out these procedures. Frequently they find themselves also teaching the teachers, as it is part of the role of the reference librarian to be an expert in the literature coming off the presses and to acquaint the faculty with new resources. Within the library staff they also have a special role, that of link with the acquisitions and cataloging activities. Through constant interchange of information and ideas with librarians in those specialties, they help to build better collections and better bibliographic tools. They feed back direct knowledge of the efficacy of those library devices which are designed to be helpful to the user.

Library administrators must accept the responsibility not only for overall direction of libraries but for the development of staff colleagues who can bring the library to life. They must select and encourage staff members who have the potential to share in this activity. They must give staff members both responsibility and authority to move forward in areas of special competence. The better the staff, the better the administration.

To get and keep librarians of these high qualities, especially in a period when librarians are in very limited supply, we obviously need to offer good salaries and good working conditions. To most highly qualified librarians it is even more important that we offer opportunities to use all the talents they have. They should be a part of the community in as many senses as possible. They should have the qualities that make them the natural peers of the teaching and research faculties, and they should be given every possible opportunity to use those qualities. In short, they should be bound to their work through understanding of the institutions they serve and through the satisfaction they get from being wholly used.

Partly because librarians are scarce, and paragons scarcer, academic libraries are learning to manage with a smaller proportion of professional staff and a larger proportion of nonprofessional staff. As we stretch the librarian upward into more and more demanding work, he must be adequately supported by less skilled staff. Thus, one requirement, if we are to use to the full the abilities of the trained professional librarian, is to assure him of adequate nonprofessional manpower under his direction, manpower able to carry a great part of the routine or repetitive load of any library.

Student assistants often carry a part of this nonprofessional assignment. The use of students as part-time library workers has several merits. Students often have special subject and language skills needed in library operations. Because they are available at odd hours, they are helpful in staffing busy desks at peak times. They often have technical or mechanical skills which libraries need. They are a good link with other students. From the point of view of the employed students, there are virtues too: they learn how to use all the resources of a library through familiarity with its internal workings. They earn needed money. In many instances, they find library work as a career an inviting prospect, so the sagacious use of student assistants may work to the advantage of both the library and the student.

A few college and university libraries have achieved this kind of staff strength. The practice of exposing professional novices to a variety of internal operations is one procedure which has helped to breed excellence in staffs. Continuing education through workshops, seminars, and professional organizations pays good dividends. Participation in self-studies of libraries or of colleges is another way in which the potential contributions of individual staff members have been recognized and used. Faculty status, which carries both prestige and responsibility, is a strong force in attracting and holding good personnel. Freedom to experiment, after careful planning, has often resulted in the professional growth of the librarians involved, as well as in improvements in the library itself. Staff meetings and other devices for the dissemination of information and the exchange of ideas are profitable if well handled. Given the right librarians to start with, the opportunity to become enmeshed in overall library concerns and in the interlocking concerns of the library and the institution seems to be the essential stimulus to ever-increasing excellence of library service and staff growth.

Library Organizations

Closely related to staffing matters is the work of such organizations as the American Library Association. As the scope and function of this association and of other library and professional organizations are the subject of a separate paper, no details concerning these areas of library activity will be examined here. But emphasis should be laid, I believe, on the value these associations have for academic libraries and librarians.

In many colleges, the professional staff of the library consists of four or five persons only. They can become isolated from other academic librarians. At the same time, they may have a deep interest in participating in and contributing to broad activities but find themselves powerless to participate except through the brotherhood of library organizations. Whether the professional staff is small or large, they and the libraries they serve need to be brought into contact with each other and with issues and interests of a very comprehensive nature. Librarians need not only an understanding of what is happening in higher education but a real understanding of what is happening in the whole library world, and they need to be personally involved in issues outside the limits of their own campuses. And the large issues that can be effectively dealt with only through unified action by groups and associations badly need the contributions of academic librarians everywhere.

Cooperative Ventures

There is so much reporting of academic library research and experimentation in the current professional literature and at professional meetings that most of us cannot keep abreast of developments. One thing that could surely work to the betterment of our competence as librarians might be a second twenty-four hours a day in which to keep ourselves informed!

Among the movements in the American library scene that are important to the improvement of library service are ventures in interinstitutional cooperation. There have been hundreds of such ventures, and many have failed because they have been idealistic rather than realistic. Where cooperation succeeds it does so because there has been objective analysis beforehand, the acceptance of practical goals which really could be achieved, and recognition of the fact that all cooperation has to be measured in terms of local gains and losses, with gains planned to exceed losses. The aim of cooperation among institutions or directly among libraries is to obtain diversity and quality which no institution can obtain alone.

Many groups of colleges have formed associations for mutual benefit. Typically, each institution has high goals in education, but its taste may exceed its financial capacity to provide all the richness of educational program it wants for its students. By working together, some of these groups of institutions have been able to develop programs of common good and to attract funds which permit joint enterprises of distinct value.

One such organization is the Great Lakes Colleges Association, a conference of twelve colleges in three contiguous states. According to this association's first newsletter:

> The member institutions . . . share qualities which have made their collaboration especially fruitful. Each is fully committed to quality undergraduate education in the liberal arts; each believes in the value of the comparatively small, cohesive academic community; each is open to forms of experimentation and innovation which will wed the enduring and traditional values of the liberal arts tradition to patterns of education which will have meaning and impact in these revolutionary times. And each accepts the axiom that associative activities can and do provide educational opportunities for faculty and students that the members cannot provide singly.

The Great Lakes Colleges Association has, since its start in 1961, promoted vigorous cooperative programs in the arts, the humanities, the social and natural sciences, urban studies, library operations, and international education. Among the colleges, responsibility for specialization has been assumed, for instance, in certain fields of international studies: Japan, including the language, at Earlham College; Latin America and the study of Portuguese at Antioch; African studies at Kalamazoo College; China, including the language, at Oberlin. The librarians of these twelve colleges meet from time to time and are in fairly constant touch with one another through correspondence on matters of collection development, technical problems, services to readers, and the common interests they all share. In this organization, the library cooperation has tended to follow the institutional cooperation, but through working together on specific problems we have come to know each other well as librarians and so turn to each other for help and information on a wide variety of library questions.

It may be of interest to others to know what staffing problems we face in establishing library support for international studies. Especially when we are trying to build a good collection rapidly, and when that collection contains much material in languages unfamiliar to us, our best efforts can be foiled by our ignorance. We are not, typically, versed in non-Western languages and we lack knowledge of bibliography and the book trade once we move out of America and Europe. This is especially true in the smaller libraries where trained staff are few. In the case of Oberlin, when we undertook to expand the Chinese-language collection—literature, history, political science, and general materials—we realized that we would have to search for a specialist who understood both American library procedures and the complex field of Chinese acquisitions. Fortunately, through the grant which supports the educational program at Oberlin in the field of East Asian studies, we were able to find funds for the purchase of library materials and for the salary of a librarian ideally suited to our needs. She was extremely competent in the field of Chinese literature, educated in China and Tokyo, and a graduate of an American library school. At Earlham College, where the specialty is Japanese studies, an American staff member who had an unusual familiarity with Japanese language and literature was able to fill a comparable role.

This area of the exchange of personnel is a complex one and will be presented to this Conference by experts in that particular field. Let me simply state that librarians in the United States are deeply interested in direct cooperation with librarians in Japan and other countries; the more similar our library objectives and procedures grow, the better the opportunities are for interchange of personnel and for interaction of benefit to all our libraries.

Another consortium of small arts colleges, the Associated Colleges of the Midwest, is comprised of ten institutions in three adjoining states. This group, too, collaborates to obtain educational assets none could afford alone. Among these benefits are specific arrangements with the Newberry Library in Chicago, whereby outstanding university scholars, graduate students, and members of the faculties and student bodies of the ten colleges participate in a program of independent studies, lectures, and seminars, with this great research library in the humanities as the base. In addition, the Associated Colleges of the

Midwest are currently working out a plan that creates order out of the chaos of periodical holdings. A central stock of major publications will be created out of little-used or duplicate runs of periodicals, with the gaps filled in by purchases made possible by the sale of unwanted duplicates. Each college will continue to have, in its own library, a generous stock of active periodicals. The central stock will be readily available to all members.

Yet another type of cooperative enterprise grew directly out of library initiative. Some years ago, three strong colleges, close neighbors, surveyed their holdings in the periodical field and developed a plan whereby agreements were reached on the purchase of certain runs by one library rather than by all, schemes for circulating current issues from library to library were devised, and fragmented runs were consolidated in one location. Later a fourth library joined the original founders of the Hampshire Inter-Library Center. The benefits of this plan are clear: more titles can be afforded, there is at least one complete run of most titles available to the group, and shelf space is saved in all but the library acting as storage center. Students and faculty members have many inter-institutional library privileges.

Another variety of library cooperative has only recently been set in motion in the state of Ohio. The Ohio College Library Center is to be a central automated clearinghouse of a bibliographic nature which will assist its members in the acquisitions process, in the location of materials held by participating libraries, and in the production of catalog cards, to name only a few of the services it may provide. It is supported by contributions from more than fifty college and university libraries within the state.

In all kinds of cooperative schemes—and these are scattered samples only—there will be another type of benefit to the academic world as a whole. As bibliographic control over the holdings of many libraries is made available through a few strong agencies, it will be easier for scholars everywhere to tap these resources. It will also help to satisfy a longing that many librarians have experienced—a wish to make more easily available to readers the rich resources that are somewhat hidden from view in separate libraries. For here we go back to a central theme in our academic librarianship: the insistence on building rich library services for the good of the reader, whether that reader be the beginning university student or the most advanced scholar.

If we could put all the good things together that we find scattered among the various universities and colleges, we would have:

an institution wherein every faculty member was dedicated to and capable of superbly stimulating teaching

all students burning with intellectual curiosity and eager to learn all they can in the precious years of higher education

libraries with rich and responsive collections organized so that all users can find what they want with ease

library staffs made up of first-rate persons of diverse skills, all dedicated to the best in higher education and library service

library buildings that are beautiful, convenient, spacious, efficient, and inviting

an institutional climate in which all elements—administrators, teachers, librarians, and students—work together happily and effectively to the benefit of all

an international brotherhood of libraries in which each library contributes to other libraries.

As things stand, each library and each librarian is aware of some areas of success, some areas of striving, and some areas of serious failure. None of us today, I suspect, is satisfied with what he has been able to accomplish in his own library and for his own institution. To be cheered by our own successes and to learn from those of our colleagues is, I think, an achievement in itself. In most parts of the higher education enterprise, the quality of library service can make or break an institution. The challenge to us is to make institutions great. Inch by inch or acre by acre, I think we can do it, especially if we do it together.

Research and Education in Universities and Use of Libraries

Yasuzō Horie
Chief Librarian, Kyoto Industrial University Former Chief Librarian, Kyoto University Library

In general, libraries are for users. They are neither for themselves nor for librarians. University libraries are no exception. Their most important task is to serve the researchers and students of the universities. In order that the university libraries can function fully as service organs, facilities and equipment should be amplified, organization should be adjusted, and administration and operation should be smoothed by taking note of the following three points:

1. *Enriching the collections in a library.* A large number of books or journals alone does not mean that the library is well furnished. It is highly desirable that the organization of the collection be free of grave defects. Organizing the collection to reflect the research characteristics of the particular university is a possibility.

2. *Making newly acquired publications available to users.* On this point the important thing is to shorten the time spent for processing, which may be done to a certain degree by mechanizing operations. With today's advanced reproduction techniques, it is also possible to make unprocessed publications available for use. Some libraries have already introduced this method. Further, in an undergraduate library, the stacks should be open as much

as possible, and students should be allowed to search for books in the stacks.

3. *Gathering and quickly conveying information on the arts and sciences.* This implies, in short, that a library ceases to be a "watchman of books." A university library can do this only when it is equipped with the necessary reference tools and capable reference librarians.

The State of University Libraries in Japan

Despite the efforts of people concerned with libraries, the present condition of university libraries in Japan, judged by the above-mentioned criteria, is, regrettably, not satisfactory. There are only a few fully acceptable libraries. More specifically, many of the university libraries function as both research libraries and undergraduate libraries, but many perform neither of the two functions better than halfway.

Research libraries in the true sense are limited in number and cover only such subjects as medicine, pharmacology, mathematics, and so forth. To substitute for research libraries, there are in many cases departmental libraries, but often, in terms of facilities and personnel, they are not very functional. What is worse, departmental library materials are further dispersed and shelved by subject or in seminar rooms, and in extreme cases, which are by no means uncommon, they are even shelved in the studies of individual instructors. In such cases, the sharing of books which are common property is virtually impossible, and as a consequence there is a strong tendency toward conversion of library books to the status of private property. At the same time, the university as a whole cannot escape the evils of unnecessary duplication of orders. To sum up, the scattering of research publications, unless it is based upon an integrated scheme, naturally hinders the library from functioning properly and, in the long run, causes disadvantages and inconvenience to the researchers using the library.

The students' voluntary and spontaneous learning or study is what should be most emphasized in university students' academic life. The library is the most important place for such study, but this function of the undergraduate library is not fully carried out in many university libraries. That is to say, in general, the reading room space per student is low, few books are openly accessible, and the reserve-book system is not widely used. Even when these points are taken into consideration, the tendency is for only freshmen and sophomores to benefit, so that in extreme cases juniors and seniors are left without any place to study. This is a mockery of the library's function as a place to study.

Generally speaking, in a large university too much emphasis is laid upon departmental libraries or seminar libraries whose main purpose is to benefit instructors. As a result, the status and role of the central library are gradually declining. If departmental libraries were developed and equipped as true research libraries, this tendency would not necessarily be detrimental. That is, the central library would still retain overall responsibility for generalia and materials spanning several disciplines, for processing functions, for custodial and storage functions, and for undergraduate library functions. However, if the deterioration of the central library is unaccompanied by a clear division of functions, the availability of the library to researchers, students, and the university as a whole will be narrowed and restricted. It should be kept in mind that the library should be proud of a high usage frequency and not of the mere number of volumes it holds.

The Quality of Library Staffs

The extremely low level of reference librarians is a great barrier to library utilization, especially in a research library, but also in an undergraduate library. This is because the most important of all the services of a modern university library is the collection and speedy conveyance of information on the arts and sciences. Profound consideration should be given to the fact that the quality of reference service is very much responsible for progress in research and education.

In this connection, Japanese university libraries suffer greatly from the lack of proficient catalogers of foreign books. On an average, foreign books account for approximately 50 percent of all the books bought by the university libraries every year, and their prompt processing is not an easy task. The most serious bottleneck to book processing is classification. The reasons are that books are not written to accord with a classification table; periodic revision of the table to meet the progress of studies is not easy, and it is in many cases difficult to classify books by their titles, etc. To overcome these problems, it is urgent that librarians proficient in a foreign language gain some technical knowledge.

It is estimated that the annual increase rate for books in Japanese university libraries far exceeds the rate of economic growth. On the other hand, library utilization does not increase as much as the number of books does. Moreover, researchers consistently demand prompt library service, and students complain about small collections of books. This is indicative of the fact that university libraries do not live up to what is expected of them. To pave the way for university libraries to be fully utilized as research and educational service facilities, improvements should be made in at least the following three points:

1. *Progress from a physical structure to a functional organization.* University libraries should be reorganized from a functional point of view, and the old idea that the library is a storeroom plus a reading room should be abandoned. This conceptual revolution concerns not only the people directly related to the library but the entire university community.

2. *Progress from a quantitative to a qualitative approach in problem solving.* The quantitative approach is, for example, to increase the number of staff as the number of books increases. In contrast, the qualitative approach is to point out the nature of the problem and solve it accordingly, as, for instance, mechanizing the processing and organization of materials, introducing extensive open stacks, and so on.

3. *Better librarians.* Points 1 and 2 apply not only to libraries but also to the people working in the library. Reference service is an important task for librarians, but its level is very low in Japanese university libraries. Expert librarians should be relieved of such duties as typing or duplicating cards or pasting labels, and should become bibliographic experts in the true sense of the term.

Extending Library Use in Japanese Universities through Cooperation

Nozomu Takai
Chief Librarian, Tamagawa University Library

The university library has to serve the same aim as the institution of which that particular library is a part; in other words, it must supply library facilities and materials for educational purposes and for the research activities of professors, instructors, and students. The library helps to realize the educational policy of the university by cooperating with professors and instructors in their teaching; thus the library provides the published resources students require and gives them appropriate reference service. The library is also responsible for providing sufficient materials to enable professors to carry on their research. Therefore, the university library should aim at the organic integration of library, professors, and students, and toward the interaction of these three elements.

The university has its own idea of education. The characteristics of that idea will be manifested as they are fulfilled by the university itself; thus the institution contributes to the general culture. The same can be said of the libraries; it is by fully developing their own facilities that they can attain their particular value as parts of the university. This is the relationship between the individual and the total body, and herein lies the fundamental principle of cooperation among university libraries. Cooperation is an intrinsic function of university libraries.

Generally speaking, cooperation may mean "give-and-take" in the practical sense. When this goes smoothly, there is no problem, nobody denying or being against it; however, once that balance is broken, problems become apparent at once. Often, the demands go only one way, becoming excessive and greatly troubling others. In this case, some measures should be taken to redress the balance, and to do so there must be effective systems and organization.

Areas of Cooperation

The following areas, among others, are to be considered:

Establishment of cooperation; formation of associations, etc.
Mutual understanding; exchange of information, etc.
Common works; problems of catalogs and common working places
Union catalogs—from library catalogs to bibliographic centers
Mutual use: facilities, interlibrary loans, copy services
Collection of materials and documents
Preservation of materials and documents
Cooperation through mechanization
Reference services
International cooperation.

In this paper I would like to describe the existing situation in these areas in Japanese university libraries and note some of the problems.

University Library Associations

The proverbial wisdom of both East and West asserts that "like draws to like," and so when those who have the will to attain a certain goal reach the developmental stage, they naturally draw together to form an organization. University libraries are no different, and they form organizations in which they exist and to which they pour out their strength, in the process seizing a new life for themselves.

These associations are established under a variety of conditions. In Japan there are three types of universities—national, public, and private—and each type has its separate library association. The administrators of the private universities are split into three groups, of which two have created library research organizations. In addition, there are associations organized by specialized disciplines and regional associations. In the regional associations are found not only university libraries but also public and special libraries, as well as individuals.

All associations have their own rules and objectives aimed at developing university libraries, improving mutual understanding, and carrying out various surveys and research. With the help of these associations, interlibrary loans, for example, and other cooperative activities are planned.

Exchange of Information

The university library associations have annual assemblies and research meetings for their development and liaison activities. They publish journals and other publications such as bulletins, reports, or collections of theses. These are not only distributed to the members, but, as a rule, are made available upon request to other related organizations and libraries as well.

Many individual libraries also publish their own reports, library catalogs, and lists. These are extremely useful in cooperation among libraries, and, along with union catalogs, are useful in effecting interlibrary loans. Some of these publications can be obtained upon request, but the problem of cost sometimes limits distribution.

Union Catalogs—From Book Catalogs to Bibliographic Centers

The union catalog is the vital prerequisite to utilizing well, through cooperation, the materials in different libraries with different systems and locations. Through the union catalog, each individual library becomes a part of a total system of libraries.

By using the union catalog, of course, one can locate materials and documents in the different libraries. However, the use of the union catalog should not be restricted to this function only. It can also be used as a clue to finding and collecting fugitive materials which may appear only in the union catalog. For these purposes, we hope to develop a national bibliographic center in Japan. To this end, each library should continue to exchange bibliographic information. Continued efforts in this direction are needed.

Mutual Use: Facilities, Interlibrary Loans, Copy Services

The best example of cooperation among university libraries is interlibrary lending and borrowing. If the research worker can locate materials and documents which are not available locally, especially those which exist only in a very special collection, his work will be greatly enhanced. To facilitate this sort of function, the rules of interlibrary cooperation must be established within the association. In reality, many university libraries have already been practicing interlibrary cooperation, and a variety of rules have prevailed. However, it is desirable to

have one unified set of rules to facilitate interaction between libraries. Some of the associations of university libraries have already established their rules, and others are preparing them.

Examples of mutual use among university libraries are shown in the tables 1–3.

According to the results of a survey of twenty-five private university libraries in the Tokyo area, interlibrary cooperation—in readers' services, interlibrary loans, photocopying, etc.—is practiced by all institutions, though to varying degrees. Moreover, all libraries possess some sort of copying device.

In short, interlibrary cooperation is already practiced, and we have finally come to realize that we must devise even more effective and better ways to utilize our resources to the full.

International Cooperation

Concerning mutual use on an international scale, we already have cooperation, mainly through copy services. This is especially true in the field of medical librarianship. Exchange among cultures will become more and more extensive; many foreign books and documents are flowing into Japan, and, in return, our documents and publications are going overseas.

TABLE 1. Reference Service*

GROUP	SCHOOLS	INTRAINSTITUTIONAL READERS (Faculty, Students, Staff)		OUTSIDE READERS	
		People	Cases	People	Cases
National universities	52	225,917	239,336	10,945	11,716
Average		4,345	4,603	210	225
Public universities	14	35,423	48,169	681	597
Average		253	3,430	49	43
Private universities	98	516,833	348,406	3,422	4,278
Average		5,270	3,555	35	44
Total	164	778,173	635,911	15,048	16,591
Average		4,781	3,878	92	101

*Source of tables 1–3: *Shōwa 40-nendo Daigaku Toshokan Jittai Chōsa Kekka Hōkoku* (Tokyo: Monbushō Daigaku Gakujutsukyoku Jōhō Toshokanka) [*1965 Survey Report on University Libraries in Japan* (Tokyo: Information and Libraries Section, Higher Education and Science Bureau, Ministry of Education)].

TABLE 2. Circulation of Volumes and Readers*

GROUP	INTRAINSTITUTIONAL USE		EXTRAINSTITUTIONAL USE	
	Circulation	Readers	Circulation	Readers
National universities	2,629,934	1,618,255	20,585	10,387
Average	37,972	21,869	278	140
Public universities	396,984	248,503	2,805	1,834
Average	10,729	6,716	76	50
Private universities	2,271,038	1,296,955	4,623	9,096
Average	9,961	5,688	20	40
Total	5,477,956	3,163,713	28,013	21,317
Average	16,159	9,332	83	63

TABLE 3. Copying Facilities*

GROUP	MICRO-FILM	EN-LARGERS	MICRO-READERS	ELECTRO-STATIC COPIERS	OTHER COPYING DEVICES	OFFSET PRINT-ING	TOTAL COPIERS
National universities	75	127	269	167	432	61	735
Average	1.0	1.7	3.6	2.3	5.8	0.8	9.9
Public universities	10	18	32	26	37	5	78
Average	0.3	0.5	0.9	0.7	1.0	0.1	2.1
Private universities	54	73	181	85	282	39	460
Average	0.2	0.3	0.8	0.4	1.2	0.2	2.0
Total	139	218	482	278	1,051	105	1,573
Average	0.4	0.6	1.4	0.8	3.1	0.3	4.6

As this trend continues, cooperation becomes an absolute necessity. But a number of problems arise when all university libraries attempt to conduct exchange programs directly with all their counterparts in foreign countries. In this situation I believe we must establish a center in Japan for overseas exchanges. Where should that center be? It would be desirable to have the National Diet Library undertake this responsibility. For this purpose, not only university libraries, but also special libraries and the larger public libraries should offer their cooperation. We also expect further cooperation from overseas library organizations on this problem.

Processing and Cataloging Methods to Promote Library Utilization

Syūkō Katō
Chief Librarian,
Komazawa University

I should like to outline briefly the history and present situation of the Japanese classification codes and cataloging rules, and thereby contribute to further improvement of processing services. I wish to make clear that the following remarks are excerpted from a survey report on processing techniques[1] made on 1 April 1963 by the Japan

Library Association on the basis of my recommendation, which deals with university (but not junior college) libraries.

Classification Code

Brief history of the classification code up to 1945

In the early days of the development of modern libraries in Japan, library classification schedules were created with classified catalogs in mind, and these were based on the eight-fold classification schedule developed in 1889 by the Imperial Library (now the Ueno branch of the National Diet Library).

The first example of a shelf classification schedule based upon decimal notation was that of the Kyoto Prefectural Library, which was formulated by Yoshiro Yuasa in 1898. Yoshiro Yuasa had studied under Melvil Dewey of the United States. However, it is the Yamaguchi Library classification scheme, set up by Yuzaburo Sano in 1909, that has exerted the greatest influence upon subsequent classification in public libraries. The classification scheme of the Yamaguchi Library is based on the traditional eight-fold schedule of the Imperial Library to which decimal notation has been applied, as is clear from the following comparison of the two:

EIGHT-FOLD TABLE

I Theology, Religion
II Philosophy, Education
III Literature, Language
IV History, Biography, Topography
V Politics, Law, Economics, Social Affairs
VI Mathematics, Natural Science, Medicine
VII Engineering, Military Science
The Arts
Industry
VIII Encyclopedias, Collectanea Series

YAMAGUCHI TABLE

000 General
100 Philosophy, Religion

200 Education
300 Literature, Language
400 History, Biography, Topography
500 Politics, Law, Economics, Social Affairs
600 Mathematics, Natural Science, Medicine
700 Engineering, Military Science
800 The Arts
900 Industry

A centesimal elaboration of the Yamaguchi classification was designated as the standard one for public libraries by the Council of Chief Librarians of Prefectural Libraries (Fukenritsu Toshokanchō Kyōgikai) in 1919. However, since those prefectural or municipal libraries which opened subsequently set up their own unique classification tables, the hoped-for objective of a standard for all libraries could not be achieved.

The next attempt at standardization was the Nippon Jisshin Bunrui Hō (Nippon Decimal Classification, or NDC), set up by Kiyoshi Mori in 1929, whose main classifications were as follows:

000 General
100 Philosophy (Religion)
200 History (Biography, Geography)
300 Social Science
400 Natural Science
500 Engineering
600 Industry
700 The Arts
800 Language
900 Literature.

The classes and notation of the NDC were based upon the Dewey Decimal Classification (DDC) and its arrangement upon Cutter's Expansive Classification (EC). It was the first full-scale decimal classification code in Japan. The fifth edition of NDC was published in 1942, but by 1945 the scheme had not generated the support its adherents had expected.

Meanwhile, the libraries of the "old-system" universities and higher schools, having created their own classification tables based on the eight-fold scheme, DDC, UDC, EC, LC, and other tables, also felt the need for a standardized classification scheme. Studies of classification tables usable in institutions of the same type were undertaken in the period 1925 to 1934, but without success.

Classification code at present

The educational reform of 1945, which introduced a new system of six years of primary school, three years of junior high and three years of senior high school, and four years of college made the establishment of libraries in primary, junior high, and senior high schools mandatory. In 1949 the National Diet Library (NDL) was opened.

The vital question was: What kind of classification table was to be introduced into the school libraries? A detailed explanation of the controversy over this problem will be found in " 'Manual for School Libraries' and the NDC" by Katō,[2] "The National Diet Library and NDC" by Katō,[3] and "Reconsideration of the Classification in Large Research Libraries," by Miyasaka.[4]

Only after a great deal of discussion was it finally decided that the centesimal scale of the fifth edition of NDC should be adopted with respect to Japanese and Chinese books. The sixth edition of NDC, published in 1950, incorporated considerable changes in divisions, affecting 40 percent of the divisions in the fifth edition. In 1961 the seventh edition was published, in which about 13 percent of the divisions of the sixth edition were shifted, i.e., moved from one division to another.

Following the lead of school libraries and the NDL, public libraries as well as university libraries under the new system started to adopt the NDC, and in spite of various problems and criticisms raised against it, the NDC has come to be regarded as the standard classification in all types of libraries. Concerning this, reference may be made to "The Future of NDC," by Katō.[5]

At an early stage the NDL adopted NDC for Japanese and Chinese books and DDC for foreign books. Gradually, how-

ever, the inconvenience of dual classification and the lack of logic of a decimal system became increasingly apparent. Therefore, in 1962 a study was launched to develop a new classification scheme, which appeared in 1968. The main classification is as follows:

A. Politics, Law Administration
B. Parliamentary Publications
C. Legal Materials
D. Economics, Industries
E. Social Affairs, Labor
F. Education
G. History, Georgraphy
H. Philosophy, Religion
K. The Arts, Language, Literature
M.–S. Science and Technology
U. Learning in General, Journalism, Libraries, Bibliographies
W. Old and Rare Books
Y. Children's Books, Special Materials
Z. Serial Publications.

This classification scheme is similar to LC in that the double letters AA through ZZ denote division, and numbers 1 through 999 stand for subdivision. Classes are arranged in the order: social science, humanities, natural science, and technology, reflecting the special nature of the NDL.

This scheme has been used since April 1968 for foreign books, and since January 1969 for Japanese and Chinese books.

Classification numbers based upon the sixth edition of NDC have long been entered on NDL printed cards for Japanese and Chinese books, but, starting in 1969, new numbers, based upon the above classification table, will also be entered. It will be interesting to note how much influence this classification will have on Japanese university and other libraries in the future.

According to a survey conducted in 1964, classification schemes employed at university libraries are as shown in table 1. Among those libraries which have adopted NDC for both Japanese and foreign books, 165 are using the sixth edition, 119 are using the seventh, and 14 are using the sixth and seventh together. Among the libraries which make use of different classification codes for Japanese and foreign books, 45 are using NDC for Japanese books. Original classifications are those

TABLE 1. Classification Schemes at University Libraries

CLASSIFICATION SCHEME	NUMBER OF LIBRARIES	PERCENT
NDC (both Japanese and foreign books)	309	67.2
NDC (Japanese), DDC (foreign)	38	8.0
DDC, UDC	12	2.5
Original classification	75	15.8
Miscellaneous	40	8.5
Total	474	100.0
No answer	12	

which have been developed originally by universities dating from the prewar period, such as Tokyo University, Waseda University, and others. It should also be noted that these older university libraries originated not only for classification tables but also processing techniques.

Book numbers

The most logical method of numbering for specifying individual books in a single class is based on author or on date of publication. Table 2 shows the methods presently adopted in university libraries. The numbering of books according to the date of receipt, though illogical, has been rather widely adopted in some lending libraries for the purpose of promoting efficient circulation.

TABLE 2. Methods of Book Numbering

METHOD	NUMBER OF LIBRARIES	PERCENT
By author	302	63.8
By date of receipt	109	23.1
No number	25	5.3
Miscellaneous	37	7.8
Total	473	100.0
No answer	13	

Cataloging Rules

Basic heading and cataloging rules

There has been a tradition in Japanese cataloging systems to provide classified and title catalogs for Japanese and Chinese books and classified and author catalogs for foreign books. Title has come to be used in the retrieval of Japanese and Chinese books for the very good reason that many premodern Japanese and Chinese works did not carry information about the author, and even in the case of those that did, it was difficult to establish the author's name.

Accordingly, the title-main-entry principle is found in Japan's first code of twenty-eight articles—Wa-Kan Tosho Mokuroku Hensan Kisoku [Cataloging Rules for Japanese and Chinese Books]—adopted by the Nihon Bunko Kyōkai, the precursor of the Japan Library Association, as well as in the revised edition of thirty-two articles published in 1910 under the title *Wa-Kan Tosho Mokuroku Hensan Gaisoku [General Cataloging Rules for Japanese and Chinese Books]*.

In 1932 the Japan Library Association (JLA) published the *Wa-Kan Tosho Mokuroku Hō [Cataloging Rules for Japanese and Chinese Books]* in 169 articles, but left the choice of whether the basic heading, i.e., main entry, should be by author or by title to the discretion of each library. The following arguments resulted from this arrangement:

There is a danger of confusion arising in catalog entry practices in the future.

The vast majority of modern books indicate the author.

Readers increasingly ask for books by specifying the author.

It is increasingly difficult to distinguish books only by title, because many books have the same or similar titles.

A system of combining subject and author cataloging of books appears convenient at first glance, but this might preclude diversification and development of the subject catalog and author catalog.

Agreement should be achieved with the cataloging principles of other advanced nations.

For these reasons this set of cataloging rules did not come into force.

In 1942, on the basis of ten years of study, the League of Young Librarians (Seinen Toshokan'in Renmei) established the *Nippon Mokuroku Kisoku* (*Nippon Cataloging Rules*) in 138 articles based on the author-main-entry principle. Then in 1952, following the principle of these rules, the JLA published a new edition of the *Nippon Cataloging Rules* (141 articles); and in 1955, taking due consideration of the results of the International Conference on Cataloging Rules, published still another edition of the *Nippon Cataloging Rules* (177 articles).

Japanese cataloging rules for foreign books have been modeled after the *ALA Catalog Rules* of 1908 right from the beginning. The *ALA Cataloging Rules* of 1949 (2d edition) and the *Rules for Descriptive Cataloging in the Library of Congress,* together with additions and changes published in 1959, have all been introduced and implemented. Therefore, there is no such conflict as is found in the case of the cataloging rules for Japanese and Chinese books. A tentative survey conducted in February 1969 shows the cataloging rules being used in Japanese libraries (table 3).

TABLE 3. Cataloging Rules in Japanese Libraries

CATALOGING RULES	NUMBER OF LIBRARIES	PERCENT
ALA	110	43.2
Foreign books, 81		
Japanese and Chinese books, 29		
NCR	139	54.9
Japanese and Chinese books, 136		
Foreign books, 3		
Original cataloging rules	5	1.9
Total	254	100.0

Types of catalogs

The catalogs of university libraries, which are now being organized on the basis of the above-mentioned cataloging rules, can be classified as shown in table 4. The classified catalog is predominant in all combinations, and this can be ascribed to the fact

that circulation is a major function in university libraries.

Libraries where all material is open-shelf need not maintain classified catalogs, and are better served by dictionary catalogs (subject catalogs). But in university libraries, the present situation is really unsatisfactory. There are only thirty-five of a

TABLE 4. Types of Catalogs

TYPE	NUMBER OF LIBRARIES	PERCENT
Libraries with single-entry catalogs	34	7.2
By classification only	16	
By author only	12	
By title ony	5	
By subject only	1	
Libraries with double-entry catalogs	104	22.1
By classification and author	62	
By classification and title	10	
By author and title	24	
By author/title mixed	8	
Libraries with triple-entry catalogs	272	57.7
By classification, author, and title	217	
By classification, and author/title mixed	40	
By author, title, and subject	1	
By dictionary catalogs	14	
Libraries with quadruple-entry catalogs	42	8.5
By classification, author, title, and subject	9	
By classification and by dictionary catalogs	15	
By classification, author, title, and other means	12	
By dictionary catalogs and other means	6	
Miscellaneous	19	4.5
Total	471	100.0
No answer	15	

total of forty-six libraries which employ the dictionary catalog, while eleven use their own subject catalogs—only 9.8 percent of the total.

The reasons why subject catalogs are not much used for Japanese and Chinese books are: (1) unlike foreign book titles, subject headings appear frequently in the titles of Japanese and Chinese books; and (2) in subject cataloging the establishment of subject headings is difficult, and the cross-referencing system is complex.

The dictionary catalog of books is rather complicated for the inexperienced reader, since it uses author, subject, and title simultaneously; studies on subject and dictionary catalogs are still insufficient in Japan. Even the rules for dictionary catalogs are as yet unestablished, and neither guidance for their establishment nor training for utilization are available. This is discussed in detail by the author elsewhere.[6]

Arrangement of catalogs

The correct and adequate arrangement of catalogs is the prerequisite and indeed the very *raison d'être* of a good catalog. Three methods of arrangement are in existence, as shown in tables 5–7, all of which have various problems.

Two reasons account for the overwhelming usage of separate files for foreign and Japanese works: First, the principles of file arrangement are different, the one being based on the alphabetic principle and the other on a syllabic or character-arrangement principle. Secondly, there is a difference in readership.

It is probable that the overwhelming use

TABLE 5. Differentiation between Foreign and Japanese Works

TYPE	NUMBER OF LIBRARIES	PERCENT
Separate files for foreign and Japanese works	288	61.0
Mixed files of foreign and Japanese works	168	35.6
Miscellaneous	16	3.4
Total	472	100.0
No answer	14	

TABLE 6. File Arrangement

TYPE	NUMBER OF LIBRARIES	PERCENT
Alphabetical (Hepburn romanization)	309	69.3
Alphabetical (*Kunrei* romanization)	73	16.4
By Japanese syllabary (*Hiragana, Katakana*)*	24	5.3
Miscellaneous	40	9.0
Total	446	100.0
No answer or unknown	40	

*Symbols of the Japanese syllabary are written and printed in two forms, the *hiragana* (cursive) and the *katakana* (block).

TABLE 7. Filing Rules

TYPE	NUMBER OF LIBRARIES	PERCENT
No rules	256	62.4
Original rules	26	6.3
ALA Rules for Filing Catalog Cards	29	7.1
Nippon Hairetsu Kisoku [*Nippon Filing Rules*]	16	3.9
Miscellaneous or unknown	83	20.1
Total	410	100.0
No answer	76	

of alphabetical card arrangement based upon the Hepburn system of romanization is due to this system's long tradition. Since not a few people support and use the official *Kunrei* (Cabinet Decree) system, the standardization of Japanese romanization is a difficult problem, but unless one of the systems is definitely selected, the development of standard printed cards will be prevented.

Libraries reporting "No rules" account for 256 institutions, or 62.4 percent. Most of these are libraries with meager resources and low rates of acquisition. However, training in accurate filing should be given right from the beginning when there are only a few cards.

Reproduction of cards

The methods of card reproduction used

in university libraries are shown in table 8. Nothing is so inefficient as the purely mechanical operations, such as card reproduction, being conducted independently by each library. Especially it is inconceivable to those in other fields that in this day and age 159, or 34.9 percent, of the libraries still reproduce cards by hand. The main reason for this is that only one or two catalogs are maintained (e.g., by class and by title) and that 177, or 45 percent, of the libraries do not provide for double or added entries. Thus, these libraries need only two or three cards for one book, and it is quite natural for them to consider that handwriting best combines efficiency and economy.

However, there is a question whether satisfactory library service is possible with only one or two approaches to a book through the card catalog. One might say, moreover, that the limited number of cards used is a great barrier to the wider use of NDL printing cards.

The NDL began the distribution of printed cards in 1950, but, eighteen years later, only ninety-four college (including junior college) libraries were purchasing cards. According to a study which the present author conducted, the following criticisms of the printed NDL cards have been made:

The basic heading is the name of the author, so that these cards are useless

to libraries whose basic heading is the title.

The entry format does not agree with that of the user library.

Reproduction and distribution take much time, causing delay of technical services.

Unit price is too high (at present 3 yen, or about .008 cents, per card).

The process of ordering, receiving, and payment is too complicated.

The conclusion is, therefore, that it is more economical and efficient for each library to catalog and reproduce its own cards.

However, these difficulties are not crucial in nature. Those who are concerned should cooperate in taking the necessary measures for promoting efficiency and rationalization of technical services, to gain time and energy for other service activities.

Union catalogs

The problem of a general catalog was excluded from the study, since this is not a part of routine work. However, since it has a great importance for reciprocal utilization of university libraries, I should now like to touch upon this question.

According to the study, holdings of university libraries are as shown in table 9. Small libraries with less than 100,000 volumes comprise about 82 percent of the total, indicating that most of the university libraries reporting are attached to new (postwar) universities.

In these libraries a union catalog for the whole university is not needed, since all the library resources are collected in one

TABLE 8. Card Reproduction

METHOD	NUMBER OF LIBRARIES	PERCENT
Printing and reproducing (for both Japanese and foreign books)	226	49.5
Miscellaneous, unknown	35	7.5
Handwriting (for both Japanese and foreign books)	126	27.6
Miscellaneous, unknown	33	7.3
Mixed use of these two	37	8.1
Total	457	100.0
No answer	29	
Use of NDL cards (as of February 1969)	94	

TABLE 9. University Library Holdings

NUMBER OF VOLUMES	NUMBER OF LIBRARIES	PERCENT
Up to 50,000	264	54.1
50,000– 99,999	134	27.7
100,000–199,999	57	11.7
200,000–299,999	14	2.8
300,000–400,000	11	2.4
500,000 or more	6	1.2
Total	486	100.0

place. When, however, materials are held at various locations and campuses, a union catalog is a must. It is worthy of note that several years ago Tokyo University Library set up a union catalog covering all libraries on its campuses.

There is also a pressing need for a union catalog which covers both the major university libraries and the NDL. For this purpose, union catalogs must first be set up in each university and then correlated with those of other universities. It thus goes without saying that catalog entries must be uniform and that this makes a general and thoroughgoing review of the catalogs of each and every library all the more necessary. The compilation of union catalogs inside and outside the university is admittedly a difficult job, but it must be accomplished for the sake of academic progress and the rationalized utilization of library resources.

In this present age of innovation, it is difficult to foresee the extent to which technical services in the library will be improved through the introduction of electronic computers. However, it is our sincere hope and expectation that the day will come when the library resources of one university will be readily available to any other library through standardization in cataloging and technical advancements.

Personnel

I have suggested that great innovations are expected through the introduction of electronic computers. At the same time, we should recognize that considerable time will be required for all the various library services to be changed by computers, and I believe it likely that technical services will be maintained as at present for some time to come. On this basis, I should like to touch upon the problems of personnel for technical services and the rules of processing under the present circumstances.

Technical services

Technical services are not limited to newly acquired materials, but for the sake of simplicity let us consider the relation-

ship between the number of items received annually and the number of processing personnel as disclosed by the survey.

VOLUMES ACQUIRED IN THOUSANDS	CORRESPONDING NUMBER OF CATALOGERS
.1	1.0
.5	1.5
1	2.0
2	2.8
3	3.4
4	3.6
5	4.7
6	5.2
7–9	7.6
10	10.0

These statistics do not, however, show the quality of library personnel (years of specialized and unspecialized experience) or the nature of the work, nor is the standard processing ability per person per day specified. It is thus difficult to judge whether the number of personnel is adequate for the number of books received.

Processing

Few university libraries have a staff manual. Questioned on possession of written rules of processing, libraries replied:

Yes	35	(7.9%)
No	406	(92.1%)
Total	441	(100.0%)
No answer	45	

Even though the NDC and NCR are available for classification and descriptive cataloging, it is possible to reject them because of special conditions existing in a given library, and this indeed appears to be the case in many libraries. Even though technical services may be performed by efficient and experienced personnel, there is still a need for detailed rules for processing to secure unity and prevent discontinuity due to changes of personnel.

Conclusion

I have outlined the classification codes and cataloging rules of Japanese university libraries, certainly a very complicated and diversified matter. Long-established universities are obliged to change their processing techniques from time to time, adding to the complexity. However, it is obvious that the present condition is a hindrance to rationalization of services and effective utilization of libraries. University librarians should take measures to rectify matters through concerted study. I am convinced that cooperation on an international level is impossible without cooperation within the country.

Formulation of plans for improvement

I should like to present three suggestions for the improvement of technical services:

1. *Establishment of goals for university library development.* Librarians often maintain that the library is the heart of the university. However, I wonder if university libraries have enough of the attributes of the heart to perform its function. We should contemplate the basic causes of poor library resources, arbitrary processing methods, unsatisfactory catalogs, and inadequate cooperation among libraries.

With regard to processing, once a certain system is established, it cannot be changed. Frequent changes in system merely delay services and confuse users. There is an intractable conflict between continuity of processing and efficient use. A few years ago, however, Dr. Keyes Metcalf was instrumental in bringing about significant changes in the Tokyo University Library; this can also be realized at other university libraries. Without touching on the matter of classification, Dr. Metcalf pointed out the need for, and actually set up, a union catalog, an achievement of incalculable value.

Of course it would be desirable to have a complete reform of classification and catalogs simultaneously, but due to the lack of funds for Japanese university libraries, this is very difficult or even impossible. Therefore, we should conceive a target which is attainable under the present circumstances.

2. *Comprehensive review of the present situation.* Not only do classification codes and cataloging rules vary from university to university; processing techniques are often not unified even on one campus, especially if the university is an old one. This inconsistency and inefficiency causes endless trouble to all concerned, so that those in charge of libraries should launch a comprehensive and thoroughgoing review of actual conditions. It is a very difficult job indeed, but the effort should be made.

3. *Responsibility of the chief librarian.* The chief librarian should play a leading role in establishing goals and in conducting a comprehensive review of actual conditions, formulating plans for improvement, drawing up a budget, and obtaining its approval.

In Japan the training of specialized personnel is insufficient, and it is difficult to secure trained personnel in sufficient numbers for technical services. Librarians should aid in the training and in other ways work to better the library under the leadership of the chief librarian.

Understanding on the part of the university administration

The fact that the library has a central and vital function in the university should be recognized by the university administration. Generally the administration is enthusiastic about plant expansion, enrollment increases, and the establishment of new departments, but indifferent to the expansion of library facilities and to increases in the library budget. Administrations will appropriate the funds necessary for the establishment of new divisions but tend to shelve proposals to increase stacks and seats or to hire more librarians, or proposals for binding, to say nothing of re-cataloging and reorganization, of materials.

A certain university library with an annual budget of over 100 million yen (about $270,000) has a processing backlog of several years due to a shortage of librarians. In such circumstances, we sincerely hope for understanding and cooperative action on the part of the administration. At this same university a favorable situation prevails in that experience as chief librarian is prerequisite to election as president. One would hope that the position of chief librarian would not be regarded as a mere stepping-stone to the presidency but rather that the president, through his experience as chief librarian, would truly understand the library's position as the heart of the university, and would take special pains to make the library a place conducive to scholarly endeavor and meaningful education.

Cooperation by faculty members

Faculty members should also share the realization that the library is the heart of a university. Library resources are the bread of life for faculty members, who are frequent users of the library. Since students do not receive training in library use during high school, faculty members should provide guidance in retrieving relevant materials. At present the only opportunity for students to learn how to use the library is during orientation. Cooperation by faculty members is badly needed in order for the library to function smoothly.

Utilization by students

Student use of libraries has been rather limited. One can think of various possible reasons for this, including inadequate training in library use. Since most high school libraries allow open access and do not prepare catalogs, students have no idea what a catalog is, let alone how to use it. They thus cannot use a university library and dislike the effort required to retrieve material.

While some university libraries have open access to all or part of their resources, nearly all those with more than 100,000 volumes operate on a closed-stack basis. We therefore hope that training in library use will be strengthened at the high school level. At the same time, universities should make some study of library science and bibliography compulsory in the first two years. Also, libraries should provide a sufficient volume of resources and should take all measures to make an increased use of libraries possible. The faculty members should devise new methods to promote the use of libraries. Only thus can university libraries be effectively utilized.

NOTES

[1]"Tosho seiri gijutsu ni kansura chōsa hōkoku [Survey Report on Book-processing Techniques]," *Gendai no Toshokan* [*Modern Libraries*] 3, no.3:146–59 (1965).

[2]Syūkō Katō, " 'Gakkō Toshokan no Tebiki' to NDC ['Manual for School Libraries' and NDC]," *Toshokan Zasshi* (*Library Journal*) 44, no.1:4–9 (1950).

[3]Syūkō Katō, "Kokuritsu Kokkai Toshokan to NDC (The National Diet Library and NDC)," *Toshokan-kai* (*Library World*) 2, no.2:58–66 (1950).

[4]Itsurō Miyasaka, "Daichōsa toshokan ni okeru shoka bunrui no saikentō (Reconsideration of the Classification in Large Research Libraries, with Special Reference to the Case of the National Diet Library)," *Toshokan Kenkyū Shirīzu* (*NDL Library Science Series*) no.7: 96–163 (1962).

[5]Syūkō Katō, "NDC no shōrai (The Future of NDC)," *Toshokan Gakkai Nenpō* (*Annals of the Society of Library Science*) 14, no.1: 1–15 (1967).

[6]Syūkō Katō, "Kenmei mokuroku no unmei (Personal View about the Future Progress of Subject Catalogs in Japanese Libraries)," *Toshokan-kai* (*Library World*) 19, no.6:218–28 (1968).

Cooperative Activities in Developing University Library Resources

Iyoji Aono
Tōyō University

As a point of departure I should like to start with the usual conceptions of what library resources in Japanese university libraries ought to be. The question of ideal library resources can undoubtedly be approached from many points of view, but here I should like to limit my discussion to the problem of the efficient development of library resources viewed as an aspect of cooperative activities undertaken by libraries.

Needless to say, the library resources of a university constitute the fundamental apparatus indispensable to the university's educational and research activities. Theoretically, the resources should be so constituted that there will be neither excesses nor deficiencies in positively meeting any changes in scholarly research and challenges from any quarter. For these reasons, university librarians endeavor to collect useful and pertinent material to fulfill not only current needs but potential demands as well.

How successful has this effort been? Today, approximately twenty years after the inauguration of the new educational system for universities and colleges, we have 377 four-year universities and 468 two-year colleges. Needless to say, all these institutions have come to regard ownership of libraries as a necessary condition of college status. Each of these libraries has been collecting, actively or passively, a substantial amount of material every year, and many universities, in fact, now have excellent collections. In truth, however, with some exceptions these libraries cannot be regarded as being satisfactory, whether as collections for particular universities or as comprehensive collections of library resources. This shows that many university library collections are inadequate not only in terms of their overall comprehensiveness but also in terms of the relative strengths of parts of the collections.

There are many reasons for this state of affairs, one of the first being that the universities do not have clear, basic policies on development of library resources. The few universities which have codified policies on acquisitions may be regarded as exceptional. A second, fundamental reason is that the budget allocations for library resources are very limited. This is not to say that university libraries have been reluctant to procure the necessary funds to purchase resource materials. In fact, on every possible occasion libraries have made demands for funds, either individually or collectively, upon university officials and relevant agencies. In some instances these actions have produced favorable results. Reliance on such conventional means, however, will probably mean that libraries will not be able to advance beyond developing resources to meet the most immediate and pressing needs of the day. From the long-range point of view, the systematic development of those library resources which are truly needed by the universities therefore becomes a problem not amenable to easy solution.

In this situation I should like to propose that, to strengthen and augment Japan's university library resources in a substantial way, libraries consider as a real possibility the idea of library cooperation to be carried out in a bold fashion and on a massive scale. This proposal is suggested by such precedents as the Farmington Plan, the Scandia Plan, the Center for Research Libraries, and the Deutsche Forschung Gemeinschaft. All of these are cooperative ventures seeking to develop library resources in a substantial manner.

It is not easy to decide which method is the best or what kind of organization or form of activity is most appropriate. For example, a certain university library may have a unique collection of high scholarly value and may find it necessary to improve its holdings. If there exists a vigorous system which provides financial and material assistance to the library in a relatively unencumbered manner, the system should be able to work with considerable effectiveness in the development and processing of library resources in overall terms.

Let me cite another example. It can hardly be said that libraries in Japan assiduously engage in selecting and collecting such little-used materials as university and academic research reports, proceedings, symposia, statistical reports, studies, government documents, etc. The same can be said about completing back files and procuring all essential bibliographies. It is precisely these types of materials, however, which by and large form the basis of and are indispensable to research activities in a university library. It is for this reason that most libraries expend considerable energy in collecting such materials. But since in most cases acquisitions policy is vague and uncertain, the resulting collections are inevitably incomplete. Moreover, these resources by their very nature are so extensive that they impose additional burdens on library directors who must grapple with difficult problems of space allocation.

If we were to undertake a national survey of current holdings of little-used materials, we would probably become aware of the following phenomena: Certain materials are held in duplicate by many university libraries, and others that are needed are not retained by any. Again, of the duplicate copies held by many of the libraries, certain specific parts are commonly lacking to all. This poverty in the midst of plenty—the holding of certain books in unnecessary amounts, and the lack of required materials in all—finds analogies in the life and environment of contemporary

Japan. Be that as it may, there is no good reason why this kind of anarchy in the collecting of materials should continue to be overlooked, particularly in Japan's university libraries, where there are chronic deficiencies in book budgets. This is why I previously noted that library collections are not only inadequate in terms of comprehensiveness, but also in terms of makeup.

We know, however, that there have been several pioneer examples of cooperative library undertakings, as I have mentioned earlier, which can provide solutions to the present problem. Would not, for example, the organization and function of a Center for Research Libraries be helpful to us, even though we are not certain whether the CRL model would be operable in a Japanese version? The main requirement for such a plan is funds, and this presents a most difficult problem. There are other difficulties to bear in mind. That is, the history of cooperative undertakings by university libraries in Japan has been rather brief, and we have had so little practical experience that we remain in the developing stage. Therefore, we often tend to be too cautious and passive in putting ideas into practice, and this might well have a negative influence on new plans for cooperative undertakings.

Although there are many difficulties, we need to take up the matter of the organization and development of library resources as a realistic problem from a broad-ranging point of view, transcending the narrow framework of individual universities. The implementation and success of one cooperative undertaking will lead to a higher stage of cooperative undertaking; in any event, it will add courage to our timid approach. I believe that ultimately it will become the basis of encouragement in the use of university libraries.

Part 4

EVALUATING UNIVERSITY LIBRARIES

Evaluation of American University Libraries

R. C. Swank
Dean, School of Librarianship,
University of California, Berkeley

My purpose in this paper is to describe the manner in which American university libraries are commonly surveyed and evaluated. Many Japanese librarians are acquainted with the American literature of this subject. I will contribute nothing new, but I will try to synthesize the American experience.

Survey techniques of one kind or another are probably as familiar to the Japanese as to the Americans, since both peoples are accustomed to taking stock of themselves. As Lewis Leary, Professor of English and Comparative Literature at Columbia University, wrote:

> ... the time for surveys comes at a time of pause, when something is finished, when progress has been made as far as possible in one direction, when the end is in sight, and it is clear that one goes no farther that way; when exciting individual effort is no longer pro-

ductive, so that one must meet in conference.[1]

The survey always brings new minds and methods to bear upon old problems when one path is dead-ended and a new path must be opened.

The survey technique is commonly used in government, business, industry, education, agriculture, medicine, and other fields when there are problems to be solved. The scientific basis of the survey has long been established, and the textbooks of social science research frequently devote chapters to its methodology. My subject is the application of the same methodology to university libraries, the urgent problems of which are worthy of the same attention.

The history of library surveys in general has been sketched by Guy Lyle.[2] In this paper I shall limit my discussion to evaluations of individual university libraries, although much of the material would be applicable also to surveys of groups of university libraries.[3]

Purposes

The specific purposes of surveys, as will be seen, may vary widely, depending upon the condition of the library, the nature of the problems to be solved, and the motives of the officials who want the job done, but the general purpose is almost always the same: to offer solutions to pressing problems, to improve conditions, to correct faulty conditions, and to plan for the future.[4] Problems are defined, conditions are assessed, and recommendations are formulated. New perspectives and standards of comparison are sought.

Behind this general objective, however, there may often be found a more specific, though not necessarily explicit, motive. Each survey has its own point of view, or angle, or axe to grind. The first, and perhaps the most significant, question is who wants the survey made: the library staff, the library director, the faculty, the president, or an external governing or accrediting body? Who sets the stage, who states the problems, who selects the surveyors, to whom is the report to be submitted, and for what audience is it to be written? Who suggests the people to be interviewed? The gamut of possibilities ranges from general surveys to which all parties are mutually agreed to surveys implicitly calculated to fire the librarian. Let me illustrate.

Members of the library staff may promote surveys to improve internal conditions in their own departments or to bring pressure to bear on the library administration. The librarian, on the other hand, may promote a survey to overcome staff resistance to needed changes of policy, procedure, and organization. He may wish to pave the way for some kind of major change in the library program, such as the move into a new building. Or he may want to persuade the faculty and the president that greater financial support is essential to the improvement of library resources and services. The faculty library committee, in turn, may be unhappy about the resources, the services, or the administration of the library and may call for a survey as a means of influencing the librarian, the president, or both. The president may seek to correct a long-term deteriorating library situation or to gather ammunition for a fund-raising campaign. An external agency, such as an accrediting authority, may require a library survey as part of its evaluation of the university as a whole. In many instances, of course, and happily so, the question of who wants to do what to whom does not even arise; the desire for solving problems, improving conditions, correcting faulty conditions, and planning is shared by all parties —the librarian and his staff, the faculty, the president, and the interested external agencies.

It is important for the surveyor to assess the specific motives, covert as well as overt, of any survey and then to proceed in as unbiased a way as possible. He needs to know, as Lowell Martin wrote, whether he has been called as witness for the prosecution or for the defense.[5] Is he a friend of the court, called upon to help make the case for a line of action already determined, to give authority to conclusions already reached? Or is he expected to provide new insights, gather new data, seek new interpretations, reach new conclusions, and recommend new lines of action? Only in this last role can he use the survey method in its most creative and fruitful form.

Problem Areas

There are general surveys that undertake to study the university library in all its major aspects: governance, administrative organization, personnel, acquisitional and cataloging processes, circulation, reference, and other services to readers, book and journal collections, use, buildings and equipment, financial support, cooperative arrangements with other libraries, and so on.[6] The best-known pattern or model for general surveys in the United States is that established by Louis Round Wilson and his cosurveyors, particularly Maurice F. Tauber, during the 1930s and 1940s.[7] These are elaborate book-length studies, replete with statistical and other data and with extensive lists of detailed recommendations. But many surveys are limited, or give emphasis, to one or more of those major aspects. That is, they are surveys, for example, of the technical processes alone, or the book collections, or personal policies and practices, depending upon the specific problem areas that need to be examined.

Following is an outline of these problem areas, each of which may be surveyed separately or as parts of general surveys:

Governance, for example, the legal status of the library in the university: Statutes governing library operations. Relationships of the librarian to the university administration, to the faculty, and to the student body. Attitudes of the governing board. Authorities delegated to the librarian.

Administrative organization, for example, administrative structure and practice within the library: Line and staff functions. Span of control and delegations of authority and responsibility. Departmentalization of the main library. Nature and functions of departmental, or faculty, libraries and their relationships to the main library. Cooperation among departments. Centralized acquisition and cataloging processes.

Personnel, for example, number and qualifications of staff: Distributions among clerical, subprofessional, and professional classes of staff. Recruiting practices. Classifications and pay plans. Job analyses. Status. Privileges and fringe benefits, such as vacations, retirement programs, health insurance, and sick leave. Morale. Staff organizations. Voice in the formulation of library policies and procedures.

Technical services, for example, efficiency of acquisitional, cataloging, binding, and other technical processes: Choice of book dealers and subscription agencies. Exchange agreements with other libraries. Systems of cataloging and shelf classification. The control of serial publications. Binding policies and practices. Circulation rules and charging systems. Problems of cost, production, and elapsed time associated with the incorporation of books into the library system and in paging and reshelving them after use. Mechanization of routine library operations, such as accounting, order procedures, catalog production, and circulation and serials control.[8]

Readers services, for example, nature and extent of the help given by the library staff to students and faculty in their use of the library: Reference and bibliographic services. Assistance in the use of the library catalogs. Selective dissemination of information. Interlibrary loan services. Messenger services.

Book collections, for example, general size and quality of library resources: Responsibilities for book selection. Book selection policies, and fields of existing strength and weakness. Reference and bibliographic resources. Number and kinds of periodicals and other serial publications currently received. Condition and completeness of back files of journals. Resources in microform. Motion picture films, lantern slides, phonograph records, and other audiovisual resources. Adequacy and allocations of book funds.[9]

Library use, for example, who uses various units of the library, how much, and for what purposes: Characteristics of the faculty and student body and specifications of their book and information needs. Departmental and main library use. Frequency of the use of different categories of resources. Factors affecting use, such as accessibility of the books, teaching methods, and lending regulations. Faculty and student satisfaction with library services. Other sources of books and information and the relationship of these sources to the library. The role of the library as one of many methods of communication.

Buildings and equipment, for example, the suitability of the buildings for library purposes: Aesthetic values. Physical relationships among departments. Convenience for students and faculty. Adequacy of seating for readers, of stack space for books, and of work space for staff. Toilets, elevators, and other utilities. Lighting. Ventilation. Protection for rare books and manuscripts. Availability of microform readers and copying equipment. Location of the library on campus.

Financial support, for example, adequacy of the budget: Percentage of university operating expenditures allocated to the library. Expenditures per student, per faculty member. Allocation of library funds among books, personnel, equipment, and supplies. Binding budget in relation to book budget. Sources of funds, public and private. Fundraising opportunities and efforts. Accounting methods.

Cooperative arrangements, for example, the sharing of resources among university and other libraries through interlibrary loan and photocopying: Agreements on specialization in collection building. Centralized and cooperative acquisitions and cataloging systems. Establishment of cooperative storage libraries for infrequently used resources. Reciprocal privileges of access by faculty and advanced students to libraries in a cooperative system. Regional and national information networks.

These examples are intended only to suggest the varieties of problem areas that are susceptible to survey approaches in a university library. Again, they may be studied separately or all together, according to the needs at hand.

Criteria

Any survey that assesses conditions and recommends improvements is by definition evaluative. The process of evaluation requires reference to, or comparison with, some criterion or standard of value. Let me offer an analysis of the kinds of criteria that are frequently used in American university library surveys. There are, first, criteria that are internal to the university and, second, those that are external.

Internally, there are first the goals of the university; toward their achievement the success of the library may be measured. In what fields does the university aspire to offer undergraduate and graduate instruction and conduct advanced research? What kinds of teaching methods does it encourage? Is independent library study one of its goals? To what kinds of students does it cater, and for what careers are the students to be prepared? What philosophy of education does the university espouse? The answers to such questions provide the basic frame of reference within which the library must be evaluated.

A second internal criterion is the library needs of the faculty and students, that is, of the community of scholars actually served by the library. Such needs might be, but are not necessarily, consistent with the formally expressed goals of the university.

A sociological, psychological, and usually statistical approach to the library's clientele may be required to establish the characteristics of that clientele, its information needs, and its satisfaction with library resources and services. In certain problem areas, especially the quality of the book collections, faculty judgment is likely to be the primary criterion, because of the faculty's unique familiarity with the collections and their knowledge of the literature in their fields.

Externally, the most common criterion is the performance of libraries in other universities. One may select a group of universities that are comparable in purpose, size, curriculum, and other factors relevant to library needs and services, then measure the library that is being surveyed against the libraries of that group. Comparisons may be drawn in any of the problem areas outlined above, such as financial support, size of book collections, number of current periodical subscriptions, salary scales, and statistics of use.

A second external criterion is the library standards developed and published by the professional library associations. These are guides to desirable practice as derived from long experience and wide observation of library programs throughout the country. They provide an authoritative base line for the analysis and interpretation of survey data. Some specific standards may be quantitative, such as the expenditures for library services per student; others may be qualitative, such as status of the librarian in the university's administrative hierarchy. The usefulness of professional standards is controversial, and the standards must always be applied with caution to individual library situations. While there are no such standards in the United States for university libraries, the ALA standards for college libraries (four-year undergraduate colleges) were published in 1959[10], and the ALA standards for junior college libraries (two-year community colleges) were published in 1960.[11]

A third external criterion may be called the principles of good administration and management. These principles are sometimes elusive, and some of them may be incorporated into the professional standards mentioned above. But without reference to professional standards, the surveyor may often appeal to the science of administration for accepted theories of organization and procedure, in reference to which the library situation may be evaluated. The academic disciplines of business administration and industrial management, as they have developed in recent years, are increasingly relevant to the problems of large, complex library organizations.[12]

Finally, an external criterion of great importance is the well-informed judgment of the surveyor. He is himself a standard, because of his successful experience, his recognized competence, his store of pertinent knowledge, his demonstrated objectivity, and the authority of his publications. The perceptions of good practice that a Louis Round Wilson, a Keyes Metcalf, or a Verner Clapp can bring to a survey before it has begun can be more persuasive in some situations than a whole volume of statistics and flow charts.

It is with reference, then, to one or another of these criteria—the goals of the university, faculty and student needs, the libraries of comparable universities, professional library standards, the principles of administration and management, and the judgment of the surveyor—that library conditions are commonly evaluated.

Surveyors

I turn now to the persons who conduct the survey. The choice may vary according to the problem areas to be studied, the criteria to be applied, and the depth and duration of the study.

A single surveyor—the expert—is frequently employed, particularly for short-term, more or less subjective evaluations of library conditions. It is often said that an experienced observer can learn a great deal in the span of several days, but to learn appreciably more, he would have to devote many months to intensive study. Some one-man surveys do extend over long periods, but the use of teams of surveyors is a common alternative.

Teams of surveyors offer the advantages of diversity of background and knowledge and of the counterchecking of interpretation and judgment. Most of the major general surveys of university libraries in the United States have been done by two or more people, sometimes working in tandem and sometimes as chief and assistant surveyors, after the style of Louis Round Wilson. Teams of surveyors have also frequently been used for intensive evaluations of such special areas as the technical services.

The American Library Association has long contracted to sponsor surveys under certain conditions. An ALA survey must be requested by the official body under which a library functions. This body must determine in some detail the purposes of the study, the areas to be covered, and the information to be derived, and it must provide the budget. The surveyors, usually a team, are selected with the approval of the executive director of the American Library Association. A written report must be prepared, and this report must be published.[13] Surveys may also be sponsored by government agencies, philanthropic foundations, and other groups under such conditions as may be agreed upon.

In recent years management consulting firms have been employed for many library surveys, because of their methodological expertise. A few firms, such as Nelson Associates of New York, have conducted so many library surveys as to have acquired considerable knowledge of library problems, particularly in the technical and cooperative (i.e. network) aspects of the field.[14] The methodological competence of the management consulting firm may be needed when librarians themselves lack the competence required for conducting a study, although the frequent unfamiliarity of the management firm with libraries and librarianship can negate that competence and result in superficial and misleading recommendations.

A similar problem obtains with electronic data processing consulting firms, which have also been engaged to study the clerical and technical procedures of university libraries with a view toward the mechanization of acquisitions processes, catalog production, circulation control, or serial control. A special competence in computing machines and programming does not ensure successful library applications because of the great differences between library goals and operations and those of business and industry, with which the data processing consultants are usually most familiar. But again, some data processing firms, such as System Development Corporation of Santa Monica, California, are developing expertise in library problems and employ librarians as permanent members of their research staffs.

For the study of some special problem areas, other types of nonlibrarian specialists may be employed as surveyors. An architect, for example, may be engaged to survey the building conditions and needs of the library.[15] An accountant may be hired to survey the fiscal procedures and controls of the library. An educator might study the relationship of library services to teaching methods. For other purposes an illumination or ventilation engineer may be needed.

In addition to outside library experts, working singly or in teams, and to nonlibrarian specialists, such as management and data processing consultants and architects, the surveyors may be the university's own staff. That is, the university may conduct a self-survey of its libraries. The library staff, for example, may organize a systematic inquiry into its own problems, as Professor Hideo Kishimoto of Tokyo University did some years ago. Classic examples of the self-survey in the United States are those of the libraries of the University of Pennsylvania,[16] Harvard University,[17] University of Chicago[18] and Columbia University.[19] Although the major work of gathering and organizing the data is done by the university staff, an outside consultant may sometimes be engaged on a short-term basis to advise on the planning and methods of the study and to help with the final interpretation of the data and the formulation of plans for future action.

Although many self-surveys are general in scope, such as the one at Columbia University, the self-survey is particularly well suited to evaluations of library resources, as in the Chicago and Pennsylvania surveys noted above. It can be argued that in any problem area no outside expert can learn as much about a library as the university's own faculty and staff already know, but this argument is especially valid in the area of book and journal resources. The Pennsylvania survey was conducted by faculty, who were presumed to be better acquainted with the strengths and weaknesses of the existing collections and with the needs of the curriculum than anyone else could possibly be. The outside surveyor can only arrive at superficial estimates in a few subject fields that are known to him, collect quantitative data, and then call upon the faculty and staff for more informed qualitative judgments.

Methods

The methods used by surveyors, whether outside librarians, consulting firms, other specialists, or the university's own faculty and staff, may vary according to the funds available, the length of time allotted to the study, and the depth or intensity desired. A survey may last two days or two years; it may be casually subjective or elaborately objective; its report may consist of a brief letter or a series of weighty volumes. Yet many of the same techniques of data gathering, such as the personal interview, are likely to be found in all surveys, regardless of their depth. There follows a brief account of methods that are commonly used.

First is the historical method. How did existing library conditions arise? Probably no experienced surveyor, even if he is spending only two or three days on a campus, will neglect to assess in some degree the main lines of the historical development of the university and the library. The reports of more elaborate surveys may contain entire chapters on historical backgrounds.

Second are the various methods of collecting descriptive data that are common to social science surveys of all kinds. Statistical sampling techniques have, of course, reached a high level of sophistication and are frequently employed by library surveyors:[20]

Documentary. The published and other available documents comprise a major source of descriptive data. Included are reports, budgets, manuals, statutes and other regulations, personnel records, committee minutes, and the like. Documents from other libraries and general reports of a statistical or other nature about the libraries of a region or country may be used for purposes of comparison. A great deal of data about library policies, book collections, personnel, production, and services can often be found in existing documents.

Questionnaires. The questionnaire is an all too familiar device, I assume in Japan as well as in the United States, for collecting new data. The structure, uses, and limitations of questionnaires are well covered in many social science textbooks. Checklists of one kind or another may also be viewed as a kind of questionnaire in that, for example, in evaluating a book collection, standard bibliographies or especially compiled lists of desirable books in particular fields may be checked against the library's holdings to query strengths and weaknesses and to produce lists of desiderata. An impressive battery of questionnaires was devised for the Columbia University survey.[21]

Observation. The surveyor may also collect data and impressions simply by looking at conditions and watching processes. The experienced surveyor develops an acute sense of what to look for and how to interpret it. He can, for example, often reach a broadly accurate conclusion about the general condition of a cataloging department just by seeing it, or about library use just by watching the readers. In more specific situations, he may observe in detail every step in a process, such as book mending.

Interviews. Interviews may be arranged with selected administrative officers, library staff members, faculty members, and students. They may be conducted with individuals or with groups, such as faculty committees. Some are unstructured; others are controlled by means of schedules of questions or topics to be consistently discussed during each of a series of interviews. Even the precise wording of each question may be determined in advance, as in a questionnaire. Interviews are often necessary in following up questionnaires or checklists, in confirming or revising data obtained from documentary sources, and in exploring attitudes that cannot with discretion be put into writing.

Special methods. Other methods may from time to time be required to collect data about particular conditions. For example, the records of book orders may be sampled to measure delays in the ordering process or to identify the vendors with whom orders are placed. The library catalog may be systematically examined to assess the quality of the cataloging or the accuracy of catalog card filing. Or the circulation records may be analyzed to establish who borrows books, what kinds of books are most frequently borrowed, or the frequency with which solicited books cannot be found in the book stacks. The kinds of special data collecting that might be required are as disparate as the kinds of problems that can occur in libraries.

A third general method, which is also descriptive but employs special techniques of analysis and interpretation with reference to principles or standards of efficiency, may be loosely called scientific management. Theories of organization may be evoked, processes may be flow-charted, and time and motion studies may be conducted to assess cost effectiveness. A recent generalization of this method is known as systems analysis, which is "a formal procedure for examining a complex process or organization, reducing it to its component parts, and relating these parts to each other and to the unit as a whole in accordance with agreed upon performance criteria."[22] Objectives are specified, the process is analyzed, and alternative strategies for efficiently realizing the objectives are explored. Both quantitative and qualitative measures are employed.

Operations research, which is a method closely related to systems analysis, is characterized by its emphasis on mathematical models of operating systems—models designed to predict the results of changes in any of the operations or conditions of a system. Several distinguished advocates of operations research, such as Ferdinand Leimkuhler, an industrial engineer at Purdue University, have adopted libraries as complex subjects for the application of their methods.[23]

Systems analysis and operations research are popularly associated in the United States with surveys explicitly conducted for the design and application of automated systems. This association is unfortunate. While automation, or mechanization, has certainly been the motive of many systems analyses of libraries, the honest systems analyst or operations researcher will insist that his methods are generally applicable to all kinds of operating systems, manual or mechanized. It has often been said that a library systems analysis, undertaken for the purpose of mechanization, has uncovered so many possible improvements in manual operations that mechanization is rendered unnecessary or undesirable.

Fourth is the experimental method, which has played a very minor role in the evaluation of university libraries. Yet, in elaborate general surveys or intensive studies of particular problem areas, carefully planned controlled experiments with imaginative new organizational or procedural patterns could be an effective way of solving problems, improving conditions, correcting faulty conditions, and pointing the way to the future.

Results

It is difficult to say how effective library surveys have been in American university libraries. What improvements have actually occurred that can be attributed to the surveys as against other forces, such as conclusions already reached before the surveys were requested? Yet there is widespread agreement that the results are positive, and additional scores of universities, whatever their motives might be, continue to request surveys.

The major evaluation of the results of American university library surveys is E. Walfred Erickson's *College and University Library Surveys 1938–1952.*[24] Erickson

queried twelve universities that had been surveyed during the fourteen-year period about actions related to every specific recommendation in the survey reports. He discovered that almost 60 percent of approximately 775 recommendations in the twelve surveys had been carried out completely or in large part, and that another 10 percent had been achieved to a small degree. In only 15 percent of the cases were the surveys definitely considered to have exerted no influence in the achievement of the recommendations. In most cases, according to Erickson, following a survey library organization had been improved, budgets had been increased, technical processes had become more efficient, and readers' services had been bettered. Yet, in a review of Erickson's evaluation, Marion Milczewski seriously questioned his conclusions.[25]

Referring back to my comments about purposes, I could suggest not unreasonably that the conditions, the motives, and often the specific directions of change have often existed before a survey was planned, and that the survey merely elaborated, detailed, and refined (i.e., improved) the quality of changes that would have occurred without the survey. Also, the political values of the survey are often important and sometimes paramount. Whether the survey in itself is the major cause of change is perhaps irrelevant; it is clearly one very effective instrument among all the other instruments and forces that lead to change in highly complex, real-life library situations.

The published reports of library surveys, moreover, comprise by now a significant part of American library literature. They are studied by library school students, analyzed by library directors, and perused by university officials and faculty members throughout the country for ideas that might be relevant to library problems in general. They contribute a wealth of information about the goals, the resources, the processes, and the services of university librarianship, and they are examples of methodologies, good and bad, for library studies.

But let us acknowledge that, in fundamental ways, we still do not have the insights and the methods to evaluate the essential products of library services, such as the nature and extent of library use in all of its ramifications, the kinds and amounts of information actually disseminated, and the impact of that information on education and research. We still cannot really demonstrate that increasing the library budget by any particular amount would result in predictable improvements in the university's program. The end products of the library, that is, its effects upon education and research, still evade our capacity to analyze and measure, and therefore to evaluate.

In the United States, library and other information-handling systems are coming to be viewed as crucial to the welfare of our society. In the scientific community huge sums of money are being spent on the control of existing information, lest control be lost with disastrous results. An increasing proportion of the total learning of mankind is accessible only by means of the written record, since the capacity of individuals to comprehend that learning remains more or less constant, while the totality of learning continues to overwhelm them. Yet again, the broad social effects of library and other information services still elude us. Libraries can be surveyed usefully by comparison with the criteria listed above, but their ultimate role in societies of the future has yet to be defined.

NOTES

[1]Lewis Leary, "The Complete Librarian: A Partial View; An Afterword," in Maurice F. Tauber and Irlene Roemer Stephens, eds., *Library Surveys* (New York and London: Columbia Univ. Pr., 1967), p.250.

[2]Guy R. Lyle, "An Exploration into the Origins and Evolution of the Library Survey," in Tauber and Stephens, *Library Surveys*, p.3–22.

[3]For an example of a survey of several university libraries see William H. Carlson, *The Development and Financial Support of Seven Western and Northwestern State University Libraries* (Berkeley: Univ. of California Pr., 1938).

[4]Maurice F. Tauber, "Survey Method in Approaching Library Problems," *Library Trends* 13:19 (July 1964).

[5]Lowell A. Martin, "Personnel in Library Surveys," in Tauber and Stephens, *Library Surveys*, p.124–25.

[6]For a study of the results of twelve general surveys see E. Walfred Erickson, *College and University Library Surveys, 1938–1952* (Chicago: ALA, 1961).

[7]See Louis Round Wilson and Maurice F. Tauber, "Public Relations: Evaluation through Records, Reports, and Surveys," in *The University Library* (2d ed.; New York: Columbia Univ. Pr., 1956), p.552–85.

[8]An example of a survey of technical services is R. C. Swank, *Report on Selected Problems of the Technical Departments of the University of Illinois Library* (Univ. of Illinois Library School Occasional Papers, no.42, [Urbana: 1955]).

[9]For examples see the section on self-surveys.

[10]ACRL Committee on Standards, "Standards for College Libraries," *College and Research Libraries* 20:274–80 (July 1959).

[11]ACRL Committee on Standards, "Standards for Junior College Libraries," *College and Research Libraries* 21:200–6 (May 1960).

[12]See the chapter on "Administrative Organization" in Wilson and Tauber, *The University Library*, p.114–22.

[13]Tauber and Stephens, *Library Surveys*, p.261–62. An example of an ALA survey is found in L. R. Wilson and R. C. Swank, *Report of a Survey of the Library of Stanford University, for Stanford University . . . on Behalf of the American Library Association* (Chicago: ALA, 1947).

[14]A characteristic study is Nelson Associates, Inc., *Prospects for Library Cooperation in New York City: Planning for More Effective Utilization of Reference and Research Resources: A Report* (New York: Nelson Associates, 1963).

[15]Donald E. Bean, "Survey of Library Buildings and Facilities," in Tauber and Stephens, *Library Surveys*, p.90–108.

[16]Bibliographical Planning Committee of Philadelphia, *A Faculty Survey of the University of Pennsylvania Libraries* (Philadelphia: Univ. of Pennsylvania Pr., 1940).

[17]Keyes D. Metcalf, *Report on the Harvard University Libraries: A Study of Present and Prospective Problems* (Cambridge: Harvard Univ. Library, 1955).

[18]M. L. Raney, *University of Chicago Survey, Vol. VII: The University Libraries* (Chicago: Univ. of Chicago Pr., 1933).

[19]Maurice F. Tauber et al., *The Columbia University Libraries* (New York: Columbia University Pr., 1958).

[20]See Tauber, "Survey Method," p.15–30.

[21]Tauber and Stephens, *Library Survey*, p. 262–75.

[22]C. A. Quadra, ed., *Annual Review of Information Science and Technology* (New York: John Wiley and Sons, 1967), p.37. See also Robert Hayes, "Library Systems Analysis," in John Harvey, ed., *Data Processing in Public and University Libraries* (Washington, D.C.: Spartan Books, 1966), p.5–20.

[23]See Ferdinand F. Leimkuhler, "Operations Research in the Purdue University Libraries," in *Automation in the Library: When, Where, and How* (Lafayette, Ind.: Purdue Univ. Libraries, 1965), p.82–89. Dr. Leimkuhler spent his sabbatical year, 1968–69, as visiting professor at the School of Librarianship, University of California at Berkeley.

[24]Erickson, *College and University Library Survey*. See also L. R. Wilson, "The University Library Survey: Its Results," *College and Research Libraries* 8:368–75 (July 1947).

[25]Marion Milczewski, review of *College and University Library Surveys* by E. W. Erickson, *College and Research Libraries* 23:357 (July 1962).

Japanese University Library Standards and Surveys

Toshio Iwasaru
*Associate Director,
Kyoto University Library*

Amidst the confusion and turmoil following the end of the war in August 1945, the Fundamental Law of Education (*Kyōiku Kijun Hō*) and the School Education Law (*Gakkō Kyoiku Hō*) were promulgated in March of 1947, indicating a starting point for the new education. However, these fundamental laws have no clause referring to university libraries.

The National School Establishment Law (*Kokuritsu Gakkō Setchi Hō*) of 1949 is the only law which touches clearly on national university libraries, and it says, in Article 6, "A national university shall have a library attached to it." Accordingly, in the National School Establishment Law Enforcement Regulations (*Kokuritsu Gakkō Setchi Hō Shikkō Kisoku*) of 1949, Articles 12 and 13 make reference to a chief librarian, a branch library, and a branch supervisor. Article 12 states that the chief librarian of the university-attached library "should be a professor of the university. However, if the case so requires, an administrative appointee may become the chief librarian." Thus, in principle, a professor serves as the chief librarian. The provision that a university-attached library may have a branch is written into Article 13, and it is further stated that the branch supervisor "should be a professor or an assistant professor of the university. However, if the case so requires, an administrative appointee may become the branch supervisor." Here again, the principle is expressed that either a professor or an assistant professor should serve as branch supervisor.

Yet such legal grounds are given only to the libraries of national universities. There is no legal requirement that public and private universities have libraries. It is only in Article 37 of the University Establishment Standards (*Daigaku Setchi Kijun*), an October 1956 ordinance of the Ministry of Education which states the standards for approval of new universities, that a library is listed as one of the facilities that a university should have. Paragraph 4 of the same Article refers only to the numbers of seats prescribed for reading rooms.

As has been pointed out, the legal treatment of university libraries is very inadequate. In view of this, movements arose aiming at solving many of the problems of national, public, and private university libraries. A proposal entitled "Daigaku Toshokan Hō Yōkō Soan (Draft Principles for a University Libraries Law)" by Mr. Miyogo Ōsa[1] resulted from one such movement, but had no further development.

University Library Standards of 1952

The School Education Law of 1947 defines all the schools from the kindergarten to the university. After this law was issued, the University Ordinance (*Daigaku Rei*), which had defined all the universities in Japan and which applied to all of them except the Imperial Universities, was abolished, and subsequently the National School Establishment Law replaced the Imperial University Ordinance (*Teikoku Daigaku Rei*), which applied only to the imperial universities.

Though all the prewar laws concerning universities were abolished, the School Education Law set forth only general guidelines. This caused the Ministry of Education to make a new set of university chartering standards based upon the new system. For this reason the University Chartering Standards Establishment Conference (*Daigaku Setsuritsu Kijun Settei Kyōgikai*) was organized as early as November 1946. In May 1947, however, the opinion that such standards should be set by a voluntary conference of all the universities in the country and not be under the control of the Ministry of Education became strong enough to bring about the reorganization of the Conference as the University Standards Association (*Daigaku Kijun Kyōkai*), a voluntary organization of universities. Later the standards which were adopted by this association became the standards for the University Establishment Committee (*Daigaku Setchi Iinkai*), an advisory body to the Minister of Education, in its investigations at the time of chartering new universities under the new educational system.

Since standards for a whole university cannot set forth in detail the standards for libraries, there was a strong desire to have independent university library standards, not only for facilities and materials, but also for organization and all administrative aspects. So, beginning in January 1948, the Library Research Committee of the University Standards Association started to discuss and examine university library standards. Great expectations were held for the results, as it was thought the standards would establish the foundations for postwar re-establishment of university libraries. Contrary to such expectations, however, the University Library Standards which were presented four years later, in June 1952, contained not much more than "the minimum requirements for a library," as stated in the code itself.

These standards consist of five sections: (1) library administration, (2) facilities, (3) books and materials, (4) organization and administration, and (5) expenses. A quantitative standard is mentioned only under the heading of expenses, which says, "All the expenses of the library shall be more than 4 percent of total university operating expenses," and "Purchasing costs for books and materials should be at the highest about 50 percent of all the expenses of the library."

In spite of the fact that these standards were the only ones concerning university libraries, they had little effect upon libraries because (1) they had no legally binding power, since they were set not by the Ministry of Education but by the University Standards Association, and (2) they indicated only the minimum requirements. Likewise, the standard assumed to be the most liberal or progressive, that is, the Article which stated that "in principle, the chief librarian shall serve full-time, and the position must be regarded as equal in significance to that of a university department head," could have no real influence in changing the situation in the direction of the recommendation.

Principles for Improvement of University Libraries

Since the University Library Standards (1952) set up by the University Standards Association could not play a leading role in the development of university libraries, a new guiding principle which would define what a university library should be under the new concept of a university was greatly needed. In response to this demand, the Higher Education and Science Bureau of the Ministry of Education issued, in January 1953, a document entitled *Kokuritsu Daigaku Toshokan Kaizen Yōkō* [*Principles for the Improvement of National University Libraries*]. The preparation for this statement of "Principles" started in July 1951, when the Research Group on the Improvement of National University Libraries (*Kokuritsu Daigaku Toshokan Kaizen Kenkyūkai*) was organized in the Ministry of Education. In October 1952 a report of their research and discussion was submitted to the Ministry. This report, which became the document issued in 1953, did not take the form of a set of standards, but was rather a list of practical guidelines to aid university libraries in their efforts to "fully consolidate for greater efficiency."

The statement of "Principles" covers: (1) organization and administration of the university library, (2) staff organization, (3) establishment of a library science course, (4) organization and cataloging of books, (5) service to students, (6) service to faculty members, (7) facilities, (8) book standards, (9) number of staff members, (10) accounting and budget, (11) inter-university usage, and (12) opening of the university library to the public. The explanatory section of the "Principles" shows quantitative standards for number of books, number of staff, and expenses. In this respect the "Principles" had a greater practical effect as a guideline for improving university libraries than did the former laws or standards.

As for private universities, an attempt was made "to elucidate what the university library should be and to set standards for the fulfillment of objectives"[2] at a plenary session of the Association of Private University Libraries (*Shiritsu Daigaku Toshokan Kyōkai*) in November 1953. Three years later, in May 1956, a document entitled *Shiritsu Daigaku Toshokan Kaizen Yōkō* [*Principles for the Improvement of Private University Libraries*] was issued.

This differed from the "Principles" for national universities in its detailed description of both library facilities and qualifications for full-time librarians. Further, the Association of Japanese Private Universities (*Nihon Shiritsu Daigaku Kyōkai*), the sole organization of private universities, issued a document in March 1963 relating to private university libraries entitled *Shiritsu Daigaku Toshokan Un'ei Yōkō* [*Principles of Management of Private University Libraries*]. In regard to public university libraries, the Council of Public University Libraries (Kōritsu Daigaku Toshokan Kyōgikai) drew up a statement in November 1961 entitled *Kōritsu Daigaku Toshokan Kaizen Yōkō* [*Principles for the Improvement of Public University Libraries*]. In the same year, *Shiritsu Tanki Daigaku Toshokan Kaizen Yoko* [*Principles for the Improvement of Private Junior College Libraries*] was drafted by the Association of Japanese Private Junior Colleges (Nihon Shiritsu Tanki Daigaku Kyōkai). With regard to special libraries, the Council of Japanese Pharmaceutical Libraries (Nihon Yakugaku Toshokan Kyōgikai) issued in 1963 a statement called *Yakugaku Kankei Gakubu Toshokan Setchi Kijun* [*Standards for the Establishment of Pharmacological and Related Libraries*].

Thus there are several sets of "Principles" for university library improvement in Japan, but there is great variation among them. Table 1 compares the figures that appear in the "Principles," except for those of the private junior college libraries and the pharmacology libraries.

The first thing to notice in this table is the variety in methods of calculating the number of staff members. The principles for national university libraries regard the number of books as one factor for its calculation, while those for private university libraries take the number of reader spaces, and the principles of management of private university libraries take the number of departments in the university and the number of serials as factors. The method of calculation for the number of general affairs staff members is not mentioned in the national university "Principles," but the two private university "Principles" state it as 10 percent

TABLE 1. Principles for Library Improvement—Comparison of Figures

	NATIONAL UNIV. (1953)	PRIVATE UNIV. (1956)	PRIVATE UNIV. LIBRARY MANAGEMENT (1963)
NUMBER OF READER SPACES FOR STUDENTS	10%–20% of students	10% of Students (2m²/student)	10% of students (2.32m²/student)
NUMBER OF VOLUMES	Up to 1,000 students: Humanities 50,000 Natural sciences 30,000	Ca. 1,000 students: 50/student	Ca. 1,000 students: Liberal arts colleges 50,000 or more Science-technology colleges 30,000 or more
	With every increase of 1,000 students, add: Humanities 10,000 Natural sciences 5,000	Ca. 5,000 students: 40/student Ca. 10,000 students: 35/student	Over 1,000 students: for every additional 200 students add: Liberal arts colleges 2,000 Science-technology colleges 1,000 (This standard is the same as that for national universities)
SERIALS	No standard	Number of current subscriptions: Colleges 400 titles or more Universities 1,000 titles or more	Number of current subscriptions: 300/dept. (More than 50 are to be foreign serials)
ANNUAL ACQUISITIONS	More than 2 vol./ student	Ca. 1,000 students: 5% of current holdings Over 1,000 students: 3–4% of current holdings	2–3 vol./student

of all the processing and service staff members. And yet, according to the *Daigaku Toshokan Jittai Chōsa Kekka Hōkoku* [*Report of Survey Data on University Libraries*] (1968), the average number of general affairs staff members among national, public and private universities reaches 30 percent of all the processing and service staff members.* This makes it clear that the figure, 10 percent, which is indicated in the "Principles" does not describe the real situation. In any case, the fact that methods of calculation for the number of staff members

varies depending upon the "Principles" used shows how difficult it is to set a standard for the number of staff members. The basis for considering the appropriate number of staff members will have to be changed drastically when the mechanization of library work and greater specialization among libraries become real factors.

*A calculation based on full-time staff members alone. The figures are 34 percent for the national and private universities and 25 percent for the public universities.

TABLE 1. Principles for Library Improvement—Comparison of Figures* (Con't.)

	NATIONAL UNIV. (1953)	PRIVATE UNIV. (1956)	PRIVATE UNIV. LIBRARY MANAGEMENT (1963)
NUMBER OF STAFF MEMBERS	Processing and servicing: 10 for 1,000 students and 50,000 vol. For every additional 1,000 students add 2 For every additional 20,000 vol. add 1 For annual acquisition of 5,000 vol. add 1	Processing: 2 for annual acquisitions up to 1,000 vol. For every additional 1,000 vol. add 1 Circulation service: 2/50 reader spaces General affairs: 10% of all the processing and circulation staff members	Processing: 2 for annual acquisitions up to 1,000 vol. For every additional 1,000 vol. add 1 Circulation service (except reference staff): 2 for 1,000 students or dept. For every added department add 1 For every additional 1,000 students add 1 Serials staff: 1 for up to 300 titles For every additional 300 add 1 General affairs: 10% of all the staff members in other sections (No standard as to the number of reference staff members.)
BUDGET	10% of university operating expenses (excluding hospital, research, laboratories, and graduate school)	5% of university expenses	University & liberal arts colleges 8–9% of total university operating expenses College of science and technology 6–8% of total university operating expenses
	Breakdown: Personnel expenses 50–60% Material expenses 30–40% Maintenance costs 10%	Breakdown: Personnel expenses to be equal to material expenses Maintenance costs to be 10% of other library expenses	Breakdown: Personnel expenses 40–50% Material expenses 40–50% Maintenance costs 10–20%
ILLUMINATION	No standards	100 lux on reading tables 50 lux in stacks	150 lux on reading tables 100 lux in stacks

*All the figures given as standards in the *Principles for the Improvement of Public University Libraries* are the same as those in the *Principles for the Improvement of National University Libraries*; hence, they are not listed in the table.

Surveys of University Libraries

What are the actual conditions compared with the qualitative standards shown in the "Principles"? There are three general studies and sets of statistics on Japanese university libraries: *Gakkō Kihon Chōsa* [*Basic Survey of Schools*] and *Daigaku Toshokan Jittai Chōsa Kekka Hokoku* [*Report of Survey Data on University Libraries*], carried out by the Ministry of Education, and a study by the Japan Library Association (JLA).

The study that was started earliest is the *Basic Survey of Schools*, which focuses upon library collections but does not give the whole picture of university library activities. The Ministry of Education therefore undertook a detailed study, starting in 1966, of the actual state of university libraries. The results of this study, *Report of Survey Data on University Libraries*, was published in 1968 by the Ministry of Education.

On the other hand, the library survey conducted by the JLA includes not only university libraries, but also the National Diet Library and public libraries. The survey has been done annually since 1955, and the results are published every year by the Association under the title *Nihon no Toshokan* (Statistics on Libraries in Japan).[3] This JLA survey is not as all inclusive as the 1968 report by the Ministry of Education, but it is useful because of its consecutive history and its reporting on each library. The Ministry of Education's report merely shows the total figures for each group (national, public, and private university libraries) under each item. Therefore, it is important to make use of both reports.

Now let us compare the figures of the aforementioned standards and those appearing in the research reports. First come the data on seating capacity. As shown in table 2, the national universities are slightly below the standard in terms of reader stations, but in area per student they are more spacious than the public or private universities. The public and private universities meet the standards for reader stations, but not for area per student.

Concerning the size of the library collections, the national universities have the highest ratio, 110.2 books per student; the public universities exceed their standard of 50 books per student by having 76.7, but the private universities have only 25.4 books per student, far below the standard.

TABLE 2. Data Based on Research Reports

UNIVERSITIES	NUMBER OF SEATS; AREA PER STUDENT	ANNUAL INCREASE IN NUMBER OF VOLUMES PER STUDENT	NUMBER OF VOLUMES PER STUDENT (1966)	BUDGET (1965) 1,000 YEN (UNIT)		
NATIONAL	9.1% 2.4m^2	5.2	110.2	Personnel Material Other operating expenditures	¥1,085,355 2,685,753 447,249 ¥4,218,357	(25%) (59%) (16%)
PUBLIC	12.0% 1.9m^2	4.8	76.7	Personnel Material Other	¥ 150,229 252,437 41,198 ¥ 443,864	(34%) (57%) (09%)
PRIVATE	11.2% 1.8m^2	2.0	2.54	Personnel Material Other	¥1,007,795 2,021,622 244,730 ¥3,274,147	(31%) (62%) (07%)

However, not all a university library's books are stored in one central library and freely accessible to the students. The number of open-access books in the national universities is about 4.2 million (16 percent of all titles); in the public universities, 610,000 (20 percent); and in the private universities, 2.6 million (14 percent). Included in the open-access areas are reserved and reference books, and even if all the open-access material is considered as available to students, it accounts for no more than 20 percent of all the library collections. This corresponds well with the fact that expenditures for library materials for students (476 million yen) are 19 percent of expenditures for library materials for faculty research (2.4 billion yen).

There are no statistics which show the ratio of total library expenses to total university expenses. The study by the Ministry of Education does not mention the expenditures for regular staff members, and the one by JLA does not give total university expenditures. Though the ratio of the total expenditures of the university library to the total university expenditures is not available, each total figure for personnel, material, and other expenses may be obtained from the JLA report.

According to the various standards for university libraries, an approximately equal amount is to be allocated to personnel and material expenses, while other expenses should be about 10 percent of total outlay. In practice, however, the JLA study shows that the expenses for material are generally far more than those for personnel, and double the amount or sometimes more in the case of national and private universities. Though the standards indicate that maintenance and administration costs should be 10–20 percent of all library expenditures, the present figures are 16 percent for national, 9 percent for public, and 7 percent for private universities. There are many opinions as to what items to include in maintenance and administrative costs, but if all expenses except those for personnel and materials are included, then the figure of 10–20 percent indicated by the standards will have to be further examined if it is to be revised on a more realistic basis.

Evaluation of University Libraries

Library evaluations are of two types: self-evaluation by librarians themselves, and evaluation by outside experts. The most common self-evaluation is in the form of an annual report by the chief librarian submitted to the president of the university. This is common in the United States, but is the practice in only a few Japanese universities.

Apart from annual reports, it is customary, where necessary, to make evaluations based upon study of a special problem within the library. With respect to evaluation by outside experts, each library may invite experts if necessary, and apart from this, annual evaluations are made by the University Library Inspection Commission (Daigaku Toshokan Shisatsu Iin), appointed by the Ministry of Education.

Evaluations by the Commission started in autumn 1965. Each year the Commission selects several libraries from national, public, and private universities and actually goes to inspect them. If there is any room for improvement, the Ministry of Education then sends a notice to the president of the university to which the library belongs. To be sure, the notice works as a mere recommendation with no binding power. The problems of a library may be discussed directly with the expert members of the Commission, who can give useful advice and suggestions. Thus the Commission plays an important role in evaluating and improving university libraries.

Generally speaking, evaluation covers administration, library materials, staff, budget, utilization of the library, reference services, facilities, and so on. Now let us take a brief look at the situation of Japanese university libraries under each item, in the hope of developing a new viewpoint on evaluation by comparing the Japanese and American situations.

First, as regards administration, since the Enforcement Regulations of the National School Establishment Law of 1949 stated that the chief librarian is, in principle, to serve concurrently as a professor, there has been no reference to full-time chief librarians, except in the University Library Standards of 1952. According to the May 1966 study, there was not a single full-time chief librrarian or branch supervisor among the 188 serving in the national universities. There were only 26 full-time chief librarians: 1 in a public university and 25 in private universities. This was no more than 5 percent of the total number (461) of chief librarians and branch supervisors.

A Japanese university library consists of a central library, a branch, and the various departmental libraries. In Japan the branch is placed under the administration of the central library, but, on the other hand, the departmental libraries are independent. Dr. Takahisa Sawamoto described five types of combinations of these three.[4] The first type is the simplest, a central library without a branch or any departmental libraries. The second type is that in which each library within the university is independent. This is a typical pattern of decentralization. In the third type the central library is too small and poor to perform such library functions as book processing or to provide reading room service. This type is characterized by its transitional nature. The fourth type has both the central and the branch libraries carrying out regular library functions. However, the staff of the branch is under the control, not of the central library, but of the branch supervisor. Nominally such a library is centralized, but in practice it is close to decentralization. The fifth type has both the central and the branch libraries performing library functions, with the staff of the branch under the direct control of the central library—a centralized type.

These are the basic types. In practice university libraries combine all these types to produce many in-between types. Among the basic five, the first type accounts for the greatest percentage of national, public, and private universities—32 percent, 69 percent, and 73 percent, respectively. The next largest in both national and public universities is the fourth type—18 percent and 14 percent. The second most prevalent in the private universities is the fifth type (12 percent), and next is the fourth type (8 percent). The least prevalent throughout the three university groups is type three.

A brief comparison of the actual situation with respect to standards for collections and budgets in university libraries has already been made. Though university libraries as a whole maintain twice as many Japanese and Chinese books (67 percent) as foreign books (33 percent), this difference in percentage is decreasing year by year. The annual book acquisitions ratio of Japanese and Chinese books to foreign books was 62 percent to 38 percent in 1966.

In connection with the size of staff, table 3 shows the results of a study made in May 1966 of the number of full-time librarians, the number of students or faculty members per librarian, the number of books, and similar items. In this table it may be seen that the number of students per librarian in a private university is three times that in the national universities. Yet it is difficult to draw a conclusion from this fact alone.

The percentage of staff members according to kinds of work is shown in table 4.

TABLE 3. Data Supplied by May 1966 Study

UNIVERSITIES	NUMBER	FULL-TIME STAFF MEMBERS	STAFF/ UNIVERSITY	STUDENTS/ STAFF MEMBER	FACULTY MEMBERS/ STAFF MEMBER	BOOKS/ STAFF MEMBER	INCREASE IN BOOKS/ STAFF MEMBER
NATIONAL	74	2,384	32	111	13.3	10,469	498
PUBLIC	37	304	8	143	17.4	9,633	607
PRIVATE	235	2,332	10	347	12.5	7,940	649

TABLE 4. Percent of Staff Members in Each Kind of Work

UNIVERSITIES	PROCESSING	READING ROOM SERVICE	REFERENCE SERVICE	MISCELLANEOUS AND ACCOUNTING
NATIONAL	35.9	18.3	3.7	15.1
PUBLIC	38.0	23.7	1.3	13.6
PRIVATE	37.5	26.1	4.4	7.9

If we compare tables 3 and 4, it can be said that the private universities give most weight to, and allocate more staff members to, processing and reading room service, since they have far more students and have a greater increase in books per librarian than do national or public universities. Contrary to this, national and public universities assign nearly twice as many staff members to miscellaneous and accounting work as do the private institutions. The percent of reading room area as compared to total assignable space in the library, as well as the allocation of staff members, shows the importance that private universities attach to library service. In a national university, the reading room accounts for 42.8 percent of the library site; in a public university, 49.3 percent; and in a private university, 56.8 percent.

Since the war much interest has been directed to the university library buildings themselves. This tendency was clear in the 1956 *Principles for the Improvement of Private University Libraries* and the 1963 *Principles of Management of Private University Libraries,* which explained in detail the uses of library buildings and facilities, though only a brief mention of this had been made in the 1953 *Principles for the Improvement of National University Libraries.* Following this trend, a committee on university library facilities was organized by the Ministry of Education in the autumn of 1963, and three years later, in 1966, the Ministry of Education adopted the *Daigaku Toshokan Shisetsu Keikaku Yoko* [*Principles of Planning of University Library Facilities*], which was the fruit of the committee's discussions. This set of "Principles," on the basis of analyses of

the university library's organization, function, and work, considered what facilities are necessary to a university library. However, there are no basic quantitative standards mentioned as to, for example, the reading area necessary per student or the office area necessary per staff member.

A brief summary has been made of the various standards, the studies of actual conditions, and the evaluation of university libraries. What, then, is the relationship between these three? Are the standards and evaluations no longer needed if actual conditions correlate completely with the standards? Does evaluation only mean describing how reality meets the measure of the standards?

It is very simple indeed to have quantitative evaluation based upon quantitative standards. One thing worth noting here, however, is the fact that the conditions to be measured by quantitative standards are numerous and diverse. Each university library has its own tradition and environment. Therefore, to evaluate each unique library by a quantitative standard cannot solve any problem of that particular library, but can only point out some deviations from the general tendency. It is in this that quantitative standards and, therefore, quantitative evaluations are limited.

The aim of evaluation is to improve a library by understanding the true state of the present situation and the strong and weak points of the library. Quantitative standards do help in recognizing actual conditions, but they alone cannot show any means for improvement. Thus, qualitative evaluation must come into the picture.

What are the required standards for qualitative evaluation? Here there are no common standards that can be applied to any library in the manner of the quantitative standards. Each library has its own aim or ideal to work for, and the library works and exists to realize the aim. Therefore, it is possible to evaluate the library by determining to what extent its well-defined ideals are being realized. This is qualitative evaluation. Evaluation can set forth ways and means for improvement only when it is qualitative.

NOTES

[1] *Toshokan Zasshi (Library Journal)* 55, no. 8:252–54 (1961).

[2] *Shiritsu Daigaku Toshokan Kaizen Yōkō,* preamble.

[3] The early issues of this survey, published entirely in Japanese, bear the added English title *Libraries in Japan.*

[4] Takahisa Sawamoto, "A Comparative Study of the Organization of Japanese University Libraries," *Library and Information Science,* no. 6:179–204 (1968).

Part 5

PROFESSIONAL
EDUCATION
OF LIBRARY
PERSONNEL

Current Problems
and Prospects
in American
Library Education

Lester Asheim
*Director, Office for Library
Education, American Library
Association*

I have been asked to discuss in general terms some of the recent developments that have occurred or are occurring in library education in the United States. This is not a difficult assignment; there is a great deal of ferment and activity on the American library scene, and the only real problem is to know where to start and how to end a list of recent developments. Nevertheless, I hesitate to carry out my assignment without making one small proviso concerning what I have to say. The developments, trends, and activities to which I am going to refer are, as the title of my paper makes clear, specifically related to the library situation in the United States. There is no implication in my presentation that what is happening in the United States is a model for Japan or for any other country.

This reservation is prompted by my long-standing commitment to the proposition that libraries are social agencies, products of the society and the period in which they operate, and responsive to the needs of their time and place. Thus most of the developments to which I will refer reflect developments in American society as a whole, and not just those in libraries alone. The Japanese reader will, I am sure, see many parallels between the American scene and his own, but all my material will not have relevance for his situation. I trust that he will accept this presentation as it is intended: as a description but not a prescription; as a survey of the situation in one country and not as an example held up for emulation, unless it meets the needs and the circumstances of other societies.

One other reservation should be stated: Although I am a member of the American Library Association staff, I speak here in my personal, not my official, capacity. My remarks represent my own reactions to the current American library scene; they are not meant to be an ALA statement on American librarianship, nor do they speak for all American librarians. Another reporter might well interpret the situation in quite a different way.

Perhaps one of the most important influences on libraries and library education in the United States has been the current concern with *information as such*, quite apart from the format in which it is presented. In recent years there has been a growing recognition, especially in government, industry, technology, and the sciences, of the need for information which either cannot wait for publication through traditional channels, or will not normally be carried in the traditional forms of publication. The widespread use of the term "information retrieval" to describe what is often simply traditional reference and bibliographic work reflects this changed approach, as do the new devices, the computers and other machines, that have been called in to get at bits of information from all kinds of sources and in forms other than the books and monographs which once stood for the librarians' major stock in trade.

Throughout this discussion I am proceeding on the assumption that the new names and the new devices, the new approaches and the new skills, the new audiences and the new agencies related to this need for information are simply expansions and enrichments of the basic business of the librarian—added to the scope of his responsibilities, but not an entirely different discipline separate from the librarianship of tradition. This is certainly one area where not all American librarians—and certainly not all information scientists—would agree with me. But if it becomes necessary to speak of documentation centers, information centers, storage and retrieval, documentalists, and information scientists in this paper, I see these comprehended in the terms with which we are familiar: libraries, librarianship, and librarians. If you accept the premise that the skills of the librarian are an essential and basic part of what is now called information science, you can see that this new dimension carries important implications for the education of librarians, even though they may eventually call themselves by

another title and perform their functions in an agency no longer called a library.

No small challenge to the library schools of the United States has been the necessity to put traditional library knowledge into the context of information science, and to incorporate a knowledge of the new technology into the pattern of library operations. We have tried to meet this challenge in several ways. One of them has been to create new schools of information science, separate from the existing library schools and concerned only incidentally with the library applications of information-science principles. Another approach has been to introduce separate information-science programs within the library school; often these lead to a separate degree, but certain parts of the program are identical with that leading to the library degree. A third approach has been simply to tack on some courses in information science to the traditional library school curriculum, leaving the existing library courses unchanged. And a fourth has been to restructure the entire library school curriculum and to introduce principles of information science wherever they have relevance in the traditional subject courses, as well as through new courses. This last approach, called the "integrative approach," is the hardest, but to my mind the most promising, solution. It would be incorrect, however, if I were to leave you with the impression that it is typical of most library schools in the United States. The most typical approach has been that of adding courses to an otherwise unchanged curriculum—patching up rather than restructuring. One or two newly created schools have been successful in designing their curricula from the beginning to encompass the necessary changes throughout, but it is more difficult to do this in an established program, where faculty competences and faculty prejudices add a further hazard to an already complicated procedure. I think this will slowly change as new people with new backgrounds come into the field of practice and into the schools. The present period in library education is one of transition, not of final achievement.

Let me touch very lightly upon some of the implications for library education if the integrative approach is to be introduced. To take only one example: In the fields of cataloging and classification, it becomes necessary to recognize the means that are now available for creating computer-based catalogs, for storing information in a new form in machines, for returning to printed catalogs capable of combining the advantages of the book catalog and the card catalog, for the implications of centralized cataloging, and many similar developments which change the way we do things and even the need for doing them at all. The old-fashioned classification courses, which taught a particular classification scheme instead of the theory of classification, no longer suffice; on the other hand, I am not ready to accept the direction already taken by some schools which leads to the abandonment of a required course in classification in favor of a course in computer techniques. For if the librarians have a great deal to learn from the information scientists, it is equally true that the information scientists have a great deal to learn from librarians.

A lot of time has been wasted on both sides reinventing the wheel; we are beginning to recognize that what is already known should be used wherever it is pertinent, not rejected out of hand before we know what its pertinence is. The graduates of our library schools should know what is useful and what is not in the old as well as in the new; they should be capable of evaluating the application of new approaches and new techniques in the light of what experience has already taught us; they should not be intimidated by new jargon and bold promises, simply because they have not learned what questions to ask about them.

This same principle applies in all areas of the librarian's concern: in the selection and acquisition of materials; in reference work; in the organization and interpretation of library materials for users; and certainly in the planning of library systems and services. This means that the librarians of tomorrow must become familiar through the schools of today with the many other forms besides books, periodicals, and the media of print in which information can be carried. It means learning how to get at kinds of information which have never traditionally been used in libraries before. I am not alarmed by the inclusion of films, phonorecordings, tapes, pictures, and other such communication media; libraries have dealt with these for a long time, and we must now simply learn to deal with them more intensively, efficiently, and intelligently than we have had to do in the past. I welcome the increasing use of reprography and microforms, for these indeed may be a far more revolutionary influence upon library collections and services than the introduction of new media as such. But there is a move to take responsibility for information in such areas as interoffice memoranda, in-house releases, and confidential and unpublished materials, including even conference and office discussions, which begins to move outside the realm in which I am comfortable. I do not say that libraries may not one day be concerned with these (special libraries already are and have been handling many of them), but I worry about what happens when the librarian begins bugging the confidential staff meeting and wiretapping private telephone lines between scientists and scholars because information pertinent to research may be included in such privileged discussions. This is an exaggerated description of what is contemplated, of course, but there are those who do not see it as an impossible eventuality.

Another very important development has been the increasing attention paid to the importance of management and administration in library operations. In the United States we have been inclined in the past to consider appointment to an administrative post to be as much an honor as a responsibility, and to use such appointments as a reward to those librarians who have worked in the library a long time or who have demonstrated their competence in other areas of librarianship, like bibliographic or reference work, which may never have called upon them to exercise administrative skills. This means that administrative appointments have often had unfortunate effects: Frequently they have lured good specialists in areas of library knowledge to abandon what they do best to get the salary and prestige of the administrator; and they have often resulted in very poor management because the person has been given the responsibility without any thought to his qualifications for carrying it out. Librarians are beginning to see management and administrative skills as essentials in the librarian's expertise which are insufficiently dealt with in traditional library school curricula. There is an urgent and growing demand for more formal courses in administrative principles and practices and for more informal workshops, institutes, seminars, and other postgraduation learning opportunities, to help already practicing librarians to sharpen their administrative competence. There is even a move to hire administrators rather than librarians to take charge of libraries. I do not mean by this the kind of honorary appointment of a scholar or man of letters to the directorship of a library which has been typical all around the world; I mean the selection of a person with general qualifications as an administrator, quite apart from the subject matter or field in which they will be applied, hired to be an administrator as such, with or without library experience. There are many, at least among students of administration, who believe that a good administrator can administer anything, and there have been enough examples of the failure of a good librarian to administer a library well to give some credence to the view that an administrator without library background will run a better library than will a librarian without administrative skills. This is a hotly debated point in the American library scene.

The response of the schools has been, predictably: (1) to introduce courses in the general principles of administration in addition to, and sometimes even in place of, courses in the administration of particular types of libraries, and (2) to design more concentrated and special opportunities for instruction in the principles of administration for librarians already in the field. The major audience for postgraduate education of this kind has been what we call "middle management"—already qualified library staff members who now carry some administrative responsibility below the level of the chief administrative officer (such as department heads and administrative assistants), who find they need intensive instruction to make up for lacks in their previous professional education.

It is worth noting that these two interests —in information science and the new technology on the one hand, and in more effective administration on the other—have come together in what we call "systems analysis," which in oversimplified terms may be described as the analysis of all the relevant possible choices of procedures for handling a problem with a view to selecting the one which will provide the most efficient, economical, and useful solution. This is a logical and systematic approach to any administrative problem (very close to what used to be called scientific management), but in the United States it has come to be popularly associated with the comparative analysis of different *machine* solutions to problems. In my view, this is a distortion of the meaning of systems analysis, which should look at all possible solutions, including those involving machines but not limiting itself to them. Since many library problems are more efficiently managed without recourse to machines, an exclusively machine-oriented analysis could frustrate the very purposes it was designed to serve. Systems analysis, in the broadly inclusive sense, can be not only a useful tool of administration, but also an effective way to teach administration in library schools. I am happy to see it appearing more and more frequently in the course descriptions of library schools, but must admit that it is still overlooked by some schools or applied in the narrow, machine-oriented sense in others.

Another extremely important influence upon American library education has been the phenomenal increase in the interest of the federal government in library development. (As an aside, it should be noted that federal support might never have reached the scale and intensity it has if it had not been for the efforts over many years of the library profession acting together through the American Library Association. The power and value of a strong, large, and actively supported national association of librarians, which can speak for all librarians with one voice, is nowhere better illustrated than in this successful effort to gain governmental recognition and support.) The first big step forward in federal aid to libraries came with the passage of the Library Services Act in 1956, which was designed specifically to assist the extension of public library service to rural areas which were without such service or were inadequately served. I will not attempt to trace the changes and expansions of that legislation to cover library construction as well as services, metropolitan areas as well as rural, and libraries of all kinds as well as public. Nor will I attempt to analyze the great number of other pieces of federal legislation which, while not always specifically library legislation, contain titles and sections which recognize the role of libraries and offer financial assistance for their development and improvement. Suffice it to say that in the fiscal year 1968 there were nine major pieces of legislation which contained library-related programs totaling several billion dollars of potential support for library construction, for purchase of books and other library materials, for training programs and programs of library education, for support of students and the improvement of teachers, for expansion of services, for experimentation and research, and for a great variety of other special purposes related to libraries.

The result has been, of course, a tremendous increase in the demand for qualified librarians to carry out the expanded services made possible by federal funds. This in turn, of course, has increased the demand for programs of education which will produce them in larger numbers, through both the enlargement of existing library schools and the creation of new ones.

The present situation in librarianship presents an ironical paradox. The demand for qualified librarians has been so far in excess of the number of graduates being turned out by the library schools that we now suffer a severe shortage of librarians at the very time when there are more programs of library education and more students being graduated in librarianship than ever before. The good aspect of this competition for qualified personnel appears in improved salaries, improved working conditions and prestige for librarians, and more attention on the part of institutional administrators to the importance of graduate schools of librarianship in their universities. This is what we have long been trying to achieve. But there is a bad side to our present fortunate situation, which appears in the rapid and not always well-planned proliferation of programs of library training. For example, there are 39 library schools in the United States that have met ALA standards and are accredited, but there are probably more than 400 programs being offered at both the undergraduate and postgraduate levels, many of them far below our professional standards, with more coming into being each year. Out of these programs are coming, not only people who will work in libraries, but many who will carry the title "librarian." Please notice that I make a distinction between "people who work in libraries" and "librarians." It is not a distinction made by the general public, but it is one that our profession is going to have to make, and demonstrate through performance, if we are to survive as a profession rather than as a semiskilled trade.

One effect of the librarian shortage has been to stimulate more cooperative ventures and more centralization of processes and services. The movement toward these had already begun in response to the demands for a higher quality of service than small and inadequately supported libraries could afford to supply. But when this demand for quality is coupled with an insufficiency of manpower, it becomes mandatory to explore ways of obtaining better results with fewer people. Shared cataloging, centralized purchasing, cooperative storage schemes, networks of reference services, library systems, joint use of personnel— all of these are now widely accepted methods of meeting this challenge. Traditional library school courses, based upon the administration and organization of libraries before this development occurred, are not attuned to the demands of the new pattern of services. Library schools must now devise curricula which will prepare people who are flexible and open-minded enough to work within these changing kinds of organizations; who are hospitable to the new procedures that cooperative undertakings may introduce; who are capable of relinquishing certain responsibilities and practices to which they are accustomed to gain more important advantages; and, above all, who are able to plan, organize, and implement services and operations on this wider scale.

Another effect of the shortage of librarians has been to stimulate interest in the possibility of redefinition of tasks and responsibilities in libraries and the reorganization of our present structure of library positions to permit the use of persons with less than the full master's degree (which is the first professional degree in librarianship recognized by the American Library Association) to do many of the tasks and chores that must be done in libraries. One rapidly growing class of such subprofessional workers is the one we call "library technical assistants" (or "technicians"), to whom can be given many of the routine and repetitive tasks of library operation which can be readily mastered at the level of the secondary school graduate or within the first year or so of college. Our junior and community colleges (covering two years of schooling after graduation from secondary school) have been the major locus for these programs of technical training, but the movement is still too new to evaluate fairly and successfully. That there is room on many library staffs for technical assistants at this level cannot be doubted; what is not yet certain is whether the kind of training now offered is best suited to the need. Meanwhile, many academic research projects are under way, and many libraries are conducting their own research in an attempt to analyze the tasks performed in libraries, to determine how much and what kind of training and/or education is required to perform these tasks properly, and to devise new programs of training and

education to meet the need. A notable project of this kind, now in the second of its projected five years, is called the School Library Manpower Project, being carried out by the American Association of School Librarians with a grant to the American Library Association of over $1 million from a private foundation.

Such research and the philosophy of library service and library education which underlies it have important implications for the future of library education in the United States. One attempt to prepare for the changes in thinking that will have to come about is a statement issued by the Office for Library Education of the American Library Association, under the title "Education and Manpower for Librarianship," in the October 1968 issue of the *ALA Bulletin*, pages 1096–1118. In this statement new classifications of personnel at both the subprofessional and the professional levels are suggested. If these recommendations do find favor with the profession at large, their implementation will require new programs of training at the undergraduate level for people below the professional level in library staffs; an upgrading of present programs of professional education; and an increase in the number and quality of programs beyond the master's degree, leading not only to the doctorate, but to advanced specialist qualifications for increased responsibilities in many areas of librarianship.

This focus upon education beyond the master's degree reflects not only the changing job structure in libraries but also a general tendency in American life toward greater specialization, more intensive demands upon the educated, and increasing awareness of the value of continuing education for everyone, not only for job purposes but for the general enrichment of life. If the number of people who continue to educate themselves, both through formal classes and informal means, continues to grow, the demands made upon libraries, both public and academic, for the materials of self-instruction and self-enrichment will increase as well. To be able to serve a public of this kind adequately, it will obviously be necessary for librarians to meet the same standards of continuing growth and advancement.

Obviously, with so many important changes occurring or imminent in library education, it has become necessary to think much more seriously about the essential ingredients of a good program of library training or education. It has been unfortunately true, particularly at the level of training of library technical assistants, that programs spring up with very little planning, insufficient physical and library facilities, inadequate faculties, and even little knowledge of the actual market for graduates of the program. So serious has this situation become that a special committee has been set up in the Library Education Division of the American Library Association to draw up criteria for such training programs as guides to those who are thinking of starting programs and as a means for judging the worth of existing ones. The suggested criteria provide some basically sound guidelines for the establishment of any kind of program of library education, and, together with the *Standards for Accreditation* used in the evaluation of graduate programs, give a good idea of what kinds of considerations American library educators consider important.

The key criteria of excellence in any academic program are quality of the faculty, quality of the students, and quality of the curriculum. The administrative organization of the school, the financial support available, the quarters and equipment that are provided, and the general intellectual atmosphere of the parent institution in which the library school is located are also important factors and must be examined in any evaluation of a school's quality, but in the end their value lies in the degree to which they contribute to an effective program of courses taught to a carefully selected student body by a highly qualified faculty.

Underlying all of this, of course, is careful planning. A first step, before a program of library education or training is established, is a sound survey of the actual need and potential demand for graduates. Just

because a university library is short of staff, for example, is not a sufficient reason to begin a library school in that university. The costs of a really good academic program at the postgraduate level (which is the level of a library school in the United States) are far too high if the result is simply to prepare ten or even fifty librarians. As a general rule of thumb, a need should be identified for at least ten years' worth of graduates before a new school is justified. For the undergraduate programs preparing library technicians, it is urged that an advisory committee be appointed made up of the employing authorities from each type of library in the geographic area to be served by the proposed program, to provide a sound survey of the actual personnel needs that the graduates of the program will fill.

A second recommendation, if there is to be a sound educational program, is that the program should have its own full-time director, and that he should not have to split his attention between it and responsibility for a library. (Only a few years ago it was not unusual for the head librarian to be the head of the library school as well; today not a single school on the accredited list is without its own full-time director.)

There should also be a full-time core faculty who can give undivided attention to teaching, program planning, curriculum design, student counseling, research and writing, and continuing evaluation of the program. It is recognized that practicing librarians can successfully be used to teach certain courses in addition to those taught by the core faculty, but they supplement the full-time faculty; they do not substitute for it. No specific number of full-time faculty members can be specified, since this varies with the number of students, number of courses, objectives of the program, and other such considerations. But it should be recognized that there is a minimum number of courses that can be offered in a useful program of library education, no matter how few students there are. In other words, smallness of the student body does not release a school from the responsibility of providing the full complement of courses necessary to the education of a librarian. None of the accredited schools has less than four full-time faculty persons in addition to the dean or director; even in the library technical assistant programs, it is a rule that the director of the program should never be the sole member of the instructional staff. Faculty qualifications, at a minimum, should include the first professional degree in librarianship, plus teaching and/or library experience.

Financing of the program should be part of the instructional budget of the parent educational institution, and not a part of the regular library budget. Financial support must be commensurate with a comparable program in any of the major disciplines or professions, and full support and a continuing commitment on the part of the university administration are essential. It is not enough to provide an extra bit of support to get a program going; there must be recognition and acceptance by the administration of continuing and probably increasing support for the program in its ensuing years.

Library materials and library space are an essential of any good program of education; they are even more obviously an essential of a program of education for librarians, where the library is not only a source of supporting materials but a vital laboratory for observation and practice. In the evaluation of a library school for accreditation purposes, for example, the accrediting team looks at both the library of the institution and the special collection in librarianship for the school itself. Both must be sufficient in quantity and quality to support a program of teaching and research at the postgraduate level in a university.

The qualifications for admission to the graduate program of a university are usually dictated by the parent institution, but most American library schools demand additional qualifications beyond those governing general admissibility. These usually include knowledge of at least one and usually two foreign languages; evidence of breadth of background in general, rather than too highly specialized undergraduate education; and a slightly higher grade-point average in previous academic work. Interest in librarianship and aptitude for it are also considered, although we have not yet found the tests or screens that provide a reliable way of measuring these.

As for curriculum, there should be a set of clearly stated objectives for the total program and a distribution of course work such that roughly 80 percent is devoted to general liberal arts education over the five years beyond secondary school, 10 percent to basic principles of librarianship, and 10 percent to more advanced courses in the area of the student's library specialization. Courses should be arranged in logical sequence, and the basic and specialized parts of the library school program should be carefully articulated, permitting the student to build upon the early courses for greater depth and breadth of understanding at the advanced level. In the United States considerable room is allowed for elective courses chosen by the student in line with his interests and previous training or experience, but such flexibility requires considerably more attention to student counseling and guidance than would be required by a more prescribed program. The *Standards* for postgraduate programs carefully avoid prescribing course content, to permit the maximum freedom to the best schools to experiment with new approaches and to introduce changes to meet changing conditions. On the technical assistant level, we are planning to suggest desirable areas of curriculum content which will serve to define what should *not* be taught at that level as much as to indicate what would be most useful. Even at that level, however, we wish to leave room for flexibility; our desire is to establish standards but not to impose standardization.

All in all, whether the program is at the undergraduate or the graduate level, whether it is a program primarily of vocational training or one of professional education, and whether it is offered in a university or in some other institution of learning, certain basic standards of support, careful planning, and continuing review and improvement are demanded, and great attention is paid to the commitment of teaching faculty, students, and the university administration to the aims of the profession and to the kind of preparation which will provide high-level service to library users. Improved service to users is the final criterion of successful education for a service profession.

When we speak of service to users, we should recognize an interesting phenomenon in library service. At the same time that libraries are reaching out to meet higher levels of academic interest on the part of a large segment of the general population, there is a movement almost in the opposite direction to provide library services to that segment of the public which has been deprived of the educational, social, and economic advantages typical of the great middle class. Again the federal government has been instrumental in identifying some of the needs of the "disadvantaged," as this group is often called, but a growing awareness on the part of the disadvantaged themselves has also called attention to society's responsibilities for them. This too has important implications for library education, since it means that librarians (at least some of them) are going to have to learn to deal with nonscholarly, nonacademic materials and needs, and with groups of users who have not in the past typically used libraries or cared about them. There is another aspect of the impact of this rising group on the library: They represent a pool of manpower which we have not yet tapped, but which could supply libraries with personnel for many jobs not yet defined and delimited to utilize their potential talents. And this again carries implications for programs of training and preparation which do not now exist in the standard patterns of education for librarianship.

A parallel phenomenon which is not in any formal way a part of the developing audience among the disadvantaged, but which does offer means—perhaps—for dealing with this audience of persons who are not book-oriented, is the rise in the amount of mass and nonprint communications media. A departure from the book

bias of traditional librarianship is one of the points of difference stressed by the new information science people. It affects the kinds of services and materials now being offered to the scholar and researcher at one end of the service continuum, and at the other end of the continuum, it could help to remove one of the major barriers we have erected between the library and a great number of people, both old and young, educated and uneducated, who turn to many other sources of information, recreation, and education besides the traditional book. Schools and school librarians have been the most outspoken advocates of a multimedia approach to the communication experience, especially in teaching and learning, and the latest standards for school librarians have virtually discarded the terms "librarian" and "library" in favor of "media specialist" and "information resources center." But public libraries, particularly in neighborhoods of low literacy, will have to be equally hospitable to the idea that the library may no longer be primarily a book agency at all, but rather a communications center for communications in whatever form works best for the particular audience. I need not spell out, I presume, the implications for library education in this development; it certainly introduces revolutionary changes in the basic curriculum in most American library schools.

I have been dealing with developments in librarianship which seem to be moving the librarian's attention to a narrower focus upon immediate local needs. Yet at the same time the horizons of the American librarian are widening to encompass not just the neighborhood, the town, or the state in which the individual library is located, but the entire world. There is a growing awareness among American librarians of the international nature of librarianship in all of its aspects. In their beginnings the American public and academic libraries were almost totally dependent upon the publication and the scholarship of other countries, since we had virtually no publication, scholarship, or literary heritage of our own. The roots of the American library movement have, therefore, always been deep in international soil, and the contents of the smallest American library will reflect, at least in English translation, an international flavor. But there has long been a bias in our outward look, which was primarily directed almost exclusively toward Europe. We are now beginning to realize how much of the world's culture and knowledge we have deprived ourselves of and are beginning to look toward a truly international exchange of information, materials, and persons to enrich and broaden the scope and the contribution that librarianship should take. Again the federal government has recognized the need for a true access to the world's literature (using that term in its most broadly inclusive sense) at least in word if not yet in dollars, and the major libraries are actively building their collections, filling gaps, and recognizing channels which heretofore have been too long neglected.

And here, of course, developments in American librarianship *do* have implications for librarianship in other countries, because of the need to transfer to a worldwide stage the kind of cooperative philosophy which is beginning to appear on the national scene. As the exchange of publications, ideas, and personnel increases across national boundaries, all parties to the exchange will be affected. We will learn from one another, we will adopt procedures from one another, we will begin to accommodate our systems to meet the special needs of one another's systems. I cannot see how such a development could be anything but good. If it is true, as I believe, that each country has developed its own brand of librarianship to meet its own needs, then it follows that each of us has cut ourselves off from some aspects of librarianship that were developed elsewhere. As the world grows smaller, and particularly as each country's special knowledge becomes accepted as part of the universal culture we all share, the total range of library developments must be tapped if we are to make effective use of this cultural store.

Training of University Library Staffs in Japan

Narau Okada
Former President, National Junior College for Librarianship

The training of library staff members had its formal beginning in Japan in 1921. "Formal" here does not refer to the commencement of library education on a statutory basis under the school education laws of the day; it refers merely to the establishment of an instructional facility called the Library Training School (Toshokan Kōshūjo). The school was a state-operated facility whose primary objective was the training of prospective employees of public libraries. Hence it was established under the administrative supervision of the Bureau of Social Education of the Ministry of Education, and was located on the grounds of the Imperial Library (Teikoku Toshokan), then the only national library in the country. The Imperial Library, the predecessor of the National Diet Library, was also under the jurisdiction of the Social Education Bureau.

The primary qualification for admittance to the training school was graduation from a middle school under the old six-five system of education, i.e., completion of eleven years of elementary and secondary education. The school required one additional year of matriculation, and, in an exotic departure for that period in Japan, was coeducational. It registered twenty to twenty-five students each year, but after the twenty-fourth graduating class in March 1945, it was forced to close temporarily because of the severity of the war then in progress.

Though the training school was primarily aimed at training specialized staffs for public libraries, the majority of the graduates looked for jobs in university and research libraries throughout the country (including

Korea, Manchuria, and Taiwan) because Japanese public libraries at that time were in such an impoverished state that they were unable to employ specialized staffs. Consequently, the curriculum of the training school had to provide an all-round library education suitable for employees of all types of libraries. Thus, cataloging and classification, which constitute the essential core techniques in all types of libraries, formed the center of the curriculum.

With the start of the war in the Pacific, collecting and processing of needed materials in various institutes and research organizations were vigorously pushed, and many of the graduates of the training school took part in this work. This was the state of affairs at the end of the war.

After the war a new library movement started in Japan. The American concept of "socialized recitation," which required access to school libraries in education, was adopted, and every effort was made to move away from the prewar "uniform education" system. Moreover, during the war researchers had come to appreciate fully how important documents and other sources of information were for their own studies and investigations. Additionally, they had discovered that it was more efficient and effective to utilize specialized personnel with library training to collect and process the needed documents than to do the work themselves. In this situation, the Ministry of Education was even more sensitive in the postwar period to the necessity of training specialized library personnel, and it therefore reopened the training school in 1947 under the new name of Library Staff Training School (Toshokan Shokuin Yō-seijo).

Furthermore, with strong support from the "library officers" dispatched from the United States to the Civil Information and Education Section of GHQ, Supreme Commander for the Allied Powers, first the Library Law (1950) and then the School Library Law (1953) were enacted. Specialized posts of "librarian" and "teacher-librarian" were designated under these laws, and at the same time the educational qualifications for these positions were clari-

fied. Thus, it is clear that by "teacher-librarian" (*shisho kyōyu*) is meant a specialist in primary, middle, and high school libraries, and by "librarian" (*shisho*), according to the Library Law, is meant a staff member of a public library, in accordance with the spirit of social education covered in Article 1 of the law.

In this situation the training of specialized staff members of university libraries had to be considered separately and from a special standpoint. This is the reason why the topic "Training of University Library Staffs" has been repeatedly discussed in meetings of the University Libraries Division during the annual conferences of the Japan Library Association. In 1952 the Research Group on the Improvement of National University Libraries established by the Ministry of Education issued *Principles for the Improvement of National University Libraries,* which outlined the problems of training university library staff members as follows:

3. Staff organization of university libraries.
   a. [Omitted here]
   b. In view of the specialized nature of their duties, staff members of university libraries should be given the opportunity of re-education and training to increase their specialized knowledge, improve techniques, and thus upgrade their positions.
   c. The Ministry of Education should make plans to train university library staff members and implement them as soon as possible.

4. Establishment of courses in library science.
   a. In order to develop academic studies of libraries and to initiate instruction in library science, courses on or departments of library science should be established in universities.

6. Improved operation of university libraries to facilitate students' use.
   a.–e. [Omitted here]
   f. Training of reference librarians should be pushed in order to provide guidance to the student at all times on the library and the use of the library.

As the willingness of the various universities to improve university libraries grew, many libraries in the mid-1950s started to establish courses on library science. However, the major objective of the courses was to train general public library staff members in accordance with the Library Law of 1950. This law set somewhat low educational standards, and the results were not especially satisfactory so far as university librarians were concerned. The establishment of the Department of Library Science at Keiō University in 1951 with strong American support a year before the "Principles" were written and the subsequent establishment of the Department of Library Science within the Division of Social Science at Tōyō University in 1959 should be noted with special interest. In 1967 Keiō University established a postgraduate (master's degree) course.

The "Principles" included 13 points concerned with the improvement of university libraries, and it was possible for some of these to be put into effect by the universities by local decision. Many, however, required the assistance of or promotion by the Ministry of Education for realization —i.e, national support. Accordingly, over a period of years the universities have petitioned the Ministry of Education for the establishment of a university library section within the Higher Education and Science Bureau for the administration or promotion of matters concerning university libraries.

The above process has led to annual four-day University Library Institutes sponsored by the Ministry of Education. Enrolling 100 librarians in each of three locations, the institutes have been offered since 1964 to satisfy the "re-education and training" demand listed in Article 3 (b) of the "Principles." To satisfy Article 3 (c) —"plans for training"—the former Library Staff Training School was elevated in status by law and became the National Junior College for Librarianship (Toshokan Tanki Daigaku) in 1964. However, this is a junior college, and its courses fall far short of satisfying the demand for the training of reference librarians, as referred to in Article 6 (f). Similarly, in 1965, a university library section, long requested by the university libraries, was established within the Higher Education and Science Bureau of

the Ministry of Education under the title Information and Library Section.

Thus, though the universities have placed heavy emphasis on the training of university library staffs, the realization of their policies by the government has been a very slow process. The fact that the single national librarians' training facility remains at the junior college level typifies this slow process. At present graduates of the junior college are increasingly unable to function even at the prefectural (public) library level. Furthermore, they are capable only of playing a supplementary role in university and specialized academic libraries. Since the Ministry of Education is fully cognizant of the problem, some kind of corrective measure is anticipated in the near future, but the problem is not amenable to a quick solution. The Ministry of Education has also reconsidered and evaluated the effectiveness of the present method of re-education or training of university library staffs, and since this matter is less complex, it is my understanding that more effective and appropriate methods will be applied soon.

On the one hand, then, we see how slow progress has been in government attempts to improve university libraries and to train university library staffs. On the other, we find that the production and distribution of scholarly publications are increasing annually at a faster and faster pace, both domestically and overseas. Consequently, demands placed on the library by academic and other researchers are increasing rapidly. Therefore, the best university libraries in our country today require "specialized staff members with specialized training in at least one discipline field, understanding of several languages, and knowledge of library science." Dr. Yosoji Itō, former president of the University Libraries Division of the JLA, has stated in an article in *Toshokan Zasshi* (*Library Journal*) (December 1965): "The method of training library staff members in our country is the Achilles' heel in the establishment of professional library service in university libraries. The training of librarians should be fundamentally reconsidered, taking as the point of departure the training of documentalists." This is indeed the case.

A breakdown of Japanese universities discloses the following pattern:

National	75
Public (municipal and prefectural	35
Private	267
Total	377 (excluding junior colleges)

All these universities, however, do not necessarily require library staffs with the same level of higher education. At present, university libraries requiring the most highly trained specialized staffs are very few in number, and no system has yet been developed to handle those with highly specialized training. However, taking into consideration the rate of development of documentation and information activities today, all the universities will require, within the next several years, specialized staffs with the highest library education. It will be too late to start training when that point is reached. Here, we who endeavor to train university library staffs face a huge dilemma as we are suspended between the present situation and the future. The problem of training university library staffs in Japan today encompasses this deep fundamental distress.

Education of University Librarians as Documentalists

Masanobu Fujikawa
Keiō University

Library educators find it virtually impossible to arrive at a consensus when they discuss the professional education of university librarians as documentalists. Perhaps this is due to differing views on the role of documentalists and of university librarians; indeed, in today's confused state of student turmoil it is even difficult to define what a university is! And to make matters even worse, we are living in an age in which "information," which encompasses virtually every aspect of man's intellectual endeavors, has become an exceedingly amorphous concept. "Information" is said to be neither energy nor matter, but at the same time is not a non-existent illusion. Speaking in all candor, I am personally bewildered by the diverse opinions and approaches to the education and training of librarians, documentalists, and information specialists. It would appear that at times their education must encompass the whole of knowledge. Thus I must confess that I am of the same opinion as Dr. Abraham Kaplan, the philosopher, who in addressing a group of librarians declared:

> Like your profession, mine also has thrust upon it, as its appropriate domain, the whole world of knowledge, the whole of culture; nothing is supposed to be foreign to us, and we ought to be prepared under suitable circumstances to be helpful with regard to any and every area of human concern.[1]

But I am not entirely pessimistic about the education of documentalists and of the institutions they are trained to serve. Universities and their libraries cannot escape the information explosion, and we as librarians or documentalists will not be content to remain, and cannot remain, forever at a low-priority level of attention in the academic world. Today university librarians are struggling to select the most appropriate materials for their collections, to process them in an adequate manner, and to render the varied services demanded of them. At the same time they are endeavoring to adopt the newer documentation techniques while absorbing the latest advances in the field of information science. It is the responsibility of those of us who are engaged in research and education in librarianship and documentation to define the existing issues and to clarify the educational principles of our profession. By so doing we can, I believe, contribute to the further development and strengthening of our university libraries.

In this paper I shall discuss my understanding of documentation and documentalists; outline desired qualifications for and education of documentalists, emphasizing their position and role in university libraries; and discuss library and documentation educators and their responsibilities.

Documentation and Documentalists

Numerous definitions of the term "documentation" have been provided by S. C. Bradford[2] and others, and it serves no useful purpose to enumerate and examine all the available definitions. We may be able to arrive at a workable definition useful for the purpose of this paper by comparing the concepts of documentation and information. When we do so, we find that we must integrate these two concepts, and at the same time we are led to a new understanding of their relation to librarianship.

It is undeniable that the term "information" has been and is interpreted in different ways, and that this has caused considerable confusion in our field. The reason seems to lie in the fact that everyone tends to define "information" on the basis of his personal understanding of the term, since it is not a neologism but an old word rich in connotation. In many cases, "information" is interpreted as being identical with information source, or with intelligence, or with knowledge as a whole. Another cause of confusion lies in the fact that we tend erroneously to oversimplify the relation between informational activities and the act of signification. In other words, finding something meaningful or relevant should be differentiated from giving a specific meaning to an object in one's mind. The problem of meaning is crucial here because it relates to all phases of classification, indexing, searching, and reference work, but unfortunately we cannot delve deeper into this subject in this paper.

As to the relation between information, documentation, and librarianship, Mortimer Taube has put it in these terms:

. . . one of the substantial differences between generally accepted library work and recently advocated documentation can be found in the difference of degree and volume of stored materials, and that relates to the notion of information . . .[3]

The term "materials" here causes a problem. A quantitative increase per se of materials (i.e., a physical increase of simple and homogeneous units) does not have any direct relationship to the problem of information. What is important is the content of the materials. At the same time, information *about* each of the materials is no less important when materials increase in number, because such information plays a significant role in finding needed items efficiently and precisely. When we consider these two aspects of information in regard to materials, the notion of information implied by Taube seems to be not too dissimilar from the central issues discussed in both librarianship and documentation. In short, documentation may be said to refer to the totality of techniques, or technological achievements, relating to access to all sorts of recorded materials, and it is, of course, the techniques which make the needed information available.

A different approach to the same problem was apparent in the Conferences on Training Science Information Specialists[4] held at the Georgia Institute of Technology in 1961–62. The term "documentation" was avoided in an attempt to lessen confusion, and instead the phrase "information science" was adopted, a phrase which sounded very fresh and unique at that time. But this substitution did not in fact solve the problem. Specialists were grouped into three categories: information scientists, technical literature analysts, and science librarians. It was recommended that uniform educational and training methods be adopted appropriate to various levels of study for specialists in each of the three categories. However, since different qualifications are required of specialists in the three groups, it is perhaps forcing matters to establish a common curriculum equally effective for all three. Despite these problems, due recognition should be given to the fact that the concept of information has been introduced to documentation work and that this has had the effect of sharpening the conceptualization of documentation and improving the quality of documentation work and of documentalists. Moreover, it should be recognized that the impetus for improvement has come not from librarians or documentalists, but from subject specialists.

A further impact of the conferences was on the position of librarians, or more precisely, science librarians, newly placed on the bottom rung of the ladder of professional qualifications. According to the consensus of the participants in the conferences, science librarians are not required to have the capacity to evaluate the contents of a given document critically, and they are expected to perform traditional library routines. In contrast, technical literature analysts are to be capable of evaluating and processing the contents of documents for scientific researchers. Information scientists occupy the highest rung, and are to devote themselves to research and scientific investigation of information itself.

We find an analogous situation in Japan. First of all, no one bears the official title of "documentalist," although there is a Japan Documentation Society (Nippon Dokumēnteshon Kyōkai) and other local documentation societies and organizations. The government authorizes the title of "information technologist," and qualifications for this are determined by the Science and Technology Agency (Kagaku Gijutsuchō).

In general, the documentalist is distinguished from the librarian by his capacity to analyze and evaluate the literature of a specialized field of science or technology, and, recently, the field of the social sciences. In contrast, the librarian is expected merely to process information sources in a variety of physical formats in accordance with established rules and codes, even if he is capable of interpreting scholarly library materials and introducing them to the researcher. We all recognize the importance of the ability to recognize, compare, translate, and digest the content of docu-

ments in many fields of knowledge and on different levels. Mathematical linguists have even tried to invade the secret recesses of metaphor and metaphorical meaning. Yet traditionally oriented librarians tend to neglect these new frontiers, leaving the field to information scientists or computer specialists. They are the ones who have taken the initiative in elaborating methods of analysis and recomposition of recorded knowledge, thus transforming our cultural assets to fit the needs of contemporary society.

This is indeed ironic. In information science we may observe that the present approach is based on finding the constituent elements of a given problem on the one hand, and determining the structure, or system, of elements which comprise the problem on the other. In traditional librarianship our predecessors sought to develop a system of grouping and identifying recorded materials by following an approach similar to that used in information science, viz., by recognizing the specific feature of a document as a whole (ordinary classification and assignment of subject headings), by analyzing content (faceted classification, analytical cataloging), and finally by finding and establishing structures (classification schemes, subject heading lists, cataloging rules).

In both information science and librarianship these approaches have been critically examined and improved through experimentation and observation. If there is an apparent difference between the two fields, it would seem to lie in the fact that in information science the articulated and algorismic approach is held in high regard, while in librarianship there appears to be a stress on subjective personal interpretation of established modes.

It is necessary to clarify the differentiating characteristics of the two fields under discussion further. In information science as it has developed to date, solutions are "sign oriented" (where "sign" is used in a broad sense, including symbols and codes and formulations). That is, proposed problems are examined and judged by formulated and established criteria, which are exact in form and distinguishable in terms of measure or scale. In librarianship, with the exception of the large domain of administration, solutions are heavily "behavior oriented." That is, proposed problems are examined and judged in terms of individual motive, inner desire, opposition to the contrary opinion, etc. Here interpretation is considered a kind of behavior. It is easier to have a closed system in the world of signs (sign systems are closed), but we are obliged to face an open system in the world of human behavior (society is open).

At least until the behavioral sciences or information science can clarify and formulate the amazing complexity of man's thinking processes and activities, librarianship will have to be directed toward the exploration of man's intellectual activities in the form of recorded materials and toward the organization of these materials in some usable structure.

Qualifications for and Education of Documentalists

Japanese librarians had the opportunity in 1963 to meet with Lester Asheim and Dorothy Spofford to discuss fundamental issues in education for librarianship. A summary of the discussions appeared in the distinguished professional journal entitled *Toshokan-kai* (*Library World*).[5] In my opinion education for librarianship has not improved as expected in the intervening six years. Perhaps the primary reason for this lack of progress is the dilatoriness of library faculty and others engaged in this field. It is easy enough to criticize the faculty in other disciplines, and to lay the blame on inadequate budgets and poor facilities. Such criticisms may be justified, but in all honesty we would have to admit that we in librarianship are not so attractive to other faculty members or to students in the university world.

In this age of the information industry, information centers, and data banks, substantial numbers of faculty and students show an intense interest in "information science" and are disturbed by the present status and trends of this "science." They are closely observing the slow changes in

and development of university libraries, and if they perceive that nothing is coming out of the treasure houses, they will turn their backs on the librarian-custodians. Newness in itself does not make a thing valuable, but new interpretations of ancient treasures are always necessary. If new approaches were not available, the works of Shakespeare and the *Genji Monogatari* [*Tale of Genji*] would have died long ago. It is time to look anew at library school curricula with open minds if we wish to preserve our universities and our libraries.

University librarians must not only satisfy the needs of the university as a whole; they must also perform the routine tasks of the librarian. Since the needs and tasks are endless, university librarians are often required to be supermen. The time has come to consider the possibility of dividing our library courses, one group being oriented toward traditional librarianship, with emphasis on knowledge of books and other library materials, bibliography, history of scholarship, administration, and management. The other group would be oriented toward documentation and information science, with the accent on subject analysis, indexing (and the strategic approach to indexing), systems design, mechanization, and computerization. The common background for these two approaches would include general linguistics, logic, communication and information theory, and, if possible, the history of thought, the history of science, and introductions to social and economic systems.

These ideas may be described in tabular form as follows:

A. Basic knowledge courses (subject knowledge would be acquired through four years of study at the undergraduate level, or by selection of a specific subject field as a minor with librarianship as a major)

  1. Fundamental courses

    a. Communications (sociological, psychological, physiological, and managerial principles)

    b. General information theory (approaches to human information processing and thinking processes)

    c. General linguistics and logic (general comprehension of symbols, codes, meaning, signification, sentence structure, and logical connections)

d. Outline of history of thought and of science and technology

e. Social and economic systems

2. Applied courses

a. General theory of classification (historical and comparative approach to past and existing classification systems as reflections of human thought)

b. General theory of indexing (historical and comparative approach; ways and means of finding and assigning tags)

c. Bibliography and bibliographies (outline of bibliography and types and examples of bibliographies)

d. Abstracts and abstracting (history; comparison with similar techniques, and preparation of sample abstracts)

e. Survey and research methods (statistical methodology; inquiry forms; interview techniques; outline of research methods in main disciplines, with examples)

B. Librarianship courses

1. Indexes and bibliographies (bibliography of bibliographies; world bibliographies; national, subject, language, and annotated bibliographies; format, arrangement, keywords, systematic characteristics of indexes)

2. Practical preparation of indexes and bibliographies

3. Classification of books and other library materials (practice of examining and using important schemes and designing classification schemes for specific purposes)

4. Selection of library materials and useful tools (introduction to various types of library materials and effective use of tools)

5. Reference service (importance of personal contact; selection and use of reference sources; recording of inquiries; utilization of statistical methods in analyzing and ordering results)

6. Administration and management of libraries, subdivided by type of library (general principles of administration and management; communication channels; standardization and unification of routine work)

C. Documentation courses

1. Indexing method (systematics; linguistic units; formation of logical connections; format; thesauri and their compilation and use; mechanization)

2. Classificatory method (deterministic and probabilistic approaches; applied mathematics; mechanization and automation)

3. Subject analysis (application of above: practice in specific fields of science and technology; annotation and reviewing in humanities and social sciences)

4. Abstracting method (application of above: practice and evaluation; possibility of mechanization)

5. Computer science (general principles; systems analysis and design; introduction to programming, and practice)

6. Information centers, data banks, and their management (personnel; records and their filing; communications; publications; efficiency and economy)

(Note: Reproduction and Printing may be added under either B or C.)

The Faculty and Their Responsibility

The makeup of the faculty will, of course, depend on which of the courses described above are selected for inclusion in the curriculum. Whatever the specific institutional setting, faculty members should not be recruited exclusively from among those who have had experience in only library science, library work, or documentation. It would be extremely desirable to establish a librarian training institute in a university where specialists and scholars in the fields described above are immediately available. Their approaches to problems and teaching methods may differ from the traditional approaches in librarianship and documentation, but we can expect from them valuable contributions to knowledge in our field as they concentrate on our common endeavor, viz., the promotion of intellectual activities.

The faculty, whatever its composition, is faced with a number of problems in Japan today. First and foremost is how to elevate and broaden the intellectual interests of the students. This is in part related to teaching methods, but more critically it involves the problem of course content. It is very important that we attempt to liberate the library and librarianship from the isolation in which they appear to find themselves, both in the world of learning and in society at large. The relative irrelevancy of libraries on the campus and in society may be particularly marked in Japan, but it may also be true to some extent in Western countries. The liberation will have to be accomplished both by librarians from the inside and by the public from the outside as they come to recognize the value of libraries and utilize them more fully. In this sense, librarians will find very useful allies in faculty members attracted to their discipline from other departments and faculties within the university.

This type of interdisciplinary cooperation has been attempted in the United States and elsewhere, but the effectiveness of such efforts is unknown to me. In Japan it should be tried and evaluated. (At the Keiō University School of Library and Information Science interdisciplinary cooperation has been tried for two years and will be further expanded in the future.)

A second problem faced by faculty members is how to combine theory and practice. Quite often we are criticized for a one-sided emphasis on theory to the exclusion of developing the practical capabilities of our students. To this my answer is fourfold: First, capability cannot be developed by teaching. Second, theory is the intellect's most valuable invention in economizing on activities. Third, most library practices merely repeat old methods and lack potential for future development. Fourth, we are attempting to develop and graduate individuals who can go out into society to think and not merely work like ants. (I believe I may be creating many enemies by this assertion.)

The situation with respect to the problems I have been discussing appears to be quite different in the United States. In the United States we find that the library system has become an integral part of the social structure, and library technology has been geared to social activities. This, of course, is a matter of degree in the two countries, and whether it is good or bad is another problem. In any case, it seems to me that there is no great conflict or contradiction between library practices and society's expectations of the library. Accordingly, American students who have acquired practical knowledge, or who have been educated in the fundamentals of a particular discipline through four years of undergraduate education, can attempt to practice their knowledge, evaluate their experience, and attempt new methods according to their creative ability. In Japan the situation is quite different. Our graduates are often asked to explore the possibility of establishing new administrative policy, invent new classification schemes or indexing methods, or plan the introduction of mechanization, all without adequate preparation or education and with few exemplars or pioneers to guide them.

In-service training or on-the-job training should not be confused with regularly scheduled basic education in universities, but the confusion occurs quite often. However, to maintain the difference between the two while at the same time integrating them when the proper opportunity presents itself, we need first to set up a firm theoretical basis of librarianship.

Librarianship theory is not in the realm of pure science. It must be applicable to real-life situations. Educators, teachers, and researchers must have the opportunity and facilities to experiment, observe, calculate, and formulate. So far as every library stresses its particularity and uniqueness, it is virtually impossible to collect comparative data which can be used for purposes of evaluation. To a certain extent each library has its unique character, but at the same time it has a degree of commonality with other libraries. Where institutional heterogeneity is marked, no scientific investigation of the institution as a social phenomenon is possible. This can lead to lack of experimentation and theorization, which in turn will lead to enervation of the creative spirit. And where no creative thinking or activity is found, students cannot be stimulated to exercise their intellectual curiosity. In this situation, when a student is placed in a practical real-life library, he will encounter a picture of library activity at odds with what he has learned. A library technology founded on sound knowledge would not be so limited, and would always be improved in the face of reality.

In conclusion, we may say that before a profession is established, it is first necessary to develop many individuals who possess a common store of knowledge and who have attained a common level of capability. To realize our hopes and to make our field a true profession, all of us who are involved with education and training for librarianship will have to devote ourselves to extensive research and education activity in our daily lives.

NOTES

[1]Abraham Kaplan, "The Age of the Symbol: A Philosophy of Library Education," in Don R. Swanson, ed., *The Intellectual Foundations of Library Education: The Twenty-ninth Annual Conference of the Graduate Library School*, 6–8 July 1964 (Chicago: Univ. of Chicago Pr., 1965), p.16.

[2]Samuel Clement Bradford, *Documentation* (London: Lockwood, 1948) 156p.

[3]Mortimer Taube, "Documentation, Information Retrieval, and Other New Techniques," in Lester Asheim, ed., *Persistent Issues in American Librarianship: Papers Presented before the Twenty-fifth Annual Conference of the Graduate Library School of the University of Chicago*, 15–17 Aug. 1960 (Chicago: Univ. of Chicago Pr., 1961), p.91.

[4]Conferences on Training Science Information Specialists, Georgia Institute of Technology, 1961–62, *Proceedings* (1962). 139p.

[5]Masanobu Fujikawa, ed., "Toshokangaku kyōiku no honshitsuteki shomondai (Fundamental Issues of the Formation of Librarianship)," in *Toshokan-kai* (*Library World*) 18, no. 5: 148–57 (1967).

Part 6

ACQUISITION AND EXCHANGE OF PUBLICATIONS

Administration of Acquisitions and Exchange

Allen B. Veaner
Assistant Director,
Stanford University Libraries

In this paper I shall concentrate on those problems relevant to the procurement of current materials and retrospective materials still in print. I exclude from consideration the purchase of out-of-print books and micropublications, mainly because both are highly specialized topics which deserve separate papers.

Of all the materials purchased on a continuing basis by universities and research centers, books are by far the oddest. They are bought by the tens or hundreds of thousands, yet hardly any two ever resemble each other. They are obtained from thousands of vendors in nearly every country of the world. Their physical characteristics vary widely: weight, size, paper, type font, shape, color, etc. Their languages,

their intellectual qualities, and their bibliographic descriptions vary widely, and the last two items are often the subjects of controversy. No other commodity essential for the existence of a research center approaches the uniqueness of the book. This uniqueness is responsible for the charm they hold for bibliophiles, but this same individuality accounts for most of the difficulties in acquiring books.

The acquisition of library materials brings about the interaction of many parties whose interests definitely conflict. They are the selectors—curators, faculty, students, staff —the acquisitions staff, the cataloging and reference staff, the controller or agency carrying fiscal responsibility, the vendor, the international monetary system, the transportation system, and, in a few instances, the political jurisdiction.

In terms of the above interests, let us define some qualitative and quantitative differences in products and services in a typical acquisitions system as shown in table 1. This table is a highly simplified and abstract picture of a complex communication process between many parties, something that in modern parlance might

TABLE 1. Interaction of Forces in Acquisition of Library Materials

INTERACTING AGENCY, DEPARTMENT

PRODUCT, SERVICE, OR SYSTEM CHARACTERISTICS	BOOK SELECTOR	STAFF OF ACQ. DEPT.	REFERENCE LIBRARIANS	CATALOGERS	CONTROLLER	VENDOR	MONETARY SYSTEM	TRANSPORTATION	POLITICAL JURISDICTION	FACULTY, STUDENTS, RESEARCHERS	SERIAL DEPARTMENT
Required quality of bibliographic data	Low to medium	Medium to high	High	High	Low	Medium to high	—	—	Variable	Variable	High
Required quantity of bibliographic data	Low to medium	Medium	High	High	Low	Low to medium	—	—	Variable	Medium	High
Required delivery speed of books	Variable	High	High	—	High	High	—	Variable	—	High	High
Physical unit of processing	Vol.	Vol.; packages	Vol., set, indiv. page	Vol.	Invoice; accounts payable; budget statements; payment vouchers	Vol. checks	Checks	Packages	Vol.	Title; vol.	Vol.
Information unit of processing	Bibl. record	Bibl. record; invoice	Bibl. record	Bibl. record		Accts. receivable; invoices	—	Letters; purchase orders; invoices	Bibl. record	Bibl. record	Bibl. record
Mode of processing physical items	Unit; batch (rare)	Unit & batch	Unit	Unit	Checks	Unit & batch	—	Unit (rare) & batch	Variable	Unit	Unit
Mode of processing information & data	Unit	Unit & batch	Unit	Unit	Batch	Unit & batch	Batch (many for one)	Unit & batch	—	Unit	Unit & batch
Degree of interest in fiscal control	Variable	High	Low	Low	High	High	—	—	High	Low	High
Interest in intellectual quality of materials	High	—	High	—	—	Variable	—	—	—	High	—

be called a communication network. In practical terms, this reduces to people talking or writing to other people about the books they want, creating and maintaining records and files, updating messages from time to time, and recording the transactions.

File Management

The control center for all this activity is a set of files, usually consisting of an outstanding order file, a file of invoices, and historical records of expenditures, such as budget statements. Some systems will contain additional files which in effect index the master file by date, vendor, purchase order number, or local account number. Maintaining and searching a large multilingual file is an extremely difficult task and requires a high order of management skill. It is in the area of file management that some computer assistance may be helpful, though at this time there is very little experience in handling large computerized files of bibliographic data. Little is known about the psychological aspects of file searching, but it is apparent that the proficient searcher is the key to an efficient manual acquisitions system which must necessarily provide a limited number of access points to each record.

In connection with file organization, it is useful to record a new and recent trend. For a long time acquisitions files were maintained in a primary sequence by author and secondarily by title, following the pattern of the conventional card catalog. Today more libraries are adopting a straight title sequence, partly to combat filing difficulties and partly out of the realization that there is no reason why a temporary control file should slavishly imitate the dictionary catalog.

Problems of Fiscal Control Systems

Wide price variation is one of the factors which distinguishes book purchasing from any other buying in research centers, and it complicates fiscal control. Now, some faculty members and book selection experts behave as if there were an infinite supply of money, but in this age of expensive reprints and keen competition for out-of-print titles, tight fiscal control is essential. In some libraries this means hiring a bookkeeper to maintain an independent, separate accounting system, in which each commitment or payment transaction is logged. The manager of the acquisitions system must take care not to delegate book-purchasing authority to the bookkeeper; a nonlibrarian should not be accorded the power to halt an outgoing purchase order.

In most large organizations there is a substantial time lag in processing invoices because of the great number of documents and the batch processing method. Even if a computer is available, invoice documents must still be keyboarded before they can be handled by computer. It is doubtful that we will soon see the development of internationally standardized invoice documents printed in both human- and machine-readable form. The handwritten or typed invoice is going to be with us for a long time.

Another problem with the invoice turns on the processing unit; for the buyer the preferred processing unit is the title, but for the seller it is the invoice. To process a consolidated invoice for payment, the buyer has to determine what portion of that invoice is assignable to his several bibliographic and fiscal records. In particular, the buyer may have to apply portions of various book funds to one invoice, a process that is time-consuming and cumbersome. The internal transfer of monies from various budgets to write a single check in payment of one invoice adds to the controller's overhead. One solution is to permit the library to commingle funds into a few large budgets and then make quarterly reconciliations to the multiplicity of funds supplying these budgets. It is a generous and understanding controller who will permit this. A few vendors provide individual invoices for each title purchased; this eliminates the problem, but such a service is only available from very large vendors. Therefore, the combined invoice is also going to be with us for a long time.

Selection and purchasing, then, are ideally one-for-one processes. As soon as fiscal and invoice processing enter the data stream, however, the processing mode shifts to many-for-one: many books and many book budgets, one invoice. When these same invoices enter the controller's shop, processing is reversed and becomes one-for-many, i.e., one consolidated check is written to pay many vendor invoices. The blank-check plan is an attempt to maintain a one-for-one processing mode throughout the acquisitions cycle. A blank check valid for some upper limit, usually $100, is sent to the vendor as an integral part of the purchase order form. The vendor fills in the exact amount of payment, and the canceled check is used to post the budget statement. An advantage is that the vendor is paid promptly and accurately; a disadvantage is that the vendor has to handle a large number of checks. The checks are usually valid for a limited time, and there could be problems with books that are out of stock or awaiting reprinting; they might be ready for delivery after the blank check is no longer valid. Also in some institutions the controller is reluctant to delegate his check-writing authority, or he may worry about the security of negotiable checks not under his direct control.

Librarians should be wary of permitting establishment of excessively restricted gift or endowment funds, regardless of their size. In some fields the income might greatly exceed the cost of all the material published in a decade; in other cases the restricted field may be so highly specialized that it becomes difficult to find material to buy. So in the end the donor is unhappy, the librarian is unhappy, and the controller must maintain a fund that is not very active.

Despite advances in electronic data communication, there is little likelihood that the book trade will soon be free of paper handling. There are too many different legal and managerial requirements among institutions, and developing countries will probably be dependent on manual data processing for some time.

Patterns of Book Purchasing

The classical pattern of book procurement has turned upon individual selection and ordering from announcements, advertisements, and national and trade bibliographies. Where budgets are severely limited (as in small public libraries) this method is practically obligatory, but for current materials, college, university, and research libraries are turning more and more to the approval order system, sometimes designated the "blanket order plan." In this scheme the selectors draw up a profile which characterizes the desired acquisitions plan within a given discipline or language. Actual selection of titles is then turned over to the vendor. Of course, to support this system the vendor must employ broadly educated selectors who know something about the academic program in a given institution. Periodically he ships to the library his selection of newly published titles and the local selectors winnow the material by actual examination—no doubt the best way to pick books. The approval system has a built-in 100 percent return privilege for any title not desired by the customer. In effect, the vendor is gambling that returns will not exceed some maximum percentage beyond which his handling costs would make the arrangement unprofitable.

The approval plan has two great advantages for the buyer: (1) he is assured of delivery immediately after publication of one copy of each new title of interest to him, thus practically eliminating the risk that a book may go out of print before an order can be placed; and (2) the book never enters the buyer's fiscal or bibliographic control system unless it is accepted. The buyer pays only for those books which he keeps; no refunds or credits need to be negotiated. Some vendors even prepare multiple copy control slips for a library's retention to assist in file maintenance and technical processing.

A major reason for this shift is the recent very great expansion of publishing and acquisitions. Colleges and universities are growing at seemingly alarming rates; the federal government in the United States has been greatly assisting the purchase of library materials under the Higher Education Act of 1965. The acquisitions rate in American academic libraries doubled in the six years between 1960 and 1966. Library schools have been unable to supply enough professionals to man acquisitions services, and there has been no easing of the recruitment problem with clerical support staff. These forces have combined to overwhelm the library's conventional ordering and receiving procedures, some of which may not have been rationally planned. There is much evidence that many traditional acquisitions procedures lack rationality; were it not for the establishment of approval plans, the whole acquisitions process in many libraries might have collapsed entirely.

The approval plan is not without some risks. One obvious problem is the quality of the vendor's selection. There is a risk that one may miss desired books or receive titles not really wanted. The only remedy is constant monitoring by local selectors and proper feedback to the vendor; without this an approval plan is likely to fail. A second risk to be weighed is the probability of inferior books getting into one's collection. However, elimination of the labor of selecting current items, searching them in the files, and typing purchase orders more than compensates for a few bad books.

A third problem with the approval plan is the possibility of conflict with long-established standing orders, especially if standing orders have been scattered among many vendors. The ideal arrangement is to take the approval plan and the standing orders from the same vendor, but if this is not possible, an exclusion list can be helpful to the chosen vendor.

The adoption of an approval plan may require some departures from traditional practices. I have heard of one library which wants to maintain a file of all the approval titles it has returned "just in case the vendor claims payment for a returned volume." This defeats a prime advantage of the system, whereby one's files need control only the items actually accepted. In those rare cases where the vendor submits an invalid claim, it is usually cheaper just to pay the invoice rather than keep superfluous records.

A variant blanket order plan is Stechert-Hafner's Latin American Cooperative Ac-

quisitions Program (LACAP). This plan is dependent upon traveling agents who try to cover the principal publishers and bookstores in each country. These itinerant agents also need to know the authors because in Latin America authors often negotiate directly with printers and distribute books from their own homes or offices.

In the United States certain libraries are required by law to work within a jurisdictional purchasing department or are compelled to purchase library materials by bidding. The expertise of the purchasing agent is invaluable for economizing on the commercial products essential for running a research center; he buys the blackboards, the consumable supplies, the furniture, etc. However, his staff almost never has the linguistic competence and the bibliographic tools to provide a book-purchasing service to the library. He also may lack motivation, since his customary purchasing is much farther from an academic program than is the library's work.

The bidding system usually goes hand in hand with the requirements that libraries obtain their books through a centralized purchasing department. Except for large quantities of the same title, we know, of course, that it is unrealistic to ask for bids on single copies of library materials. There are two powerful reasons for staying away from the bid system: first, it almost forces the buyer to do business with a single vendor; second, it is simply inefficient to bid for single, unique items which are relatively low in unit cost.

There is yet another hazard in the bid system—a danger that has been particularly troublesome in the United States. This is the problem of the unqualified vendor. The unqualified vendor needs only a typewriter, a telephone, a small office, and a few clerks. By bidding low, he tries to obtain an exclusive contract. From then on he acts only as a clearinghouse, consolidating book orders from various sources and forwarding them to the publisher, usually with instructions that the ordered items be shipped directly to the destination. There are several advantages to this scheme, and all accrue to the benefit of the vendor: since he stocks no books, he needs no warehouse; he can easily avoid hunting for an out-of-stock book by simply reporting to the library that the book is not available and canceling the order. The problem became so acute that several years ago the American Library Association and the National League of Cities jointly sponsored a study of book purchasing in the United States. A principal recommendation of the report, which will be published shortly, is that libraries supported by jurisdictions be exempt from bidding requirements and allowed to use their experience and judgment in choosing vendors.

Exchanges

There are whole categories of material available only by exchange, either because certain publications are not distributed in the book trade or because the book trade in a given nation is not well developed. In countries like the United States where labor costs are high, exchange is one of the less efficient methods of obtaining materials, owing to the great amount of correspondence needed to negotiate each exchange. It is also laborious to post records of exchanges, and such records must be kept for a long time to resolve controversies. Determining the economic value of a given exchange can sometimes take on the character of a delicate diplomatic negotiation. The "scorekeeping" aspects of exchange can be troublesome and irritating. It is hard to balance an exchange of goods where the traders differ substantially in prosperity. My own feeling is that if national currency policies permit, the advanced countries should give first preference to regular purchase routines, falling back on exchange only if the partner suffers hardship through lack of hard currency.

Various methods are employed to balance accounts between partners: page for page, volume for volume, or the "priced" exchange. In the last-named method each partner agrees beforehand to the equivalent cash value of certain publications, and a fictitious ledger is posted to keep account of the "money," although no cash ever changes hands.

Procurement by exchange is necessarily slower than direct purchasing, if only because of the normal time lag in correspondence. Additionally, communications and postal services in developing countries may be slow. Sometimes when the person in charge of exchange leaves, he takes his correspondence with him, and his successor has no record of prior negotiations. Political instability contributes to the difficulty of maintaining continuity of exchanges.

Press runs in developing countries may be small, and current material may go out of print before it can be obtained by exchange. One effective countermeasure is to secure the services of a resident or regional agent who is well informed on the needs of your library. Owing to the vastness of its international exchange operations, the Library of Congress is able to employ such persons, who can see to the selection, wrapping, addressing, and shipping of desired materials.

Some materials are not well suited for exchange. Irregular serials are among them. Even regular, dependable serials are difficult because in most cases the subscription supplied from the advanced country will be obtained through a subscription agency, while the periodical itself will be sent direct from the publisher. This multipath flow makes it hard to maintain continuity. Nevertheless, subscriptions are much in demand by partners, just because they tend to be expensive and can easily drain off scarce hard currency.

The use of exchange for domestic procurement is declining and is considered an archaic practice by many. Commonly a library obtained a quantity of its own institution's publications at a favorable price and exchanged them with other libraries which did essentially the same thing. Because of the aforementioned high overhead costs of correspondence, both lost in the process.

Reprint Procurement

Reprints present two special problems, one bibliographic and one financial. Some reprinters persist in issuing reprints with titles differing significantly from those assigned to the original works. In my opinion, this constitutes a malpractice, because one can find oneself buying an expensive reprint of a title already in the library. The buyer should be wary of reprints advertised with scant bibliographic information, and, if expensive, the titles should be searched with redoubled persistence until their identity or lack thereof is definitely established.

Besides the risk of wasting resources on titles already in the library, the financial problem is additionally aggravated by the high price of reprints and by the widespread practice known as "fishing." "Fishing" is the issuance of prospectuses and announcements without bona fide intention of publishing the reprint unless a large enough market is indicated by responses from purchasers. Often a special prepublication price, which is difficult to turn down, is offered. There is a risk of tying down sorely needed funds in anticipation of needing them for the reprints when they arrive; if the reprints are never issued or are issued many years later, the library's purchasing power for other materials has been impaired. The bold solution to the problem is to call the reprinter's bluff and order the material without encumbering funds. The other solution is to learn from the experience of others and get to know who are the dependable reprinters.

Rapid expansion of educational institutions is making reprinting a very attractive business. Because reprinters concentrate mainly on material no longer protected by copyright, their capital investment is minimal: a good, clean copy of the original, suitable for photomechanical reproduction, a plate-making camera, offset-printing facilities, and a bindery. Hence one can find the same title reprinted two or three times by different reprinters working from different copies of the original document. When this happens, prices may vary widely, and the buyer may benefit from the competition.

In the past many libraries willingly lent books to reprinters without compensation, only to find the reissued works offered at prices judged exploitative. Also, in a few cases, to meet the needs of photomechanical reproduction processes, books have been damaged by reprinters. As an aid to libraries and reprinters, the American Library Association has adopted a set of guidelines, "Lending to Reprinters," in which are set forth basic principles of good practice for both the library and the reprinter. This statement has been published in the Spring 1967 issue of *Library Resources & Technical Services* (11:229–31).

Centralized Technical Processing Services

In the United States the introduction of systems analysis and computer applications is furthering an already popular pattern of organizing acquisition and cataloging work, namely, the formation of unified technical processing departments. Here the aim is to minimize doing the same job twice or more, mainly in searching for authoritative bibliographic data and in transcribing found data. This centripetal tendency is particularly beneficial for larger systems which need to supply purchasing and bibliographic services for outlying units which lack the staff or bibliographic tools for processing.

Essentially, the establishment of any centralized service by definition creates a large-batch operation. The larger the batch, the less the unit processing cost, but the greater the turnaround time. It is the "large-batch" characteristic which is responsible for the generally slow response time of centralized services. This phenomenon partly explains the performance difference between a library acquisitions department and a bookstore. Popular titles, whether from trade or scholarly presses, often appear very early in bookstores. But compared with the university or research library, the bookstore's procurement efforts are spread over a much narrower range of titles; hence it sometimes appears to students and faculty that the campus bookstore is more efficient than the library. However, bookstores buy titles in quantity, often directly from the publisher; therefore, they often skip the middleman who caters to the library market. The college or university bookstore may show spectacular success with a relatively small number of titles, but very few of them have the talent or bibliographic tools to dig out the more obscure and difficult-to-obtain publications. Here is where the service facilities of the jobber outweigh a few extra points of discount.

An important new development is the growing popularity of commercial services which supply not only books but also complete bibliographic data and processing services—even complete catalogs. In the United States it is possible to obtain from a single source book, plastic book cover, spine label, book pocket, charge card, and catalog cards for many in-print titles likely to be purchased by school and public libraries. For books which sell in large quantities, such services are obtainable far more cheaply than those any library could provide with its own resources.

When one adds the rapidly growing tendency to ship books by air freight to the possibility of utilizing the computer to process bibliographic data, one comes up with a powerful combination which could challenge the economic viability of local technical processing in the academic library. In the United States it appears a likely trend that the large vendors may become not only retailers of books but also retailers of complete bibliographic services based upon a quickly obtainable machine-readable record distributed by the nation's wholesaler—the Library of Congress.

Personnel Selection in Acquisitions

Searchers are the heart of any acquisitions system. Their recruitment and training are a challenging task for several reasons. A wide range of language and subject competence is needed, a combination not easy to obtain. Many of the personnel requirements are contradictory: constant alertness combined with the ability to withstand monotony, for example. There are certain intangible characteristics of the good searcher; he is a persistent, dogged sleuth, perhaps resembling somewhat the dedicated police inspector. But searchers must not be *too* perfectionistic. Good supervisory practice calls for a chief bibliographer or head of the searching unit to sort incoming book requisitions into batches, which are then distributed to the searchers in accordance with their language facility and experience. A searcher should not receive a new batch of requisitions until all the previously assigned searching work has been completed. This will serve to prevent searchers from burying the hard searches in their desk drawers and doing only the easy ones.

Searchers require a good deal of physical stamina; a searcher may walk greater distances each day than an airline stewardess. Finally, a searcher must be willing to work for a relatively low salary. This last factor constitutes a real personnel problem for the manager and for the library profession. In some institutions the nature of the searcher's responsibilities is not well understood by nonlibrarians; hence, searchers are sometimes treated as low-grade clerks. If this happens, turnover will be high, costly duplication of orders will result, and important titles will not be obtained by the library. To forestall such possibilities, the work of the searcher should be carefully documented and thoroughly explained. Good searchers are not easy to recruit, and the good ones need to be nursed carefully. If searchers' salaries can be improved, then the manager must also strike some balance with the professional staff, few of whom will be willing to consider full-time careers as searchers.

Student wives seem to make good searchers—perhaps because they have already searched and found husbands! At any rate, they are often recent college graduates, well trained, alert, fast learners, energetic, and economically motivated. Such a candidate is well worth the risk of short-term employment. The worst risk is someone who is emotionally unstable or a misfit who imagines that the library is a convenient refuge from stress. In a large organization, it is well to consider cautiously anyone who requests a transfer to the library from some other part of the institution.

What is true for searchers applies equally to filers. To fix responsibility in filing work, it is convenient to assign a specific part of the file to one individual for maintenance. This will motivate employees to care about the job they do.

Toward World Bibliographic Control

Global bibliographic control, which would be of immeasurable value to acquisitions work, appears to be well on the way to reality with establishment of the Shared Cataloging Program, administered by the Library of Congress. Shared Cataloging brings under early bibliographic control several hundred thousand new publications each year. Within the past few years it has enabled American academic libraries to increase their utilization of central bibliographic records from about 50 percent to nearly 75 percent. This program has further enabled accurate bibliographic data to enter the processing stream at a much earlier date, in some cases even before the books arrive in the library, which is naturally of great assistance to all technical processing operations. Effectiveness of the Shared Cataloging Program is due entirely to the magnificent spirit of harmony shown by the national bibliographic centers throughout the world—a tribute to international cooperation.

Research Resources— Acquisition of Government Publications

Yukihisa Suzuki
Head, Asia Library,
University of Michigan

"The twenty years since the end of the Second World War," said B. P. Kanevskij, head of the International Exchange of Publications Department, Lenin State Library of the USSR, "have confirmed the importance of international scientific and cultural relations for the consolidation of peace and understanding between peoples." A successful development of closer cultural and scientific contacts including the exchange of publications, is a basic prerequisite for better relations in the international community.

The purpose of this paper is to describe the present state of acquisition and exchange of publications, especially Japanese titles that support Japanese studies programs in the United States, and to suggest, quite hopefully, measures for improvement. It is not intended to present a detailed analysis of the needs for Japanese government publications, nor is it planned to discuss such crucial problems as selection and reference of government publications, their cataloging, classification, and arrangement in a library, or the historical development of controls over them. I wish merely to present some personal observations on Japanese government publications in connection with Japanese studies in the United States.

Since the termination of World War II there has been a steady and impressive growth among Americans of scholarly and public interest in Japanese studies. The same can perhaps be said about American studies in Japan. Furthermore, one noticeable development in recent years has been the increasing demand not only for Japanese titles for Japanese studies per se, but also for the results of scholarly research produced in Japan in every possible academic discipline. Specifically, demands for Japanese publications on China, Korea, South Asia, Southeast Asia, and other parts of the world have increased and thus consume a substantial slice of the book budgets of major East Asian collections.

Let us briefly examine East Asian collections in the United States and Canada. In approximately fifty-four major American libraries (as of June 1967) there exist:

Chinese	2,734,820
Japanese	1,521,734
Korean	96,677
Other*	19,110
Total	4,372,341.[1]

*Including Manchu, Mongol, Hsi-hsia, Moso, but not Tibetan and Western Languages.

The survey conducted by the Committee on East Asian Libraries shows that some 300,000 volumes were added to these fifty-four collections during the year July 1967–June 1968, representing a 35 percent increase over the total acquisitions for the previous year, and costing some $1.3 million for materials and $2 million for processing and services. The total holdings, as of 30 June 1967, reached 4.4 million volumes, with 80 percent of the total concentrated in fifteen major collections, as shown in table 1.

We expect Japanese collections to be growing at the rate of at least 120,000 volumes a year. The total dimensions of these research resources are very sizable. American interest in Japanese studies is vitally dependent upon a free and adequate flow of published materials, and as the number and sophistication of the American specialists on Japan increase, the volume of acquisitions will naturally grow in size and complexity.

The comments presented in this paper will naturally emphasize the sorts of problems that complicate and render difficult attempts of American libraries and scholars to procure research materials. All these problems, we are aware, have equally vexatious analogs when viewed from the standpoint of Japanese libraries and scholars seeking to acquire materials in the United States.

American libraries and scholars are interested in acquiring two broad classes of printed materials from Japan: trade publications and government publications. The volume of publications in Japan is shown in table 2.[2] It is quite evident from this table that during these nine years 30–40 percent of monographic publications and 30–50 percent of serials were official publications of the Japanese national and local governments or their related agencies. This ratio of government to trade publications should be noted with interest, as it is precisely in this phase of acquisitions activity that American libraries and scholars have been confronted with difficulties. Even though not totally without problems, trade publications are relatively easily available for acquisition through Japanese commercial dealers and agencies. The definition of the term "government publications" which I have adopted in this presentation is the one given in some of the classical publications on the subject.[3]

Government Publications as Source of Scholarly Information

Perhaps one of the basic questions asked for clarification is: Why are government publications so crucial? To this we can simply reply that the publications of any government "constitute a great library covering almost every field of human knowl-

TABLE 1. Holdings in East Asian Collections

COLLECTIONS	CHINESE	JAPANESE	KOREAN	OTHERS	TOTAL
Library of Congress	357,120	470,582	29,179	6,258	863,139
Harvard	289,635	103,083	17,626	3,688	414,032
California (Berkeley)	159,996	122,231	11,707		293,934
Columbia	168,514	86,645	6,550	1,000	262,709
Chicago	157,473	34,976	512	3,700	196,661
Princeton	168,267	25,344	833	2,050	196,494
California (UCLA)	140,079	40,000	462		180,541
Michigan	81,000	90,370	745		172,115
Hawaii	68,367	83,966	6,921	339	159,593
Yale	100,190	46,019	1,728		147,937
Hoover	86,747	42,350	1,549		130,646
Washington	96,098	25,147	6,113	629	127,987
Cornell	110,094	10,261	(200)		120,555
British Columbia	94,847	19,710	101		114,658
Toronto	71,500	17,950			89,450

TABLE 2. Japanese Publications

YEAR	MONOGRAPHS		SERIALS		NEWSPAPERS
	COMMERCIAL*	OFFICIAL	COMMERCIAL	OFFICIAL	
1958	22,665	8,320	5,526	4,311	3,093
1959	16,088	6,294	8,080	4,931	3,339
1960	15,112	5,747	8,568	5,693	3,330
1961	12,315	2,630	4,680	2,068	912
1962	12,702	3,092	5,170	2,063	971
1963	13,244	3,230	5,604	2,279	960
1964	12,909	3,493	5,430	1,879	968
1965	13,740	3,399	5,510	2,045	985
1966	15,092	3,528	5,786	2,073	1,066

*Including juvenilia.

edge and endeavor."[4] Many of the publications are "transcripts of original records and constitute primary source material in the history of government administration and activities."[5] They are "amongst the oldest written records, and if measured by their influence on civilization, are probably the most important of all living records."[6] They "form one of the most extensive and valuable sources of information on practically every phase of human activity," and it would be "almost impossible to conceive of a subject which, in one form or another, has not been discussed in publications" issued by governments.[7]

In the present century governments and government-supported institutions play a direct and dominant role not only in the fields of natural science and technology, but also in the social sciences and humanities. Reports and other publications resulting from these participations naturally constitute a source of information, and access to them has become a serious concern for all of us in higher education. We will not hesitate to go even further and say that demands for government publications and source materials are the barometer for judging the degree of sophistication in area studies. When studies of other nations still remain in the embryonic stage, perhaps some introductory and outline types of secondary source publications may be sufficient, but any advanced study of other

nations cannot progress without depending upon government publications.

When a student proposes to work on a comparative study of voting behavior in several different chosen prefectures, for example, librarians must scrounge for *Senkyo no Kiroku (Official Records of Election)* and *Senkyo Kekka Shirabe (Official Records of the Results of Election)*, published by the prefectures. For a student of the Allied Occupation of Japan, *Oboegaki Shūsen Zaisei Shimatsu [Records of Financial Settlement at the Time of the End of World War II]*, issued by the Ministry of Finance, would be an indispensable source. *Chūka Jimmin Kyōwakoku Soshikibetsu Jimmei hyō [Classified Table of Personnel of the People's Republic of China]* by the Cabinet Investigation Bureau would be a valuable tool for the study of Mainland China if it were made available. There are also innumerable local histories which would undoubtedly strengthen a Japanese collection.

No serious research should depend upon or be restrained by the availability of research material. Indeed, we librarians constantly feel that there is never enough material to meet the insatiable demands of our clientele, especially when an institution (University of Michigan) embarks on such an elaborate project as Robert E. Ward's "Study of the Political Modernization of Japan," which is to identify trends and patterns of political change in postwar Japan (see appendix A).

Difficulties in Acquisition of Government Publications

The acquisition of these valuable government publications, in both the United States and Japan, has proved to be the terror and nightmare of librarians and the despair of almost everyone who has needed them for research. The needs of American scholars in Japanese studies for government publications have often been expressed in binational conferences.

In the Second Japan–U.S. Conference on Cultural and Educational Interchange, held in Washington, D.C., 16–22 October 1963, the American Committee stated:

American libraries have great difficulty in learning about government and non-commercial publications, which in many cases are of the utmost importance to scholars; moreover, by the time they discover and order any, the stock is often exhausted.[8]

It suggested "the formation of a binational continuing or standing committee, comprising government, librarian, and scholar members, to study the situation and devise measures to facilitate the flow of such publications to America." At the same time, recognizing that "the processing and custody of a massive flow of government publications to depository libraries would be difficult with present resources," it urged that "financial support from the government (perhaps in the form of work scholarship) be considered for the basic added expense."[9]

The final communiqué of the Third Conference, which was held in Tokyo 2–7 March 1966, stated:

Both Japanese and American libraries encounter difficulties in dealing with materials from the other country. While their difficulties are different, both library systems could benefit through a program of exchanges of library personnel and mutual help in their training, and in the selection and acquisition of materials.[10]

The report of the Fourth Conference read:

A major unsolved problem for American libraries and individual scholars is obtaining Japanese government documents, and even bibliographic information about them. . . . Americans never hear of a great proportion of these, and even when referenced to a document have great difficulty in obtaining it. A major effort is needed in identification, and facilities for purchase and for exchange, including a reduction in the "not for sale" (hibaihin) category.[11]

Naturally, these inherent difficulties have made it difficult for most of the Japanese collections in the United States to meet the needs of researchers and instructors satisfactorily. The situation would be worse had we not the cooperation of many Japanese institutions. For this, on behalf of all the East Asian collections in the United States, I should like to take this opportunity to express deep and sincere gratitude, to the National Diet Library especially, for cooperation and efficient assistance. I recall that in November 1968 the University of Michigan asked the NDL for assistance in procuring a copy of *Chūgoku ni okeru Kōgyō Gijutsu no Genjō Bunseki* [*Analysis of Industrial Engineering in Communist China*] issued by a certain association. A microfilm copy was received exactly one month later from the library's Division for Interlibrary Services. We hope that American libraries will be able to reciprocate some day with the same efficiency. This one example will suffice to show that as long as a working bibliographic control exists, even these "fugitive" publications can be made available quite expeditiously.

Shortly before their departure for Japan in 1967, the members of the first ALA mission sent a questionnaire to twenty-one Japanese collections in the United States, which asked: "Are there demands from your clientele for Japanese government publications? If so, what kind of government publications?" Nineteen of the twenty-one replied, "Statistical works of all kinds."

Different approaches to acquisitions problems have been tried with varying success, following the old maxim in acquisitions: "Buy if you can, but beg, borrow, or steal if you must." All the needed and available Japanese titles available on the market are purchased as much as possible, but since the geographic distance does not permit borrowing or stealing, the only resort has been to beg. Table 3 shows what types of government publications were solicited during 1967 by an American library which is

TABLE 3. Classified List of Japanese Government Publications Solicited by the Asia Library, University of Michigan*

Local histories, including histories of local assemblies, and archaeological studies	190
Statistics	
National	4
Local	53
Labor	7
Bibliographies	
Subject bibliographies	8
Catalogs of libraries and special collections	58
Subject indexes	6
Exhibit catalogs	2
Politics	
Occupation of Japan	2
Laws, statutes, etc.	5
Elections, national and local	32
Police system	1
Constitutional history	5
Public opinion survey	1
Histories of government agencies	2
Annual reports	27
Education	
History of universities and colleges	3
Surveys	5
Directory	1
Sociology and anthropology, including folk art and folk songs	14
Area studies	
Modern China	4
Other Asian countries	4
Natural science	
Natural disasters	7
Agriculture, irrigation	8
Birds, animals, etc.	4
Humanities	
Japanese language	6
Music	2
Miscellaneous, such as:	
Documentation, Japanese papers, etc.	15

*Over 70 percent of these requests have been filled satisfactorily.

not an official depository library for Japanese government publications. (There are two *official* depository libraries of Japanese government publications in the United States: the Library of Congress and the library of the University of California at Berkeley.)

As Robert E. Ward of Michigan pointed out, one very curious, baffling thing about the problem is that "it has been given very little systematic attention in Japanese library or bibliographic circles."[12] This writer has not been able to locate a single article on Japanese government publications in *Toshokan Zasshi* (*Library Journal*), the official organ of the Japan Library Association since 1907. Articles by Yoshitarō Tanabe,[13] Tsutomu Kuroki,[14] and Kanehiro Kondō[15] constitute the very few treatments of the subject. Difficulties, or "the inadequacies and shortcomings of the present disorganized system [of handling government publications]," as a Japanese writer puts it, was "pointed out by an unknown foreigner" in 1956.[16] The proposal by an English scholar was discussed at a cabinet meeting, and the Prime Minister recommended that the idea of establishing an organization to handle government publications exclusively should be studied.[17] Not long after this event, Seifu Kankōbutsu Sābisu Sentā [Government Publications Service Center] was established in Tokyo.

In the paper of Ward and Suzuki, three types of problems are described that "confront the American library or scholar seeking to acquire Japanese official publications: (1) identification, (2) facilities for purchase, and (3) facilities for exchange,"[18] and continued:

Where the problem of identification is concerned, there is currently only one bibliographic source that purports to give a more or less complete listing of Japanese official publications. This is *Zen Nihon Shuppanbutsu Sōmokuroku* (Japanese National Bibliography). The current (as of 1967) issue lists only official publications appearing before 1964. A 3-year gap of this sort is normal and in itself constitutes a very difficult problem for the scholar interested in more recent official publications, statistics and viewpoints. In addition to this major, if laggard, source there are several more current bibliographic lists of official publications, the best known and most widely used of which are probably the *Seifu Kankobutsu Geppō* [Monthly catalog of government publications] and the weekly accession list of the National Diet Library known as *Nōhon Shūhō* (*Current Publications*). But between them these list substantially less than half of the items actually published by the Japanese Government and its agencies. Some more correct and definitive catalog would be of enormous assistance to both American and Japanese scholars who make professional use of official publications.[19]

The deficiencies of those bibliographies, as far as the listing of government publications is concerned, is clearly shown in table 4.

TABLE 4. Number of Titles Listed in *Zen Nihon Shuppanbutsu Sōmokuroku* (ZNSS) and *Kanchō Kankōbutsu Sōgō Mokuroku* (KKSM).

YEAR	ZNSS	KKSM
1951	4,477 vols.	
1952	5,510	17,000 vols.*
1953	4,367	9,000
1954	5,161	9,800
1955	3,224	9,300
1956	4,799	9,000
1957	6,515	9,200
1958	9,725	10,000

*Includes titles published between September 1945 and December 1950.

Zen Nihon Shuppanbutsu Sōmokuroku is the national bibliography of publications deposited in the National Diet Library under Article 24 and Article 25 of the National Diet Law Library.[20] It is simply a catalog of titles received by the national library. *Kanchō Kankōbutsu Sōgō Mokuroku* [*Comprehensive Catalog of Government Publications*], which unfortunately ceased publication with Volume 8 (1958), was compiled with the information furnished by the branch libraries within each ministry. Naturally it included many titles which were not deposited with the National Diet Library, and thus was more inclusive. To support research and instructional pro-

grams, it is vital to have bibliographic information as comprehensive as possible. Also, in this day and age of highly developed photoduplicating methods, it has become even more important to know, again, what has been published by whom and when and who has it. This writer, therefore, proposes that the publication of *Kanchō Kankōbutsu Sōgō Mokuroku* be resumed at the earliest convenience.

It will be worthwhile to quote here the recommendations by Professor Ward made at the meeting of the Japanese Sister Committee of the Cultural Conference in August 1966:

1. Preparation of detailed catalog of public publications in Japan
2. Clarification of the scope of the publications to be increased and the scope of the publications to be exchanged with the publishing organizations individually under the present inclusive exchange as provided by the current agreement between the two governments
3. Clarification of the scope of public publications to be exchanged (for example, whether publications by local offices of the central government agencies and local public bodies should be considered or not)
4. Study of the method for improving percentage of Japanese public publications offered to the National Diet Library
5. More effective use in the U.S. of public publications etc. sent by the Japanese government under the inclusive exchange program. (They are deposited at the Congressional Library and Berkeley Library of University of California.)[21]

While I thoroughly subscribe to all these recommendations, at this point I would point out the importance of the fourth one. One of the worst stumbling blocks in Japan, as in the United States, in exerting some effective control over this important source of research materials has been the constant attempt to secure multicopies when so many restrictions make it virtually impossible. The cold fact is that the National Diet Library, the official agency for distributing Japanese government publications among foreign institutions, has itself been facing difficulties in receiving even a majority of publications issued by the government and its agencies. The NDL has been regularly issuing *Nohon Shūhō* (*Current Publications*), announcing what has been received and expeditiously making available to us whatever is announced on the list, as stated above. If all this evidence is put together, then, to this writer, the most basic, urgent task for all of us concerned is to appeal to the government to make sure that at least one copy of whatever is published is deposited with the NDL.

At this point a few items need clarification. First of all, some Japanese libraries and librarians have not remained completely negligent, indifferent, or inactive on this matter. "Government Publications" was adopted as the feature theme for discussion at the meeting of the Local Legislative Libraries Division of the All-Japan Library Conference at Kanazawa in 1967. The Division for Interlibrary Services of the NDL, in addition to services to foreign institutions, has compiled numerous bibliographies with an attempt to extend some bibligraphic control over government publications, such as: *Kuni ga Henshū shita Shuppanbutsu o Kankō shita Kankei Dantai to Shuppansha Ichiran* [*List of Agencies and Publishers Who Issued Publications Compiled by National Governmental Offices, September 1968*]; *Gyōsei Shihō Kaku Bumon Shibu Toshokan ni okeru Shochō Kankōbutsu no Shūshū Hōhō ni Kansuru Chōsa Kekka Ichiran* [*Report on the Studies of Acquisition of Branch Libraries in Executive and Judiciary Branches of Government, September 1967*]; *Seifu Kankōbutsu Tenji Mokuroku* [*Exhibit Catalog of Government Publications, 1966*]; a list of publications of *gaikaku dantai* [external organs of the ministries]; and others.

Thus the voice for better accessibility of these "fugitive" publications seems to be getting stronger. It is gratifying to hear that November has been designated officially as *Seifu Kankōbutsu Fukyū Gekkan* [National Government Publications Distribution Month]. The editorial of a recent issue of *Shuppan Nyūsu* [*Publishing News*] reads:

Some measures should be taken to have government publications better known to the public and for their accessibility and distribution.

. . . Among government publications there are many research reports and statistical figures only the government and its public agencies can compile. It is very unfortunate that the general public cannot use them. The people have the right to learn the policies, source materials, and statistics of the country. We sincerely wish that . . . the publications of the governmental agencies, which are supported by the people's tax money, would be made widely available to them.[22]

In reference to the fifth recommendation quoted above, our Japanese collections have not been totally blameless. When libraries have reached the point of coordinating what has been and is proposed to be received, instead of scrambling for scarce items on the market, efforts and programs for coordination should be more fully developed. Often government and institutional publications under the exclusive depository arrangement have become the institution's private property, often with restrictions placed upon their circulation. For example, all serials, statistics, yearbooks, and official documents issued by governmental agencies are classified as noncirculating. The depository libraries have never made it known what has been received under the arrangement, thus causing additional burdens on the office in charge of exchange. It should be recommended that the definition of "depository library" be reviewed and its responsibilities carefully defined. In a research library, acquisitions cannot be separated from cooperation, especially when we deal with scarce items like government publications.

All during these discussions on government publications, this writer has been recalling the old wisdom of "those who live in glass houses should not throw stones." As our distinguished Japanese scholars and colleagues must have already experienced, the state of government publications in the United States is not at all as clean and immaculate as some foreign observers often think. The Government Printing Office in Washington is only one of more than 340 government printing plants scattered across the country and overseas. In 1962 the staff director of the Joint Committee on Printing "estimated that from 60 to 65 per cent of all government publications were produced outside GPO."[23]

The basic problem here is that over half the publishing done by the federal government of the United States has been done in offices other than the Government Printing Office. Consequently this vast, vital segment of publication falls outside of any organized system of bibliographic control of distribution. No longer is there a centralized source from which all government publications may be acquired.

The Depository Library Act of 1962 marked the first general revision of the laws governing the distribution of United States government publications to designated depositories since the enactment of the General Printing Act of 1895. Certain flaws are still recognized in the Act of 1962. It is important to note here that both the American Library Association and the Association of Research Libraries have shown keen interest in implementing an effective bibliographic control of non-GPO materials. The American Library Association has within its Reference Services Division and Resources and Technical Services Division the Public Documents Interdivisional Committee to "plan for a survey of federal and state documents, centering on the availability and use of them; to complete a proposal for submission for authorization to seek funds."[24] ARL also has a special committee, the Committee on Non-GPO Publications, to tackle this problem.

Prior to the enactment of the law in 1962, the Joint Committee on Government Publications of the Association of Research Libraries, the American Library Association, the American Association of Law Libraries, and the Special Libraries Association formulated the Documents Expediting Project (popularly known as "Doc Ex"), which was organized in 1946 to facilitate the procurement and distribution of government documents of all types for interested public, university, and special libraries. The focus of this project was on the documents which are not distributed by the Superintendent of Documents or which are difficult to obtain through the usual channels. The project has been administered by the Library of Congress as a section of the Exchanges and Gift Division.

By 1967 subscribers to this cooperative centralized service reached a new high of 136.[25] Since 1946 the project has supplied subscribing libraries with nondepository publications that are unavailable elsewhere. In fiscal 1967 these subscribers received some 214,000 items sent through established channels; an additional 48,000 items were sent in response to 11,323 individual requests. The project made a successful effort to obtain a greater number of the publications issued by the 49 Senate, House, and joint committees of Congress and by 25 of the more important subcommittees. In 1966 arrangements were also made to receive and distribute some 40 new series or groups of publications issued by agencies in the executive branch. During the same year the Exchanges and Gift Division compiled lists of surplus United States government publications which were sent to the project members to enable them to fill gaps in their collections, a move which brought 880 individual requests for 21,456 volumes and issues.[26]

Even all these projects have been only partially successful, perhaps due mainly to the increasing output by governmental agencies. Still, strong, persistent efforts of scholars and librarians must be made on this vexatious problem to bring about some tangible results eventually. The present situation in the United States is not totally satisfactory. However, if ALA and ARL, two most respected, powerful professional organizations, had not taken a positive step, the situation would be more chaotic.

I can only quote from an article by a foremost specialist in the United States on government publications:

Today, with the federal government financing three-fourths of the national research effort and moving swiftly into massive support of education, the negative effects of its chaotic and incomplete printing, publishing, and distribution programs are serious. The problems connected with these programs, while not susceptible to easy or cheap solutions, can be overcome provided vigorous, high-level attention is focussed upon them. In any case, their resolution should not be beyond the capacity of a government which can count the number of chickens in Sagadahoc County and send rockets to the moon.[27]

NOTES

[1]Association for Asian Studies, Committee on East Asian Libraries, *Annual Report for 1967–1968, table 1.*

[2]*Zen Nihon Shuppanbutsu Sōmokuroku (Japanese National Bibliography), 1958–1966* (Tokyo: Kokuritsu Kokkai Toshokan, 1961–68).

[3]Anne Morris Boyd, *United States Government Publications* (3d ed., rev. by Rae Elizabeth Rips ([New York: Wilson, 1949]), p.1; "Some Problems of Government Publications," in ALA Committee on Public Documents, *Public Documents* (Chicago: ALA 1936), p.28–29; Yoshitarō Tanabe, "Nihon no kanchō kankōbutsu no genjō [Present State of Japanese Government Publications]," *Kokuritsu Kokkai Toshokan Geppō [National Diet Library Monthly Bulletin]*, no.35 (Feb. 1965), p.3; Tsutomu Kuroki, "Seifu kankōbutsu no shūshū to teikyō [Acquisition and Treatment of Government Publications]," *Toshokan-kai (Library World)*, 18, no.2:56–57 (July 1966)).

[4]Laurence F. Schmeckebier and Roy B. Eastin, *Government Publications and Their Use,* rev. ed. (Washington, D.C.: Brookings Institution, 1962), p.1

[5]Ibid.

[6]Boyd, *United States Government Publications,* p.1.

[7]Everett S. Brown, *Manual of Government Publications: United States and Foreign* (New York: Appleton, 1950), p.4.

[8]*Japanese Studies in the United States* (Second Japan–U.S. Conference on Cultural and Educational and Cultural Interchange, p.3. September 26, 1963), p.1.

[9]Ibid., p.2.

[10]*Final Communiqué* (Third Japan–U.S. Conference on Cultural and Educational Interchange Document G) p.3–4.

[11]*Progress Report: Educational and Cultural Relations between Japan–United States 1966–1968* (prepared by the Executive Secretary, American Committee on United States–Japan Educational and Cultural Cooperation, March 22, 1968), p.19–20.

[12]Robert E. Ward and Yukihisa Suzuki, "A Proposal for a Binational Investigation of the Interchange of Official Publications between the United States and Japan," unpublished paper for the Third Japan–U.S. Conference on Cultural and Educational Interchange, p.3.

[13]Tanabe, op. cit. (see footnote 3).

[14]Kuroki, op. cit. (see footnote 3).

[15]Kanehiro Kondō, "Seifu kankōbutsu no ichigenka to Insatsukyoku [Centralization of Government Publications and Printing Bureau]," *Seifu Kankōbutsu Geppō [Monthly Bulletin of Government Publications]* 10, no. 4–5:4–7 (April 1966); ibid., 10, no.6:4–11 (May 1966).

[16]Ibid., 10, no.5:9.

[17]Ibid., p.8.

[18]Ward and Suzuki, "A Proposal for a Binational Investigation," p.3.

[19]Ibid., p.3–4.

[20]Article 24. Of each book, pamphlet, periodical, map, motion picture or other work, printed or otherwise reproduced by or for any other agency of the government in an edition of five hundred (500) copies or more (except confidential matter and blank forms), fifty (50) copies shall be furnished immediately to the National Diet Library for official use and for use in international exchange for the publications of other governments and in other international exchanges. Of such works reproduced in editions of less than five hundred (500) copies, a number of copies less than fifty (50) shall be furnished to the National Diet Library in accordance with regulations to be made by the Chief Librarian.

Article 25. As for publications other than those mentioned in the foregoing article, the Chief Librarian shall cause the publishers of these publications to deposit a specimen copy of each work in the National Diet Library; in compensation for such deposit the Chief Librarian shall give the publisher without delay that issue of the periodically published catalog of all works published in Japan which lists the deposited work.

[21]*Japanese Progress Report to the Fourth Japan–U.S. Conference on Cultural and Educational Interchange,* p.39.

[22]*Shuppan Nyūsu,* no.1383 (21 Nov. 1968), p.1.

[23]U.S. Congress, Senate Committee on Rules and Administration, Depository Libraries, Hearing, 87th Cong., 2d Sess., as quoted in Clifton Brock, "The Quiet Crisis in Government Publishing," *College and Research Libraries* 26, no.6:481 (Nov. 1965).

[24]*ALA Bulletin*, 62, no.10:1205 (Nov. 1968).

[25]*Annual Report of the Librarian of Congress for the Fiscal Year Ending June 30, 1967* (Washington, D.C.: Library of Congress, 1968), p.42.

[26]*Annual Report of the Librarian of Congress for the Fiscal Year Ending June 30, 1966* (Washington, D.C.: Library of Congress, 1967), p.38–39.

[27]Brock, "The Quiet Crisis," p.489, 531.

American Studies Today—
The Middle of a Revolution

Lawrence W. Towner
Director and Librarian,
Newberry Library, Chicago

When the invitation to attend this important Conference came, I was particularly delighted. It released in my mind a perfect jumble of things I should like to talk about with Japanese scholars and librarians concerned with the study of America. Alas, I fear that very little order has been made out of that perfect jumble. Among the things I thought of was one of the first important books I read in my special field of American history, Roy Hidemichi Akagi's *The Town Proprietors of the New England Colonies*, published in Philadelphia in 1924 and still the standard monograph on the subject. Another was a recollection from the period when I was editor of the *William and Mary Quarterly: A Magazine of Early American History* between the years 1955 and 1962. The most rapidly growing sub-

scriber among foreign countries was Japan, and Japanese readers often wrote to me with queries and requests for help. Now there are twenty-two Japanese subscribers to this quite specialized historical magazine. Quite clearly, an interest in American studies is no new phenomenon in Japan.

When one attempts to describe and analyze the state of American studies today, one must attempt to describe the middle of a revolution, a very difficult thing to do. It is like other revolutions; one is not sure when it started, where it is going to end, and just what stage of it one is in. Moreover, there are several revolutions going on at once. But perhaps, if we look back over the past twenty-five years, we can grasp some of the essentials of some of those revolutions pertinent not only to American history as a discipline but also to American history and literature as a collecting area for libraries.

First and most significant, there has been a revolution in the interpretation of American history by students of that subject. It is not easy to describe succinctly and, as with the other revolutions, the end is not in sight. But that does not prevent our trying. Prior to World War II, American historiography was dominated by the great Populist or Progressive historians. They were Charles A. Beard, Vernon Louis Parrington, and Frederick Jackson Turner. Much of the history of America written in that period was a working out, in one way or another, of the broad themes these men had laid down in their key works. Broadly speaking, their interpretations pictured American history as a struggle between the haves and the have-nots; between the rich and the well-born, the creditor, the businessman, and the slaveholder, on the one hand, and the agrarian, debtor classes, often in combination with urban workers, on the other.

The period of American history, for example, that saw the creation of the nation —the separation from Great Britain and the laying of the foundations of the present government, that is, the period from 1763 to 1789—had a widely accepted interpretation handily described as the Becker-Beard hypothesis. These men saw the American Revolution not only as a fight for home rule but also as a fight over who should rule at home. Lined up against each other were not only the patriots and the British—the goods and the bads, respectively—but also, within American society, the poor against the rich, the West against the East, the agrarian classes against the commercial classes—also the goods and the bads. In colony by colony, state by state, this was found to be the case. The Revolution itself, it was held, was led from above but pushed from below.

The Articles of Confederation, which provided for a great deal of local autonomy, were found to be the perfect expression of the Revolutionary spirit, and the Constitution that came in 1787 was in turn a perfect expression of a Thermidorian reaction. It was viewed as the instrument of the creditors, the Eastern merchants, the bankers, and the traders, who designed it to keep power out of the hands of the common people. From this vantage point, the rest of American history was viewed as the struggle of the farmers and workers (and slaves) to wrest economic and political democracy from the reluctant hands of the rich and well-born. In short, it was the working out in the ages of Jefferson, and Jackson, and Lincoln, and Roosevelt, and Wilson of the Declaration of Independence's statement that all men are created equal.

After World War II the historians who had been trained in the old Populist or Progressive school still taught this interpretation, not only of the Revolution, but of American history in general. A new generation of historians put all this under attack, however, again using the Revolution as an example. The seemingly solid and durable Beard-Becker interpretation of the internal revolution was undermined from every side, and the walls came tumbling down. Beard's classic *An Economic Interpretation of the Constitution*, for example, was the subject of two major assaults: one by Robert E. Brown, who took the work chapter by chapter and refuted its findings, and the other by Forrest E. McDonald, who did all the research Beard said ought to be done and found Beard wanting. Studies of the British Empire, of the ori-

gins of the Revolution, of the colonies and states before, during, and after the Revolution revealed that the Beard-Becker hypothesis was too simplistic, too unsophisticated, too wrong to hold the period together. Their interpretation of the Revolution fell into chaos, from which no single historian or group of historians has been able to rescue it.

What arose in the 1950s instead of the old Populist-Progressive view of American history has been labeled, not too inaccurately, I think, as "consensus" history. That is to say, some of the leading historians, Daniel Boorstin, for example, tended to emphasize the common grounds, the common ideas, and the agreements of the American people throughout their history and to de-emphasize the sharp conflicts so well described by the earlier historians. To what extent this transformation of American history was the product of a felt (if unperceived) need of Americans to draw together in the face of an implacable foe in Eastern Europe and in the face of unprecedented world responsibilities for which we were not clearly prepared, it is hard to say. Future historians will undoubtedly explore this aspect of the American mind relentlessly, but we are still too close to it, probably too much a part of it, to be able to understand what happened and why. But that there was a major shift in emphasis can hardly be ignored.

I want to pause here in my necessarily sketchy and crude description of the revolution in interpretation. That revolution is continuing, and there are some new developments, but they can be discussed better after we examine some of the technical revolutions of the last twenty years with regard to the availability of historical and literary materials.

For two decades, much of what has been written in American history, and, I suspect, in American literature, might be described as deeper and deeper analysis of smaller and smaller points. Partially this is a consequence of the great proliferation of historical and literary studies. It has often been almost antiquarian in character—a study of the past without direction from the questions of the present. But one salutary aspect of this intensified study of America's past has been a turning to great editorial projects. These decades have certainly been the second great age of editing in America, rivaling the great age in the nineteenth century which saw the publication of so many documents in American history. There are some important pre-World War II precedents that one ought to touch on if space were not limited, but we can start with the greatest editorial project of them all, *The Papers of Thomas Jefferson*, edited by Julian P. Boyd. This project proposes to edit and publish not only all the letters and other writings of Thomas Jefferson, but also all the letters *to* Thomas Jefferson. Hence the word "Papers" rather than "Writings" or "Works" in the title. When completed, this project will run to some fifty volumes, and it will be, undoubtedly, the greatest documentary biography ever written.

Following the lead of the Jefferson project, there are now, as you know, several other great series, including the papers of James Madison, Benjamin Franklin, the Adams family (not just one generation but four), Alexander Hamilton, John Jay, John Marshall, and, soon, George Washington. Altogether there will be some 250–300 volumes of the papers of the founding fathers. Other publication projects, including the debates on the Constitution, both in the Philadelphia Convention and in the state conventions, the papers of the first Congress, and the like, will make the Revolutionary era possibly the most fully-reported period in the history of any country. Nor is this development confined to the Revolutionary generation. Other historical figures, such as Polk, Wilson, Theodore Roosevelt, Franklin Roosevelt, Grant, and Lincoln, are or have been subjects of editorial projects of greater or lesser magnitude.

It will come as no surprise to this group when I say that editing has also become a major preoccupation of students of American literature. The "new bibliography," as exemplified by the work of Professor Fredson Bowers of the University of Virginia, has made the establishment of a text—which is a necessary preliminary to subject editing—an immensely complicated and scientific affair. One needs to learn a whole new technique and a whole new language to comprehend the method editors have evolved. Using this method, the Modern Language Association—some 26,000 members strong—has set up a vast editorial project to make available, often for the first time, editions of the complete works of the great nineteenth-century American literary figures. Nathaniel Hawthorne, Edgar Allan Poe, Herman Melville, Walt Whitman, Mark Twain, William Dean Howells, Ralph Waldo Emerson, Henry David Thoreau, Stephen Crane, and Washington Irving are marching in ever-growing sets across the shelves of every university and college library in the land. Some 220 volumes are planned. When the works of these literary figures have been exhausted, no doubt other authors will be subjected to the same editorial process to provide the best possible edition of their literary works. Editing, in short, has become a major preoccupation in the scholarly world concerned with American studies, literary as well as historical.

Concurrent with the editorial revolution, there have been technical revolutions in methods of reproducing materials that are stupendous in their consequences. Let us look again at the period of early American history for our examples. Thirty years ago it would have been nearly impossible to go beyond a master's degree, if indeed that far, in early American history without visiting for several months those great Eastern libraries where the printed and manuscript records of seventeenth- and eighteenth-century America are concentrated. Harvard, Yale, and Princeton, the Library of Congress, the Massachusetts, New York, Pennsylvania, and Virginia historical societies, and the great private libraries, such as the American Antiquarian Society in Worcester, Massachusetts, or the John Carter Brown Library in Providence, Rhode Island, were musts on the lists of every student of early America.

Now, however, a revolution has been taking place. Microfilm and other forms of microprint, Xerox and other forms of copying, and photo-offset printing—all partially responses to the tremendous market created for all forms of printed material by the fantastic increase in the number of students and faculty members in our colleges and universities—have made it possible to write a creditable dissertation in early American history in almost any university in the land.

For example, as you all know, the great bibliography of materials printed in America before 1800 is that compiled by Charles Evans at the turn of the century. This chronological list of all published books and pamphlets has been an indispensable tool since the first volume came out. Now, of course, thanks to the American Antiquarian Society, almost all these books can be seen in any university library on microcard. Similar projects have made the newspapers and magazines of early America equally accessible, so that for an expenditure of probably under $25,000 any library in the world can have at its disposal everything published in what is now the United States prior to Thomas Jefferson's first term as President.

Further, much of the material published by historical societies and state governments in the nineteenth and early twentieth centuries pertaining to early America, long out of print, is now being reprinted in one form or another. The great demand for this kind of material by new libraries and the fact that the originals usually are printed on poor paper has created an economic market that will not be denied. For a well-spent $100,000 or so and a great deal of bibliographic searching it will soon be possible to have available everything except the unpublished manuscripts concerning early America in one's university or college library.

And even that exception has increasingly become subject to exceptions. I have already mentioned the project to edit and print the papers of the Adams family, but in anticipation of that publication venture, the Adams Papers Trust and the Massachusetts Historical Society, some fifteen years ago, made available for purchase by any library the entire great body of Adams papers on microfilm. More recently the National Historical Publications Commission has begun the systematic publication on microfilm of important manuscript materials pertaining to American history wherever they may be found, in private or public institutions, throughout the land. Sitting in my study in Chicago, I can read even now the papers of many of our presidents, along with some of the important parts of the manuscript collection of, for example, the Massachusetts Historical Society, such as the papers of Timothy Pickering and Robert Treat Paine.

These developments, of course, were necessarily preceded by years and years of work on finding aids for manuscript materials, among which should be mentioned Philip Hamer's *A Guide to Archives and Manuscripts in the United States* (New Haven, Conn.: Yale University Press, 1961); the Modern Language Association's *American Literary Manuscripts* (Austin; University of Texas Press, 1960); and, of course, the great ongoing *National Union Catalog of Manuscripts.*

The rapid growth of the availability of materials on American history and literature has, of course, put a vast burden upon college and university libraries. Not only have costs of individual items gone up significantly, but, more important, the number of items published in any given year pertaining to American history and literature and culture has grown staggeringly. Concurrent with this revolution, however, has been a paperback revolution liberating both the teacher and the student from the restrictions of any given library's holdings and, at the same time, eliminating the libraries' need to purchase large numbers of copies of single books for course work. A single copy of most books, or at most two, is really all that is necessary. Teachers in American studies now build their courses around paperback books, and students can now afford libraries that their professors at one time could not get or afford. My own children, for example, have larger libraries than I had when I started teaching twenty-three years ago.

The increasing numbers of students and professors studying American history, literature, and culture is reflected not only in a greater output of books (which a library must acquire) but also in a great output of articles and other materials published in periodicals. As a consequence, not only has the circulation of such established magazines as the *American Historical Review,* the *William and Mary Quarterly, PMLA,* and the *Journal of American History* increased greatly, but also the number of new magazines has increased. Periodicals specializing in American Jewish history, American labor history, the history of the American Negro, the histories of various states, and in such new disciplines as American studies are a few that come to mind at once. These new periodicals produce an added strain on any library attempting to provide resources for American studies. Clearly, students and scholars need to have access to all periodical literature, if only to avoid the unnecessary duplication of effort in their researches.

This means that old libraries are faced with quickly expanding budgets for periodical literature and that new libraries not only have to acquire the current magazines but also must somehow acquire back issues of old ones. This latter problem is being met by technological advances in reprints. Many magazines, such as the *William and Mary Quarterly,* are now available through such organizations as Kraus Reprints, Inc. and on microfilm. Reprinting, in fact, has become a major industry within the printing industry.

I mentioned in connection with the growth of periodical literature the subject of American Studies with a capital "S." This is a phenomenon whose *major* growth I associate with the postwar period. No one except its initiates are quite sure exactly what "American Studies" means, and some of us who are not initiates are not sure that the initiates know. At its best it indicates that we must have training in literature as well as in history, in architecture and in the history of science—a kind of cultural anthropology of modern man—if we are to understand American society in all its complexity and richness. It is a kind of "area-study" approach like that

developed in the United States for enriching our understanding of other areas by bringing to bear on them all the techniques and resources of many disciplines. At its worst, one suspects it to be a manifestation of hyperpatriotism and neoisolationism sponsored by a few idiosyncratic rich men who believe that concentration on American Studies is a necessary antidote to such strange foreign *isms* as Communism and Socialism. However one interprets American Studies, its existence surely reflects the fact that America has become a major world power—"the new Romans," as a Canadian recently called us. America is a subject worthy of intense preoccupation and study, if not just for its intrinsic merit, then simply because it has become the most powerful (and perhaps most dangerous) nation on earth.

Into this peaceful, if industrious, scene of "consensus history," major editing projects, proliferation of monographic studies, new technologies of reproduction, and the growth of American Studies, now intrudes the rude and ugly face of controversy, which, I suspect, will do much to revitalize the study of American history and (perhaps) of literature as well. To go back to my opening question of interpretation, I refer to the continuing revolution in the meaning of America's past as understood by America's present. This revolution is not easy to describe.

Recently I was chairman of the American Historical Association's Annual Meeting Program Committee, which had responsibility for organizing some seventy-five scholarly sessions. In my brief report on that program, I opened by saying that someone said history doesn't teach us a damn thing about the present; instead the present tells us the kind of questions we have to ask of the past. I think this is true, and the critical problems American society is now trying to face have not only opened up new fields of historical inquiry, they have also begun to subject the so-called "consensus" history to a hard-hitting attack from what is now called the "New Left."

New fields of inquiry, rejuvenated old fields of inquiry, concern first of all the great domestic problems of American society. Urban studies are now being pushed on almost every American campus. There is a growing interest in the history of the family. Negro history has become transformed into black history, and black history programs, with black instructors, books written by blacks, and classes attended by blacks, seem now to be the sine qua non for survival of any academic administration or, indeed, institution. But perhaps more important than any other current problem facing American society has been the ruthless, unhappy, and tragic mistake of Vietnam. This war has produced a greater division in American society than anything since the American Civil War. Without question, without fear of being proved wrong, I predict that in the future, if we have a future, we will view the war in Vietnam as a great watershed in American intellectual and cultural history, as well as in politics and international diplomacy.

As a consequence of the failure of American society to solve its domestic problems (partly, I think, or even in large part, because of its tremendous involvement in Vietnam), the youngest generation of American historians have found my generation's writings sterile expressions of the Establishment. At its best our historical writing is found to be irrelevant, and at its worst it is viewed as a mask for an imperialist, aggressive, exploitative, capitalist society. The consensus which they see it depicting they believe to be imaginary, and its authors are to them the witting or unwitting tools of an industrial-military complex which dominates the society. There have not been many products of this historical view—it is not yet a school—and I know of none in the field of literature as yet, though they will come.

Among the works of the "New Left" historians are two collections of essays that deserve careful examination: Barton J. Bernstein's *Towards a New Past: Dissenting Essays in American History* and Alfred F. Young's *Dissent: Exploration in the History of American Radicalism*. The latter work is a perfect example of today's problems informing our view of the past, in this instance, the protest movements that began with the civil rights issue. Dissent is important today. It is important, therefore, to demonstrate a tradition of dissent to give it a kind of legitimacy that the more conservative elements in our society would deny. Bernstein's book, on the other hand, gathers essays by historians who question, from the Revolution to the present, the received interpretations of the past.

If the consensus historians can be characterized as those who stress the wide range of agreement among Americans throughout our history, the "New Left," as revealed in these works, can be characterized as those who stress the points of conflict. These conflicts, in their view, have not necessarily resulted in improvement in American society. The consensus historians view American history as a general upward spiral toward greater democracy, toward a better life for everyone, toward greater improvement for the downtrodden. They are optimistic, in short. The New Left is pessimistic in its view of the outcome, thus far, of American history and is sometimes inclined to believe that a fundamental reconstitution of American society may be necessary if wrongs are to be righted and democracy prevail.

The temper of this different emphasis can be gauged from a recent review by one of America's great historians, Professor C. Vann Woodward of Yale, author of the widely read and influential *Jim Crow in America* (among other books). Woodward's liberal credentials are impeccable. Like the rest of us, he accepted the liberal interpretation of the antislavery movement which reduced the great abolitionist William Lloyd Garrison to the level of a noisy troublemaker, intransigent, radical, and therefore ineffective in bringing about the actual abolition of slavery. It was the antislavery moderates that accomplished that goal, they said; Garrison, if anything, may have been an impediment. A recent study—*Means and Ends in American Abolitionism: Garrison and His Critics on Strategy and Tactics, 1834–1850*, by Eileen S. Kraditor—finds in Garrison's very intransigence, his uncompromising unwillingness to be a moderate on the subject, his insistence on being heard, the stuff of a hero.

As Vann Woodward put it in his review of this book:

> His big thing was that abolitionism was a *radical* and not a reform movement, that slavery, and the social dogmas that justified it so thoroughly permeated American society and government, North as well as South, that the eradication of the institution and its ideological defenses. . .was a root and branch operation. On that he never equivocated.

Garrison warned that slavery was a sin and that, if the Constitution supported slavery, then the Constitution ought to be destroyed, and the society which fed on slavery ought to be reconstituted. As Vann Woodward points out, our new self-conscious awareness of the extent to which we are still a racist society makes the recently revised interpretation of Garrison seem painfully and tragically true.

As I said at the beginning of this brief essay, where the revolution in interpretation of American history will end no one can tell. It is possible that America will see itself a little more clearly as a consequence of the "truths" the New Left is trying to see and to make American society see. On the other hand, we may not pay sufficient attention to this new view of ourselves. That is, we may not pay sufficient attention *in time*, and our own imperfect understanding of ourselves and our past may lead to our undoing. This great noble experiment which had, and may still have, so much promise for mankind, will then end in failure. It would not be mankind's first failure. It could be mankind's last.

Problems of Obtaining Publications for the Japanese Student of American Studies

Hiroshi Shimizu
Director, Rikkyō University Library

American Studies, as a subdiscipline of "area studies"—which aims at a comprehensive investigation of a particular geographic area—is a relatively recent introduction to Japan. The Institute for American Studies (Amerika Kenkyūjo) of Rikkyō University was not established until 1939, and this was the first step in the institutionalization of American Studies in Japanese universities. There was an initial flow of publications from the United States to the Institute, but this flow was cut off as diplomatic relationships between the two countries deteriorated and war ensued.

After World War II the Japanese people developed a heightened interest in American systems, institutions, ways of thinking, social life, culture, economy, and the like. In the immediate postwar period any publication about the United States sold well regardless of quality. In addition, American Cultural Centers were established throughout Japan, and students and ordinary citizens, as well as research workers interested in America, began to use these facilities of the U.S. government. These centers contributed greatly to introducing the people to and making them knowledgeable about American culture. In the intervening years American Studies has continued to develop as a discipline in Japan, but there has been less than ideal coordination among the specialists.

Accordingly, there has developed a keen awareness of the necessity for better interdisciplinary understanding and cooperation to advance the studies further, and it was in this climate that the American Studies Foundation (Amerika Kenkyū Shinkōkai) was established. This was designed to provide financial support for Japanese specialists in American Studies and also made possible the revival of the Japanese Association for American Studies (Amerika Gakkai). This association had actually been organized immediately after the war, and had published the monthly *Amerika Kenkyū* (*American Review*), as well as the six-volume *Genten Amerika Shi* (*Documentary History of America*), but had been forced to suspend activities because of financial difficulties. The association at present boasts 250 members, but there are in fact many more scholars and individuals who have a scholarly interest in America. The percentage of courses devoted to American Studies in the humanities and the social sciences in various universities has increased remarkably in the postwar period, and the number of students majoring in American Studies has also increased. Needless to say, the publications required by these students are numerous and diverse.

It is said that Japan's economic revival and consequent rise in international status have benefited research facilities and researchers, but the effects have not necessarily been satisfactory. The surface prosperity that one finds in Japanese society scarcely penetrates to the area of academic studies, and researchers find it difficult even to acquire needed publications. Despite the fact that in the postwar period there has been available in the United States a wealth of new and out-of-print Americana, including reprinted journals, financial difficulties stand in the way of the acquisition of these extremely expensive reprints and back numbers. Furthermore, it sometimes happens that local researchers in distant areas are not even aware of these publications because of an insufficiency of information about them.

In general, in Japan it is difficult to acquire most U.S. federal and state government publications, the journals and other publications of national and local academic associations, and a variety of journals and newspapers. Doctoral dissertations are even more difficult to acquire. Accordingly, Japanese researchers are agreed that some means must be devised so that they can receive prompt and accurate information about these publications as quickly as possible, and then procure them inexpensively and with certainty.

In 1968, with the support of the American Studies Foundation and Tokyo University, the Center for American Studies (Amerika Shiryō Sentā) was established on the Komaba campus of Tokyo University. This is open to any student of American Studies in Japan, and books and materials for their use are currently being collected. The Center has just commenced operations, however, and the number and quality of the materials available are now grossly inadequate for the announced objectives of the Center. In the future it is expected that it will become the center in Japan for materials relating to American Studies.

There exist other research centers in other universities which are closely related to the Center for American Studies. These are designed to provide facilities to individual researchers or to research groups. Hence researchers can, by utilizing facilities located in the large centrally located metropolitan universities as well as in local universities, advance their studies. Liaison among researchers and coordination of their efforts are promoted through these centers.

It is essential, however, that these central and local centers and libraries establish ties with one or more research centers in the United States. At present whatever liaison exists is largely on an individual person-to-person basis, but this results, among other things, in great inconvenience and inequality of opportunity, especially for younger researchers.

Those of us who are engaged in American Studies research are of the opinion that our resource needs can be met only to a limited extent by the American Cultural Centers. To cope with the very serious demands being made on researchers today, we wish to ask the American side to establish some sort of central clearinghouse to provide information on the kind of hard-to-procure publications discussed earlier (the information should include, if possible, critical evaluation of contents).

Such a clearinghouse would enable Japanese research centers, the National Diet Library, and other institutions in Japan to receive news of American governmental and trade publications, as well as of the publications of nonprofit agencies and academic organizations. If these publications were deposited in the research centers or the National Diet Library after acquisition by purchase, gift, or exchange, it would be possible in most cases for Japanese researchers to satisfy their resource needs in Japan without having to inquire of American sources. In the absence of such a special service at the present time, I find from personal experience that a great deal of my own research time is taken in informing fellow researchers and students about available materials and even in helping them by lending or copying documents available in the Rikkyō University Library.

It may well be that our colleagues in the United States in American Studies or in Japanese Studies are faced with the same, or worse, problem. Therefore, I believe it would be extremely desirable to establish a clearinghouse to facilitate the exchange of information about publications and to aid in the collection of the needed materials.

Acquisition and Exchange of Government Publications in Japan and the United States

Ryūkichi Harada
Tōhoku University

At an earlier stage in human history the tidal wave of the Industrial Revolution brought about sweeping changes in society. Today we are similarly confronted with the initial waves of the "information revolution," which appears likely to produce changes on an equally massive scale. These initial waves can be readily observed in many areas of society where they are already beginning to cause change. Universities and libraries, which are our primary concern, are inherently wedded to information, and hence must bear the brunt of the waves of the new age. Moreover, they have the very grave responsibility of reinforcing the waves of change and letting them stream out to society. Accordingly, the activities of universities and libraries must be positively and vigorously expanded and intensified. In this situation libraries, as the central organ of information processing in the university community, will naturally be forced to redouble their efforts toward functional improvement, particularly in the fields of the acquisition of research materials and information retrieval.

The acquisition of government publications presents a particularly serious problem to university libraries, since such publications in recent years have shown marked improvement in quality and have greatly increased in number, with the result that they have become indispensable sources for university research. Moreover, there have been clear trends in university research toward specialization and toward microscopic and macroscopic investigations of society, with particular focus on contemporary society instead of on classics and history as in the past. These trends have strengthened the ties between university libraries and government publications, which today contain vastly improved statistical data, mammoth technical plans, survey data on widespread social trends of the day, etc.

National and local governments in all countries have long published documents and a variety of printed materials. The development of democracy has promoted the view that government bears the responsibility of making these materials widely and easily available, and many policies have been implemented to this end. Moreover, governments are now required to prepare precise policies, particularly in the economic sphere, and detailed surveys and studies are now held to be indispensable in such fields as traffic, technology, and means of livelihood. Accordingly, governments have become, in a certain sense, survey research agencies, and their reports cannot be ignored by the academic world. In this manner government publications have improved in quality and increased in quantity, and have come to be regarded as indispensable in policy planning and in the drafting of legislation. Just as these studies are important for the intraministry and domestic (or prefecturewide) purposes of the government, so too are similar studies important for the extraministry and foreign purposes of the government. That is, the making of policy appropriate to other countries (or to prefectures) has come to be based on the acquisition and study of the government publications of other countries. In this situation it is clear that the exchange of government publications with foreign countries is analogous to the international exchange of academic journals and publications conducted by universities, and that this has come to be an extremely important enterprise.

Over the past twenty years or more amicable relationships have been maintained between Japan and the United States, and the exchange of information has proceeded quite smoothly. Despite the expectations of the governments and peoples of the two countries, however, it cannot be said that the exchange of government publications has always been satisfactory, and there is therefore an urgent need to improve the situation. This long-standing problem is a particularly serious and difficult one for the university libraries of the two countries. To find a solution to this problem is surely an important objective.

Since the principal cause of the problem lies in differences within the two countries with respect to the supply and distribution of government publications, our first step should be to clarify the existing situation. To this end I shall first delineate the differences between Japan and the United States with respect to government publications, and secondly examine the points at which government (national central) libraries and university libraries differ in their approach

to the problem. I shall conclude by pointing out those issues deriving from these two analyses which require solution.

Differences between Japanese and U.S. Government Publications

Both the Japanese and U.S. governments annually issue a large volume of publications, but differences in the actual state of affairs account in part for difficulties in the exchange and acquisition of these publications. We shall first, then, clarify the situation in the two countries, paying special attention to the differences; secondly, we shall compare the two from an overall point of view and analyze their virtues and shortcomings; and, thirdly, we shall analyze the differences in the basic character and functions of government publications in the two countries.

The differences in the actual state of affairs of government publications in Japan and the United States can be considered from four points of view. First of all, we have a class of material printed and circulated by a ministry or a bureau for internal use only. Such material may require confidential handling, and normally is not available to the public. In the United States, however, a substantial number of these works are listed, if only by title, in the *Monthly Catalog of United States Government Publications* and other sources, and in principle some are available by purchase. In Japan, on the other hand, they are not even listed in catalogs, and the Accounts Law (*Kaikeiho*) forbids their sale.

Second, the agencies officially created to print government publications are the Printing Bureau of the Ministry of Finance in Japan and the Government Printing Office (GPO) in the United States. It is significant that the former is under the jurisdiction of the Ministry of Finance, while the latter operates under the jurisdiction of the Congress. Moreover, it is in their functions that these agencies differ substantially, both qualitatively and quantitatively. Established by the Printing Act of 1895, GPO enjoys broad authority as the government printing agency. It is the world's largest printer, in

1963 producing over a billion volumes and selling 53 million. At the same time, it is engaged in the compilation and publication of a detailed monthly bibliography and index of government publications, and it distributes some 10,000 titles to approximately 1,000 depository libraries in accordance with the Depository Library Act of 1962. Thus it is literally *the* agency for the printing, publishing, processing, and distribution of government publications in the country.

In Japan the volume of printing and publishing is substantially lower. Distribution is through sales outlets under the direct management of the Printing Bureau, while publicity is handled by the Council for the Dissemination of Government Publications (Seifu Kankōbutsu Fukyū Kyōgikai). The Council, made up of officials from the various ministries and agencies, is attached to the Prime Minister's Office. The compilation of bibliographies is entrusted to the Acquisitions Division of the National Diet Library (NDL). This fragmentation of function eloquently points up the weakness of the system in Japan. Even more revealing is the low volume of printing and publishing. In 1961 some 150 titles were published. In September 1962 some 422 titles (410 books, 12 serials) were available for sale. The total number of titles published during the twenty-one-year period from 1946 to 1966 was 1,517. These figures clearly indicate that the Printing Bureau is not much more than a printer of bank notes, stamps, and postal cards.

There are reasons for this quantitative weakness. It is scarcely an exaggeration to say that the Japanese government, both at the national and local level, has created private information sales agencies. I exaggerate, of course, but I exaggerate to make a point. The government through its powerful agencies amasses information of very high quality on a broad scale and in great detail, but very little goes to the Printing Bureau. Rather it flows to private printing-publishing companies disguised as such-and-such a "society" or "association," there to be manufactured and sold to bookstores at elevated prices. Of course, this practice in many cases may merely illustrate the

government's commitment to the dissemination of information, but when we consider the value of the information so dispensed, we must conclude that something has gone awry with the system. Since another speaker will examine this point in greater detail, I will refrain from further comment.

The third difference between the two countries lies in the systems for the collection and deposit of government publications. In the United States about 600 libraries have been designated as depository libraries since the passage of the Printing Act, and in principle these libraries receive government publications free of charge for the use of the public. The number of these depository libraries has recently been increased to 1,000 under the terms of the previously mentioned Depository Library Act. In Japan the only equivalent to these depository libraries is the National Diet Library. Counterbalancing NDL is, however, the Library of Congress, and we can therefore say in effect that there is no depository library system for government publications comparable to that found in the United States. Thus, in this respect the two countries differ by the absolutely chastening ratio of 1,000:0.

Here is clearly revealed the heart of the problem of acquiring the government publications of the United States and Japan. The full recognition of these differences is the first step toward improvement—improvement which can probably best be effected by Japan's establishment of a system paralleling that of the United States. Until this basic problem is solved, it is obvious that Japanese university libraries, individually or collectively, can only come up with makeshift, second-best solutions regardless of the amount of research and energy expended.

The depository system in the United States is based on two ideas: that the Congress bears the responsibility of reporting its activities to the people, and that the people, by receiving these reports, will exercise oversight over Congress and the administration through the electoral process. These ideas are evident at the heart of the Depository Library Act, which stipulates that there shall be at least two depositories in each of the senatorial election districts (i.e., the 50 states) and two in each congressional election district (less than 500). It is to be regretted that these ideas have not flourished—nor, of course, have they been implemented—in Japan. Perhaps tradition still casts its baleful influence, for in prewar days the Imperial Library (Teikoku Toshokan), the predecessor of NDL, acted as a repository for publications collected for purposes of censorship by police stations throughout Japan under "peace-and-order" measures administered by the Police Bureau of the Ministry of Home Affairs.

In Japan the Government and the National Diet require that the people submit information free of charge, but do not supply free information to the people. There is a common thread running through the tendency for a Diet member, once elected, to disregard his campaign promises, and the tendency for information, once collected by the government and the National Diet, to stop there. The information, transmuted into national policy, is simply directed to the people; officials do not consider it necessary to report the information as information to the people. But apart from such issues, which bear directly on democratic government, we as librarians are also perturbed by the problem of the preservation of the information and data gathered by the government. In the present situation government publications are located in only one place—NDL—and a major disaster involving the destruction of Tokyo could mean that not even one complete set of Japanese government documents would be left in Japan, or anywhere else, for that matter. The situation is quite desperate and demands improvement.

The fourth difference between the United States and Japan relates to the mechanism of sales. In the United States the GPO sells publications directly by mail, and every effort is made so that people can learn easily about the publications, and can easily order and acquire them. In Japan, on the other hand, there are a number of government publications service centers in the major cities, as well as several dozen outlets in various prefectures where such publica-

tions may be purchased. It is not possible to say that the one system is superior to the other in all respects. But from the point of view of government publications as a bridge between the people and their government, we may very well conclude that the American system, which at first glance seems not to be especially accommodating, proves to be unexpectedly appropriate, while the Japanese system is not necessarily superior. The service centers are under the direct management of the national government, but the sales outlets in the prefectures in many cases handle government publications on a time-available basis when requested by local bookstores, and they are not usually very convenient for individual customers. These stores also sell non-Printing Bureau publications issued by the so-called "auxiliary publishers" (*gaikaku shuppansha*), but these are not cataloged, they are not clearly distinguished from trade publications, and their prices vary. All of this contributes to an unpleasant aura surrounding these publications.

We have thus far been discussing the differences between Japan and the United States with respect to government publications, and now I should like to turn my attention to the advantages and disadvantages of the two systems. First, in production the United States enjoys an advantage in the centralization of publishing in the GPO, whereas Japan suffers from the substantial diversion of publishable materials into "auxiliary" organizations. Second, in depositories, the United States clearly enjoys a 1,000:1 or 1,000:0 advantage over Japan. Third, in sales the U.S. system of direct mail selling can be counted as superior to the Japanese system of indirect store sales.

In view of the facts of the situation discussed above, the United States superiority on these points appears undeniable. On the other hand, if pressed one can note certain points in which the Japanese system is superior. I have not undertaken a comprehensive study here, but I believe that we can generally assume that Japan enjoys the following advantages:

First, since the federal government of the United States does not enjoy any degree of authority over the individual states, the contents of government publications do not match those produced under the centralized government of Japan. The central government of Japan divides the nation into several regional blocs, where it places branch offices; moreover, it exercises tight control over the prefectural governments to an extent unknown in the United States. From the constitutional point of view this can be regarded as a plus for Japan and a minus for the United States.

Second, in the United States there are no national universities, public universities being supported by states and municipalities. Private universities enjoy a position of ascendancy. In this situation, most university publications remain outside the framework of government publications. In Japan, on the other hand, there is a substantial number of national universities, and in contrast to the United States, they dominate the universities operated under local government or private auspices. Large numbers of academic publications in the national universities representative of Japanese scholarship are included among government publications. In 1966 the Ministry of Education published some 535 serials, of which most were scholarly journals of the national universities. This accounted for the largest number of publications by any ministry or agency and amounted to 50 percent of the total. Under proper conditions of production and deposit, this can be counted as a credit to the Japanese and a debit to the U.S. system.

The third and least studied point is that in the United States there exists a relatively small group of influential societies, independent of the government and the universities, which issue authoritative publications. In Japan the weeding-out process among scholarly societies has not proceeded that far, and the specialized departments of the universities each tend to create "auxiliary" societies. These comprise a mixture of strong and weak societies, and in many of the first-rank universities influential general journals of national stature are published. These do not belong in the category of the government publications of universities, discussed above, which are issued with

government funds. However, they are supported in one way or another by the national universities, with the editors and sponsors realizing from the outset that they will be operating in the red, even though they can rely to some extent on society dues, donations, and the like. Strictly speaking, these journals lie outside the purview of government publications, but since they are centered at national universities, the possibility exists that they can be amalgamated and treated as government publications. As the consolidation of academic societies and the amalgamation of journals proceeds apace, and the Printing Bureau and the depository system are further developed, the supply of Japanese government publications will also be improved, so that most of them will become available to university libraries. The shortcomings of the United States system can prove to be an advantage to Japan.

Keeping these six advantages and disadvantages in mind, let us now summarize the actual situation of government publications in both countries from the point of view of their concentration and dispersion. Briefly, in the United States production is concentrated while users are scattered; in Japan the users are concentrated and the producers are dispersed. In the United States there is a relatively smooth and linear flow in the circle comprising Citizens-Congress-Government-GPO-Depository Libraries/Direct Sales-Citizens, resulting in strengthening the center of production and increasing the number of users. In Japan there does indeed exist a similar circle, consisting of Citizens-National Diet-Government-Printing Bureau-NDL/Sales Outlets, but in fact there exists another route which can be schematically described as follows: Government-Certain Auxiliary Organizations-Certain Bookstores-Some Citizens-National Diet. This invites the tendency for some individuals to seek out and stealthily acquire and use various and sundry publications. There have been numerous cases where such works as compilations of laws and statutes—which the government, as a matter of course, should be officially printing through the Printing Bureau—have, at least in part, been entrusted to trade publishers. These are not deposited in NDL, although they are sold in the bookstores, and government agencies must purchase them at national expense.

These differences in practice between the two countries arise from a multiplicity of causes, as discussed earlier. From the standpoint of information science, we may conclude that in the United States there is the idea that information per se—that is, "knowledge resources"—is valuable, and that it should as a matter of principle be circulated and made public. In contrast, in Japan the value of information per se is inadequately recognized, and the underlying idea is to treat information as something to be put to practical use, especially put to use by powerful organizations in isolation and in secrecy by a relatively small elite. Both producers and users tend to regard information in this light, and it is necessary to take this kind of thinking into consideration when devising appropriate countermeasures.

Differences between Government and University Libraries

The central and local governments of Japan and the United States for the most part operate central libraries which collect and preserve material and offer a broad range of services to three categories of users: legislative bodies, executive and judicial agencies, and the citizenry at large. Especially prominent are the two national central libraries, the Library of Congress and NDL, which engage in vigorous collecting activities under the special rights granted to them as the libraries of record in the two countries. Local government libraries lag far behind these two, and university libraries cannot match their activities. The overwhelming superiority of the national libraries in the collection of government publications is to be expected. This arises first from the fact that just as governments establish diplomatic apparatuses for the mutual exchange of ambassadors and ministers, so, too, for reasons of diplomatic form and administration of special rights, governments establish central libraries to collect their own government publications in order to exchange them with the national libraries of other countries. A second reason is that in drafting legislation a government cannot disregard past actions, and government documents must of necessity be examined in the determination of national policy. It is for these two reasons that the national central libraries of a nation naturally occupy a special status.

However, when the national library places too heavy an emphasis on its functions as a governmental library for the nation, as described above, it also naturally follows that this will lead to a variety of undesirable results. For one, publications are not people, and if they are merely exchanged, acquired, and accumulated as a kind of ritual, then the whole procedure will become nothing but a formality and the government library will lose all its functions as a library. It will become a storehouse for old publications without even the functions of an archive. Vigorous collecting activated by a book-reading, information-gathering spirit will come to a stop, and the library will be unable to respond to the needs of the people. It will, on the contrary, tend to isolate itself from the people.

Moreover, in principle a policy may be said to come into existence as a result of a single clear decision in time, whereas, in contrast, information has a certain reach in both time and in space and characteristically can be selected and studied from a variety of points of view. While policy/ government seek a singular solution, information/publications possess a plural content and plural uses. We want information/ government publications, in principle, not only to be used to solve the specific problems of government, but also to be broadly and deeply understood and utilized by the intellectual community in a variety of practical and theoretical endeavors. This means that even though they are products of the government, so long as they are publications it no longer suffices merely to place them in government libraries; they must also be deposited in university libraries.

In the modern age universities have expended an enormous amount of energy in collecting information/publications. Their exploitation is regarded as a fundamental mission of universities, and we need not stress the fact that researchers have come to treat information as a commodity, reprocessing it to create new, original information. Information must be acquired and reprocessed before it can create an active kingdom of knowledge, and no institution is superior to universities in reprocessing capability. Universities have long been active in the exchange of scholarly publications, and their accomplishments are far in advance of government libraries'.

Today government publications have been strengthened both in quantitative and qualitative terms, and it is therefore only natural that both the general public and universities are demanding the information they contain more than was the case in the past. This vast group of information users does not feel that the government is making the most effective use of the one set it utilizes piecemeal only for the purpose of drafting legislation or making policy, nor are they happy with this situation. Moreover, the informed layman expects that in the examination of legislation and policy the government will rely on the interest and studies of the citizenry and academia. Thus, the distribution of government publications should not be restricted to government libraries but should be broadened to university libraries, and thus be available to the people in all their diversity. In international relations the exchange of ambassadors and ministers is a good thing from the point of view of formalities and information acquisition (in the narrow sense), but this exchange of plenipotentiaries is clearly not enough. As a result, consulates and consul generals are also exchanged by mutual agreement. Similarly, it is necessary to provide service to the citizens so that they can understand and study the available information (in the wide sense of that word). Government libraries are, to be sure, at least in form provided both for the general populace and researchers, but they are difficult to use.

If the time comes when university libraries will be opened to the populace at large and researchers and ordinary citizens can rub shoulders as they utilize government publications, then we can expect that there will be a tremendous advance in the "gross national information" and in the "gross national knowledge" resulting from the reprocessing of the information. The tremendous U.S. superiority in this area may be seen by the fact that, of the depository libraries for government publications other than the Library of Congress, at least 400 of the 600—the figures may be somewhat out of date—are university libraries open to the public.

Moreover, the fact that the United Nations has designated a number of university libraries in Japan as depositories is exceedingly momentous. University libraries inevitably possess a certain regionality, while at the same time they possess a universality which ties them to the entire world. In short, they possess individuality. These university libraries have clearly demonstrated that because of their regionality they can and do collect specialized local publications which the national central library is unable to acquire. In some cases they also make arrangements with officials who are graduates of the local university for the kind of exceedingly detailed program of acquisitions which brings in material en bloc, including even ephemera not collected by the central library. The best policy would be to encourage this kind of local development while at the same time energizing the power of the university libraries.

In summary, although the question of the exchange and acquisition of government publications by the university libraries of Japan and the United States have been given considerable attention in recent years, there still remain a number of difficult problems to be resolved, and these must be tackled in an aggressive manner by enlisting the enthusiasm and cooperation of the parties directly concerned. I have emphasized the points in which the two countries differ and have discussed the production, the acquisition, the publicity on and distribution of government publications, as well as the specialized status and roles of universities and university libraries. I should like to close by citing four areas which require improvement:

1. *Strengthening the central printing agencies of government.* The strength of the GPO in the United States is well known, but it should be further strengthened, and in Japan the Printing Bureau requires a radical broadening of both its capacity and authority. The "auxiliary" publishing organs of government agencies must be held in check, while at the same time a direct sales system is adopted.

2. *Strengthening the exchange centers of university libraries and government publications and improving public accessibility.* Many U.S. university libraries operate efficient book exchange centers and government publications reading rooms, but others are incomplete or inadequate and require strengthening. In this respect Japan tends to be exceedingly underdeveloped or surprisingly backward, and it is vital that the library world take a new look at this situation. It would be difficult to make demands on the government if libraries themselves are unprepared.

3. *Broadening and strengthening the depository library system.* The U.S. Depository Library Act has developed an enviable system, and since Japan has practically nothing equivalent to it, we should consider modeling our system after the United States system. We hope for the warm support of the United States. That is, we should like to have our friends consider whether, if one complete set of Japanese government publications were available, it should be sent to the United States or be placed in a depository library in Japan independent of NDL. Again, we should like to have several libraries in Japan designated as depositories for GPO publications in the pattern of UN depositories, thus shaming the Japanese government into taking action. There must be created in Japan a network of multiple depositories in keeping with national needs. In all probability university libraries will be central to the network, and will certainly serve as a vital adjunct to NDL.

4. *Further exploring the question of collecting, exchanging, and procurement of the publications of U.S. state, county, and municipal governments and universities.* This should probably not be termed a conclusion, since it is rather a question which arises from the speaker's inadequate preparation. The fact is that this is regarded as a very important matter by Japanese active in the study of the United States, and we should like to have some instruction on the procedures involved. It would be desirable, in fact, to organize a system which would provide comprehensive and readily available information on these publications. University libraries in particular are in need of this kind of service. Earlier I discussed the Japanese situation with respect to such publications and, while the coverage is incomplete, we can say that a substantial percentage is covered in catalog listings.

In closing, if I may venture a personal opinion, I believe that the supply of government publications should be increased and that they should be collected in quantity in keeping with the needs of the "information age." This cannot be overdone. Making such publications available to the public and to universities is an urgent matter. Even if Japan is a small country and lacks the resources to deposit government publications in all domestic universities, the government still has an obligation to consider depositing the publications in several or several dozen universities. I believe that constant assistance from the United States along these lines will in the end bring about the best results for U.S. university libraries as well.

Availability of Government Publications in Japan

Yasushi Sakai
Director, Division for Interlibrary Services, National Diet Library

It is often said that Japanese government publications are not easily procurable by libraries, academic institutions, and researchers, both here and abroad. The purpose of this paper is to explain the present situation with respect to government publications in Japan and to present a possible solution for discussion.

When we refer to government publications in Japan, we ordinarily use the term in one of two ways. In the narrow sense of the term we mean those publications defined in the Cabinet Conference understanding of 2 November 1956, entitled "Improving the Distribution of Government Publications." Here we find reference to "printed matter edited by government agencies for sale or distribution." It goes without saying that by "government agencies" is meant only organs of the executive branch, since the statement declares elsewhere that "legislative and judicial agencies, as well as other governmental agencies, shall be called upon for cooperation."

In the broader sense, the term includes any publication edited, written, supervised, printed, or published by a government agency. The term "government agency" here, of course, includes not only executive but also legislative and judicial organs. It is this latter definition which is most generally used.

To avoid ambiguity, the *Kokuritsu Kokkai Toshoken Hō* (*National Diet Library Law*) promulgated in 1948 uses the expression "various agencies of the state" (*kuni no shokikan*) in the article regulating deposit copies. All publications produced by or for various government agencies are to be deposited in the National Diet Library for its internal use and for international exchange. Confidential files, blank forms, models, and other simple forms are excluded. On the other hand, books, pamphlets, periodicals, music scores, maps, works produced by film techniques, works transcribed as phonograph records or through other mechanical means of reproducing sound, and works reproduced as documents or drawings by printing techniques or other mechanical or chemical methods are all included. The phrase "various agencies of the state" covers:

Legislative organs: the House of Representatives, the House of Councilors, and the various agencies thereof

Executive organs: the Cabinet and the various agencies thereof; the administrative agencies of the nation provided for in Article 3 of the *Kokka Gyōsei Soshikihō* (*National Government Organization Law*); affiliated organs and other agencies stipulated in Article 8; local branch offices and bureaus stipulated in Article 9; the National Personnel Authority and various agencies thereof; and the Board of Audit

Judicial organs: the Supreme Court, lower courts, and various agencies thereof, and Inquests of Prosecution

Various corporations, as follows:
Japan National Railways
Japan Monopoly Corporation
Nippon Telegraph and Telephone Public Corporation
Atomic Fuel Corporation
Japan Housing Corporation
Forest Development Corporation
Special Ship Equipment Corporation
Water Resources Development Corporation
Overseas Technical Cooperation Agency

Local Public Enterprise Finance Corporation.*

The definition of "government publications" used in this paper is based on the National Diet Library's interpretation of the term.

Present Situation of Government Publications

In Japan the printing and publishing of government publications is not centralized in one agency, as appears to be the case with the GPO in the United States and HMSO in Great Britain. The agency responsible for printing and publishing government publications is supposed to be the Printing Bureau of the Ministry of Finance. The Printing Bureau also prints Bank of Japan notes, various kinds of treasury bonds such as government bonds, revenue and postage stamps, and postcards. Furthermore, it is charged with editing, printing, and publishing the *Kanpō* (*Official Gazette*), *Hōrei Zensho* [*Japanese Laws and Regulations in Force*], *Kokkai Gijiroku* (*Proceedings of the National Diet*), government publicity documents, etc.[1] Out of the tremendous volume of books, periodicals, survey reports, etc., prepared by various ministries and agencies, those which are handled by the Printing Bureau account for a very small percentage—only 160 titles in 1967. Government agencies had the rest printed by private printing companies or by other bodies. As for distribution, these publications were circulated within a particular ministry or to other ministries and agencies at the publishing ministry's discretion.

Official and Private Conceptions of Government Publications

In the past the prevailing notion concerning publications and data compiled by

*The various corporations listed here are totally financed by the government, and the right to appoint officials in these organizations is in the hands of government. These organizations are subject to audit by the Board of Audit.

government agencies was that they had been prepared—with the exception of publications issued for publicity or propaganda purposes—for the purpose of facilitating the administration of the state. The notion that such materials should be made widely available to the sovereign people was not necessarily strongly held. We may say, moreover, that the people themselves—with the exception of certain specialized researchers—had an exceedingly small interest in government publications. Heightened interest in government publications, in fact, is a post-World War II development. The fact that the rapid rise in interest developed first in the field of economic recovery and industrial reconstruction is easily explained, given the condition of the state of the economy in the aftermath of the war.

The government "establishment" in a sense may be regarded as a kind of gigantic research organization, and the reports and data which it compiles and publishes on the basis of its research have an extremely high reliability. Government publications are indispensable sources of information in determining the thinking and direction of a nation with respect to economic recovery and industrial reconstruction. On the other hand, however, the government agencies entrusted with the studies simply are not organized and staffed to meet the demand for their reports. In this situation it has been the National Diet Library (NDL)—the legal depository of government publications—which has borne the brunt of the demands of the day. As a consequence, the Special Libraries Association (Senmon Toshokan Kyogikai) was organized in 1952 under the good offices of NDL.

One of the most important projects which the Association (which includes the major research libraries and research organizations in Japan) initially undertook was the division of the nation into regions and the establishment of regional documents centers. These centers were intended to promote the easy utilization of government publications, and today there exist seven such regional materials centers, as shown in table 1. Each year exhibitions of government publications are sponsored in the centers at which a catalog entitled *Seifu Kankōbutsu Tenjikai Mokuroku* [*Catalog of the Exhibition of Government Publications*] is distributed. This is one of the important catalogs for the understanding of government publications.

TABLE 1. Regional Documents Centers, February 1969

REGION (CITY)	TOTAL RESOURCES	NUMBER OF MEMBERS
Kantō (Tokyo)	126,927	211
Kansai (Osaka)	127,989	82
Chūbu (Nagoya)	90,230	41
Kyūshū (Fukuoka)	80,387	41
Hokkaidō (Sapporo)	69,790	32
Tōhoku (Sendai)	64,184	12
Chūgoku (Okayama)	48,927	21
Total	608,434	440

As an indication of popular interest in government publications, a public opinion poll conducted in 1967 by the Public Information Room of the Prime Minister's Office may be cited. This poll was conducted 16–20 June 1967 at the request of the Printing Bureau of the Ministry of Finance to investigate the general public's knowledge of government publications. Some 3,000 respondents were selected by random sample from holders of residency cards in 106 cities with populations of more than 100,000. Poll takers visited the subjects, and the actual number of respondents interviewed was 2,262, for an interview percentage of 75.4 percent. The results of the poll were as follows:

1. Are you aware of the term "government publications"?
   Yes 37%   No 63%
2. Have you ever read a government publication (excluding *The Official Gazette*)?
   Yes 21%   No 79% { Have seen 13% / Have never seen 66%
3. Have you ever seen the *Seifu Kankōbutsu Geppō* [*Monthly Report of Government Publications*]?
   Yes 7%   No 93%
4. Where have you seen government publications? (Asked of the 7% who have seen the *Geppō*)
   At office 19%
   At ministries and agencies 61%
5. Have you ever utilized government publications? (Asked of the 7% who have seen the *Geppō*)
   Yes 24%   No 76%

Content and Form of Government Publications

Government publications are usually divided into two categories: "official use documents" (*bunai shiryō*) and "general documents" (*ippan shiryō*). They can also be divided on the basis of the purpose of publication into six categories:

1. Documents compiled to facilitate directly the administration of an agency, or in drafting plans of an agency
2. Documents compiled as records for posterity
3. Documents in the form of reports, reference materials, or directives submitted by or to the government or ministries and agencies
4. Documents in the form of reference materials or directives to local public bodies and other agencies
5. Documents embodying results of research and investigation in fields of responsibility of an agency, and
6. Documents for publicity for domestic and foreign use.

Government publications can also be classified in terms of the manner in which they are published as follows:

1. Those which are compiled and published at the expense of an agency
2. Those which are compiled and published at the expense of an agency with additional copies sold by the Printing Bureau of the Ministry of Finance
3. Those which are compiled at the expense of an agency with the agency paying for only those copies which it needs and with the remaining copies being sold by extra-agency bodies (*gaikaku dantai*), and
4. Those which are compiled or edited by an agency (sometimes only nominally), but which are printed and published by an extra-agency body. In such cases,

copies which the agency needs may be purchased or may be reserved as a gift.

From the point of view of distribution, government publications can also be divided into three categories: (1) those "not for sale" (*hibaihin*), distributed free of charge within an agency or to other agencies concerned; (2) those "sold at cost"; and (3) those available as "general trade" publications. Finally, from the point of view of printing, documents can be classified as movable-type, typed, and mimeographed publications.

Government publications which are available at service centers for government publications are limited mainly to those "general documents" which are designated for "general trade distribution." Thus the present situation is unsatisfactory for researchers and investigators, since the service centers do not have all the publications, and moreover the number of copies is very limited.

Measures Taken to Promote Distribution of Government Publications

As I have indicated, the demand for government publications had been increasingly voiced by industrial and research organizations, but our government did not take this problem seriously until a foreign, not a Japanese, scholar voiced his concern. In 1956 the British sociologist R. P. Dore came to Japan to study agricultural life here. He pointed out deficiencies of organization in the publication and distribution of government publications in our country, and suggested in views aired in the press the need for improvement, calling upon the government to take the necessary steps. The weaknesses pointed out by Professor Dore were exactly to the point, thus causing repercussions in the various agencies concerned. The issue was taken up by Tanzan Ishibashi, then Minister of MITI (Ministry of International Trade and Industry), and this led to a government decision, issued on 2 November 1956 in the form of a "Cabinet Conference understanding," to improve the diffusion of government publications. As a consequence, a Council for the Dissemination of Government Publications (Seifu Kankōbutsu Fukyū Kyōgikai) chaired by the Director of the Public Relations Office of the Prime Minister's Office, and including those responsible in the various agencies for information and publicity, was organized. This Council publishes the *Seifu Kankōbutsu Geppō* [*Monthly Report of Government Publications*] and operates directly the Government Publications Service Center (Seifu Kankōbutsu Sābisu Sentā) in Tokyo. Moreover, government publications service stations have been set up as nongovernmental agencies in each of the prefectures. At present, there are six service centers and fifty service stations.

This series of measures taken by the government improved the diffusion of government publications to a certain extent. However, government publications which are exhibited or sold at service centers are those arbitrarily selected and provided by various ministries and agencies from among publications published with budgeted funds, and therefore the scope and number of copies available are regrettably limited.

In addition, there exists a body called the Liaison Conference for Strengthening the Diffusion of Government Publications (Seifu Kankobutsu Fukyu Kyoka Renraku Kondankai). This organization, consisting of private publishers which issue government publications at government request, works to promote the wider dissemination of government publications. At present thirty-eight publishers belong to this organization, which publishes each year for distribution to members only a listing entitled *Kaiin Hakkō Tosho Mokuroku* [*Catalog of Books Published by Members*].

Interpretation of Regulations for NDL Deposit

The inadequacy of funds for printing and the practice of extra-agency publishing have cast a baleful influence on the deposit of the legally stipulated number of copies at NDL (30 copies in press runs of 500 or more). NDL interprets the phrase "publications published by various agencies of the state or for various agencies of the state" as including:

1. Publications prepared (edited, compiled, translated, or investigated) by state agencies and published not by the agencies but by outsiders
2. Publications compiled under the supervision of state agencies where the agencies are judged to be responsible for deciding the content of the publications
3. Publications which appear to be compiled and published by extra-agency bodies located in state agencies but which are judged to be actually compiled by governmental agencies
4. Publications whose compilation is obviously commissioned by governmental agencies
5. Publications which are compiled by an organization at the request of or as a proxy for a government agency, where the agency subsidizes the publication, or purchases a substantial number of copies, or in some cases provides gifts for the publication, and
6. Publications prepared by government agencies in cooperation with outsiders.

Deposit Copies at the NDL

According to a study of the deposit of government publications, the number of copies received by NDL during 1967 from various government agencies and local public bodies was 6,921 book titles and 2,654 serial titles. Of these, publications by central government agencies (excluding national universities) amounted to 2,851 book titles and 695 serial titles.

It is extremely difficult to determine how many government publications are published, but those who are concerned generally estimate that annual book production is approximately 2,500 to 3,000 titles. Therefore, we may conclude that about 90 percent of the publications which see print are deposited in the NDL. Hence we believe that these publications can satisfy most of the demands of researchers, either through reproduction or some other means of service.

The problem is that the legal provision for the deposit of thirty copies of each title is not satisfactorily fulfilled, and the

deposit, of course, forms the foundation for the international exchange of government publications. It is very natural that the flow of publications to overseas exchange partners is uneven. In the international exchange of government publications, however, the Library of Congress (LC) is accorded the highest priority, with the result that its receipts of Japanese government publications should practically match those of NDL. Researchers in the United States should take note of this point. Perhaps LC ought to, as a first order of business, develop ways in which these resources can be actively utilized.

Guides to Government Publications

For the general reader who approaches government publications, tools such as catalogs are indispensable. It is regrettable that there is no complete catalog listing all government publications in our country. We have the following catalogs at present; all are incomplete:

1. *Nōhon Shūhō* (*Current Publications*). Accessions list of works deposited in NDL. Published by the National Diet Library. Weekly. 10p. (average issue). Sold by the Printing Bureau of the Ministry of Finance.

   This is a prompt report covering all domestic publications received under the National Diet Library Law. A quick report on newly published work, it is most comprehensive. It is very useful in obtaining prompt and comprehensive knowledge of the latest publications of government agencies.
2. *Seifu Kankōbutsu Geppō* [*Monthly Report of Government Publications*]. Compiled by the Commission for the Dissemination of Government Publications; published by the Printing Bureau of the Ministry of Finance. 36p.

   This was called the *Seifu Kankōbutsu Mokuroku* [*Catalog of Government Publications*] until 1961, when the present title was adopted. This catalog lists those publications and documents edited or compiled by various ministries, agencies, or governmental organizations which are presented to the Public Relations Office of the Prime Minister's Office in accordance with the Cabinet

Conference understanding of 2 November 1956. The publications listed in this catalog are exhibited at government publications service centers, and some are for sale. Publications are divided into periodicals and nonperiodicals; they are subarranged by issuing agency. Each entry lists the title of the publication, the publisher, price, postage fee, and note on primary contents. This monthly report is available free of charge upon application to a government publications service center or to a government publications service station, although 25 yen in stamps must be included per copy to cover mailing costs.

3. *Biblos*. Edited and published by National Diet Library. Monthly. 24p. Copies published by Yūrindo, Inc. are for sale at 600 yen per year.

The periodical *Biblos* is published to maintain liaison between NDL and its branch libraries, as well as with government libraries and special libraries. In each issue there is a monthly report, at the back of the book, on publications of central government agencies. The publications listed are substantially the same as those carried in *Nōhon Shūhō*.

From vol.13, no.1, through vol.17, no.8, this periodical featured a special section called "Introducing Postwar Government Publications." This was a convenient source of information on major government publications.

4. *Seifu Kankōbutsu Sōmokuroku* [*Union Catalog of Government Publications*]. Published by the Printing Bureau of the Ministry of Finance every other month. 50p.

This is a bimonthly catalog of those government publications printed by the Printing Bureau of the Ministry of Finance which are for sale. It is published at the beginning of February, April, June, August, October, and December. The works are arranged by subject: Jurisprudence, public peace and order, personnel affairs, compensation, welfare, labor, finance, the economy, commerce and industry, foreign relations, agriculture and forestry, education, transportation, communications, construction, local autonomy, etc. The name of the editor or the author, an abstract, size, the number of pages, frequency, fixed price, postage, etc., are listed for each title in the publication. The abstracts are especially detailed. The publications contained in this catalog are for sale at government publications service centers. This catalog is distributed free of charge at government publications service centers and government publications service stations, but it is not available by mail.

5. *Seifu Kankōbutsu Shinbun* [*Government Publications News*]. Published by the National Official Gazette Sales Cooperative (Zenkoku Kanpō Hanbai Kyōdō Kumiai) twice a month. 6p.

New government publications for sale are introduced in detail in this newspaper, which furnishes a truly convenient and quick way to gain firsthand knowledge of government publications. 30 yen per copy, 720 yen per year.

6. *Zen Nihon Shuppanbutsu Sōmokuroku* (*Japanese National Bibliography*). Edited and published by the National Diet Library. Annual. (Copies for sale are published by the Printing Bureau of the Ministry of Finance.)

This catalog of all publications published in Japan is compiled in accordance with provisions of the National Diet Library Law. It contains all government publications as well as publications by local public bodies deposited at NDL.

7. *Kankōchō Shuppanbutsu Mokuroku* [*Catalog of Publications of Ministries and Agencies*]. Edited and published by the National Diet Library. Annual. Not for sale.

This catalog is an offprint of the "Ministries and Agencies" part of the *Zen Nihon Shuppanbutsu Sōmokuroku*. It covers the ministry and agency publications deposited at NDL according to Article 24 of the National Diet Library Law. It divides publications into books and magazines and arranges them by issuing agency.

8. *Seifu Kankōbutsu Tenjikai Mokuroku* [*Catalog of Exhibition of Government Publications*]. Jointly edited by the Special Libraries Association and the National Diet Library; published by the Special Libraries Association. Annual.

This is a catalog of the exhibition of government publications held at various places annually under the sponsorship of the Special Libraries Association. It includes the publications of central ministries and agencies, public enterprises, government-related agencies, extra-agency bodies, etc., covering the period from the November two years preceding the exhibit to the December of the preceding year. The sale price is 150 yen per copy.

9. *Hakusho, Nenkan, Nenpō, Jittai Chōsa Hōkoku, Roppō Mokuroku* [*Catalog of White Papers, Yearbooks, Annual Reports, Reports on Fact-Finding Investigations, Six Legal Codes*]. Edited and published by the National Official Gazette Sales Cooperative. Annual.

This is a catalog of those white papers, etc., which are the most widely used of all government publications. 30 yen for each copy.

10. *Seifu Kankōbutsu Fukyū Kyōka Renraku Kondankai Kaiin Hakkō Mokuroku* [*Catalog of Publications Issued by Members of the Liaison Conference for Strengthening the Dissemination of Government Publications*]. Edited by the Liaison Conference and published by the National Official Gazette Sales Cooperative. Annual.

This is a list of publications published by the members of the Liaison Conference. This conference consists of thirty-eight private publishing companies which publish government publications. The catalog is distributed only to member organizations, and is not for sale.

11. Library bulletins, monthly reports of documents, catalogs of holdings, etc., published by branch libraries of the National Diet Library. Below are listed the primary reports or catalogs which contain individual agency publications:

National Personnel Authority Library (Jinjiin Toshokan)	*Tosho Geppō* [*Monthly Report of Books*]
Statistics Bureau Library (Tōkeikyoku Toshokan)	*Shiryō Geppō* [*Monthly Report of Documents*]
Administrative Management Agency Library (Gyōsei Kanrichō Toshokan)	*Tosho Geppō* [*Monthly Report of Books*] (Published every other month)
Defense Agency Library (Bōeichō Toshokan)	*Kanchō Shiryō Tsūhō* [*Bulletin of Documents of Governmental Agencies*]
Economic Planning Agency Library (Keizai Kikakuchō Toshokan)	*Keizai Kikakuchō Hakkō Shiryō Mokuroku* [*Catalog of Documents Published by Economic Planning Agency*]
Science and Technology Agency Library (Kagaku Gijutsuchō Toshokan)	*Shiryō Geppō* [*Monthly Report of Documents*]
Ministry of Foreign Affairs Library (Gaimushō Toshokan)	*Shiryō Geppō* [*Monthly Report of Documents*]
Ministry of Finance Library (Ōkurashō Bunko)	*Ōkurashō Kankei Shuppanbutsu Mokuroku* [*Catalog of Publications Concerned with the Ministry of Finance*]
Ministry of Health and Welfare Library (Kōseishō Toshokan)	*Shiryō Geppō* [*Monthly Report of Documents*]
Ministry of Agriculture and Forestry Library (Nōrinshō Toshokan)	*Nōrin Tosho Shiryō Geppō* [*Monthly Report of Books and Documents of the Ministry of Agriculture and Forestry*]
Ministry of International Trade and Industry Library (Tsūsan-Sangyōshō Toshokan)	*Shiryō Dayori* [*Information on Documents*]
Ministry of Postal Services Library (Yūseishō Toshokan)	*Tosho Mokuroku Geppō* [*Monthly Report of Catalogs*]
Ministry of Labor Library (Rōdōshō Toshokan)	*Shinchaku Annai Oyobi Shiryō Mokuroku* [*Information of New Publications and Catalog of Documents*]
Supreme Court Library (Saikō Saibansho Toshokan).	*Tosho Geppō* [*Monthly Report of Books*].

To complete this listing of guides to Japanese government publications, I should like to mention two catalogs which are no longer published. They are *Kanchō Kankō Tosho Mokuroku* [*Catalog of Books Published by Government Agencies*] and *Kanchō Kankōbutsu Sōgō Mokuroku* [*Union Catalog of Government Publications*].

Kanchō Kankō Tosho Mokuroku commenced publication in December 1927 as a quarterly issued by the Cabinet Printing Bureau. The prospectus stated: "We can easily learn about the government publications of Great Britain and the United States by referring to the monthly catalogs published by the printing agencies of the two countries, but paradoxically we have great difficulty in learning about our own government publications." It is obvious from this statement that the catalog was modeled after those of the GPO in the United States and HMSO in Great Britain. This catalog subsequently became a monthly publication, but during World War II it fell victim to the paper shortage and ceased publication in November 1943.

Kanchō Kankōbutsu Sōgō Mokuroku [*Union Catalog of Government Publications*] was compiled by the National Diet Library. This library administers branch libraries located in the ministries and agencies of the executive and judicial branches of government, and thus affords a mechanism for cooperation among government libraries. The acquisition of government publications issued by ministries and agencies is through these branch libraries. One of the concrete mechanisms for cooperation between NDL and its branches was compilation of the *Kanchō Kankōbutsu Sogo Mokuroku*. The first volume was published in 1952, and publication continued through vol.8 (1960). Thereafter the entries were incorporated into *Zen Nihon Shuppanbutsu Sōmokuroku*. This catalog listed an extremely broad range of publications, including, of course, printed works and also mimeographed materials not normally distributed publicly. It was extremely well received by researchers, and even today there is a desire that it be revived.

Difficulties in Procurement

There are a number of reasons why Japanese government publications are difficult to acquire, and the main reasons may be described in the following terms. First, in the organization of the national government no system has been set up to centralize the printing and distribution of publications. Instead, we have a long history of individual agencies placing orders for printing with trade publishers, or of entrusting the printing and publishing to extra-agency bodies, with agency funds budgeted for this purpose. Apparently this has not always been the case in Japan, particularly in the early stages of the Meiji Restoration. Thus, in the fifth year of Meiji—on 20 September 1872—a Printing Bureau was established in the Council of State (Dajōkan Inshokyoku) and was charged with the responsibility of printing and distributing all government publications. Three years after its establishment, however, the Printing Bureau became a unit of the Bureau of the Mint, and a new policy was adopted which provided that "all works except confidential and other indispensable publications of government agencies are to be turned over to private publishers." This same policy holds today.

Second, in the government agencies themselves the bureaus and divisions produce publications indiscriminately, and no mechanism exists to process and control these in a centralized way. In extreme cases, it is not unusual for individuals in a particular bureau to be completely unaware of the publications issued by a neighboring bureau. Worse still, it is difficult for ministries to control documents produced by their external organs or by their local offices. In recent years in many cases the archives section or the publicity section of a ministerial secretariat has taken on the responsibility of processing and controlling such documents. But for the most part there is trouble enough in controlling the publications and documents produced within the ministry proper, and control does not extend to the products of external organs and local offices. NDL has branch libraries in the central ministries, which provide the library services necessary for the conduct of the business of the ministries and agencies. At the same time, the branches are responsible for collecting and acquiring all the publications and documents produced by the ministry or agency, and thus they work to procure government publications for NDL. Even in this situation, we are aware of difficulties in the comprehensive collecting of all publications and documents produced by the several ministries and agencies.

Third, the publishing programs of the ministries and agencies are inadequately funded. Put in other terms, in the budget allocations for printing allotted to the ministries the demands of general users outside the government have not been taken into consideration. There is not only a chronic insufficiency of funds for printing purposes; it is a fact also that while the types of publications increase yearly, and printing expenses also rise each year, the rate of increase in the budget allocations for printing is extremely limited. In this situation, the solution devised has been publication and sale of publications by extra-agency bodies. In other words, a ministry compiles a publication, prints only the number of copies needed by the ministry with its own funds, and permits the rest to be published under the name of an extra-agency body. Alternatively, the ministry may only edit the publication, while the printing and publishing will be done entirely under the name of the extra-agency body. The ministry will then purchase the required number of copies. Thus there are many ways in which ministries relate to extra-agency bodies in their publishing activities, but, in short, by distributing through an extra-agency body, a sufficient number of copies is produced to satisfy demand, and profits are set aside to finance other publications. Among such extra-agency bodies are some with some substance, but others are only nominal publishers. In toto there are several hundred such bodies.

Survey of Extra-Agency Bodies and Their Publications

In 1953 NDL conducted a survey of extra-agency bodies issuing publications and found that at that time there were some 110 organizations publishing about 400 titles. A second survey, conducted in February 1969, was distributed to 580 organizations. Of the 300 replies received, 236 organizations reported that they were issuing publications totaling some 1,800 titles, while the remaining 64 reported inactivity in this area. The survey thus reveals the extraordinary increase in publishing of government publications by extra-agency organizations.[2]

System for Easy Access to Government Publications

From the domestic point of view the following three principal measures would probably ensure readier access to government publications:

1. *Comprehensive deposit of copies in the National Diet Library.* The comprehensive deposit of government publications in NDL would result in their inclusion in *Nōhon Shūhō* (*Current Publications*), *Biblos,* and *Zen Nihon Shuppanbutsu Sōmokuroku* (*Japanese National Bibliography*), and this would permit a comprehensive approach to these publications. Moreover, their accessibility would be assured through photoreproduction or other means.

2. *Comprehensive collecting of materials produced within ministries through branch libraries of NDL.* The researcher regards as important a variety of materials not normally deposited in NDL—for example, mimeographed materials circulating prior to their issuance as printed documents. Here we must look to the strengthening of the collecting of intraministry materials by the branch libraries. In fact, when the *Kanchō Kankōbutsu Sōgō Mokuroku* [*Union Catalog of Government Publications*] was being compiled and published by the Branch Libraries Division of NDL, the branch libraries made strenuous efforts

to collect all intraministry documents so that they could be listed. Thus, mimeographed documents were included, and even if copies were not deposited in NDL, they were housed in the branch libraries and listed in the monthly accessions lists issued by the branch libraries, and hence made known and available to users.

3. *Quick compilation of a broad catalog of government publications.* We must, of course, depend on NDL for such a compilation. In this situation we should undoubtedly consider reviving the *Kanchō Kankōbutsu Sōgō Mokuroku.*

From the international point of view, the following points need to be considered:

1. Full exploitation in the United States of available Japanese documents. Both quantitatively and qualitatively an excellent supply of Japanese government publications is currently being sent to the Library of Congress.

2. Strengthening cooperation with the National Diet Library, and

3. Possible establishment of an organization in Japan to procure the government publications of Japan.

Proposal for Procuring Government Publications

As I have stated earlier, any drastic solutions to the problem of free access to government publications cannot be quickly achieved. It is possible for domestic users in Japan to examine or acquire through one means or another those publications which they need, but this is not possible for foreign readers. I have attempted some experiments on the feasibility of microfiche reproduction and distribution with the cooperation of the National Cash Register Company. The results show that given a certain number of orders—a minimum of fifty—the outlook is good for quick and economical service.

SUBJECT OF EXPERIMENT:

Rōdō tōkei chōsa geppō [Monthly Labor Statistics and Research Bulletin], vol.20, no.4; 60p. 120.00 yen (postage: 12)*

COMPILER:

Rōdō Daijin Kanbo Rodo Tokei Chosabu (Labor Statistics and Research Department, Minister's Secretariat, Ministry of Labor, Japan)

PUBLISHER:

Rōmu Gyōsei Kenkyūjo (Labor Administration Institute)

COST OF PRODUCING MASTER: 500.00 yen

COST OF COPIES:

1–10: 150.00 yen per copy
11–49: 120.00 yen per copy
50– 100.00 yen per copy
*360 yen = $1 U.S.

Where the number of titles rises to the range of 100–300, and the number of orders to the 100–300 range, the cost per copy declines to 65.00 yen. Three days are required for reproduction. Approximately 100 pages may be placed on a single microfiche.

These studies show that the price per customer when 50 orders are received amounts to 110 yen—based on a copying cost of 100 yen, to which is added a proportionate cost of producing the master of 10 yen (500 yen divided by 50)—and this is almost the same as the price of the original (120 yen). If the number of copies produced increases, there should be a further decrease in the price.

To carry out such a project, at least the following two measures might be required:

1. *The establishment of an office (in Tokyo)* jointly supported by interested institutions in the United States. This office would be responsible for selecting those government publications deemed necessary in the United States, determining the number of copies to be reproduced, ordering, shipping, payment, etc. Might it not be possible for the American Cultural Center or the Tokyo office of the Library of Congress to be charged with the responsibilities of such an office?

2. *An agreement to lend materials for microfiche production* involving NDL, its branches, the Printing Bureau of the Finance Ministry, Government Publications Service Centers, and other agencies.

In seeking to effectuate such a project, an important problem and one that requires further study requires resolution, namely, the matter of copyright for those works published by extra-agency organizations. (This is, of course, not a problem with pure government publications, which may be reproduced as microfiche.) A number of solutions may be available, such as the payment of a certain sum to the publisher for each microfiche produced.

NOTES

[1] *Ōkurashō Setchihō*, [*Ministry of Finance Establishment Law*] Part 2, Affiliated Organizations: Article 16, Printing Bureau.

[2] *Kuni (Chūō Kanchō, Kōkyō Kigyōtai, Seifu Kankei Kikan, Seifu Kankei Dantai) ga Henshū, Kanshū shi, Seifu Kankei Dantai, Shuppansha ga Hakkō shita Kankōbutsu Ichiran. List of the Publications Compiled by or under Supervision of the Government of Japan (Central Government Agencies, Public Corporations, and Extra-departmental Organizations) and Published by Extra-departmental Organizations (Gaikaku Dantai) or Commercial Publishers.* Preliminary ed. (Tokyo: National Diet Library, 1969). 1v.

Part 7

EXCHANGE OF PERSONNEL

Exchange of Librarians: Past Practice and Future Prospects

Warren M. Tsuneishi
*Chief, Orientalia Division,
Library of Congress*

One of the first American advisers to the Japanese government urged almost 100 years ago "that libraries and museums be supported as a necessary adjunct to cultural progress."[1] In 1871, when this advice was given—a scant three years after the Meiji Restoration—"cultural progress" in Japan meant, above all, the modernization of the educational system. Horace Capron, the American adviser, recognized clearly the fundamental role played by "libraries and museums" in education. It is probably safe to say that ever since that time, practically every American library adviser, consultant, and teacher who has gone to Japan has tendered essentially the same advice: Libraries as an essential component of the educational system must be given due priority in overall developmental programs for the advancement of the cultural life of the people. In the twentieth century, as educational horizons have broadened and the learning process has come to be regarded as a never-ending one stretching from the cradle to the grave, libraries have come to be more widely appreciated as a key social institution in the preservation and transmission of the accumulated knowledge of the human race. And with the so-called "knowledge" or "information explosion" of recent years, libraries have moved even more prominently into the limelight as the nerve centers of an increasingly information-oriented society.

As we have noted, the essential message of libraries as central to the educational and information system, broadly defined, has been carried over the years by a succession of librarians who have found their way to Japan, perhaps most recently by Douglas W. Bryant of Harvard University in the series of lectures presented during 1963 on the modernization of university libraries.[2] The message also has been carried back by Japanese students matriculating in American universities and by Japanese observers of the American library

164

scene, particularly in the post-World War II period.

The American Contribution

When we look at the flow of American librarians to Japan and of Japanese librarians to the United States, it would appear at first blush that the "exchange" is entirely one-sided, with all the benefits of interchange accruing only to the Japanese side. As we shall see, however, while the exchange of librarians may perhaps be characterized as being weighted heavily in favor of Japanese librarianship, by no means has the benefit to American librarianship been negligible. The interchange, moreover, is undergoing modification as educational and cultural standards and needs in both countries themselves change, and we can already see an equalizing trend appearing in the exchange.

In modernizing her library system, Japan has inevitably relied heavily on foreign expertise, especially that supplied by American librarians. In the winter of 1947–48, for example, the United States Library Mission of Mr. Charles Harvey Brown, representing the American Library Association, and Mr. Verner Clapp,[3] then Chief Assistant Librarian of the Library of Congress, traveled to Japan and under exceedingly difficult conditions worked for the establishment of the National Diet Library. Echoing the sentiments of General Horace Capron some three-quarters of a century previously, the Japanese toastmaster in a dinner honoring Mr. Brown and Mr. Clapp praised the energy of the two American consultants and concluded: "We are firmly convinced that the National Diet Library will be a cornerstone for the construction of a democratic and a cultural Japan."[4] Once again libraries were placed, rightfully, at the center of the cultural life of the nation.

Perhaps the next major accomplishment of American librarians in Japan was the organization and development of the Japan Library School of Keiō Gijuku University by Professor Robert L. Gitler and his associates.[5] Recruited by the American Library Association to undertake the task, Professor Gitler assembled a staff of faculty members which was entirely American. Subsequently, distinguished American library specialists have been and continue to be invited to Japan as visiting professors at the Japan Library School. According to Professor Sawamoto of Keiō:

These Americans not only gave instruction and guidance to the students in their classes but also served as professional consultants for Japanese librarians. Their influence on and contributions to Japanese librarianship were and continue to be tremendous. No progressive steps in this field in recent years have been without their impact—direct or indirect.[6]

But not only have we seen a movement of American librarians from West to East; traveling in the opposite direction have been many library students, librarians, and professional leaders, singly and in groups. Any number of distinguished Japanese librarians who have visited American libraries come readily to mind, from Fujio Mamiya, in 1915 to our distinguished co-panelist, Professor Takahisa Sawamoto, whom I first came to know through our mutual association with the Columbia University Graduate School of Library Science. In 1968 the Japan Special Libraries Association sent an inspection team headed by Mr. Heizō Miyata, Executive Secretary of the Kansai Chapter of the Japan Special Library Association, to observe exemplary special libraries. But perhaps the most important and the most influential of the group tours was the U.S. Field Seminar on Library Reference Services for Japanese Librarians, conducted during the fall of 1959 and headed by Miss Naomi Fukuda, then of the International House Library, but since November 1968 a transplanted Curator of the East Asian Collection at the University of Maryland. Sponsored by an ALA committee chaired by Mrs. Frances Neel Cheney of the Peabody Library School, the seminar met in several cities across the length and breadth of the country, taking a sample of representative libraries and their reference services, and observing American systems of library cooperation and education for librarianship.[7]

A decade later we are finally reciprocating. In many ways the American delegation to this binational conference may be regarded as a counterpart to the 1959 field seminar, only this time it is the *Americans* who have come to study the characteristics of *Japanese* libraries and librarianship. Put in another way, the binational conference is merely the latest expression of the American library profession's abiding interest in Japanese librarianship.

The Counterflow—Japanese Contributions

But in all candor we must admit that the American interest has been largely in terms of the teaching of and proselytizing for the cause of American librarianship, with results, it is hoped, which have been beneficial to Japanese librarianship.[8] Has there then been no contrary flow of Japanese library experts to advise American librarians on matters on which the Japanese happen to be uniquely qualified?

Put in these terms, which are those of the American model of "technical aid and assistance," the answer must be in the negative, and hence the superficial appearance previously noted of an "exchange" program heavily weighted to benefit the Japanese side only. But when we look at the flow of individuals from a somewhat different point of view and examine certain highly specialized aspects of American library development, we find that the exchange has not, after all, been so unbalanced, and the Japanese contribution has not been minimal. Let me cite as one example the development of Japanese-language collections in over fifty American research libraries during the past sixty-some-odd years. The obvious fact here is that these collections could not have been developed without the direct and indirect assistance of Japanese scholars, bibliographers, and librarians.[9]

The collecting of Japanese-language books and manuscripts on a comprehensive basis in the United States originated in purchases made by Professor Kan'ichi Asakawa of Yale University for both the Yale Library and the Library of Congress in 1906. As a result of this trip, Dr. Asakawa, the first Japanese scholar to hold a professorship in a major American university, acquired for the Library of Congress some 9,000 works in all fields of Japanese literature. Six decades ago, when only a handful of Americans could speak and write Japanese, the collecting of Japanese books in this quantity was breathtaking in its audacity and foresight. Through the ensuing years the Japanese collection at the Library of Congress grew slowly, and only commenced to develop systematically with the appointment of Dr. Shio Sakanishi as Chief Assistant in Japanese to the Orientalia Division in 1930, where she served until 1941. Her work in developing the collection in the humanities and the arts is amply recorded in the annual reports of the Librarian of Congress.[10] Still another Japanese bibliographic specialist who contributed greatly to the organization and cataloging of the Library of Congress collection was Masao Senda. Traveling and working under funds supplied by the Rockefeller Foundation, which was committed to the promotion of Asian studies in the United States, Senda worked as a Japanese cataloger from 31 January 1939 to 19 June 1941. This was at a time when Japanese studies in the academic world were in their infancy, and Senda therefore can be counted as a pioneer in the cataloging of Japanese-language publications in an American library.[11]

Another major Japanese collection is that of the East Asian Library of Columbia University in New York. This is a rich treasure of library materials illustrative of all aspects of Japanese civilization, and it serves the metropolis of New York as well as the academic community of Columbia University. It is largely the work of Ryusaku Tsunoda, a graduate, like Asakawa, of Tokyo Semmon Gakkō, the predecessor of Waseda University. Professor Tsunoda began his lifelong career as bookman, teacher, and sage in Hawaii in 1909, and, after moving to New York, commenced a lifelong connection with Columbia University, today one of the principal centers of Japanese studies in the United States. In appreciation of Tsunoda Sensei, one of his devoted students has written:

> He came not only to learn but to teach. He came with something of Japan to give, and at the same time a greater capacity to receive. . . . Thus to Hawaii and New York, he brought his knowledge, his books, his search for truth and his love for other seekers of learning. On one of his trips from Japan he brought to New York a valuable collection of books, contributed by Japanese friends, businessmen and the Imperial family, with which he founded in 1928 the Japanese collection at Columbia, the first of its kind in America. This pioneering work reminds us again of those early Japanese monks Saicho, Kukai and Ennin who brought back books from China and with them founded the great centers of monastic learning in Japan. . . . His collection has continued to grow, under the care of devoted students, but to the end of his life it remained an intimate concern of his.[12]

Books are the flower of any civilization, and if it were not for the devoted endeavors of bibliophiles like Asakawa, Sakanishi, and Tsunoda, American libraries would be the poorer in their resources for the study of Japanese culture.

Just as the Russo-Japanese War of 1904–5 stimulated American interest in Japan—to the point where the Library of Congress commissioned Asakawa to purchase books for its collections—so World War II worked to promote the systematic and scholarly study of Japan and Japanese civilization. As a consequence, in the post-World War II period, Japanese studies programs have mushroomed in American universities and colleges. Today there are perhaps as many as 60 colleges and universities in the United States offering courses in the Japanese language, and many more offering lectures in the history, art, literature, religion, politics, and government of Japan without requiring of the students a knowledge of the language. One result of the burgeoning academic interest in Japan has been an expansion in the depth and breadth of Japanese-language collections in American university libraries. Major deposits ranging in size from 18,000 volumes to close to 500,000 volumes can now be found in some fourteen institutions, and minor collections are available in some forty libraries. All of these collections are characterized by rapid, if uneven, growth.

The very rapid expansion of these collections during the past quarter of a century could not have been accomplished without the expert knowledge of Japanese scholars and librarians, either citizens of Japan or trained in Japan. Selecting at random from among these librarians, we may mention, for example, Miss Miwa Kai, Assistant Librarian and Head of the Japanese Section of the East Asian Library, Columbia University, since 1944; Mr. Shigeharu Isobe, from 1959 to 1967 Assistant Librarian of the Harvard-Yenching Chinese-Japanese Library, Cambridge, Massachusetts, and now Librarian, Jikei Ika Daigaku; Mr. Tamotsu Takase, Deputy Curator of the East Asian Collection, Hoover Institution, Stanford University from 1955 to 1968; Mr. Andrew Kuroda, Head, Japanese Section, Orientalia Division, Library of Congress; Miss Ai Kawaguchi, Head of the Japanese Language Section, Shared Cataloging Division, since 1968 and an LC employee since 1956; Mr. Yukihisa Suzuki, Head, Asia Library, University of Michigan; and Mr. Hiroshi Mori, Japanese bibliographer at the University of Michigan during the period 1965–68. To repeat, the development of Japanese collections in the United States—which are regarded as the best outside of Japan, and which may be said to constitute a cultural resource of the first importance to American scholarship—could not have taken place without the work of these and other individuals from Japan.

Today there are an estimated 110 professional librarians in the United States working exclusively or primarily with the acquisitions, cataloging, and reference servicing of Japanese-language publications. Of these, by far the largest concentration—some 50 individuals—are to be found in the various departments of the Library of Congress. A recent study shows that of the 50, only 13 possess library science degrees; 31 are now or were born as citizens of the United States; 11 retain their Japanese citizenship; 6 are citizens of the Republic of Korea; and 2, of the Republic of China. In other words, only about one-fourth of LC's professional librarians working with Japanese-language publications have been trained as librarians or bibliographers, and a substantial percentage have not taken undergraduate or graduate courses in Japanese history, literature, or language. Typically they have come to the Library with their primary qualification being mastery of the Japanese language. In other words, the demand for Japanese librarians is so high and the supply so limited that the sole qualification for employment as librarians in many cases has been competence in the language. Thus, when we inquire into the educational background of the majority of LC's professional librarians, we find individuals with college majors in business administration, religion, liberal arts, and the like, but very few with majors in Japanese studies or library science.

Lack of adequate training is by no means the sole problem. In a survey of the personnel needs of East Asian collections conducted in February 1969, the following distribution of vacancies for Japanese librarians was reported:

UNIVERSITY OR RESEARCH LIBRARY	POSITION VACANT
Chicago	Cataloger
Hawaii	Cataloger
Hoover Institution	Deputy curator (Japanese)
Iowa	Cataloger
Kansas	Cataloger
Michigan	1 Bibliographer 1 Cataloger
Minnesota	1 Cataloger
Washington (Seattle)	Bibliographer
Library of Congress	Ass't. head, Japanese Language Section Subject cataloger: Religion Subject cataloger: Science Catalogers (number of vacancies indeterminate).[13]

There are at least thirteen positions now vacant (as against fourteen in 1967), and the chance that they will be filled by Japanese-language librarians now being trained in the United States is not very great. In this situation, American librarians can only turn to their colleagues in Japan for assistance, either through short-term "exchanges" of librarians—for example, requesting the services of a bibliographer or a cataloger for a two-year period—or through the traditional export of librarians and subject experts on an extended, even permanent, basis.

Ideally, the qualifications for Japanese librarians working in American libraries would include fluency in Japanese and English, library and bibliographic training and expertise, and a strong subject background in some aspect of Japanese civilization (e.g., history). For cataloguing positions, we might wish for extensive experience; for the position of bibliographer, thorough knowledge of general bibliography as well as expertness in one or more specialized subjects, for example, Japanese economics and sociology. Whether such individuals are available remains to be explored.

There is yet another type of expert potentially needed, although actual demand has not yet arisen. That is subject specialists to study and evaluate existing Japanese collections as visiting consultants. They would then make recommendations to fill obvious gaps and supply the necessary guidelines for the systematic future development of the collections. The truth of the matter is that such experts are few and far between in the United States, and even if more were available, few libraries could afford to hire them on a permanent basis. One finds in large research libraries the employment of subject bibliographers whose primary function it is to develop the collections in a systematic and rational fashion. Thus, we may have a "humanities bibliographer," a "science bibliographer," and a "social science bibliographer" working in the acquisitions department of a university library. In contrast, we will often find in the East Asian field a single curator, with perhaps an assistant curator and one or two catalogers who are responsible for developing and servicing the Chinese and Japanese collections of a library in all subject disciplines. The curator might be expected to have full competence in Chinese and Japanese bibliography, history, literature, language, politics and government, education, economics, etc. This is manifestly impossible, but the economics of university libraries have not yet permitted any other alternative. In this situation, the short-term consultant may well provide at least an interim solution. Hiroshi Mori at the Asia Library of the University of Michigan and Miss Naomi Fukuda at the University of Washington Far Eastern Library have provided such expertise in the past.[14]

Still another area in which there is a potential demand for Japanese experts is in library education. Because of the inadequate preparation of some staff members employed in Japanese libraries in the United States and because of the great additional need for trained librarians with Japanese-language competence, attempts have been made to overcome these deficits by arranging for specialized courses in Japanese bibliography, acquisitions, cataloging, and reference services. These courses would be given as a part of the regular curriculum of library studies in a graduate school or through the organization of specialized summer institutes. Thus, courses in Japanese bibliography have been given at the Universities of Michigan, Chicago, and Columbia for several years as part of the Asian Studies programs. The University of Hawaii Graduate Library School has during the past two years offered courses in technical services and bibliography in Asian libraries.

More recently two summer programs have been developed, the first an Institute on Bibliographic Services in East Asian Studies, to be conducted 9–20 June 1969, at the University of Wisconsin, Madison, Wisconsin, under the direction of Professor Dorothea Scott, and the second an Institute for Far Eastern Librarianship, to be held from 23 June to 1 August 1969, at the University of Chicago Graduate Library School under the direction of Dr. T. H. Tsien. Both are funded by the U.S. government under the Higher Education Act of 1965. Financial and legal barriers may stand in the way of the participation of Japanese library educators in these summer institutes funded by the U.S. government, but ideally specialists from Japan and China ought to be invited to offer their expert knowledge in areas of their special competence.

To round out this discussion of the needs of the library and information science profession in the United States for professional assistance from Japan, we shall mention two recent developments, one in the field of the application of computers to the mechanization of bibliographic records, and the second in the area of the exchange of scientific information and materials.

As the American leader in the field of library automation, LC has undertaken a Machine Readable Cataloging (MARC) program, which, at present, is capable of handling roman-alphabet records only. In the production of printed cards or bibliographic listings by computer, for example, the system at present is designed for input and output in languages using the roman alphabet only. Records in all other languages—for example, Russian and Japanese—must first be converted to roman letters. The problem of the machine manipulation of non-roman-alphabet records remains to be solved, and it is here that American librarians must look for aid to Japanese librarians and information specialists. We can look nowhere else, since to my knowledge no other country has the proper mix of language problems and computer facilities. Perhaps our colleagues in the Japan Information Center for Science and Technology who cannot evade the issue of the machine handling of records in a variety of scripts, because they *must* deal with the Cyrillic and Sino-Japanese scripts, can show the way in leading us out of this particular wilderness.[15]

The need for Japanese expertise in the fields of science, technology, and medicine has long been recognized, as shown by the experience of the National Library of Medicine in procuring the support of the Keiō Medical School Library in the operations of the MEDLARS program. Moreover, the governmental United States–Japan Committee on Scientific Cooperation in its programs for the exchange of scholars and the exchange of scientific information and materials has proceeded on the assumption that bilateral cooperation on an equal basis in the sciences would be of inestimable value in advancing science in both countries, and this has appeared to be the case.[16]

To summarize, as we have seen from this brief survey of American and Japanese contributors to library development in both countries, the "exchange" between the two countries has decidedly proved to be of mutual benefit, although, to be sure, in different ways and with varying force. The American contribution has been greatest in the broad areas of library administration, processing, and education, while the Japanese contribution has been in the highly specialized area of Japanese-language-collection development and control.

Mechanisms for Interchange

Internationally minded American librarians are legion, and the international programs of the profession reflect a concern which ultimately finds its rationale in the proposition that knowledge and books know no artificial boundaries of geography or nation. An overview of the worldwide concerns of American librarians has been described in an article by Mrs. Marietta Daniels Shepard entitled "International Dimensions of U.S. Librarianship."[17] Included is a wide-ranging discussion of the role of the American Library Association and of the national libraries—the Library of Congress, the National Agricultural Library, and the National Library of Medicine—in the promotion of international library activities and movements of librarians across national borders.

Because in recent years American librarians have become increasingly involved in overseas activities on the one hand and concerned about the development of foreign-language resources in domestic libraries on the other, the American Library Association sponsored a conference in 1967 to determine "who was doing what" in these areas. The report of that conference describes the international activities of the principal U.S. government agencies—the national libraries, the U.S. Agency for International Development, etc.—, international agencies such as UNESCO, and private organizations like the American Library Association, the Medical Library Association, the Ford Foundation, and the Council on Library Resources.[18]

The details of existing mechanisms for exchange—how and where to apply for available grants for study and travel, sponsoring agencies, qualifications, etc.—are amply described in published guides such as UNESCO's *Study Abroad*[19] and need not detain us here. However, of special interest to librarians desiring to travel to the United States are the programs described in Dr. Lester Asheim's study, "Sponsored Tours for Foreign Librarians in the United States," first presented at a conference in Honolulu in 1966 and appended in this work as Appendix B. The study has been updated with information supplied by the current director of the ALA International Relations Office, Mr. David Donovan. Here we find descriptions of State Department programs to promote the exchange of librarians, such as the Multi-National Librarian Project, which provides study tours of brief duration for young librarians. The Jointly-Sponsored Library Project, on the other hand, places mid-career librarians in American institutions for professional experience for a one-year period.

While the need for such programs is acute, unfortunately funding difficulties have sharply curtailed the actual movement of librarians during the past year or so. Other avenues remain open, however, such as the Fulbright exchange program, which might be exploited better by librarians than it has been in the past. In view of the decreased funding of exchange programs by both government agencies and private foundations, it would appear that new avenues must be found to further this endeavor. In this connection it behooves us to be alert to all possibilities, no matter how remote. There appears to be, for example, an active movement of people in the international sister cities program. Honolulu, for example, is affiliated with Hiroshima, Kyoto with Boston, and San Francisco with Osaka, etc.[20] Why should not librarians be included in the periodic exchange of individuals between sister cities?

Of more immediate and direct importance are the following existing mechanisms for international contact and exchange:

1. American Library Association
International Relations Office
1420 N. Street, N.W.
Washington, D.C. 20005
Director: David Donovan
   International Relations Committee. Committee for Liaison with Japanese Libraries.

   Chairman:
      Thomas R. Buckman
      University Librarian
      Northwestern University Library
      Evanston, Illinois 60201

This committee is specifically responsible for liaison with the Japanese library world; the present binational conference is one expression of its interest and concern.

International Relations Round Table
Chairman (1970):
   Morris A. Gelfand
   Queens College
   Flushing, Long Island
   New York 11367

This division of ALA provides staff members with foreign-language competence to man a hospitality desk at ALA conferences. It sponsors a reception and informal gathering at the annual conference for foreign guests. It also publishes a directory of American librarians who have served overseas. The third edition of *Foreign Service Directory of American Librarians* is available from the University of Pittsburgh Book Center, 4000 Fifth Ave., Pittsburgh, Pennsylvania 15213, at $3 a copy.

2. American Association of Law Libraries
53 West Jackson Blvd.
Chicago, Illinois 60604

   President:
      Earl C. Borgeson
      Harvard Law Library
      Cambridge, Massachusetts 02138
      Langdell Hall

Foreign Liaison:
   Kate Wallach, Chairman
   Foreign and International Law
   Louisiana State University Law
      Library
   Baton Rouge, Louisiana 70803
   Albert P. Blaustein
   AALL Representative to the Council
      of National Library Associations
   Rutgers Law Library
   New Brunswick, New Jersey 08903
   Kurt Schwerin
   AALL Representative to the International Federation of Library
      Associations and to the International
      Association of Law Libraries
   Northwestern University Law Library
   619 Clark Street
   Evanston, Illinois 60201

3. American Society of Information Science
(Formerly American Documentation
   Institute)
2011 Eye Street, N.W.
Washington, D.C. 20006
Executive Director: James E. Bryan

4. Association of Research Libraries
Foreign Acquisitions Committee
Chairman:
   Philip J. McNiff
   Director, Boston Public Library
   Boston, Massachusetts 02117

This committee is concerned with all aspects of problems faced by American libraries in acquiring and bringing under bibliographic control publications from foreign countries.

5. Association for Asian Studies
Committee on East Asian Libraries
Chairman:
   Weiying Wan
   Head, Asia Library
   University of Michigan Library
   Ann Arbor, Michigan 48104

This committee is specifically concerned with the problems of East Asian (Chinese, Japanese, Korean) collections in the United States.

6. Library of Congress
   Dr. Jean Allaway
   International Relations Officer
   Library of Congress
   Washington, D.C. 20540

The Library of Congress administers the Jointly-Sponsored Librarian Project of the Department of State.

7. Medical Library Association
   919 North Michigan Avenue
   Chicago, Illinois 60611

   Executive Secretary:
   Mrs. Helen Brown Schmidt

   Foreign Liaison:
   Mr. John B. Balkema, Chairman
   MLA Committee on International
      Cooperation
   Johns Hopkins University
   1900 East Monument Street
   Baltimore, Maryland 21205

8. National Agricultural Library
   U.S. Department of Agriculture
   Washington, D.C. 20250

   Director: John Sherrod

   Foreign Liaison:
   Kevin J. Keaney
   In-Service Training Officer
   National Agricultural Library
   Washington, D.C. 20250

9. National Library of Medicine
   8600 Rockville Pike
   Bethesda, Maryland 20014

   Director: Martin M. Cummings, M.D.

   Foreign Liaison:
   Martin M. Cummings, M.D.

   Note: The NLM has a contractual arrangement with Keiō University for
   indexing selected Japanese periodical
   literature and for the acquisition and
   cataloging of Japanese monographs.
   Seven people from the staff of Keiō
   University have been trained at the NLM
   in indexing, searching, and cataloging
   operations.

10. Special Libraries Association
    235 Park Avenue South
    New York, New York 10003

    Executive Director: George H. Ginader

    Foreign Liaison:
    Mrs. Vivian D. Hewitt, Chairman
    SLS International Relations Committee
    Carnegie Endowment for International
       Peace
    United Nations Plaza at E. 46th Street
    New York, New York 10017

11. State library associations

    Note: There are at least three state li-
    brary associations in the United States
    active in assisting foreign librarians to
    visit American libraries for brief or ex-
    tended periods of time. The work of

foreign liaison is done on a voluntary
basis, and there is no provision for travel
funds and other expenses. Librarians with
full professional qualifications and with
fluency in English may be assisted in
contacting particular local libraries in the
states of California, Illinois, and New
York:

California Library Association
Committee on International Exchange
   of Librarians
1741 Solano Avenue
Berkeley, California 94707

Illinois Library Association
Foreign Exchange Program
Chairman:
   Carlos Cuitino
   The Goss Company
   5601 West 31st Street
   Chicago, Illinois 60650

New York Library Association
Committee on the Appointment of
   Foreign Librarians
Chairman:
   John Solomita
   Queens Borough Public Library
   89-11 Merrick Blvd.
   Jamaica, New York 11432

12. University of Pittsburgh
    Graduate School of Library and Informa-
    tion Sciences
    Pittsburgh, Pennsylvania 15213

    The Graduate School administers the
    Multi-National Librarian Project, for-
    merly administered by the International
    Relations Office of ALA.

As we can see from this brief listing,
which by no means exhausts those agencies engaged in international activities, the
points of contact are many, and unfortunately the coordination of effort among
the organizations is less than ideal. There
is, for example, no single clearinghouse for
foreign librarians seeking information about
American libraries. Nor does there exist a
placement service for librarians seeking
either short-term or long-term employment
in American libraries, despite the real need
for such librarians. This is an area which
requires further study, but the probability
of the establishment of a single coordinating mechanism between the United States
and Japan does not appear very high now
or in the foreseeable future.

Prospects

It is time to summarize and look to the future. I shall leave it to my Japanese colleagues to describe their personnel exchange needs in detail as they see them, and shall merely note here what appears to be obvious from my vantage point. That is, I should imagine that the movement of American professional librarians and educators to Japan will continue, though on a somewhat reduced scale. It would be extremely desirable and ultimately more productive if these Americans developed some facility in, even mastery of, the Japanese language. I should imagine further that the flow of Japanese students and observers to the United States may well continue, perhaps even at an accelerated pace, especially as the library world moves from manual to machine methods of bibliographic control. The information needs of both American and Japanese society, both hyperindustrialized and both moving into the postindustrial, information-oriented society of the future, are essentially the same, and cooperation through exchange of personnel and of technology would appear to be in the best interests of both countries.

In the United States we can increasingly expect to rely more heavily on specialists from Japan in the development of our Japanese-language library resources. During the past year the Library of Congress has reached out to NDL for assistance in the preparation of LC printed cards for currently published monographs listed in the Nōhon Shūhō. This is merely one example of the kind of bibliographic expertise we in the United States will increasingly seek from Japanese librarians. In the future, too, there exists the possibility of requesting consultants in Japanese bibliography, library education, and collection evaluation, as well as in science, technology, medicine, and information science.

The interchange of persons, then, will be tailored to fit the particular needs of both countries, and we can therefore expect to move increasingly toward mixed teams of professional librarians, information specialists, and subject and linguistic specialists. One need only examine the makeup of the Japanese and American delegations to this conference, comprising specialists in all these areas, to see the direction in which we are moving.

NOTES

[1] In a letter from General Horace Capron, U.S. adviser to Kiyotaka Kuroda, then Deputy Commissioner for the colonization and development of Hokkaidō, dated 25 Aug. 1871 and cited by Kumahiko Takebayashi, "Meiji jidai toshokan no tembyō," *Toshokan Kenkyū* 9; no.3:392–94 (July 1936).

[2] For abstracts of papers on the future of university libraries and on impressions of Japanese university libraries see D. W. Bryant, "Kindaika o mezasu daigaku toshokan," *Toshokan Zasshi* 57, no.11:495–99 (Nov. 1963).

[3] Mr. Clapp's signal achievements in the immediate postwar period were recognized by the award by the Government of Japan in the autumn of 1968, during the 20th-anniversary celebration of the National Diet Library, of the Order of the Sacred Treasure.

[4] *Kokuritsu Kokkai Toshokan ni Kansuru Shiryō, dai 3-shū* (Tokyo: Sangiin Chōsabu, 1948), p.157.

[5] Robert L. Gitler, "Education for Librarianship: Japan," *Library Trends* 12, no.2:273–94

(Oct. 1963). This article also contains an excellent summary of the early pioneers in Japanese library development with special attention to overseas influences.

Alice Lohrer and W. V. Jackson, "Education and Training of Librarians in Asia, the Near East and Latin America," *Library Trends* 8, no.2:243–77 (Oct. 1959).

Takahisa Sawamoto, "Education for Librarianship in Japan," *American Libraries: Report of the U.S. Field Seminar on Library Reference Services for Japanese Librarians* (Tokyo: 1960), p.129–34.

[6] Ibid., p.132.

[7] Their English-language report was published in 1960 under the title *American Libraries: Report of the U.S. Field Seminar on Library Reference Services for Japanese Librarians*. The Japanese report published in the same year under the title *Amerika no toshokan* (Tokyo: Amerika Toshokan Kenkyū Chōsadan). For an interpretive account of the Field Seminar, see Yukihisa Suzuki, "As They Saw

Us," *California Librarian* 21, no.2:87–92, 118 (April 1960).

[8]The possibility that American models of librarianship may not be entirely applicable in another cultural environment should not be overlooked. See, for example, the series of perceptive lectures by Lester Asheim in his *Librarianship in the Developing Countries* (Urbana: Univ. of Illinois Pr., 1966). Dr. Asheim warns against succumbing to the illusory notion that what is good for Americans is good for everyone else.

[9]In his paper on research resources for the present conference Mr. Yukihisa Suzuki presents an overview of the characteristics and size of Japanese-language collections in American libraries. For a bibliographic guide to articles and books on Japanese collections see W. L. Y. Yang and T. S. Yang, *Asian Resources in American Libraries: Essays and Bibliographies* (New York: Foreign Area Materials Center, Univ. of the State of New York, State Education Dept., 1968), p.69–76.

[10]A. W. Hummel, "The Growth of the Orientalia Collections," *Library of Congress Quarterly Journal of Current Acquisitions* 11, no.2:80–81 (Feb. 1954).

[11]For an account of his experiences, see Masao Senda, "Beikoku Giin Toshokan Tōyōbu shokumuki," *Toshokan Kenkyū* 15, no.1: 57–73 (Jan. 1942).

[12]W. Theodore de Bary, "A Tribute to Ryusaku Tsunoda," in *Ryusaku Tsunoda Sensei, 1877–1964*, p.11. (Note: This booklet, which appeared in 1966, bears no imprint. It was issued in connection with the establishment of the Ryusaku Tsunoda Memorial Book Fund, c/o Professor Donald Keene, Columbia University, New York.)

[13]The survey was conducted by Dr. T. H. Tsien, Head, Far Eastern Library, University of Chicago, for the Committee on East Asian Libraries of the Association for Asian Studies. The information cited here is contained in a letter from Dr. Tsien to this writer dated 24 Feb. 1969.

[14]See, for example, Naomi Fukuda, *Libraries for Japanese Studies: Report of a Survey* (Tokyo: International House of Japan Library, 1963).

[15]For a survey of efforts to date in the United States to handle Chinese characters by computer systems, see Frank A. Kierman, Jr. and Elizabeth Barber, "Computers and Chinese Linguistics," *Unicorn* 3:31–73 (Jan. 1969). *Unicorn* is a preprint series issued by the Chinese Linguistics Project and Seminar, Green Hall Annex, Princeton University, Princeton, N.J. 08540.

[16]*United States–Japan Committee on Scientific Cooperation: the First Five Years, 1961–1966* (Washington, D.C.: Govt. Print. Off., 1967). (Dept. of State publication 8210. East Asian and Pacific series, 158).

[17]Marietta Daniels Shepard, "International Dimensions of U.S. Librarianship," *ALA Bulletin* 62:699–710 (June 1968).

[18]*Who Is Doing What in International Book and Library Programs: Conference Proceedings, October 9, 1967* (Washington, D.C.: International Relations Office, ALA, 1967).

[19]Students interested in subsidized study and educational travel abroad should consult *Study Abroad: International Guide: Fellowships, Scholarships, Educational Exchange, 1966–1968* (16th ed.; Paris: UNESCO, 1966).

For programs of U.S. governmental agencies, see *A Guide to U.S. Government Agencies Involved in International Educational and Cultural Activities*, compiled by the Policy Review and Coordination Staff, Bureau of Educational and Cultural Affairs, Department of State (Washington, D.C.: Govt. Print. Off., 1968), (Dept. of State publication 8405. International Information and Cultural series, 97.)

The following quarterly journal carries articles on the work of private and governmental organizations engaged in interchange of personnel: *International Educational and Cultural Exchange*, published quarterly by the U.S. Advisory Commission on International Educational and Cultural Affairs; for sale by the Supt. of Documents, Govt. Print. Off., Washington, D.C.

[20]List supplied by Town Affiliation Association, 1612 K Street, N. W., Washington, D.C. 20006. This association issues the monthly *Town Affiliation News*.

Historical Background

The prewar period

Exchanges of Academic Librarians between the United States and Japan

Takahisa Sawamoto
School of Library and Information Science, Keiō University

When we examine the interchange of academic library personnel between the United States and Japan, we are embarrassed to find that the traffic has been so one-sided, that is, predominantly a flow from the American side to Japan. It has been inevitably so for many reasons. In this paper, an attempt is made: (1) to review the historical evidence of exchanges of academic library personnel between the two countries; (2) to analyze some of the trends revealed in these materials and to comment on some current problems and needs; and (3) to say something about prospects for the future.

After the beginning of the Meiji period in 1867, Japanese academic developments were strongly influenced for many years by European countries, especially Germany, England, and France. Since 1945 Japan has been showered by American cultural and academic gifts.

Japanese academic librarianship has been, in a sense, the most retarded sector of our library world, at least partly because our schools have been clad in the armor of European academism. It is only in recent years that substantial numbers of administrators and professors, as well as influential older university librarians, have taken an interest in American modes of library service.

During the period from 1639 to 1854, Japan closed her doors to all foreign countries except Holland and China because of the exclusion policy of the Tokugawa shogunate, and international cultural exchanges were virtually suspended. Yukichi Fukuzawa, well known as a scholar and as the founder of Keiō Gijuku University, visited Western countries in 1860 and 1863, and his observations on Western libraries in the first volume of his *Seiyō Jijō* [*Conditions in Western Countries*] (1866) are considered to be the first on this topic to reach Japan. Another early historical document on Western libraries is *Tokumei Zenken Taishi Bei-Ō Kairan Jikki* [*Report on Visits to American and European Countries by the Envoy Extraordinary and Ambassador Plenipotentiary*] (1878), in which descriptions of European national libraries are found.

It is interesting to note that Seiichi Tejima, who later became the chief librarian of Tokyo Library, Japan's first national library, was listed as an interpreter in the suite of Tomomi Iwakura, the Envoy Extraordinary and Ambassador Plenipotentiary. Fujimaro Tanaka, a high official of the Ministry of Education, took Tejima with him when he was dispatched to the United States in 1876 to study American educational institutions and exhibitions. In 1884 Tejima went alone to England to observe British librarianship.

In the half century from 1890 until 1940, more than thirty Japanese librarians can be listed as visitors to the United States and/or European countries to study librarianship or observe library practices abroad. Most of them were from the public-library field. Some of these individuals—including only those who visited the United States and excluding those who had very little or no influence on Japanese academic library developments—are listed chronologically here:

PERIOD*	NAME	INSTITUTION**
1888–90	Inagi Tanaka	Tokyo Library
1902–03	Kichiro Yuasa	Kyoto Prefectural Library
1909–10	Mankichi Wada	Tokyo Imperial University Library
1914–39	Chieko Hirano	(Boston Art Museum Library)
1915–16	Miyahiko Mori	(Mainichi Press Library)
1922–42	Shio Sakanishi	(Library of Congress [LC])
1926–28	Kiichi Matsumoto	Imperial Library
1926–28	Miyogo Osa	South Manchuria Railway Co. Library
1929–33	Yujiro Nakajima	(Kwansei Gakuin University Library)
1934–40	Naomi Fukuda	(LC, International House of Japan Library)
1937–38	Hiroshi Kawai	Tokyo Imperial University Library
1938–41	Masao Senda	(LC, Tenri University Library).

*Period of stay; in some cases includes visits to European countries.
**The institutions with which they were affiliated before they went abroad, except for those in parentheses, which are the Japanese or American libraries in which they worked after completing their studies.

Of the above, some are worthy of more than casual mention. Seiichi Tejima selected Inagi Tanaka to study librarianship in the United States from 1888 to 1889 (eleven months) and to investigate British library practices from 1889 to 1890 (eight months). He conducted his American studies—the first Japanese to do so formally—at the Harvard University Library, the Library of Congress, the Boston Public Library, the New York Public Library, and others. On his return to Japan, he succeeded Tejima as the chief librarian of Tokyo Library for twenty-eight years. He made contributions to Japanese librarianship in the area of library management.

Kichirō Yuasa, of Kyoto Prefectural Library, who went to the University of Chicago to study librarianship for the academic year 1902–03, was the first to urge the establishment of a library school in Japan.

Mankichi Wada, chief librarian of Tokyo University Library from 1897 to 1923, visited the United States and European countries in 1909–10. His influence was great not only within his own institution but in the entire Japanese library world. He took leadership in the development of education for librarianship by establishing a course in librarianship in his university.

Miyahiko Mōri, who studied at the Library School of the New York Public Library, after his graduation in 1916 worked with the Maninichi Press as head of its library. He organized a library study group and published books on librarianship.

Shio Sakanishi, who did graduate study at the University of Michigan and who remained in the United States for almost twenty years, spent the latter half of these two decades at the Library of Congress, where her contributions to the development of a good Japanese collection were tremendous. She was a pioneer in showing the potentialities of Japanese librarians to American librarians.

Kiichi Matsumoto, the chief librarian of the Imperial Library, of which the Tokyo Library was the antecedent, visited the United States, England, and Germany from 1926 to 1938 to study national library policies. He devoted himself to development of a central national library system and to revision of the Library Ordinance to permit the realization of his objectives.

Miyogo Ōsa, who worked with the South Manchuria Railway Company Library, went to New York to attend Columbia University's School of Library Service in 1926. After completion of his studies there in 1928, he returned to Manchuria and headed the company's libraries in Fushun and Dairen, successively. After the war he taught in Tokyo at the Education Ministry's Training Institute for Librarians, and in 1964–65, after having held other library positions, he worked at the Library of Congress with Japanese manuscripts.

Yūjirō Nakajima, after graduation from the Peabody Teachers College Library School, returned home to work at Kwansei Gakuin University Library, Nishinomiya.

Naomi Fukuda, a graduate of the library school of the University of Michigan, stayed in the United States for six years, working at the Library of Congress until 1940. She has contributed to American librarianship not only through her work with the Library of Congress Japanese Section but also as a consultant and liaison agent for visiting librarians in Japan since the war. She organized a model library in the International House of Japan, and in her capacity as its librarian has helped many Japanese librarians and promising students who wished to study in the United States. At the same time she has given sincere and effective help to American librarians staying in or visiting Japan. She organized and led a project called the U.S. Field Seminar on Library Reference Services for Japanese librarians in 1959. She has made several trips to the United States to investigate the status of Japanese collections in American research and educational institutions, and her reports on and recommendations for such Japanese collections have been highly valued. In late 1968 she accepted a position as visiting curator of the East Asian collection at the University of Maryland.

Hiroshi Kawai, a librarian at Tokyo Imperial University, spent one year studying mainly American librarianship and briefly visited British, French, German, Swedish, and Italian libraries. While in the United States, he audited courses by Professor Lucy E. Fay and Ernest J. Reece at Columbia and by Professors Louis Round Wilson and Pierce Butler at Chicago. He was critical of the American trend toward the centering of librarianship in public libraries. He suggested in his commentary report on his observations that Japan needed to formulate its own concept of librarianship after a comparative analysis of American and European librarianship.

Masao Senda, with the support of the Rockefeller Foundation, stayed in the United States two and a half years, of which the latter one and a half were spent at the Library of Congress as cataloger of Japanese materials. He deserves to be remembered with Dr. Sakanishi, Miss Fukuda, and other librarians who still are working for the development of Japanese collections in the United States.

Besides librarians, a number of Japanese scholars who have visited or lived in the United States have been able to help American institutions by suggesting sources of information on Japanese culture. One of the most distinguished of these was the late Professor Ryusaku Tsunoda, whom I met at Columbia University in 1963. He established the basis of the Japanese collections in the East Asian Library at Columbia in the late 1920s. Without his endeavors Columbia surely would have been unable to possess the splendid Japanese collections it has today.

Examination of library personnel interchanges in the prewar period reveals that no notable American librarians visited Japan for close contact with Japanese academic librarians. At the same time, most of the Japanese librarians who visited the United States had as their objective the absorption of American librarianship, and thus, with few exceptions, they had little time or incentive to contribute to the American side. Nor was the interest of American society in Japanese culture such as to create any great demand for aid by Japanese librarians. In a few instances, however, such as the Library of Congress and at Columbia University's East Asian Library, some Japanese librarians or scholars did find ways to contribute to the development of Japanese collections and to their technical processing. Some of these Japanese librarians who began such labors in this period are still continuing their effort.

The postwar period

During the war and for some time after the surrender of Japan in 1945, educational and research activities in Japan were thrown into almost total confusion, as were other normal activities in national life. No less than others, research workers and scholars in academic institutions inevitably had to spend most of their time in seeking food and other necessities to survive. Not unnaturally, academic libraries and materials for their collections seemed to have little importance. Research dwindled, and publication of research results all but vanished. It was a dark age indeed for academic librarians. During the period from 1945 to 1950, no visits of Japanese librarians to the United States are recorded.

Although the administration of occupied Japan was nominally under the Allied Powers, it was the United States, which contributed the largest military forces, that naturally exerted the greatest influence on the ways in which the policies for the rehabilitation of our country were implemented. The fundamental objectives were two: the demilitarization and the democratization of Japan. One of the paths to democratization was democratization of education, including reforms which involved considerable changes in the concepts and operations of educational institutions.

Early in the occupation period an education mission from the United States visited Japan. Its report, published in 1946, not only emphasized the important role of the library in education but also called for the training of professional librarians. Four years later, a second American education mission again pointed out the importance of libraries, this time especially in institutions of higher learning. Between the visits of these two education missions, a United States cultural science mission had surveyed Japanese universities and, in its recommendations, called attention to fundamental deficiencies in libraries and urged the training of better professional librarians.

Again early in the occupation period, Ralph Shaw came to Japan to advise the administration of the Ministry of Agriculture and Forestry Library on the organization of a national agricultural library. He visited Japan a second time in 1963.

The Education Division, Civil Information and Education Section, of SCAP (Supreme Commander for the Allied Powers)

Headquarters, interested itself in libraries and librarians, and the Information Division operated CI&E libraries, first in Tokyo and eventually in about twenty other major cities. These libraries were administered by American professional librarians who not only served the general public but also gave assistance and advice to scholars and academic librarians. These, as well as other librarians in various capacities with the American forces, lectured from time to time in short-term institutes for practicing librarians. Appearing at the Institute for Librarianship held at Tokyo University in July 1948 were, for example, the following librarians: Paul Jean Burnette, speaking on "Current Trends of American Libraries"; Louis W. Doll, on "The History of American College and University Library Developments"; and Jane McClure, on "Education for Librarianship." The Education Division sponsored a series of six institutes for educational leadership in library science from 1949 to 1951, with the participation of American professional librarians as leaders, among them Susan G. Akers.

Prior to the establishment of the National Diet Library in 1948 and during its planning stage, Verner Clapp and Charles H. Brown in 1947 and Robert B. Downs in 1948 were invited to Tokyo to act as advisors. They also took great interest in the problems of academic libraries in Japan and had tremendous influence on librarians through formal talks and informal conversations. "Departmental Libraries in Universities," a lecture given at Tokyo University by Downs in July 1948, for example, was translated into Japanese and published in an issue of *Toshokan Zasshi* (*Library Journal*). Downs also investigated major Japanese universities to determine which of them would be best suited as the home for the projected Japan Library School. Keiō Gijuku University was eventually selected.

The official establishment of the Japan Library School came in April 1951. Prior to the opening of the school, Robert L. Gitler, the founding director, arrived in Tokyo in the evening of the last day of 1950 and devoted the next three months to preparations for the first such school at the university level in Japan. Some twenty-one American professors at the school over the years not only have instructed and guided the students enrolled in their classes but have also acted as consultants in various fields of librarianship. Among those well remembered by university librarians because of their special contributions toward helping to solve academic library problems are Robert L. Gitler (1951–56 and 1961), Frances N. Cheney (1951–52), Bertha Frick (1951–52), Everett T. Moore (1952–53 and 1967–68), George S. Bonn (1954–55), Guy R. Lyle (1957), Thomas P. Fleming (1963), and J. R. Blanchard (1964). The last three were invited to the school for a special three-year program for the training of life science librarians in universities and research institutions in Japan.

A concrete illustration of what can take place in an academic library with the help of distinguished American librarians is provided by the changes which have occurred at Tokyo University. The late Dr. Hideo Kishimoto, then the director of the nation's largest university library, invited Dr. Keyes Metcalf in 1961 and Douglas W. Bryant in 1963 as consultants. On the basis of their advice, the university adopted a program to enhance library services by revising the organization and functions of the library and remodeling some of the facilities. The main library building received many improvements, and better library services have been provided.

From 1959 through 1968, more than one hundred American librarians visited Tokyo, some of them for fairly long stays and others very briefly, some of them with specific professional objectives and others just dropping in without any particular professional purpose in mind. Among them have been: John T. Ma (1966), Ernst Wolff (1967), Miwa Kai (1961, 1968), Richard Irwin (1963), Warren M. Tsuneishi (1963), G. R. Nunn (1964), Yukihisa Suzuki (1964, 1967, 1968), Joyce Wright (1965), Hide Ikehara (1965–68), James R. Morita (1966), Masato Matsui

(1966), and Suzuko Ohira (1968). All of these came to Japan to acquire Japanese and other Oriental materials, to gather information about sources for such materials, or to further related purposes. This is one of very few fields in which Japan has made and can make some contributions.

In the same period about a dozen American librarians from such federal agencies as the Library of Congress and the National Agricultural Library came to Japan. They included L. Quincy Mumford (1963), John G. Lorenz (1967), Foster E. Mohrhardt (1963, 1966, 1967), Hisao Matsumoto (1968–), and again Warren M. Tsuneishi (1967).

A list of American professors in library and information science and administrators of academic libraries who visited Japan during the said period includes about forty names. In addition to Metcalf and Bryant and the names on the faculty of the Keiō Library School, the following are worthy of mention: Jack Dalton (1959), R. H. Logsdon (1959), Raynard Swank (1960, 1961), David Heron (1960, 1961), Lawrence Clark Powell (1960, 1966), J. Periam Danton (1960, 1963), Maurice Tauber (1961), Sarah K. Vann (1961, 1963), W. N. Locke (1962), Constance M. Winchell (1962), Earl C. Borgeson (1963), Lester E. Asheim (1963), John R. Russell (1966), Thomas Buckman (1967), Leon Carnovsky (1967), Lowell Martin (1967), William S. Dix (1967), Louis C. Branscomb (1967), Irving Lieberman (1968), Robert M. Hays (1968), Joseph Becker (1968), and again Foster E. Mohrhardt. Some of these came to Japan representing the American Library Association or its divisions. Some visited the Japan Library School to give lectures to the students at its assembly periods and/or attended informal meetings of small groups of university librarians to exchange ideas.

Visits to the United States by Japanese librarians were resumed in 1950. Among those who went in the early 1950s are the following academic librarians:

PERIOD	NAME	INSTITUTION
1950	Hisanosuke Izui	Kyoto University Library
1950–51	Shigehiko Funaki	Ueno Library Training Institute
1950–51	Hideo Karasawa	Keiō University Library
1950–51	Takeo Urata	Tokyo University Library
1951	Masai Watanabe	Niigata Prefectural Library (Juntendo Medical Library)
1951	Hiroshi Yamanaka	Hiroshima University Library
1951–52	Masao Nagata	Niigata University Library
1951–52	Masao Yoshida	National Diet Library (NDL)
1951–52	Yurio Kobayashi	NDL
1952	Narau Okada	NDL
1953	Kojiro Yoshioka	Tohoku University Library

Among the above, Masao Nagata, who audited courses at the University of Chicago Graduate Library School, should be specially cited because he later introduced to Japanese librarians the thoughts of Pierce Butler on librarianship. Takeo Urata, from the Tokyo University Library, was the first after the war to receive formal education for librarianship in an American graduate library school as a full-time student.

To close the 1950s, mention must be made of a very significant project for the interchange of library ideas called the U.S. Field Seminar on Library Reference Services for Japanese Librarians. The project was supported by the Rockefeller Foundation and sponsored by the ALA International Relations Office. A total of nine Japanese librarians were selected and organized into a team. For over a year prior to the actual visit, they studied the literature of American librarianship in general and American ways of reference services, and simultaneously intensified their familiarity with Japanese library circumstances through seminar sessions in Tokyo and in the Kansai (Osaka-Kyoto) area with distinguished consultants and colleagues. After this intensive preparation, the group crossed the Pacific and inspected during a two-month period in 1959 the facilities and services of more than seventy American libraries of various types. They were also the beneficiaries of seven ALA-sponsored field seminars with distinguished specialists in which their findings were reviewed and consolidated.

The group members were so well prepared and organized that they learned much more than other less well-prepared visitors might have done in so short a period. Upon their return to Japan, they imparted their findings to their Japanese colleagues through talks and publications. Among the members of this group, which was led by Naomi Fukuda, were such academic librarians as Toshio Iwasaru (Kyoto University Library), Sumio Gotō (Nihon University Library), Yasumasa Oda and Heihachirō Suzuki (NDL), Haruki Amatsuchi (formerly Japan Science Council Library), and this writer.

In connection with the plans for improvement of the services of Tokyo University Library, not only its director, the late Dr. Kishimoto, but also such staff members as Iyoji Aono, Tadashi Otokozawa, and Reiko Tomono visited the United States to inspect the services of American libraries in 1960. In connection with the establishment of a new medical library at the same university, Takeo Urata and Yoshio Tsuge went to America to inspect American medical library buildings in 1957. For a new development of the university's agricultural library, Toshio Sasaki was dispatched to study library science at Columbia in 1961–62, and Taizō Inokuma and Daitsu Satake were sent in 1962 to investigate American agricultural library services.

An interesting case is that of Keiō University, oldest and most influential of the private universities in the country, which also has been meeting the challenge of library problems. In 1957, six years after the establishment of the Japan Library School in its Faculty of Letters, Keiō's administration finally recognized that better library facilities and services were essential to the proper functioning of the university. Guy R. Lyle and John M. Cory, both then on the faculty of JLS, Raynard C. Swank, then the Director of the International Relations Office of ALA, and other librarians who visited the Keiō campus gave timely and stimulating advice to the administration. In 1960 a special committee was organized to help in the formation of a new program. With a grant from the Rockefeller Foundation and with the cooperation of ALA, a group of administrative officers and librarians toured American universities in the fall of 1963 for observation and consultations.

On his second visit to Japan in 1967–68, Everett T. Moore provided advice which was taken into deep consideration by the administration. A tentative plan drawn up several years previously was re-examined by a long-range planning committee under the chairmanship of Saku Satō, concurrently director of the university libraries, and a definitive report on the fundamentals for the development of new "research and education information systems," including the existing library system, was approved by the administration in 1968. The new program for research information systems is to be put into effect from the fall of 1969. In this consolidation of new ideas, the university owes much directly or indirectly to the advice and suggestions provided by many American librarians and professors.

The Scientific Information Office, predecessor of the Information and Academic Library Section of the Ministry of Education, was successful in obtaining funds in the 1964 budget to send two directors of national university libraries to America and Europe to investigate their university libraries. Ryutaro Kato, Director of Nagoya University Library, and Mutsuo Takahashi, Director of Osaka Gakugei University Library, were the two selected for the project. Provision of such funds to send university library directors and librarians

each year unfortunately has not been realized.

In 1966 Tōhoku University Library sent Osamu Kanaya, its director, and Ryūkichi Harada, Associate Director, to visit U.S. university libraries to study their services and building planning.

Yoshitomi Okazaki, of Hitotsubashi University Library, went to the United States and studied and practiced at Boston University Library and elsewhere in 1967–68 on the Jointly-Sponsored Librarians Program, and Hiroshi Tanabe, of Tokyo University Library, went in 1968 on the Multinational Group Librarians Project. Both programs are sponsored by the State Department.

In the field of medical librarianship, considerable development is apparent. Inspired by the late Dr. Yoshio Kasama, director of the Keiō Medical Library in the early 1950s, Yoshinari Tsuda has made great contributions to the improvement and advance of Japan's medical libraries. He went to the United States first in 1952–53, studying at the University of Illinois Library School and interning in medical librarianship. He completed his library studies at Illinois on his second trip, in 1959–60, and received practical training in indexing at the MEDLARS in 1966. Kazuo Fujii of Osaka University's Nakanoshima Library, which has medical library services, joined Tsuda for observation of American medical librarianship in 1960.

In addition to these two medical library leaders in Japan, quite a few other medical librarians have studied in the United States. They include Tetsurō Sakamoto, Osaka University, who studied at Western Reserve University Library School (1960–61); Takao Fukudome, Keiō Medical Library, who studied at Columbia University Library School (1963–65); and Yasuhiro Tokumura, Osaka University, who studied at Peabody Library School (1963–65). For medical library internship or trainee programs, Takashige Satō, of Kyūshū University Medical School Library, went to the United States in 1963; Yoshio Shibuya of Kōbe Medical School Library, in 1966; Kōji Nagao of Tōhoku University Medical School, in 1966; Tamiko Matsumura of

Keiō, Medical Library (special internship in indexing and searching at the MEDLARS, National Library of Medicine) in 1967–68; Kōji Nagao of Tohoku University Medical Library, in 1968; and Keinosuke Imamura of Tokyo University Medical Center Library, in 1968–69. At present, Keiō Medical Library is contributing to the MEDLARS program by providing input information on Japanese medical articles and other matters.

In the field of agricultural librarianship, Keiichirō Harada, formerly a member of the Ministry of Agriculture and Forestry Library, was the first to be formally trained in an American library school and in the USDA Library. He is now contributing at the FAO Library. Toshio Sasaki, previously mentioned in the paragraph on the Tokyo University Agricultural Library; Tamotsu Itō, Information Specialist at the National Institute of Animal Health; Akio Satō, of the Ministry of Agriculture and Forestry Library; Etsuko Takeyoshi, bibliographer of the Tokyo office of the International Rice Research Institute; Yutaka Kobayashi, of the Japan Information Center of Science and Technology, and I attended the third conference of IAALD held in Washington, D.C., in 1965. On our way back home, we visited American agricultural libraries. Japanese librarians concerned with agricultural sciences are willing to work toward the development of an international cooperative project comparable to that found in medical librarianship, but it may take a little more time for qualified librarians to be numerous enough in Japanese agricultural libraries to permit meaningful international contributions.

Keeping in mind the possibility of establishing a new library school, the development of professional library education programs, and similar matters, Tōru Miyaji, Director of Osaka University Libraries, together with Akira Tabohashi, University Library Specialist in the Information and (Academic) Libraries Section, Ministry of Education, made a trip in 1967 to observe American library schools and to discuss problems in education for librarianship with deans and faculty members.

If there is to be expansion of education for librarianship, the supply of qualified instructors must be increased, and this can be done in part by singling out promising young faculty candidates who will complete degree programs in American schools of library and information science. Keiō is extremely fortunate in having its library school staffed by such faculty members as Masanobu Fujikawa and Masao Nagasawa, both with degrees from Peabody, and Shigeo Watanabe and Toshio Hamada, with degrees from Western Reserve.

Since the 1950s, increasing numbers of graduates of Keiō Library School have been going to the United States to further their studies in librarianship. More than 50 of its almost 750 graduates have gone in the past 15 years, and about 30 of these 50 have entered American graduate library schools and completed their degree programs. Among the library schools attended are those at Columbia University, Drexel Institute, Rutgers University, Simmons College, Syracuse University, Florida State University, George Peabody College, University of Chicago, Rosary College, University of Illinois, University of Michigan, Western Michigan University, Western Reserve University, University of California at Berkeley, UCLA, University of Denver, University of Washington in Seattle, and the University of Hawaii. The majority of these graduates of the Keiō Library School are currently working in university libraries and scientific and technological libraries.

To close this section on Japanese-American exchanges, it is appropriate to invite attention to an interesting cooperative program, called the "internship program," which was inaugurated between the University of Maryland and Keiō Library School in 1965. According to the provisions of the agreement, the Japanese trainee for this library internship is to be selected from among candidates who possess such qualifications as: (1) a bachelor's degree in library science, (2) competence in English, (3) some familiarity with cataloging and classifying Japanese materials, and (4) an interest in helping an American university organize and catalog its Japanese collection. Most of the trainee's time is to be spent on a Japan-related project in the library of the University of Maryland. The trainee will also be encouraged to enroll in two courses per semester in the university's library school, but the internship does not include transportation. One of the major responsibilities of Keiō Library School is to select candidates appropriate to the project and to recommend them to the administration of the University of Maryland Library. Despite initial difficulties, we are pushing ahead with confidence that the program already has brought benefits to both the University of Maryland Library and Japanese librarianship. The third trainee, Shigeru Morisono, of the Keiō Main University Library, is now at the University of Maryland Library.

In the above account, the roles played by some distinguished Japanese librarians may have been unintentionally overlooked. The emphasis has been on showing that many people in the Japanese library world have been to the United States to study librarianship professionally, to engage in actual library services, in some cases to help American libraries develop their Japanese-language collections, to contribute to international projects, and so forth. What the facts demonstrate, however, is that American contributions have predominated over contributions from Japan. That there have been some Japanese contributions and that there are possibilities of others constitute a source of gratification.

Past Trends and Current Problems and Needs

Before the war the academic community in Japan was more closely associated with its European counterparts than with the American. Accordingly, not many librarians visited the United States. As Japan-related studies in the United States were in their infancy, the need for Japanese library materials was not very great. A few Japanese trained in librarianship in the United States, however, remained there to develop and process Japanese materials in the Library of Congress. Otherwise, such interchange as existed came from the American side.

Dependence on the United States continued for a time after the resumption of personnel interchange between the two countries following the war. That it has lessened may be seen in connection with one of the most significant developments in the postwar Japanese library world, the establishment of a professional library school at Keiō in 1951. The school initially depended entirely on American faculty members, but it soon began to move toward and has now achieved self-sufficiency, imperfect though it may be as yet.

Other significant developments in Japanese librarianship were the establishment of the National Diet Library in 1948 and of the Japan Information Center of Science and Technology in 1957, both of which have been providing useful tools and information not only to Japanese but also to American libraries. Some of their librarians, who were trainees in American university libraries as well as in the Library of Congress, were found to be able to render substantial assistance to collections of Japanese language materials.

Still another change in Japan, although slow, has been the awakening of Japanese university librarians to service-centered librarianship. The American ideal of good services to library users was most quickly comprehended by special librarians in Japan, but it is now permeating university libraries. In other words, although it has taken time, university libraries now are more likely to accept the American service concept than they were in past years.

On the American side of the picture, the scholarly concern with Japanese culture has greatly increased. Research efforts have substantially deepened and widened in range. Accordingly, scholarly demands for materials about Japan and her culture have expanded tremendously and have forced, and are still forcing, the librarians associated with Japanese collections to work harder and harder. The shortage in qualified personnel in Japan-related collections in the United States must now be quite serious.

Recent rapid developments in information services in the fields of science and technology, not only in America but also in Japan, also affect relations between the libraries and librarians of both countries. A special cooperative project has started in medical librarianship. To fulfill our share of work in this project, we soon realized that it was imperative to prepare highly professional manpower.

Yet another pertinent trend is the change in the attitudes of the United States government and of American foundations toward assistance to Japan. Many of the Japanese librarians who have visited the United States in recent years for observation and study have been enabled to do so with grants from the State Department or from such private American sources as the Rockefeller, Ford, and Asia Foundations and the China Medical Board. There is now a distinct tendency for such grants from American resources to diminish. Since there are few Japanese foundations interested in supporting library personnel exchange programs, and since the Ministry of Education has failed to prevail on the Ministry of Finance to grant its budgetary requests for funds to cover foreign travel expenses for university librarians, what was once a broad highway has now narrowed to a small path.

In addition to the above trends, a new achievement in library mechanization adopted by the Japan Information Center of Science and Technology should be mentioned. In JICST's computerized system, regular Japanese texts using 1,861 *kanji* (Chinese) characters and 158 *kana* (Japanese syllabary) symbols can be handled in machine-readable form. The system can cope with a total of 3,000 characters, including, in addition to Japanese *kana* and *kanji*, the roman, Russian, and Greek alphabets, as well as Arabic and roman numerals and some symbols. In connection with the MARC project of the Library of Congress and the shared cataloging program of the Library, this ingenious development in Japan has a tremendous potential. Further details of this are presented by one of my colleagues in another paper.

It has been very often said that what is good in one country may not necessarily be good in another country of a different culture. This may be true, or it may not. When the matter under discussion is related to Japanese studies, it seems more than likely to be true. When the matter has to do with science and technology, it seems less likely to be so.

First of all, the language difference between the countries causes a variety of problems. Japanese library trainees and students in library science must have competence in English if they are to acquire the principles and techniques of American librarianship. This is absolutely essential for Japanese studying library and information science in America. Most of the American librarians and library teachers who have visited Japan, on the other hand, have not had much understanding of written or spoken Japanese. Had they been competent in Japanese, they would have acquired more from Japan and could have been more helpful and effective in advising Japanese librarians. From time to time we receive inquiries from American library school graduates on the possibilities of their placement in Japanese libraries. Even in cases where we must acknowledge that their qualifications and experience in librarianship are more than satisfactory by American standards, a Japanese library administration would hesitate to place them in its library because of the language problem. Since most Japanese libraries cannot afford to provide interpreters to be constantly at the side of American librarians who have no Japanese language ability, the problem would seem to be insurmountable. It must be even greater, however, for Japanese library trainees or librarians in America because interpreters for them are not likely to be available.

Since the need for the help of Japanese scholars and Japanese librarians has become greater in American academic libraries, we often receive inquiries from them for Japanese librarians or library trainees. It is rather difficult to find a person who has a broad knowledge of Japanese culture and the materials concerned and who at the same time is competent enough in English to serve satisfactorily. Generally speaking, it is easier to find a person competent in English among those Japanese librarians who are interested in Western civilization. In a library trainee exchange program, at the stage when we find a candidate librarian qualified in terms of intellect, skills in librarianship, subject matter in a broad sense, and language, we often meet procedural difficulties. Usually American institutions require such a library trainee to stay with them at least two years, while the average Japanese library to which the candidate librarian belongs is not willing to grant leave for so long a period. If the statement in the initial contract says "at least one year or longer," the administration of a Japanese academic library would take the matter into consideration. There is less likelihood of assent if the statement requires two years from the beginning.

The training of instructors in library and information science has been an urgent need in both countries. In Japan very few instructors are qualified in terms of professional training. A systematic exchange program must be organized for the training of teachers, with special provision for those in information science. An acute decrease of grants in recent years has created difficult barriers to the sending to the United States of candidates for teaching positions in this profession in Japan. The training of Japanese university librarians and departmental librarians in American university libraries and departmental libraries has been proved to be valuable, but this has also been cut back because of diminishing funds.

For the training of professional librarians and library and information science teachers, individual exchange programs must be drawn up most carefully. In this area American librarians and teachers will play a most important role. At one time it was possible for a team of American library science instructors to visit Japan and to teach Japanese students, as in the early stages of the Keiō Library School. Although this had a great influence on Japanese librarianship, there can be no repetition of such an experience because of the large amount of money needed. Hereafter, individual visits of American professors in library science and information science under the Fulbright program would seem to be as much as can be expected. Although it is very difficult to plan such a professor's visit three years ahead according to the procedures of the Fulbright Educational Commission, at present there is no easier way. To train young Japanese librarians and teacher candidates, the Fulbright grants also offer the best available opportunities.

In the fields of science and technology, more cooperative programs between the two countries are needed. In the medical disciplines, we need more Japanese medical librarians properly trained in handling the information in Japanese medical literature, so that we can send more and better input information to MEDLARS. In the agricultural sciences, Japan has ranked fourth in the world in the volume of agricultural literature produced and second in the volume of literature concerning fisheries. As her agricultural library manpower is in very short supply, however, we need first to recruit and educate capable agricultural librarians in Japan and then to arrange for training of the best of them in the United States, so that we can contribute to the world's agricultural information systems. In the fields of the physical sciences and technology, some achievements have been made by the establishment of JICST. Although this is rather well supported by industry, more funds should be provided by the government to expand its services to scholarly users. Training of its information personnel is still an urgent need.

The fact that so many characters are used in Japanese-language texts has created a fundamental problem for information specialists in mechanizing the processing of recorded materials in Japanese. Although it is still in an experimental stage, the new computer system adopted at JICST using a *kanji* teletypewriter and a *kanji* teleprinter as input and output devices has shown great potentialities for use by large

American academic libraries that possess Japanese materials. There are still many problems in this system to be solved, and the close cooperation of librarians and information specialists of both countries is required to meet the developing needs of these who seek information in Japanese materials.

Future Prospects

In the course of setting forth major problems and needs in the foregoing section, we inevitably suggested certain prospects. In this section, only those prospects or needs which are considered most important will be discussed.

Through our experiences before and since the war, we have learned beyond question that library personnel exchanges are very important and useful in the development of library collections and services for academic users in both countries. In general, however, the exchange has been one-sided—that is, the main flow has been from America to Japan. Nevertheless, despite many past and current obstacles and problems, we have had a great number of exchanges of persons concerned with the development of academic library and information services.

In the coming years we should continue to have exchanges of persons for the future development of academic library services, but in all probability the number of such exchanges will be reduced, mainly by the limitation of available funds. It is, therefore, necessary to select individuals for exchange programs from the standpoint of maximum effectiveness.

When a visit for observation of achievements in either country is believed desirable, it would be helpful to organize a team consisting of different specialists, such as experts in librarianship and information services, professors in subject fields, and administrative officers of universities and academic libraries. The effectiveness of a visit by a team consisting of various types of librarians who have prepared themselves for their objectives before the actual visit has been proved, as we saw in the case of the U.S. Field Seminar on Library Refer-

ence Services for Japanese Librarians. It is true that four eyes see more than two. Although it is a very hard task to organize different types of people into a team and have them prepare themselves before the event, the effects of such a well-prepared program will be worth the effort. One caution in connection with the selection of members is that it is not always necessary to include a professor-librarian of a university library who is about to retire.

There will continue to be a need for interchange of individuals. Since American sources of financial aid for Japanese have been reduced, our young candidate students who want to study in the United States will have to face very keen competition for grants. At the present time, the Fulbright grants are the most popular among university graduates. Usually, however, it is very difficult for a young librarian who has been engaged in practical library work and who has been away from English studies for some years to obtain such a grant. Thus an arrangement such as that with the University of Maryland, for which the Keiō Library School has been serving as a liaison office and a recommendation agency for Japanese candidates, must be recognized as being very useful for both sides. If the conditions are satisfactory, such arrangements will contribute to meeting the needs of both American university libraries and young Japanese librarians.

The distinctive exchange contract in the field of medical sciences, which has been made between MEDLARS, NLM, and Keiō Medical Library, will continue, and it is certain to be expanded since both sides are finding the results very useful. In the field of agricultural librarianship, there is the possibility that a similar contract can be concluded between NAL and the Japanese Government, which plans to establish a national central agricultural library. However, it may take time to materialize. Needed is a preparatory period of some years during which the knowledge and skills of Japanese agricultural librarians and documentalists can be raised to meet the highest international standards.

Physical sciences librarianship in Japanese universities is still in an embryonic stage. The Japan Information Center of Science and Technology, however, has forged far ahead to meet the information needs of Japanese industry. It has developed a mechanized system to process information expressed in Japanese. This technological advance is one of the few achievements we have to offer to the United States, and it will in the future have a tremendous impact on research libraries there, since it permits the handling of Japanese materials not only in science and technology but also in other fields.

The Council for Science and Technology, organized in 1958, is now keenly interested in national policies on the development of national science information systems. Subcommittees of the Council were organized in early 1969 to work on drafts for a national plan. At this moment we need very much to study and observe American achievements. Along this line, more Japanese scientists and information specialists are certain to go to the United States to inspect the national information network for science and technology.

To conclude, Japanese specialists still will need to study American librarianship and information science in a substantial way, and especially is this so in information services for scientists and technologists. Because of the diminishing funds allocated to Japan by American private foundations, however, the number of library personnel exchanges must be reduced. Under governmental and industrial support, however, visits to the United States by Japanese scientists and information specialists may increase. In any case, individuals and missions must be both wisely selected and well prepared for effective exchanges. Work-study exchanges of librarians will be most useful if arranged in close cooperation between American and Japanese institutions.

Part 8

NATIONAL BIBLIOGRAPHIC CONTROLS

National Bibliographic Controls and Requirements for Automated Bibliographic Output

John G. Lorenz
Deputy Librarian of Congress,
Library of Congress

All large-scale enterprises, certainly all national enterprises, depend for their success on a widespread acceptance of standards. We are all familiar with the necessity for standardization in the engineering and technological fields. Effective mechanical, electrical, or electronic devices, with all their multitudes of component parts and with all the complexities of the interaction of these parts, would be impossible without standardization of measures, whether they be measures of distance, measures of power, measures of wave lengths, or whatever. A national system of railroads would be impossible without a standard gauge for the tracks on which they run, without stan-

dard coupling devices for the cars, without precisely defined scheduling, and without standard signals controlling the switching of the trains. In the communications field we could have no national and international telephone system without the standardization of an immense array of items of equipment, circuits, and switching devices, and of area, exchange, and patron codes. Radio and television broadcast and reception likewise would be utterly impossible without agreement on an almost incredible variety of technical details.

The need for standardization in the field of the information sciences, bibliography, and library work may not be as immediately obvious as it is in the technological fields, but it is fundamental nonetheless. Here we are concerned with communication between human beings, and not only with the technical means of communication but with the substance of the communication itself—sometimes even with its significance and meaning. If we are to communicate information to one another, we must have a language of communication. We must agree on terminology. We must have standard ways of identifying and describing the items that form the substance of our communication. We must agree on what details are important and what are not. We must develop systems for providing access to bibliographic units according to their informational content and for grouping like items together and in juxtaposition with items that are closely related. Having done all this, we need to standardize the techniques by which we communicate this array of organized information to the electronic maze of the computer for storage, for manipulation, for print-out, and for retrieval in response to the varied needs of users of the information.

I will begin my survey of bibliographic controls in the United States by tracing the development of national bibliographic standards, after which I will describe our work in developing standard formats for converting bibliographic information to machine-readable form for national and international dissemination, thus enabling all who have access to computers to use their powerful resources for producing information needed for all sorts of special requirements.

One of the first developments, both chronologically and in order of importance, was the gradual formulation over many years of standards for bibliographic description, i.e., of rules for cataloging. The rules which are now followed by Anglo-American libraries in their descriptive cataloging are easily traced to Charles A. Cutter's *Rules for a Dictionary Catalogue,* first published in 1876 as Part II of the U.S. Bureau of Education's special report on *Public Libraries in the United States of America.* Rules in force at the Library of Congress prior to that date were followed until the end of 1899, when the card catalog that had been begun in 1865 was discontinued. This catalog consisted of cards bearing manuscript entries and mounted clippings from the earlier catalogs that were printed in book form. In July 1898 entries for books received by copyright were first printed, and a new catalog on standard-size cards (7½ x 12½ cm) was started. For this work the rules adopted were those of Cutter, with a few emendations from the ALA catalog rules of 1883. At first the catalogers merely annotated

interleaved editions of the printed rules as particular rules were interpreted or expanded in use. When this method became unsatisfactory, the assistants made manuscript card copies of all rules and instructions issued to them. These rules were arranged alphabetically according to catchword headings, which provided a form convenient for reference; their use influenced the later decision to issue all the rules in this form.

The printing and distribution of catalog cards immediately aroused more than academic interest on the part of other librarians in the Library of Congress rules and practices, an interest that led to printing in similar fashion and distribution of the LC supplementary rules. These were printed on standard-size cards in three series: "Numbered rules," "Dated rules" (intended primarily for the use of LC catalogers in that most of them related to cataloging routines), and "Provisional rules," which were either temporary in nature or of purely local interest and application, but which were sold in the same manner as the other rules. It was planned to publish the supplementary rules in pamphlet form also from time to time, but only one such publication was issued, the fourteen page "Supplementary Rules on Cataloging 1–11," which included the eleven rules issued on cards between 20 April 1903 and 26 January 1905. Card rules continued to be printed, as expediency dictated, until the early 1930s.

Interest in cooperative and centralized cataloging led to the appointment in 1900 of a committee of the American Library Association to formulate standard cataloging rules which would be in accord with the LC system. The chairman of the committee was J. C. M. Hanson, Chief of the Catalog Division of the Library of Congress, who by his position was particularly well qualified for the assignment and who was willing to make many concessions in the LC practice so that it would conform to the requirements of the ALA code. The advance edition of the *ALA Catalog Rules* was printed by LC in 1902; the final edition —delayed in the interests of a joint code of rules representing the (British) Library

Association as well as the American Library Association—was printed by the American Library Association and by the Library Association in 1908. In this publication a few of the LC supplementary rules were adopted with but slight modifications as standard rules; others were included but specified as LC supplementary rules. Thus the variations from the rules recommended as standard practice were apparent.

During the thirty-three years which elapsed between the publication of the *ALA Catalog Rules* in 1908 and its preliminary American second edition in 1941, there was continuous advancement in the standardization of cataloging, furthered by the increasing use of LC printed cards. American libraries revised their catalogs extensively, frequently at great cost, to incorporate these printed cards easily. It followed that cards prepared in individual libraries for purely local use also tended to observe LC practices with such modifications as the local situation might prescribe. In the absence of any supplementary rules from ALA between 1908 and 1941, libraries had to formulate their own rules, relying for guidance chiefly on the rules issued occasionally by LC and on such deductions relating to LC practice as could be made by using the printed cards as examples.

In 1930 the ALA Committee on Cataloging and Classification, in response to an inquiry from the Association regarding needed publications in the field of cataloging, suggested, among other projects, a revised code of cataloging rules as being of first importance. A subcommittee, the Catalog Code Revision Committee, with Charles Martel of LC as chairman, was appointed to begin work on a revision. This subcommittee was made an independent committee of the Association in 1932 "to make necessary revisions in the ALA Catalog Rules with authority to cooperate with the Library Association of Great Britain and with such other national library associations as it might think appropriate."

From the evidence before the committee, it soon became apparent that dissatisfaction with the 1908 code rested not with its inclusions but rather with its omissions.

The basic rules were on the whole satisfactory but did not meet the needs of the cataloger in the large scholarly or specialized collection.

In the meantime cooperative cataloging activities had experienced considerable growth under an ALA committee. As a consequence, a larger number of libraries became involved in the work of supplying copy for printing and distribution by LC, and the amount of copy provided by libraries previously cooperating was greatly increased. This created an urgent demand from such libraries for rules which would answer the many questions arising in the preparation of this copy. Much time was lost by individual catalogers seeking precedents in the files of printed cards, and, if this source failed, engaging in complicated correspondence with cooperating cataloging headquarters at LC. Hence, ALA decided that the new edition should attempt to cover all the needs which had been expressed by librarians throughout the country by providing new rules and extensive interpretations and examples of the application of the earlier rules.

The preliminary American second edition, published in 1941, expanded the rules of 1908 to make more provision for special classes of material, e.g., serial publications, government documents, publications of religious bodies, anonymous classics, music, and maps; to amplify existing rules to cover specific cases of frequent occurrence; and to provide better examples and more adequate definitions. It was divided into two parts: Part I. Entry and heading; Part II. Description of book. The second part did not represent LC practice in all respects and did not show where variations occurred. It also failed to provide, as the 1908 rules had provided, for alternatives in those cases where the LC rules resulted in more elaborate cataloging than that practiced by most of the other research libraries in the United States.

This failure, as well as the more elaborate statements of the previous brief rules, caused severe criticism of the preliminary American second edition from administrators who anticipated that more detailed and expensive cataloging would come to be accepted as standard practice. A special committee was appointed by ALA to consider the matter before a definitive edition would be authorized. This committee, sensitive to the importance of standardization of cataloging rules and the unique position of LC as a standardizing agent because of its distribution of printed cards, and aware of the eagerness of LC itself to adopt rules which would simplify its catalog entries, divided its recommendations into two parts, corresponding to the two parts of the edition under consideration. Part I was found generally satisfactory both to the Library of Congress and to other libraries. The committee urged, therefore, that the definitive second edition of this part be published as soon as possible.

Lack of funds delayed the project, but in 1946 a new editor, Clara Beetle, was appointed by the ALA Division of Cataloging and Classification. Having been granted a leave of absence from LC, she began the editorial revision of Part I. It was published in 1949 as *ALA Cataloging Rules for Author and Title Entries*. The chief changes from the preliminary edition were: a rearrangement of the material to emphasize the basic rules and subordinate their amplifications and to make the sequence of rules logical so far as possible; reduction of the number of alternative rules; omission of rules of description; rewording to avoid repetition or to make the meaning clearer; and revision, where possible, of rules inconsistent with the general principles.

Part II was considered in the light of the fact that LC had announced its intention to issue its own rules for description. The ALA committee recommended that the decision to publish a definitive edition of this part be deferred until it could be seen whether the LC rules could be accepted to represent standard practice and thus obviate a separate code.

The rules of descriptive cataloging previously recorded at LC were not limited to the supplementary rules on cards. LC also had published two guides prepared by members of its staff. *A Guide to the Cataloguing of Periodicals,* prepared by Mary W. McNair, was published in 1918

and in two subsequent editions, the latest in 1925. In 1919 Harriet W. Pierson compiled and edited a *Guide to the Cataloguing of the Serial Publications of Societies and Institutions* (2d ed. 1931). These two pamphlets presented the basic ALA rules for the cataloging of serials, together with amplifications and examples, and included matters of procedure for the handling of such material at LC.

Precedents in cataloging served to supplement the printed rules. Assistants in the Catalog Division studied proof sheets of the printed cards to select sample cards for incorporation in their files of card rules. These served both revisers and catalogers as guides to problems which were new to them. To these files were also added decisions as circulated within the Division and informal interpretations of the rules by various revisers. These rules were disseminated solely through correspondence and only in reply to inquiries as to rules and practice. The unreliability of this unsystematic manner of developing and disseminating rules was realized most keenly when the cooperative cataloging program was expanded in the 1930s under the auspices of the ALA Cooperative Cataloging Committee. Other librarians, when attempting to follow the cataloging practice of LC, found that they did not know the LC rules and that the precedents revealed by printed cards were likely to justify considerable variations.

Rules and practice developed and recorded in this fashion tend to grow away from the principles on which they are based. Rules on cards, by their physical limitations, do not permit sufficient explanation of their underlying reasons and do not correlate the various rules that are based on one governing principle. LC decided, therefore, that the whole body of rules needed to be re-examined and presented in a systematic, rather than an alphabetic, order. This re-examination was carried on for several years, and an attempt was made to learn the needs of other libraries for certain types of catalog data. The almost unanimous opinion voiced in numerous discussions, conferences, and replies to questionnaires was that less bibliographic detail than LC had been including in its catalog entries would satisfy the needs of most American libraries, and that most of them would welcome almost any simplification that LC could afford to make.

This expression of opinion led to the publication in 1946 of a report to the Librarian of Congress by the then Director of the Processing Department, Herman H. Henkle, which presented a statement of the functions of descriptive cataloging and the principles which should underlie a code of rules to carry out these functions. The Librarian, Luther H. Evans, eager to learn whether the proposals contained in the report would be likely to meet not only the needs of LC but those of other libraries, and following a recommendation in Mr. Henkle's report, appointed a committee of representatives of LC and of the profession at large to advise him on questions and differences of opinion to be resolved. The committee's report was issued and approved by the Librarian of Congress in the fall of 1946. The chief of the Descriptive Cataloging Division was directed to draft a code of descriptive cataloging rules in accordance with the committee's recommendations, with the stipulation that the draft be submitted to the LC staff and the library profession generally for criticism. The preliminary edition of the rules was published in 1947.

Studies and criticism of the rules were invited, and individuals and groups of catalogers responded. To summarize and crystallize opinion, LC submitted the rules to ALA as a substitute for Part II of the *ALA Catalog Rules*. The ALA Committee on Descriptive Cataloging suggested some specific changes, and these were made as far as they were feasible. ALA then accepted the rules as the proposed substitute, and they were issued in 1949 as *Rules for Descriptive Cataloging in the Library of Congress (Adopted by the American Library Association)*.

The success of these simpler rules for description led to a demand for an equal simplification of rules for author and title entry. After a preliminary study by Seymour Lubetzky, then a member of the staff

of LC, the ALA Division of Cataloging and Classification resolved to attempt a revision along such lines. Mr. Lubetzky was appointed editor in 1956 and served until 1962, when he resigned and was succeeded by C. Sumner Spalding, also of LC.

The International Conference on Cataloguing Principles, held in Paris in 1961 with the encouragement and support of the Council on Library Resources, marked a major accomplishment in international cooperation in the field of cataloging and bibliography. Its discussions were based on a "Statement of Principles" that had been drafted by A. H. Chaplin along lines closely parallel to the draft rules prepared by Seymour Lubetzky for the ALA Catalog Code Revision Committee. There was very substantial agreement among the representatives of the various countries, including Japan, on the proper rules for making entries in catalogs and bibliographies. The cataloging principles agreed to at this international conference were closely examined by the Catalog Code Revision Committee in the United States and were adopted, with limited modifications, as the basis for further work on the code.

Although the rules for description had been thoroughly revised in 1949, it was found advisable to subject them again to scrutiny. The revision of these rules was worked out by LC in collaboration with ALA. Rules for the treatment of special classes of materials, such as manuscripts, maps, and music, which had been issued from time to time by LC, were also revised and included.

From the earliest stages of the revisions of the rules, arrangements were made to coordinate the work of the American committee with that of the Cataloguing Rules Sub-Committee of the (British) Library Association, resulting in an exchange of drafts of rules, working papers, and minutes of discussions. The Canadian Library Association was also an active participant in the rules through its Special Committee on Revision of the ALA Catalog Code, which studied and criticized each draft of the rules. Although agreement between the three groups was not complete, it was close enough to justify entitling the resulting code *Anglo-American Cataloging Rules.* Other library associations throughout the world were also kept informed of the progress of the work through a distribution of the drafts as they were prepared.

The publication in 1967 of the *Anglo-American Cataloging Rules,* under the joint auspices of the American Library Association, the Library of Congress, the (British) Library Association, and the Canadian Library Association, thus brought to an end, at least for a time, many years of effort toward developing practical and uniform standards for bibliographic description. It satisfied one of the prime requirements or preconditions for automating bibliographic controls on a national or international scale.

A second requirement was the development of subject controls. Here again Charles A. Cutter was the founding father. His rules for subject headings, contained in the 1876 *Rules for a Printed Dictionary Catalogue,* met with wide and almost unquestioned acceptance. They formed the basis for the *ALA List of Subject Headings for Use in Dictionary Catalogues,* which ALA published in 1895. This list was intended for use in small and medium-sized libraries, but when LC began work in 1898 on its present card catalog, it realized that it would be in the best interests of all concerned if it adopted the ALA list as the core of its own system of subject headings, with, of course, considerable expansion and modification.

At first interleaved copies of the ALA list were placed in the Catalog Division and subject headings newly established by LC were entered on the blank leaves. When this system began to break down, it was decided to publish a list of all the headings currently in use and, at regular intervals, cumulative lists of additions and changes. This pattern has continued to the present day.

The printing of the first edition of the LC subject heading list was begun in 1909 and completed in 1914. The second edition followed in 1919 and the third in 1928. These early editions included class numbers for many of the headings and contained *see* and *see also* references. They lacked, however, the "refer from" tracers, then available only at LC in manuscript or typewritten form. By 1935 some 40,000 of these tracers had accumulated, and ALA pressed for their inclusion in the next edition. In accordance with this expressed need, the fourth edition appeared in 1943 in two volumes, the second a separate list of the "refer from" tracers.

The fifth edition (1948) introduced a change of format and type size, use of symbols for references, and other stylistic changes. The sixth edition (1957) was redesigned to make it possible to produce the seventh edition by merging linotype slugs from the supplements with the standing type of the sixth edition. In the meantime, however, developments in computer and photocomposition technology offered the prospect of even greater advantages.

After experimentation had demonstrated the feasibility of the method, keyboard operators punched a paper tape which contained, for each line, its text and its format code, that is, bold face, italics, indentions, and the like. This paper tape also contained the symbols which would activate a photocomposing machine when intermixed format and type fonts were required in the body of single lines. Conversion of the paper tape to magnetic tape provided for handling of the data by a computer. Initially the computer assigned a locator number to each line, and the file was then listed out on a chain printer. After proofreading was completed, a correction routine repeated the previous steps for necessary changes and additions to produce an updated tape. The updated tape was processed by a computer which composed the text and added control information, resulting in a new magnetic tape which, after conversion to a 15-level paper tape, activated the photocomposing machine. The columns emanating from the photocomposer were mounted as pages, photographed, and printed by photo-offset. The seventh edition of the list of subject headings was published in 1966, and a completely edited tape of its 1,440 pages is now available in MARC II format in both 7- and 9-level tape. Supplements have been produced by the same computer-photocomposition techniques used for the seventh edition.

There were several reasons why automated printing techniques were chosen to publish the LC subject heading list. First of all, it is desirable to reduce the span of time between editions of the basic list and the number of supplements which users must consult between editions. With the text of the list on tape in error-free, machine-readable form, rekeyboarding of the text and reproofreading for typographical errors are largely eliminated. Preparation of copy for the eighth edition will, in effect, be accomplished at the time the copy for the supplements is sent to the printer. Therefore, the time span between the cutoff date for inclusion of new headings and publication of the next edition of the list can be narrowed to the time necessary for the press work.

Another advantage is that the potentialities inherent in the tape can be made available to others through the purchase of copies. This will create new opportunities for experimentation in computerized applications outside LC. Some librarians may wish to manipulate the tape by computer programs to produce cards specifically designed for their individual files. With proper coding of the magnetic tape record, subject heading lists in special fields of knowledge could also be extracted.

A final advantage is that of facilitating analysis and improvement of the list. If, for example, the tape for the subject heading list were coded by subject field and if plans for converting the classification schedules to machine-readable form materialize, very fruitful possibilities will open up for correlating more closely the two subject retrieval instruments, both terminologically and structurally.

The third, and last, of the requirements for bibliographic control on a national or international basis was the development of a standard system of classification. Of the many systems now in use I shall discuss only two, that of LC itself and the Dewey Decimal Classification, which originated elsewhere but is now being developed and applied by LC.

When LC was founded in 1800, its 964 volumes and 9 maps were arranged solely by size, with folios, quartos, octavos, and duodecimos in separate groups. This system remained in vogue until 1812, when the Library owned 3,076 volumes and 53 maps. In 1814 the Capitol, which housed the Library of Congress, was burned and the collection was almost completely destroyed. In 1815 the library of Thomas Jefferson was purchased by the Congress, and the classification used by Jefferson was adopted. This was an adaptation of Francis Bacon's well-known scheme for the classification of knowledge and called for the arrangement of the books into forty-four groups. The classification thus inaugurated was retained with some changes and many additions until 1897.

In that year the Catalog Division initiated a new system of classification and began the task of evolving both notation and schedules. The question of whether to adopt an existing scheme or to work out a new one was carefully considered, with the result that it was decided to make use of the best features in existing classifications and to construct from them a classification broader than any then in print. This was probably an inevitable decision. No classification system in general use at that time could have been successfully used to organize the more than 2 million books and pamphlets then contained in the collections, and LC benefited greatly from having a classification tailored to its particular needs. The LC scheme was based on the principles and in part on the notation of Charles A. Cutter's Expansive Classification, but many features of the Brunet, Dewey Decimal, and Brussels schemes, as well as others, were introduced. The first schedule, "Z, Bibliography and Library Science," was in manuscript in 1898, and by 1910 almost all the schedules had been completed, though schedules for various parts of "P, Language and Literature," were not printed until 1928, and the last major schedule, "K, Law," is only now being developed.

The classification structure thus evolved covers in elaborate detail the whole range of knowledge as represented in books. It is a flexible system, allowing for subdivision by a variety of means, even within its already minute classes. It employs decimal and alphabetic methods of notation wherever suitable and is capable of indefinite expansion. It is also a practical scheme, having been developed out of attachment neither to a theoretical concept of the organization of knowledge nor to a particular notational device but rather out of the actual process of organizing a collection of books. Though conceived by J. C. M. Hanson, its development was primarily the work of Charles Martel, chief classifier under Hanson and his successor as chief of the Catalog Division. The intrinsic advantages of the system and the availability on LC catalog cards of classifications made under it have resulted in its use by many other libraries in a number of countries.

The Dewey Decimal Classification, which applies to the organization of materials or of ideas the simple mechanism of the decimal system of numerical notation, is the nearest approach to a"universal" system for classifying materials. In the United States it is the system followed by perhaps 90 percent of all libraries, including nearly all public and school libraries. In other English-speaking countries and in countries now or formerly part of the British Commonwealth it is followed by a majority of libraries. Elsewhere it has adherents in almost every nation of the globe. It has been translated, with or without abridgment, expansion, or adaptation, into scores of languages, from Spanish, Danish, and Turkish to Japanese, Sinhalese, and Portuguese. In Europe it has been adapted and expanded under the name of the Universal Decimal Classification. Japan has developed its own adaptation, entitled the Nippon Decimal Classification. It is also used for filing systems in business and has many other applications.

The Decimal Classification was devised for the Amherst College Library by Melvil Dewey in 1873 while he was a student at that institution. It first appeared, anonymously, in 1876 as *A Classification and Subject Index for Cataloguing and Arranging Books and Pamphlets of a Library.* The second edition appeared in 1885, carrying Dewey's name and the title *Decimal Classification and Relativ Index.* Before Dewey's death in 1931, a total of twelve editions had been published. At his death, Dewey left the *Decimal Classification* copyright to the Lake Placid Club Education Foundation, a nonprofit organization that he had founded at Lake Placid, New York, to be used in the interest of library and other work. To date, seventeen full editions and nine abridgments have been published by the Forest Press of the Lake Placid Club Education Foundation.

In 1927, in anticipation of an arrangement for the assignment and printing of Dewey Decimal numbers on LC catalog cards, the editorial office of the classification was moved to Washington and given space in LC, to keep the work of editing and the work of application as close together as possible. The arrangement became a reality in 1930, when ALA established in the Library the ALA Office for DC Numbers on LC Cards. This office was so successful that in 1933 LC took over the work and has continued it ever since as a self-supporting activity, a part of its card-distribution service. In 1953 LC, under a contractual arrangement with the Forest Press, undertook the preparation of the sixteenth and subsequent editions of the classification and, for this purpose, took over the staff and files of the editorial office. Though carried on for a time in separate offices, the editorial activity and the assignment of DC numbers to LC cards were thus united in the same organization. In 1958 the two offices were combined into the present Decimal Classification Division.

It is Dewey's notation system, rather than any theoretical excellence of his arrangement and development of the world of knowledge, that has been largely responsible for the widespread acceptance and usage of his decimal classification. The notation, consisting of only ten digits and a decimal point, is almost universally understood and lends itself readily to subject synthesis with the benefit of numerous memory aids. Another valuable feature of the DC notation not shared by some other commonly used classification systems is its adaptability, the ease with which it may be applied in whole or in part to collections of books and other materials of any size or nature and expanded as these collections grow.

The development of the three types of bibliographic standards I have described —standards for entry, headings, and description; standards for alphabetical subject headings; and standards for subject classification—was, as we have seen, a long-drawn-out process, extending from the early years of this century to the present day. The application of these standards did not wait upon their full development. It proceeded concurrently, application leading to a refinement of standards in a never-ending chain.

The basic step toward standardizing bibliographic controls on a nationwide scale was taken in 1901. In that year the then Librarian of Congress, Herbert Putnam, announced the sale of LC catalog cards and their free deposit in selected research libraries. I shall quote from his contemporary account:

> The Library is beginning a distribution of copies of these cards, which has two purposes: First, to place in each local center of research, as complete as possible a statement of the contents of the national collection at Washington; second, to enable other libraries to secure the benefit of its expert work in cataloging and in printing cards for books acquired by them as well as by it, and to secure this benefit at a cost which, while a full reimbursement to the Government, is to the subscribing library but a fraction of the cost of doing the entire work independently. In pursuance of the first purpose there is being sent to certain public libraries a copy of every card printed by the Library of Congress. . . . A chief purpose of the first class of distribution is to supply libraries with information of books which they do not possess. The chief purpose of the second is to enable them to avoid expense in the preparation for use of those which they do possess. . . .
> The cost of getting any particular book into the card catalog is far greater than the public supposes. There are various elements of cost . . . But the two most costly factors are the work of the cataloger, the expert, and the work of the compositor.

> . . . Now, the interesting thing is that until now libraries have been, in effect, duplicating this entire expense—multiplying it, in fact, by each one undertaking to do the whole work individually for itself. There are thousands of books which are acquired by hundreds of libraries—exactly the same books, having the same titles, the same authors and contents, and subject to the same processes. But each library has been doing individually the whole work of cataloging the copies received by it, putting out the whole expense. . . .
> Since the Library of Congress moved into the new building expectation has turned to it. It has already the largest collection of books on the Western Hemisphere; it is increasing more rapidly than any other single collection. It receives without cost two copies of every book entered for copyright in the United States. . . . It receives an enormous mass of material through exchange. And it is buying a number of other books, current and non-current, which includes a large portion of material in current acquisition by the other libraries of the United States. It is classifying and cataloging this material on its own account. It is printing the results in the form of cards. . . . These cards are of the standard form, size, type, and method of entry. . . .
> Now it is receiving this urgent appeal: To permit other libraries to order extra copies of the cards which will cover books that they are acquiring. . . . American instinct and habit revolt against multiplication of brain effort and outlay where a multiplication of results can be achieved by machinery. This appears to be a case where it may be. Not every result, but results so great as to effect a prodigious saving to the libraries of this country. The Library of Congress cannot ignore the opportunity and the appeal. It is, as I have said, an opportunity unique, presented to no other library, not even to any other national library. For in the United States alone are the library interests active in cooperative effort, urgent to "standardize" forms, methods, and processes, and willing to make concession of individual preference and convenience in order to secure results of the greatest general benefit. . . .

A centralization of cataloging work, with a corresponding centralization of bibliographic apparatus, has been for a quarter of a century an ambition of the librarians of the United States. It was a main purpose in the formation of the American Library Association in 1876. . . .

There are many difficulties of detail, and the whole project will fail unless there can be built up within the Library a comprehensive collection of books, and a corps of catalogers and bibliographers adequate in number and representing in the highest degree . . . expert training and authoritative judgment. But the possible utilities are so great; they suggest so obvious, so concrete a return to the people of the United States for the money expended in the maintenance of this Library; and the service which they involve is so obviously appropriate a service for the National Library of the United States, that I communicate the project in this report as the most significant of our undertakings of this first year of the new century.

That the project did not fail is evident from a single statistic. In 1901 LC distributed 378,000 printed catalog cards; in 1968 it distributed over 110,000,000 cards to 25,000 libraries, firms, and individuals.

In 1902 the Librarian of Congress announced that "sets of the printed catalogue cards issued by the Library of Congress are being deposited at libraries in various parts of the country for the following purposes: (1) to enable students and investigators to ascertain whether certain works are in the Library of Congress without making a trip to Washington or submitting lists of books; (2) to promote bibliographical work; (3) to promote uniformity and accuracy in cataloging; and (4) to enable the depository library and other libraries in its vicinity to order cards for their catalogues with the minimum expenditure of labor by submitting lists of serial numbers taken from the depository cards."

It was apparently intended from the beginning of the depository system to include foreign libraries, particularly those which supplied LC with copies of their printed cards and also in cases where the sets of LC cards formed the basis for regional union catalogs. In 1903 a set of cards was set aside for the Institut International de Bibliographie in Brussels and in 1904 another for the Public Library of New South Wales in Sydney, Australia. When the depository system was largely replaced in 1946 by LC catalogs in book form, 133 libraries were receiving full or partial sets of cards or proof sheets. Three Japanese libraries were among the 22 foreign depositories.

The depository system has been continued for regional union catalogs and bibliographic centers and for institutional catalogs performing in large measure the same service as regional union catalogs. For the most part, however, LC's book catalogs took over the function formerly performed by the depository sets of catalog cards. Libraries were consulted as to their preference and needs, and nearly all of them disposed of their depository sets since the book catalogs were found to be more useful and less costly to maintain.

In 1949 LC began sending to over fifty foreign libraries depository sets of the book catalogs as a substitute for the discontinued sets of cards. This was done as an aid to scholarship, as an encouragement to the development of similar publications, and in furtherance of international bibliographic controls. The aim was to select an institution in each country which by reason of legal deposit or the comprehensiveness of its interests might be presumed to receive nearly the complete current publications of its country and hence to be in the best position to develop bibliographic controls for that country's works.

I shall return to the subject of the book catalogs, but first I should like to mention some of the significant steps taken in recent years to expand the card-distribution service. Early in the century *Publishers' Weekly*, the *Cumulative Book Index*, and other organs of the book trade began, as a service to libraries, to include the card numbers for LC printed cards as a part of the entries for all current titles listed in these media. The publication of the numbers in these current journals has made it possible for librarians to order LC cards concurrently with the ordering of the books themselves. Orders by number can be handled more quickly at LC than orders by author and title because the card stock is arranged in numerical order; thus a smaller charge is made when orders are by card number.

In 1950 an American publishing firm suggested that the benefits of this system might be extended by having the LC card number printed by the publishers on the verso of the title pages of the books themselves. Other firms quickly followed suit, and the practice has now become almost universal among American publishers. It has further simplified and expedited the ordering of printed cards, to the great benefit of libraries everywhere.

With the appearance of LC card numbers in so many new books, the Card Division was under increased pressure to have its printed cards ready by the time orders were received. For many years LC has attempted to obtain new books well in advance of their publication date so that they may be cataloged and the cards printed by the date of publication. Efforts have been made to persuade publishers to make early deposit of their copyrighted titles, with but partial success.

Various expedients were tried in the hope of correcting the situation. In 1949 arrangements were made with the *United States Quarterly Book Review* under which LC borrowed advance review copies for cataloging purposes. The results were encouraging, and from 1951 to 1953 LC maintained a representative in New York City who served as its liaison with publishers there, encouraging the publishers to send a review copy of each of their books to the *United States Quarterly Book Review*. These measures materially improved the card-distribution service, but lack of sufficient financial support compelled the discontinuance of the *Quarterly Book Review* in 1956.

During 1958–59 LC conducted an experiment to test the feasibility of a different approach. Designated as "Cataloging-in-Source," this experimental procedure was based on cataloging a book before publication and having the complete catalog entry printed in the book itself. The conclusion, as set forth in a final, comprehensive report, was as follows:

> The underlying purpose of the experiment . . . was to ascertain whether a permanent, full-scale program of Cataloging-in-Source could be justified in terms of financing, technical considerations, and utility. As regards this, the answer must be a regretful negative. The reasons for this decision . . . are chiefly the very high cost of the proposed program to both publishers and the Library of Congress, disruptions of publishing schedules, the high degree of unreliability of catalog entries based on texts not in their final form, and the low degree of utility which would result from the copying of these entries.

Meanwhile, however, three new developments had changed the picture. The first of these developments is called "All-the-Books Plan." In 1953 LC, with the cooperation of book publishers throughout the country and especially of the American Book Publishers Council, initiated a procedure under which publishers were asked to send to the library a copy of each book they published as soon as bound copies were available. When the plan was first inaugurated, only 100 firms were printing preassigned card numbers in their books and forwarding them to LC in advance of publication date. But publishers were quick to appreciate the beneficial effect of the program. They found that books could be promoted—exhibited, reviewed, and circulated—through libraries at the same time their own promotional activities were most intense. Publishers' catalogs containing LC catalog card numbers became more useful library tools. Libraries were enabled to buy more books with the money they saved by being able to purchase catalog cards by number instead of ordering by author and title. To the library profession and to scholarship this new development was significant because of the more complete and current representation of American works in the LC catalogs. It also enabled LC to fulfill its obligations better as a national bibliographic center and as the principal agency of a centralized catalog system. By 1968 the number of publishers participating in the preassigned card number program and the "All-the-Books Plan" had increased to 6,842.

The second development was initiated in 1959, when *Publishers' Weekly* began printing LC catalog entries for all the titles appearing in its "Weekly Record" listings.

To the information previously given (including the LC card number) were added the Dewey Decimal Classification number and LC subject headings. The final step was taken in 1965, when the LC classification number was also given. In addition, *Publishers' Weekly* began sending to LC its review copies of all titles not already provided by publishers under the "All-the-Books Plan." These developments have meant that LC now receives promptly a virtually complete representation of the current titles issued by the American book trade.

The third development is named the "Cards-with-Books Program." Always on the alert for ways to improve methods of distributing cards, LC investigated the possibilities of a program whereby libraries could obtain sets of LC cards with the books they purchase from distributors and publishers, rather than having to order cards separately. It was estimated that the large wholesale book distributors in the United States make about 70 percent of their book sales directly to libraries, and that current American trade books account for an estimated 80–85 percent of these sales. If LC catalog cards could be supplied to libraries along with the current American books they purchase, the libraries could realize benefits in all handling and processing operations required to put their new books into prompt use. The basic idea was not a new one. When LC launched its printed catalog card service in 1901, it was immediately suggested that a catalog card should be distributed with each new book sold, and some efforts were made along this line with only limited results. The situation had been changed by the success of the "All-the-Books Plan" and of the supplementary arrangement with *Publishers' Weekly*. Exploratory conferences with some of the book distributors and with a few publishing houses that themselves distribute books indicated a favorable attitude, and the program was launched in 1961. Within a few years nearly 10 million cards were being distributed annually by wholesale book dealers and publishers, and the program continues to grow.

Since its founding nearly seventy years ago the card-distribution service has become a mighty instrument for promoting bibliographic standards and control. But the ever-increasing work load, turnover of staff, and, above all, lack of space for card stock have hampered its effectiveness and made it apparent that a drastic overhaul is required to achieve the maximum in efficiency of operations. To that end, LC has begun a full-scale effort to mechanize the service. Much of the work of the Card Division is routine and repetitive in nature; mechanization of these procedures will result in more efficient operations and improved service. The new system has been designed to mechanize as much of the total operation as possible. New order forms with the customer number and a code indicating the type of handling desired and the card stock numbers are being read by optical scanning equipment. Once read, this information is sprayed in the form of tiny fluorescent bar codes on the back of each order slip. These bar codes are then used to sort the order slips into sequence by card number on high-speed sorting machines. The next step is the actual drawing of cards from stock. After the orders have been filled from stock, the intermixed cards and order slips are again placed on the high-speed sorters, and the cards and slips are sorted into sequence by customer number. Addresses and invoices for each shipment are printed on the computer, and the orders are assembled for manual packaging and shipment. The new system has reduced the time required to ship card orders from three to four weeks under the manual system to eight calendar days. It is also expected to effect long-range economies.

Until 1947 the card-distribution system was effected in two principal ways. One of these was through the sale of individual cards ordered by libraries and other purchasers. The other was through the placing of complete sets of cards on deposit at centers of research. The benefit which these sets conferred was indubitably great, but their maintenance was a considerable expense to LC and an even greater expense to the recipients, who had each to provide filing equipment and staff for the maintenance of the catalogs. It was suggested that it might be no more expensive to publish the contents of the cards in book form than to distribute them as cards, and that the circle of those whom the service would reach could thus be much enlarged. The success of the sale of the monumental 167-volume *Catalog of Books Represented by Library of Congress Printed Cards* up to 1942, which was sponsored by the Association of Research Libraries and published by the firm of Edwards Brothers, made the idea worth investigating. The libraries who would use the service were polled, and the *Cumulative Catalog of Library of Congress Printed Cards* was accordingly commenced in January 1947. Each issue reproduced the contents of all cards printed by the Library during the preceding month, and there followed quarterly, annual, and quinquennial cumulations of these issues. Thus, for the first time there became generally available in convenient form and at moderate cost a publication which listed at frequent intervals a substantial segment of current American and foreign publications, providing for each of them one or more methods of classification, subject analysis, and other cataloging data in terms of standard systems. It provided the basis for significant advances toward the solution of the problem of bibliographic control.

The next advance occurred in 1956, when the *Cumulative Catalog* was expanded to include the current catalog entries of other North American libraries. These entries had for many years been forwarded by libraries to the National Union Catalog in the Library of Congress, where the cards were filed in a catalog whose invaluable bibliographic information was available to scholars only through a visit to Washington or by correspondence. The expanded book-form catalog was named *The National Union Catalog: A Cumulative Author List*. It represented the most comprehensive bibliographic service ever developed and broadened the horizons of American librarianship as much as did the inauguration of the distribution of LC catalog cards more than half a century earlier.

Numerous beneficial effects have become evident. The inclusion of information about the location of the publications listed has made possible regional and national planning of acquisitions programs and reduced the unnecessary duplicative purchase of expensive works. It has led to a more equitable distribution of the burden of interlibrary loan. The ready availability of a great body of current bibliographic information has tended to reduce the costs of acquisition, cataloging, and reference work. Finally, it paved the way for the publication, now in progress in over 600 volumes, of the National Union Catalog's card record of holdings of books published prior to 1956.

If time and space permitted, I could describe the contribution made to national bibliographic controls by the other Library of Congress catalogs in book form—*Books: Subjects*, the *National Union Catalog of Manuscript Collections, Motion Pictures and Filmstrips, Music and Phonorecords*, and the *National Register of Microform Masters*. I could add a word about the *Catalog of Copyright Entries, Dissertation Abstracts, New Serial Titles, Newspapers on Microfilm*, the *Monthly Checklist of State Publications*, the *Directory of Information Resources in the United States*, the *Handbook of Latin American Studies*, the *Monthly Index of Russian Accessions*, and the *World List of Future International Meetings*. But I hope that I have given the reader some idea of the application in the United States of national bibliographic controls in the conventional forms of printed catalog cards and of catalogs in book format.

The development of nationally accepted standards in cataloging and classification, of national cataloging services, and of national controls over bibliographic resources preceded the advent of computers and their potentiality for bringing a new dimension into bibliographic services. Yet these earlier developments were really necessary before the resources of modern electronics could be effectively and efficiently applied to bibliographic problems. By the time computer applications became feasible, the bibliographic stage had been properly set.

In 1961 the Council on Library Resources provided a grant that allowed the

Librarian of Congress to engage a group of specialists to begin an investigation of methods for automated library services. The team of specialists, headed by Gilbert W. King, was asked to determine if it would be feasible to mechanize the LC bibliographic processes. The result of their effort was the report *Automation and the Library of Congress,* published in 1964. The report indicated that not only was automation of bibliographic activities possible, but that it would be highly advisable for the Librarian to begin as soon as possible a program that would actually bring about automation of the LC's central core of bibliographic records. To accomplish the recommended task, LC established the Information Systems Office.

While research was being conducted at LC, a general demand for the analysis of requirements for converting cataloging data to machine-readable form was stimulated by growing recognition that computers could serve as library tools. Because the Library of Congress was already the major American supplier of bibliographic data, there was general agreement that it should consider the production of a machine-readable catalog record.

In January 1965 LC and the Committee on Automation of the Association of Research Libraries jointly sponsored a Conference on Machine-Readable Catalog Copy. After the conference the Information Systems Office prepared a report entitled *A Proposed Format for a Standardized Machine-Readable Catalog Record,* which was intended to stimulate discussion throughout the library community. It was hoped that such discussion would lead to an agreement concerning a format standard. The response to the report was encouraging. The consensus of opinion indicated that LC should experiment with a modified version of the proposed format.

Late in 1965 the Council on Library Resources made a grant to LC for the design of a system, preparation of computer programs, and the evaluation of a pilot project. By February 1966 the planning had gotten under way, and the pilot project for machine-readable cataloging was designed and given the title MARC (for *MA*chine-*R*eadable *C*ataloging). For this project sixteen libraries were chosen as participants to receive weekly magnetic computer tapes containing bibliographic records. The selection of participants took into account such criteria as library type; availability of technical staff, funds, and computer equipment; geographic location; and willingness on the part of the institution to utilize the bibliographic data and to evaluate experience with use of the machine-readable tapes sent by LC. Since funds were unavailable to extend the number of participants, the participating libraries were encouraged to make the tapes available to other libraries. As a result, over a dozen secondary libraries participated in the experiment.

As work on the project progressed, consultations were held with representatives from the University of Chicago, Yale University, and Harvard University. It is important to note that interest was not limited to United States libraries, for representatives of the Bodleian Library at Oxford and the British National Bibliography participated in discussions at LC prior to the implementation of a United Kingdom MARC Project.

Approximately 50,000 bibliographic records were distributed during the nineteen months of the project. The experience of the participants in utilizing the records and the format was reported to LC, and the MARC format was evaluated. On the basis of the results from the pilot project as well as of LC tests and experience, work began on a new format. Additional information for the design of the new format was gathered from many visits to participating libraries, from opinions gathered through telephone surveys, and from experience reported by informal working groups. Changes proposed were discussed with the participants, with the national libraries, and with other libraries working on automation projects. The format for the pilot project was completely revised to facilitate not just one-way distribution, but general exchange of bibliographic data.

The resulting format was designated MARC II. Its purpose is to provide a single standard format that will allow for convertibility and compatibility of data between various systems. Because of the flexibility of the MARC II format, a library receiving a machine-readable record may choose to use the record as it is received or convert the record to a format specifically designed for local use. The procedures for processing and output will be governed by each local institution, while communication between institutions will simply require that records transmitted or received be converted to or from the communications format. The base structure of the format has been designed to accommodate all forms of bibliographic description. Only the content of the format will vary according to the nature of the material described.

To facilitate the exchange of records in the communications format, the Information Systems Office developed the MARC Distribution Service, which each week distributes magnetic tapes of current English-language monographic cataloging prepared at the Library of Congress. The records are available on a choice of seven-track or nine-track tape and will be recorded in an extended form of the American Standard Code for Information Interchange (ASCII). The initial distribution of MARC records includes only records for English-language monographs, but work will soon begin on conversion of records for monographs in French, German, and other roman-alphabet languages. The problems of converting records for works in non-roman-alphabet languages and for nonbook materials remain to be solved.

Practical applications of MARC records are numerous:

1. *Book selection.* The current MARC tapes are used in conjunction with other bibliographic tools to provide awareness of the publication of new books.

2. *Processing tools.* The MARC records are being used to print forms for book and purchase orders as well as lists of materials being processed. This is accomplished through the use of a special machine file of records specially formatted for acquisitions use. The acquisitions records contain information on the status of each transaction.

3. *Cataloging.* Libraries participating in the MARC system provide print-outs of appropriate records for their catalogers. The catalogers then edit the print-out and adapt the information to local requirements.

4. *Catalog cards.* Several libraries use the MARC tapes to generate standard-size cards for their catalogs.

5. *Book catalogs.* MARC records are used in conjunction with local catalog records to produce book catalogs of local holdings. In some instances the book catalogs provide holdings information for several libraries and represent initial efforts at producing union catalogs from MARC records.

6. *Control devices.* Several programs are being used to generate book cards for circulation control, book pockets, spine labels, etc.

7. *Bibliographic tools.* MARC records are being used experimentally to produce special bibliographies, subject listings, topical indexes, and similar tools.

8. *Subject authority file.* Authority file maintenance by computer is being tested through the use of a machine-readable file of the LC subject headings.

9. *Book lists.* The data contained in MARC tapes will be used to generate lists of new books for distribution to university faculty members according to area of interest or specialty. This will involve the development of a program for selective dissemination of information.

10. *Syllabus/bibliography production.* In conjunction with local records the machine-readable bibliographic data can be used to create and maintain current university course bibliographies and similar tools.

11. *Searching of machine files.* MARC tapes will be used as an experimental vehicle in the development of systems to provide searching of machine files. Possible applications of the results of this work include processing of book requests and purchase orders against a standing file of catalog records.

12. *Local catalog processing.* The MARC records will be used in experiments to develop on-line computer-aided reprocessing

of machine-readable cataloging data to adapt it to local library use.

Participants in the MARC Pilot Project demonstrated the practical applications of machine-readable cataloging records in working situations. For example, the Washington State Library used MARC records to generate a book catalog for three regional library systems. Full bibliographic information was compiled in computer-numbered sequence, and readers were directed to this information by secondary finding lists, arranged by author, title, and subject. The use of a sequential register obviated the need for interfiling new records into the main listing. Instead, sequential additions to the register, along with new finding lists, were distributed in loose-leaf form on a monthly basis. Book cards, pockets, and spine labels were also generated from the MARC records.

The University of Toronto Library tested methods of integrating MARC data into their technical processing operations. Material received through a blanket order system was checked against the MARC tape to determine if a catalog record was present. Matched records were modified when necessary to reflect local data requirements. Records added to the system were used to produce sets of catalog cards for the several catalogs in the university libraries. Reports were also transmitted to union catalogs, and the MARC record was made a part of the Toronto data base. Catalog cards produced from the machine records were arranged in alphabetized blocks ready for filing.

Several libraries demonstrated that it was possible to produce selective bibliographies from the machine records. One particularly interesting university application involved matching a faculty interest profile against the MARC records to provide a listing of relevant records in the magnetic tape. This was a practical mechanization of the traditional library service of notifying specialists of newly acquired publications. The automatic service was carried out more efficiently and at greater speed than was possible with the manual notification system.

The Fondren Library at Rice University conducted an experiment to determine what information is needed to match a title with such acquisitions information as author, title, publisher, and date. The purpose of the experiment was in part to rank the relative importance of the various search elements.

One of the most important aspects of MARC work has been the development of standards that may be accepted by the entire library community. Early in the project the MARC staff, in cooperation with the Library Typewriter Keyboard Committee, Resources and Technical Services Division of the American Library Association, established a character set. The set incorporated requirements of a keyboard for both a manual and a paper-tape typewriter. Later a set of specifications for a computer print train, designed to be compatible with the keyboard requirements, was developed with expanded upper- and lower-case characters and diacriticals. The character set requirements were determined by an analysis of existing sets and their ability to cover the handling of roman-alphabet languages. A study was made to establish what combination of additional characters would meet the highest percentage of typographic requirements. Cooperation from other libraries aided greatly in the study, and the result is a set of specifications which has been adopted by ALA. The specifications will lead to a manufacturer's design of new character sets for input-output devices.

Standardization has been emphasized in the development of MARC in such areas as format design, codes for languages, codes for countries of publication, and so forth. Such standardization, which is essential to interlibrary communication, aids in the continued attempts of libraries everywhere to avoid unnecessary duplication of design effort.

The MARC II format itself represents a standard that has been widely accepted. In addition to LC, the National Library of Medicine and the National Agricultural Library have adopted it. ALA has accepted the format as a United States library standard, and the United Kingdom machine-readable cataloging project uses the MARC II format in Great Britain.

The availability of a communications standard, coupled with standards for a library character set and related bibliographic developments, promises to open a new era when cooperation between libraries can be accomplished, both nationally and internationally. The design of the MARC format was carefully planned so that local needs could be met in any manner chosen; yet the exchange of information between one institution and another could be carried out in ways that were always uniform. The concept of the format is that records from all sources can be brought into a common frame of reference. The structure of the format is hospitable to all bibliographic description, even though the content of the format will vary according to the material described.

It is important to bear in mind that automation will continue to operate on many levels in the library world. The equipment available to different institutions varies widely in type and sophistication, while computer facilities at various locations range from very small to elaborate and powerful multiunit configurations. Because of the wide disparity from one institution to another, it is clear that libraries must work together to influence standardization. The MARC experience has shown that such cooperation is possible.

LC anticipates that in the next few years, as interlibrary cooperation increases through the use of automation, conversion of retrospective records will receive increasing emphasis. It is probably true that scientific libraries, such as medical libraries, have less need to go to records older than ten or fifteen years. However, large research libraries are not only concerned with the rapid dissemination of current information, but must also serve the needs of researchers by providing access to older materials. Considerable discussion and initial planning related to conversion of retrospective records at local installations has been stimulated by the implementation of the MARC Distribution Service. Because

full-fledged conversion at the local level would result in considerable duplication of effort, investigation of the feasibility of converting retrospective material at a central source is under way. The Council on Library Resources has funded a study to investigate the bibliographic, economic, and technical problems of centralized conversion. This study should enable the library community to look at the problems of local and centralized conversion in a more realistic manner.

I now turn to a recent development with important international implications. Described by one university librarian as "the most momentous and far-reaching development in the library world since Melvil Dewey conceived the unit card and the Library of Congress began to provide catalog cards to other libraries," the National Program for Acquisitions and Cataloging, or the Shared Cataloging Program, as it is more widely known, is a subject of interest to librarians everywhere. For the first time a program has been evolved which presents the potentials of developing a central source of bibliographic information on all materials of value to scholarship published throughout the world. The program is aptly named, because it means not only that LC shares its cataloging staff and expertise even more widely than in the past, but also that other libraries in the United States and bibliographers and libraries abroad are cooperating in this worldwide effort to coordinate the acquisition and cataloging of library materials for retrieval and use.

During the last decade it had become apparent to every library administrator that his own technical staff, difficult to recruit and retrain and limited in language and subject specialization, could not continue to classify and catalog promptly the ever-multiplying library receipts, especially of foreign-language material. Above all, this would be a wasteful operation, because this same cataloging was being done over and over in other research institutions. LC had helped to reduce this wasteful duplication through the programs I have described, but its coverage of books in English published outside the United States was not complete, and that of foreign-language titles was far from satisfactory. Since LC was already meeting a large part of the need, it seemed that the most practical approach would be to increase its acquisitions and cataloging resources and thereby create a truly comprehensive center for cataloging.

Accordingly, after consultations with LC and with its full cooperation, as well as the support of other library associations, the Association of Research Libraries proposed an amendment to the Higher Education Act of 1965, then being considered by the Congress. As a result of these efforts, the Librarian of Congress was given the responsibility for acquiring in so far as possible all library materials of value to scholarship currently published throughout the world, of cataloging them promptly after receipt, and of distributing bibliographic information through printed catalog cards or by other means.

Even before funds became available in the spring of 1966, LC began to direct its attention to the task assigned. It was early realized that cooperative efforts would be required. Accordingly, LC began to explore the possibility of international cooperation, especially in cataloging. Anticipating increases in the acquisition of foreign publications and recognizing the shortage of trained catalogers and the accelerated procedures required, LC considered the feasibility of using the entries in other national bibliographies as aids to cataloging. This possibility was explored at a conference in London in January 1966, attended by the national librarians and the producers of the current national bibliographies of England, France, the Federal Republic of Germany, and Norway. It was emphasized that LC did not seek to change the cataloging practices of other countries, but rather to utilize their products in the most rapid and feasible manner, compensating them adequately for their extra services. Not only was it agreed that it was desirable for LC to use for cataloging purposes the descriptions of books listed in the national bibliographies of these countries and of those other countries where adequate bibliographies exist, but also that it was feasible for the bibliographies to supply LC with copy for the entries in advance of publication.

The conference recognized that acceptance and implementation of the principle of shared cataloging should eventually result in a more uniform description of each publication, identified by a reference to the listing in the national bibliography of the home country. It believed that the program would speed up ordering and cataloging procedures, result in faster bibliographic control, reduce the cost of cataloging in libraries all over the world, contribute toward the increased sale of publications on an international scale, and make resources for scholarly research more quickly available.

In April 1966 the first experiment in shared cataloging was undertaken. Arrangements were made for LC to receive from the *British National Bibliography,* through a London bookseller, advance printer's copy of the bibliography entries. Concurrently the bookseller began supplying LC with current British imprints at an accelerated rate through a combination of blanket-order selections, supplementary selections by LC's own recommending officers, and, later, LC's receipt of the order slips of approximately one hundred major American libraries and selection from them for order of those materials not yet supplied to it through other means. The first catalog cards prepared under the program were printed and distributed in the spring of 1966.

After this prototype operation proved the feasibility of the approach, there followed visits to Paris, Wiesbaden, and Vienna to make similar arrangements with book dealers and the producers of the current national bibliographies. The initial results of this early experimentation with national bibliographies prompted Sir Frank Francis, then director of the British Museum, to say in his presidential address at the thirty-second Annual Meeting of the International Federation of Library Associations, held in the Hague in September

1966, that "the first experiment was a brilliant justification of this highly practical approach." If it is possible to get this cooperation fully worked out and made into a going concern, he said, "it will . . . mean that practicality is taking a hand in our affairs at last and that the dream of collaboration which has foundered so often in the past on the rocks of formalism can at last become a reality."

Following this meeting an informal conference of Eastern European national librarians was convened in Vienna to consider the development of a shared-cataloging and expanded acquisitions program for Eastern European publications. Subsequent conferences at which the program was a prime topic of discussion have included the thirty-third Annual Meeting of the International Federation of Library Associations, held in Toronto in August 1967; the International Conference on African Bibliography, held in Nairobi in December 1967; the May 1968 meeting in Geneva of the Association of International Libraries; and the August 1968 meeting in Frankfurt of the International Federation of Library Associations.

At the present time twenty-two countries are included in the program, fifteen of which (Austria, Belgium, Brazil, Denmark, Finland, France, Germany, Great Britain, Italy, Japan, the Netherlands, Norway, Sweden, Switzerland, and Yugoslavia) are covered by the ten overseas shared-cataloging offices. The remaining seven countries (Australia, Bulgaria, Canada, Czechoslovakia, New Zealand, South Africa, and the USSR) are sending prepublication data prepared for their current national bibliographies or other valuable cataloging information directly to the Library of Congress. In addition, a regional acquisitions office in Kenya is centralizing the receipt of materials from eleven East African countries and producing the quarterly *Accessions List: Eastern Africa,* the only regional bibliography from this area.

The shared-cataloging office in Tokyo is the newest of the overseas centers. Following negotiations in November 1967, officials of the National Diet Library agreed to assist LC, and preliminary arrangements were also made with a book dealer for local staff and office space. Final arrangements were concluded in May 1968, and the field director of the Japanese center took up his residence in Tokyo. NDL is supplying advance cataloging information for current Japanese publications based upon the entries to appear in the weekly bibliography, *Nōhon Shūhō.* The preliminary cards are photographed by a planetary camera in the NDL, developed, and delivered each week to the shared-cataloging office. Masters of the final printer's copy for the NDL cards are also reproduced for LC and utilized in the preparation of LC printed cards. The *kanji* text representing the body of the entry is "stripped in" on printed cards with the English portion of the text, thus expediting the printing of the final LC catalog card.

The results of this cooperative program of shared cataloging are embodied not only in LC catalog cards and (some of it) in machine-readable form on magnetic tape under the MARC program, but also in LC's published *National Union Catalog.* The program is, therefore, one of mutual benefit to libraries and scholarship everywhere. Thanks to it, cataloging production has increased from 110,000 individual titles in fiscal 1965 to over 200,000 in fiscal 1969. These catalog cards are also being made available to the more than 25,000 other libraries, firms, and individuals subscribing to LC's card-distribution service and to additional thousands of users through its published catalogs in book form. As a result, many thousands of libraries across the country are spared the expense of doing their own cataloging. They are relieved of the fruitless attempt to attain self-sufficiency in scores of foreign languages and of subject competency in all fields of specialization. This effective utilization of scarce professional talent is one of the program's most important dividends. It is also producing a standardization of cataloging information which is essential for efficient access to source materials and for their automated control. Since the cost of cataloging is necessarily very high and rapidly increasing, centralized cataloging by LC represents a national saving of many millions of dollars.

In June 1967 the Library of Congress, the National Library of Medicine, and the National Agricultural Library announced their plans for "a coordinated library automation effort" for the purpose of improving "access to the world's literature in all areas of human concern and scholarship" and the establishment of the U.S. National Libraries Task Force as the instrument for directing and coordinating this joint enterprise. They indicated their agreement "to adopt common goals" in their automation programs and to direct their efforts toward achieving "systems compatibility at the national level." Specific goals were: (1) the development of a national data bank of machine-readable cataloging information; (2) a national data bank of machine-readable information relating to the location of hundreds of thousands of serial titles held by American research libraries; and (3) the attainment of compatibility in as many areas of the three libraries' operations as possible, including compatibility in "the several authority lists of subject headings now used by the three libraries."

Three basic concepts—cooperation, standardization, and communications—are the fundamental principles in the National Libraries Task Force's program. From the beginning the Task Force has emphasized the cooperative approach. From June 1967 through December 1968 it held over fifty meetings which brought together at least two representatives from each of the three national libraries. Subgroups have been formed as required for the detailed analysis of specific compatibility and design problems. Currently the following groups are pursuing specific investigations: Acquisitions, Bibliographic Codes, Character Sets, Descriptive Cataloging, Generalized Output, Machine-Readable Format, Name Entry and Authority File, Serials Control, Subject Headings, and Systems. Later it will probably be necessary to add groups on such matters as machine-file structure, data file conversion, filing rules, and output requirements. The accomplishments in a rela-

tively brief period of time have been rather remarkable, particularly when it is recognized that many involve problem areas in which skeptics expressed doubt that any compatibility could be achieved—at least in our lifetime.

Of great importance in standardization and systems development for the benefit of research institutions everywhere is the recent announcement by the three national libraries of the joint adoption of the MARC II format for the communication of bibliographic information in machine-readable form. Agreement on this communications format is concrete evidence of the national libraries' mutual desire to extend the usefulness of their collections and services through the application of new technological capabilities wherever economically feasible. It will pave the way for further extensions throughout the research community.

A second major agreement on standards concerns descriptive cataloging, where the three libraries have decided to adopt standard practices. In announcing this agreement it was emphasized that these standards are of importance to other libraries, whether they use a manual or a computer system. Common elements were identified, those creating compatibility problems were examined in detail, and certain practices in each institution were modified to achieve a higher degree of compatibiliy among the three systems.

A third standard recently adopted is the standard calendar date code, designed to provide a standard way of representing calendar dates in the data-processing systems of the three libraries. This should also be useful in data interchange among other libraries and agencies. General use of this standard code will eliminate the confusion caused by a variety of date representations.

The Task Force has also recommended the adoption of standard character sets for roman alphabets and the romanized forms of languages not written in the roman alphabet. The work was complicated by the fact that over 70 languages in 20 alphabets are used in at least one of the national libraries and that certain diacritical marks and scientific characters must be provided for. The standard set of 175 characters, as now developed, includes many diacritical marks, together with scientific and other special characters.

Work has just been completed on the development of a standard code for the languages that represent the major body of the published literature. In other areas the Task Force is looking into the need for standards that will assure more adequate control over the technical report literature. On the basis of a pilot study of the structure of name authority files in each of the three libraries, it has been determined that a mechanized central authority file would be useful. The difference in size of the present files is an important consideration, however, and a large-scale study will be necessary. The Subject Headings Group is making progress in one of the most critical areas relating to the achievement of compatibility. Computer output programs useful to the three institutions are being examined. These include collective publications (book and card catalogs and indexing and abstracting services), on-line and off-line printing, and console output. Study to date has been concentrated on programs for human-readable printed text. Search and retrieval programs will receive attention at a later date.

A final goal toward which priority attention is being directed is the National Serials Data Program, the objective of which is the creation of a national data base of machine-readable information identifying the content and location of serial titles in research libraries. This ambitious undertaking, jointly supported by the three national libraries together with funding from the National Science Foundation and the Council on Library Resources, is an immediate outgrowth of a feasibility study conducted in 1965 by the Information Dynamics Corporation for the National Science Foundation.

This study was concerned with the need for a national inventory of serials relating to science and technology. It concluded that such a program was technologically

feasible, that it was needed, and that the Library of Congress was the institution best qualified to assume responsibility for it. Accordingly the three national libraries joined together in this effort, which was broadened to include controls over serials in all fields of knowledge. The total program is being undertaken in four phases: (1) preliminary design, (2) reduction to practice, (3) pilot project and planning for large-scale conversion, and (4) conversion and implementation of total program.

Phase 1 of this program has now been completed under the guidance of the Library of Congress Information Systems Office. A set of standardized data elements has been identified for controlling serial literature; a user survey has been completed, including an assessment of the needs of the three national libraries; and a cost-benefit study has confirmed our judgment that the eventual price tag on this program will be high. Phase 1 has resulted in the development of a definitive format for the identification, location, and service of serial literature, which can serve as the basis for an automated system. Its findings will make possible a reappraisal of our objectives.

I know that I do not need to convince the reader of the significance of serial literature to all scientific and technological research as well as to studies in other disciplines or to point out the many complications involved in the control of serials. Certainly computer technology offers an opportunity to gain more adequate control over this changeable material if we can arrive at common data elements and a standardized format and if we have the money to support the enterprise. We have learned some interesting facts from these studies. First, a machine-based national data bank should be designed to take maximum advantage of computer systems and should not be constrained by the limitations of manual systems. Second, a universal numbering scheme for serials is a basic requirement; the Task Force has been cooperating with the United States of America Standards Institute in an effort to design a scheme. Third, users' attitudes on implementation vary so widely that it is unlikely that final recommendations will please everyone. Although much more remains to be done and more resources will ultimately be required, the eventual result will be, it is hoped, a matchless tool for the bibliographic control of the millions of pieces of serial literature received by American libraries from all parts of the world.

As can be seen from this lengthy recital of the development of bibliographic standards and controls in the United States during the last seventy years or so and in my account of our attempts during the last decade to apply the potentialities of electronic computers to the service of our bibliographic needs, a tremendous human effort has been involved. It has required great vision and genius on the part of those who have led us in these efforts; it has required long, exhausting hours of investigation, research, study, discussion, and analysis by countless experts in all kinds of fields; it has required active and continuing attention by great institutions, professional associations, and commercial enterprises; but, most of all, it has required a sense of common purpose, an attitude of cooperation, and a willingness to give up some cherished preferences in the interest of achieving a broad consensus among all those involved in these important matters.

We in the United States know only too well how many problems still remain to be solved, how much study is still required, and how much our achievement falls short of our vision. Nevertheless we take heart from the accomplishments of our predecessors, from what success we have been able to achieve in our own time, and from the willingness of our colleagues abroad to cooperate with us in our mutual task of bringing to the world of scholarship and research a new generation of bibliographic tools and techniques.

National Bibliographic Control and the National Diet Library

Yasumasa Oda
*Director of Automation Project,
National Diet Library*

In the *Guide to Japanese Reference Books*, published by the American Library Association in 1966, there are nine past and four current national bibliographies listed in the national bibliographies section. Winchell's *Guide to Reference Books*, 8th edition (ALA, 1967), however, lists only three of the current Japanese national bibliographies. They are *Shuppan Nyūsu* (*Japanese Publications: News and Reviews*), published three times a month; *Shuppan Nenkan* [*Yearbook of Publications*], which is an annual cumulative edition of *Shuppan Nyūsu*; and *Zen Nihon Shuppanbutsu Sōmokuroku* (*Japanese National Bibliography*). Winchell's *Guide* does not include the fourth and most important index for the selection of books, *Nōhon Shūhō* (*Current Publications*), which is widely used in both Japan and the United States. *Nōhon Shūhō* is a bibliography published weekly by the National Diet Library (NDL), and *Zen Nihon Shuppanbutsu Sōmokuroku* is its annual cumulative edition.

The postwar U.S. Library Mission, represented by Verner W. Clapp and Charles H. Brown, made a major contribution toward the establishment of the National Diet Library and recommended that all publishers in Japan, public and private, be obligated to present newly published books to NDL, then still in the planning stage, so that it could maintain a complete national bibliography. This recommendation was made because newly published books could not be collected through a copyright registration deposit system such as exists at the Library of Congress. This was so since, under the Japanese Copyright Law, registration is not required as a procedure to obtain copyright, inasmuch as copyright becomes effective concurrent with authorship. The National Diet Library Law adopted the recommendation and requires in its provisions that at least one copy of every new Japanese publication be presented to NDL.

Nōhon Shūhō and the *Zen Nihon Shuppanbutsu Sōmokuroku* are compiled on the basis of these presentations and thus constitute more comprehensive bibliographies of new publications than *Shuppan Nyūsu* or *Shuppan Nenkan*, which list only publicly sold books and magazines. Yet it is questionable how comprehensive the two NDL bibliographies are; it has been variously estimated that they list from 70 to 80 percent of all new publications. These figures are not based on reliable sources, and because there is no way to determine the total number of new publications, they are not particularly significant. One can only say that nearly all new books sold through distributors are included in the bibliography. Although publications which do not involve distributors—such as government publications, publications by public and private groups, local publications, personal publications, and publications not for sale and not presented to the NDL—are checked and collected as much as possible, it is still difficult to conclude that all books are collected by NDL without any exceptions. It must also be added that there is no firmly established cooperation among libraries for the acquisition and processing of new publications, such as we find in the publication of the *National Union Catalog* of LC, or in the recently developed National Program for Acquisitions and Cataloging (NPAC). Despite its problems, *Nōhon Shūhō* is the most reliable current national bibliography, and it is one of the responsibilities of NDL to make it more comprehensive and reliable. One other problem requiring improvement is the delay in the publication of annual cumulative editions. For example, the 1967 edition of the *Zen Nihon Shuppanbutsu*

Sōmokuroku was published as late as April 1969.

In another paper by this author, "The National Diet Library as the Library Center of Japan" (see page 284), problems related to printed catalog cards compiled and distributed on the basis of new publications deposited in NDL are discussed. However, it must be mentioned here, too, that these printed catalog cards are prepared according to the Nippon Mokuroku Kisoku (Nippon Cataloging Rules, or NCR) and the Nippon Jisshin Bunrui Hō (Nippon Decimal Classification, or NDC) respectively. NCR and NDC were formulated with reference to the *ALA Cataloging Rules* and the Dewey Decimal Classification. In the 1965 edition NCR was revised according to the cataloging principles agreed upon at the 1961 International Conference on Cataloging Principles in Paris. The original edition had been confined to establishing cataloging rules for Japanese and Chinese books alone, but the rules were revised on the basis of the draft *Anglo-American Cataloging Rules* to make them applicable not only to Japanese and Chinese books but also to Western publications. NCR and NDC are formulated, published, and popularized as the standard cataloging and classification rules in Japan by the Japan Library Association (JLA) through its committees. NDL is cooperating with JLA by participating in the committees. NDL has been using its own independent classification since January 1969, but by showing both the NDC number and the NDL classification number on its printed cards—like the dual classification numbers on LC printed cards—it is striving to standardize the cataloging systems according to NCR and NDC and in cooperation with JLA.

In the printed catalog cards of NDL the readings of authors' names are spelled out for the purpose of standardizing entries and for convenience in filing the headings uniformly. In Japan almost all the names of persons or organizations are written in Chinese characters. One can easily understand the individual characters, but when it comes to pronouncing them, there is often trouble. For example, one phrase written in Chinese characters is familiar even to children as "Banzai!" (meaning "Long live . . . !" or "Hurrah!"). However, these same characters can be used for a surname which may be read "Nagatoshi," and this pronunciation may be known to only a limited number of persons—the bearer of the name and a few of his close acquaintances. Furthermore, there are often two or more ways of reading the same characters in names. For instance, one cannot tell, unless one asks the bearer of the name, the proper way to read a particular surname because the characters can be read as Tsunoda, Kakuta, or Sumida. A certain first name can be read as Junko, Sumiko, or Ayako. This is exactly the reason why NDL printed catalog cards indicate in the headings both the reading of the author's name and the Chinese characters for it.

NDL publishes the *Zasshi Kiji Sakuin: Jimbun shakai hen* (*Japanese Periodicals Index: Humanities and Social Science*) and *Zasshi Kiji Sakuin: Kagaku gijutsu hen* (*Japanese Periodicals Index: Science and Technology*) as monthlies. The academic reports on science and technology magazines can be found in the abstract journals, such as the *Nihon Kagaku Sōran* (*Complete Chemical Abstracts of Japan*) or the *Kagaku Gijutsu Bunken Sokuhō* (*Current Bibliography on Science and Technology*), both published by the Japan Information Center of Science and Technology (JICST), or in the *Igaku Chūō Zasshi* (*Japana, Centra Revuo Medicina*), published by the Igaku Chūō Zasshi Sha. In the humanities and social sciences there is nothing that can be called an index journal, with the exception of a few academic journals which list in their indexes articles in magazines related to their special areas. Under these circumstances the *Zasshi Kiji Sakuin* of NDL is important as an index journal. The volume on humanities and social sciences has approximately 1,500 titles and the volume of science and technology has approximately 1,300 titles of magazine articles indexed. Thus together they make up the most comprehensive index journal in Japan. However, the science and technology volume is regarded as inadequate, as this volume covers only 26 percent of the 4,929

titles listed in the *Nihon Kagaku Gijutsu Kankei Chikuji Kankōbutsu Mokuroku, 1967* (*Directory of Japanese Scientific Periodicals*). In view of this, many researchers and librarians demand an increase in the number of titles collected, and many also express strong hopes for the publication of cumulative editions.

As to the national union catalog, the Ministry of Education had begun the compilation of the union list of academic journals in the collections of the seven major national university libraries before NDL was established. This has now grown into the *Gakujutsu Zasshi Sōgō Mokuroku* (*Union List of Scientific Periodicals*), which includes the publications of not only public and private university libraries but also of major public and private research institutions, including NDL and JICST.

For bibliographies of books and translations published before 1867 and still extant, there is the *Kokusho Sōmokuroku* [*General Catalog of Japanese Books*], which has been published since 1963 by Iwanami Shoten. This serves as a national bibliography of Japanese books published before 1867 and as a national union catalog, since the locations of the books are clearly indicated. Along with these major union catalogs, NDL has been compiling a union catalog of foreign books collected at the sixteen university libraries, two public libraries, and NDL and its thirty branch libraries. In regard to Japanese books, NDL is striving to make a comprehensive collection of new publications through the previously mentioned book presentation system so that a national union catalog will not be required for publications issued after the establishment of NDL. The union catalog of foreign books is compiled and published in book form as *Shinshū Yōsho Sōgō Mokuroku* (*Union Catalog of Foreign Books*). It is compiled from catalog cards for recent accessions sent to NDL at the end of each year by participating libraries. Those books which have been published only within the past three years are included in the book catalog, the remainder being filed into a card catalog at NDL. It is, therefore, a very arbitrary arrangement.

In Japan the idea of maintaining an up-to-date union catalog in card catalog form has not gained much ground, and many people think that union catalogs must be maintained in book form. It is for this reason that a union catalog is usually published in book form, although at present NDL's lack of staff and budget does not allow all the collected catalog cards to be compiled and published in book form. Even when such an arrangement is tolerated out of necessity, an up-to-date catalog must be maintained, as is illustrated by the delay in the publication of the 1967 *Union Catalog of Foreign Books* until as late as March 1968. These delays occur because the catalog cards are sent to NDL only once a year and because much time is spent in standardizing the various forms which are received. (Also the printing is held up, because the proofreading requires much time.)

In Japan coordination among the libraries in a single university is a tremendous problem, and in some of the older established university library systems there is no uniformity in cataloging among the departmental libraries, with the result that no union catalog for the university can be compiled or maintained. Worse still, some participating libraries have no experienced foreign-book catalogers. In situations of this kind, the difficulty of NDL's compiling a union catalog by editing the catalog cards sent by participating libraries for uniformity of entry and style is immense. Furthermore, when catalog entries are standardized, there will be books which cannot be retrieved because the standardized entries do not correspond to the entries in the libraries possessing the books. It is apparent that catalog standardization is a great necessity. Another related matter of concern is that to make this truly a national union catalog, the number of libraries participating must be increased. Many voice the need to increase the number of participating libraries, but at present there is no hope of increasing the number of staff at NDL.

Many of these problems associated with NDL's national bibliographic control will probably be solved when the library automation project, now planned by NDL, is put into practice. In the 1969 budget NDL was granted a budget for the preparation of computerization, and now the prospects for the installment of an electronic computer in early 1971 have become brighter. We are now actively engaged in preparations, and the MARC project of LC will be of great help in this. It is hoped that by the time the computer is installed in NDL not only English-language monographs but also other roman-alphabet-language monographs and monographs in Cyrillic-alphabet languages will be recorded and distributed in MARC tapes. NDL will no doubt be able to realize great benefits from the use of MARC records. In Mr. Lorenz's paper (page 188), twelve examples of practical application of MARC records are raised. It is our intention to make use of the tapes for book selection, processing, and cataloging, as well as for the compilation and publication of *Yōsho Sokuhō* (*Accessions List: Foreign-Language Publications*) and *Gaikoku Seifu Kankōbutsu Ichiran* (*Accessions List: Foreign Government Publications*), both semimonthlies; *Ajia Afurika Shiryō Tsūhō* (*Materials on Asia and Africa: Accession List and Reviews*), a monthly; and the *Kokuritsu Kokkai Toshokan Zōsho Mokuroku: Yōsho hen* (*National Diet Library Catalog: Western Books*), which is a cumulative edition published by NDL on the other publications.

This author is particularly interested in the application of computers to the compilation of union catalogs of foreign books. If the MARC records can be utilized, locally produced catalog cards need not be sent to NDL, as is being done at present. Even before the LC Retrospective Conversion of Bibliographical Records (RECON) is put into operation, books published after the commencement of the distribution of MARC tapes can be included in *Shinshū Yōsho Sōgō Mokuroku* immediately. This could be done if the participating libraries were to transmit to NDL the LC printed catalog card numbers, or copies of the title pages, of books being accessioned. NDL would then be able to edit the reports by utilizing the output of the MARC records and would be spared the tasks of standardizing the entries, proofreading, etc. This would also permit an increase in the number of participants without enlarging the NDL staff.

There is a strong demand from library circles for centralized cataloging of foreign books by NDL. This can be met through the process of compiling a union catalog described above—by sending back the output of MARC records giving the cataloging information required for newly acquired foreign books reported by participating libraries. In doing this, the problems arising from differences between cataloging for the union catalog and in the participating libraries will be solved at the same time. Moreover, catalog entries which are standardized by this cataloging will contribute to the simplification of the compilation of union catalogs in university libraries and bring about a smoother coordination of different libraries within the same university.

There are many other benefits which are immediately foreseeable through the application of MARC records. By making a start with the MARC records, automation of NDL can be brought about fairly smoothly, and through the accumulated experiences of its use, the communications format of Japanese bibliographic data can be gradually developed and the foundations laid for the general automation of NDL. Once automation starts to operate smoothly, the publication of a quarterly cumulation of *Nōhon Shūhō*—which has been requested by library circles but which has yet to be realized because of the lack of staff—is possible, and delays in the publication of the *Zen Nihon Shuppanbutsu Sōmokuroku* can be easily overcome. NDL's authority file of authors can also be made available for use by many libraries. If the present broad subject headings can be changed somewhat, a very convenient and useful index in the form of a cumulative *Zasshi Kiji Sakuin* can be compiled very easily.

It is our firm conviction that NDL has the responsibility for developing a communications format for Japanese bibliographic data—that is, a Japanese version of the MARC format. The format must be at once both a library standard for Japan and internationally compatible, or at least convertible. The MARC II format has great flexibility and thus can serve as a very good model for our development. The MARC II format is being developed by LC for the purpose of recording all bibliographic data relating to materials of academic value collected energetically by LC. It should be evaluated not only as a library standard for the United States, but also for the whole world. In developing our own Japanese MARC format, it is important to consider its compatibility with the MARC II, and close contact must be maintained with LC in the process of development so that, among other things, cataloging information in the Shared Cataloging Program can also be submitted by magnetic tape.

Part 9

APPLICATIONS OF COMPUTERS TO LIBRARY MANAGEMENT AND INFORMATION RETRIEVAL

Some Aspects of Technology and Change in Relation to University Libraries

Herman H. Fussler
Director, University of Chicago Library

It will be the general thesis of this paper that libraries serving universities and other large research and educational enterprises will need to make some major changes in some of their concepts and in many of their methods of operation in the next ten to twenty years if they are to respond satisfactorily to the changing needs of readers and to other current or prospective library operating and management problems. It is further assumed that some aspects of computer, photocopy, and communication technology may be of increasing assistance to libraries as they attempt to meet and solve these problems. Although technology is likely to play a critical role in the improvement of libraries and information access,

it is also evident that technology can be applied to the wrong ends or otherwise misused. Even when appropriately applied, technology is unlikely to give us quick, simple, easy, and inexpensive solutions for complex intellectual, organizational, economic, and other problems relating to library development and information access.

Before discussing possible technical and other improvements in library services or operations, we obviously should have some common understanding of at least some of the contemporary problems for which better solutions are needed. This presents us with certain difficulties, for the most urgent current library or information access problems of one country may be quite different from those in another. Furthermore, there may be strong differences in opinion within a single country on the nature of the problems and the best methods for attack upon them. The methods of solution or improvement for similar problems may differ from country to country. These differences are likely to be particularly true with respect to the role and utilization of technology as a response to library and information access problems.

For these reasons, I should like to emphasize that the current problems and the responses that I propose to outline in this paper are those that seem to me to be among those that are important in the United States at the present time. The problems and the proposed solutions are intended to be illustrative; by no means do they cover the full range of problems facing libraries in the United States and the range of responses that are being seriously considered or attempted. Although the immediate problems and the priorities may be very different in the United States and Japan, there must surely be a common concern with the general quality and efficiency of the processes through which students, faculty, professionals in many fields, and many others can be assured of highly efficient access to recorded and other relevant literature and information.

It may be helpful to try to group some of these current problems and responses of university and research libraries in the United States under the three broad objectives that have almost always been among the primary concerns of the university library community: (1) the need to extend the body of relevant resource materials readily available to readers; (2) the need to improve the bibliographic, abstracting, review, and indexing apparatus for the effective control of publications and other pertinent sources of information; and (3) the need to improve the efficiency, the speed, the reliability, and the general responsiveness of direct library services and facilities for readers.

Despite the relatively high level of library service in the United States, there are at present enough visible stresses and strains in all three of these areas to suggest the need both for a basic re-examination of some of our concepts and operating or other changes in our methods of response. Even if specific problems and strains were not as visible as they seem to be, a deep and continuing concern with the general efficiency of our systems of library and information access would seem to be highly appropriate. Such on-going concern seems to me to be justified because I assume that the use of pertinent information in an academic environment by both students and faculty is to some degree an elastic phenomenon. In other words, the extent of the information effectively utilized by students and faculty members, under many circumstances, may vary quite sharply in proportion to the ease or the difficulty of gaining access to it. We furthermore assume that it is difficult to envisage an intellectual environment in which an individual can command or have efficient access to too much literature or information that is *relevant* to his problem at any point in time. If these assumptions are true, then the improvement of our libraries and information systems should, in time, produce improvements and changes in the basic intellectual processes of education and research to which they contribute.

Resource Access

If we examine some of the current problems in the availability of resource materials, primarily at the graduate and research level in the United States, we must first note the many quantitative changes in this situation. The number of relevant publications being produced throughout the world is increasing. Most of our universities have greatly broadened the geographic and subject scope of their interests in recent years, thus requiring access to a far broader spectrum of subjects. This expansion of intellectual interests seems likely to continue, though perhaps not quite so rapidly as in recent years. There are larger numbers of students; there are more institutions of higher education; the percentage of graduate students is increasing; and there are more faculty members interested in research.

The implications of these quantitative changes with respect to the production and use of resources have, as we all know, many serious long-range consequences. If, for purposes of long-range planning, we were prepared to add to these consequences the premise that any serious reader, regardless of his geographic or institutional location, ought to be able to gain access within reasonable lengths of time, at reasonable costs, and in a reasonably satisfactory form, to relevant material, it is evident that in the United States, at least, we have a set of serious problems requiring responses superior to those now commonly available.

Obviously, physical access to research resources must either be by means of local institutional self-sufficiency or by means of various shared-access arrangements or by means of some combination of these two approaches. In the United States there has long been a growing realization that local self-sufficiency for a reasonably broad spectrum of research needs was not economically feasible by existing methods of collection building. Verner Clapp and others have pointed out that perhaps local self-sufficiency at the research level might be achieved through an imaginative, very large-scale plan for the mass production and mass distribution of the world's scholarly literature in very large microfacsimile packages of some sort.[1] Although there have been some proposals for the distribution of large bodies of current and out-of-print, research-related material in this way, no comprehensive plan for providing local self-sufficiency at the research level through microform distribution is presently known to be under serious consideration. A number of such plans, as supplements to the undergraduate or college library, have recently been proposed. There are at least four serious problems: (1) we have yet to develop microform reading devices that compare favorably in reliability, comfort, intellectual efficiency, and general ease of use with the reading and use of full-size printed books and other materials; (2) the costs of such reading devices, if made available, would have to be relatively low to permit their widespread utilization; (3) if current publications were to be incorporated in such a distribution plan, suitable arrangements would have to be made for the reproduction of copyrighted material; and (4) the costs of such "packages" of material and the required bibliographic control apparatus seem likely at the present time to continue to be substantial.

The general concept raises some other interesting questions that deserve our attention. If there were to be a massive microform conversion of current or retrospective research materials, it should be ascertained whether extensive duplication and distribu-

tion of the entire body of such material to individual libraries would be functionally and economically as desirable as creating a central agency from which copies could be obtained rapidly when demand by individual libraries or scholars. The widespread "package" distribution of material may make the funding simpler, but could result in substantial institutional investments for materials that might be very infrequently used. Decisions would need to be made, depending upon the extent of duplication and the costs of reading devices, on whether low, moderate, or very high rates of reduction were used.

We should also note that many important retrospective research materials are no longer available in the book market, and only reprinting or microfacsimile reproduction can make such publications widely available, unless easy arrangements can be made for borrowing the originals from institutions that now have them. The physical deterioration of book papers may also be an inducement to the development of some microform-duplication approach unless, as is not unlikely, some simple, inexpensive means for the deacidification of full books becomes available. In short, the possibilities of greater self-sufficiency through various patterns of microform utilization still exist, but many difficult organizational, technical, copyright, economic, and reader utilization and satisfaction problems would still have to be solved before one could be sure of the responsiveness of such a system.

For these and other reasons, it seems fair to say that more attention in recent years has been given in the United States to the means of strengthening the national resource base by developing a variety of plans for the shared use of resources. The plans have included such diverse enterprises as: simple interlibrary lending; the Farmington Plan for current foreign publications; the so-called PL-480 acquisitions programs for the blanket procurement and distribution of current scholarly publications from certain foreign countries; the joint acquisition and storage programs of the Center for Research Libraries; a wide variety of local, state, and regional plans of varying degrees of formality for the sharing of resources; and several national plans, such as that for medicine sponsored by the National Library of Medicine, or the ERIC system for educational research literature. Since some of these plans are described in greater detail elsewhere in this volume, I will limit myself to some—possibly hazardous—generalizations on some aspects of these plans. In the first instance, it should be noted that we presently have a very large number of schemes to improve the availability of current and, in some cases, retrospective materials. These plans have widely different objectives and equally different methods of support and control. The availability of the materials provided is not geographically uniform and, even in the best of the present plans, leaves much to be desired in terms of the scope of materials available, the problems of locating wanted materials, the speed of access, costs, and assurance of access. Nonetheless there is a growing recognition of the need to build a more responsive shared-access system or systems. It should be emphasized that such systems cannot take the place of basic college or university library collections; the intention of shared-access systems is to extend such basic collections for relatively infrequently used materials. Many of the recent proposals in this area have been described as "network" systems, in which it is proposed that individual libraries be linked together in some systematic way to provide for the individual reader access in one way or another to the resources of the entire network. Usually, though not invariably, these systems are conceived of in some sort of hierarchical pattern.

Technology, both explicitly and implicitly, should play a critical role in the design of such network or interdependent library or information systems. At the present time its role is, with a few exceptions, largely in the area of providing faster communication among libraries in handling requests and reports on the availability of wanted materials and in photocopying wanted materials, either in full size or in microform. There have, however, been a number of experiments on the facsimile transmission of textual materials between libraries. Thus far electronic facsimile transmission has not proved to be particularly satisfactory, primarily because the overall costs of existing systems, in relation to the bulk of the material commonly required, has been relatively high and the quality has not always been good. Furthermore, it is evident that the major delays in providing access to textual materials between two conventional academic libraries are only to a small degree related to actual transmission time. A much greater proportion of the total access time is presently related to identifying and locating the wanted item in the source library, converting the form of text into one suitable for transmission (e.g., a microfilm or full-size photocopy in loose sheet form rather than bound volumes), and, after reception, in getting it into the hands of the reader. A sharp reduction in the costs of communication circuits, i.e., telephone lines, co-axial cables, or microwave circuits, and some further developments of terminal equipment to handle bound volumes would seem likely to be required before large-scale scholarly textual transmission can be seriously considered, except in unusual circumstances. In any case, it is obvious that careful analyses of speed-of-access requirements, limitations, and costs need to be made before responsive systems of this type are likely to be designed. A case in point is the effort to reduce transmission time, e.g., electronic facsimile vs. mail, when the great bulk of the delay in access between institutions is the result of other factors. Quick, full-size photocopies sent by air mail overnight might, in fact, satisfy many, if not most, reader needs.

There have also been many proposals for the storage, manipulation, and high-speed transfer from one institution to another of large quantities of computer-stored textual data. The costs of such storage, while declining, are still high, and the communication costs present problems analogous to those for facsimile transmission. Added to these costs are the substantial costs for the initial conversion and input of the textual data in a form suitable for computer control, transfer, and display, or print-out.

In consequence, it is evident that relatively small bodies of data can be handled in this way if the requirements justify the relatively high costs, but the prospects for large-scale storage and long-distance transfer of large amounts of full text seem at the present time rather distant.

There are at least three important general observations to be made on matters of this kind: (1) the general trend in technology, and especially in the case of computers, is to offer increasing capability at lower unit costs; (2) even with such improvements in prospect, very careful analyses of requirements, costs, and benefits may identify other alternatives in library procedures of much greater potential benefit than the immediate assumption of a technical solution; and (3) substantial increases in scholarly library interdependence to increase the level of resources available to readers seem indicated. The design of highly efficient and responsive systems of this kind will require imagination and skill, and we believe that special interlibrary centers exclusively devoted to such functions, such as the Center for Research Libraries or the National Lending Library for Science and Technology in Great Britain are likely to make important and distinctive contributions in improving the accessibility of infrequently used research resources.

Bibliographic Access

Our second general area of concern was that of improving bibliographic access and control—also a topic treated elsewhere in this volume. Not too long ago the basic bibliographic apparatus of a college or university was related primarily to the publications held by its library. While such author, title, and subject catalogs of the resources of an individual library are still critically important and very heavily used instruments, some significant changes that may alter both the costs and the relative importance of these institutional catalogs are beginning to emerge.

An increasing percentage of the basic cataloging information for currently published monographs added to the Library of Congress (LC) and other large U.S.

libraries is now being generated, published, and otherwise distributed through the efforts of LC and the two other national libraries, working in collaboration in many cases with national or other libraries abroad. These book catalogs also give information on locations of the titles listed. In addition to this widespread availability of current monographic bibliographic/locational data, the long-awaited project for the publication in book form of the *U.S. National Union Catalog* has now started. This will contain author or main entries for an estimated 11,000,000 to 13,000,000 different titles, with at least one U.S. location for each title.

The analysis and control of the contents of serial publications and journals have long been generated and published almost entirely outside the typical university library by societies, by commercial publishers, by the national libraries, by other agencies of the federal government, or in other ways, and the results are, of course, widely distributed in book or other published form. It is hoped that a national system for providing up-to-date locational information for serial publications can also soon be brought into being to maintain the information in the existing *Union List of Serials*.

We all know that in the general field of bibliographic control of scholarly and research publications, many basic improvements are still badly needed, e.g., qualitative reviews, deeper subject analysis, faster coverage, more consistent abstracting, better coordination and coverage, and the capability of easier, more complex, and more consistent searches for relevant material. Although these and other improvements are needed, the underlying changes that are already apparent with respect to the availability of bibliographic data have far-reaching consequences.

To a substantial degree, the scholar or the student working anywhere in the country will now, or in the foreseeable future, be able to identify materials pertinent to his needs, regardless of the strength of his local library. He will also be able to ascertain at least one location for most such material. It seems to me that this is a significant change. A second consequence is that the development of such systems should substantially reduce the staff that may otherwise be required for cataloging and other technical processing work in local libraries.

A third consequence has to do with the growing necessity for these basic bibliographic and indexing systems to require machine-readable data and computer-based data manipulation. This is true even though the initial product of such operations is a printed bibliography. This seems to me likely (1) to stimulate greatly and to facilitate computer-based data processing within libraries; (2) to lead toward the design and development of systems that may, in the long run, assist the reader in conducting more complex and faster searches for relevant materials than are now possible with the existing manual systems or the printed products of machine-based systems; and (3) to suggest the possibility of very radical, long-term changes in the local bibliographic apparatus and means of access to it. Having made these observations, it is perhaps equally important to observe that there are also complex intellectual, technical, and economic issues in connection with the extension, coordination, and use of these systems, as well as major problems of bibliographic scope and coverage. There are problems in data handling standards; in large file management and utilization; in error identification and correction; in the levels of content analysis; in file security; in data input, output, and storage costs; in the limited size of the character fonts that can now be handled, etc. There are serious observers of the scene who suggest that the time will come when a reader may, by means of a computer-connected console, consult complex, machine-stored bibliographic files in ways that will aid him in defining his problem, that will display or otherwise make available a list of the pertinent materials, possibly with annotations, and that may, at some time in the future, then go on to produce the pertinent text itself or request the original or a copy of it from a local library or some other source. Such systems are likely to be extremely expensive and

very difficult to achieve for some time to come and, in consequence, are likely to emerge sequentially.

In summary, it seems evident that while our systems of content or bibliographic control are in need of much further improvement, they are already ahead of many aspects of physical accessibility of the materials controlled; that the newly evolving systems are highly dependent upon computer-based data processing; that the systems have very substantial long-range potentials for substantial improvement and alteration of library bibliographic services and operations; and that the development of these systems must overcome many quite serious problems.

Library Services and Operations

The increases in the size and complexity of the body of recorded knowledge and information and the rising expectations and needs of readers have produced obvious strains for both the library and the reader. From the reader's point of view, the library often seems slow in its responses and otherwise difficult or even frustrating to use. Libraries, on the other hand, even though they are successfully selecting, acquiring, cataloging, and circulating extraordinarily large amounts of relevant material, recognize that there are often serious delays in the availability of needed material; that costs are tending to rise relentlessly; that qualified staff with the requisite languages, subject knowledge, and other skills and experience are not always available; and that variations in work loads with the academic calendar are often difficult to meet satisfactorily.

In addition, it is evident that many of the present procedures of libraries are costly to extend or to adapt to changing needs and requirements because of the complex record and other changes that are commonly required. It can be argued that libraries, as they have grown to large size, may, in a sense, become the prisoners of their complex manual data-processing systems and the resulting files. For example, the main card catalogs of many university libraries now contain several million cards.

Substantial rearrangements or other modifications in such large, complex files clearly present such serious cost problems as to be likely to inhibit major change or alteration. They may also present users with increasingly difficult access problems. Since the state of recorded knowledge is dynamic, and since universities are subject to continuing change in structure, methodology, and objectives, it is essential that we give greater attention to designing library and information access systems that will be as responsive as possible to the wide variety of reader needs—some of which are now being met very well—and that will be capable of easier evolution and change to meet, even to anticipate, future needs and requirements.

In any broad consideration of library services and resources it quickly becomes evident that such services are critically related to data processing with certain key characteristics: (1) A very high proportion of all the internal processing and other operations of libraries is based upon access to, and the maintenance of, bibliographic and related data files that describe, analyze, locate, or otherwise show the status of the materials held by a library. (2) Data from these basic files are searched, compared, extended, extracted, deleted, rearranged, matched with data from other files, or otherwise manipulated for an extremely large percentage of all the end purposes connected with library operations and are also closely associated with many aspects of reader access to a library's resources. (3) Such record generation, maintenance, and manipulation accounts for a very significant proportion of library operating costs. (4) Many, though certainly not all, of the routines or operating decisions associated with the use of these basic data files are highly formalized, i.e., many of the decisions based upon these records do not require interpretive or qualitative intellectual judgments. The decisions are usually affirmative or negative actions depending upon the nature of the internal data; for example: Does the library have a specified title or not? Is it in use or not? Is the order for it overdue or not?

It is evident that these conditions, if true, are those that, at least theoretically, match some of the basic capabilities of modern computers: (1) computers can store and manipulate at very high speeds large bodies of complex data; (2) they can use the same data base for a wide variety of end products or routines; (3) they are capable of extending, correcting, deleting, and otherwise altering records when instructed to do so; (4) they can make comparisons and other routine decisions if the decision-making rules are sufficiently formal and are based upon the internal data; and (5) they can handle, in many cases, wide variations in work load with relatively low incremental costs, and large load increases can produce sharp reductions in unit costs.

There is another basic capability of the computer that deserves recognition. It is possible for computer-based systems to be so designed as to permit the collection of significant performance data on library operations as a by-product of the operation itself. As a simple illustration, it would be possible in a computer-based, book-circulation system so to design the system that for books requested, but not available at the time of request, data could be collected on what kinds of books were most commonly unavailable; the reasons that they were unavailable; the identity of groups of readers that were most frequently unable to get material, etc. These data can, of course, be collected by manual methods, but only at very high costs. We must look to performance data on a wide variety of library operations that are generally not now available to tell how well a library is responding to many reader needs and to other kinds of operating criteria. Such data can help us to construct mathematical models of library loads and response capabilities that can lead to the design of more efficient and more responsive systems. I hasten to say that the collection and analysis of such data is a future potential of computer-based library systems since virtually none of the present computer-based operations is sufficiently developed to permit any very advanced level of performance analysis.

The consequences of the basic match between some library problems and the capabilities of modern computers has perhaps been summarized most tersely in several of the conclusions in the report of the panel that surveyed the operations of the Library of Congress:

1. Automation can, within the next decade, augment and accelerate the services rendered by large research libraries and can have a profound effect upon their responsiveness to the needs of library users.
2. Automation of bibliographic processing, catalog searching, and document retrieval is technically and economically feasible in large research libraries.
3. The retrieval of the intellectual content of books by automatic methods is not now feasible for large collections, but progress in that direction will be advanced by effective automation of cataloging and indexing functions.
4. Automation will enhance the adaptability of libraries to changes in the national research environment and will facilitate the development of a national library system.
5. Automation will reduce the cost-to-performance ratio. . . .[2]

In part because of these conclusions and other corroborative observations, the three national libraries and a goodly number of public, college, and university libraries in the United States are now attempting to mechanize or to automate some portion of their data-related operations. A powerful stimulus to further such developments will occur when machine-readable current bibliographic data become available from the Library of Congress and other sources in the MARC II format.

Because there are many different kinds of computers, different ways of using them, and different approaches to library data-processing, it is not easy to categorize the current efforts to develop such systems in the United States. It is obvious that the full spectrum of both potential and experimental application is quite broad. At one extreme there are efforts being made to test systems for on-line direct information retrieval in which there is a real-time inquirer-computer dialogue. There are a few

very limited systems for the on-line searching and retrieval or display of bibliographic or indexing and citation data, e.g., Project MAC-TIP at the Massachusetts Institute of Technology, or the National Library of Medicine-Harvard-State University of New York medical library data. There are other systems where the mode of access to indexing data is by batch, or periodic processing of a computer-stored file in response to one or a number of requests, e.g., the MEDLARS searches based upon the data generated at the National Library of Medicine. Other libraries are attempting to design and implement rather highly integrated bibliographic data systems that will use existing levels of bibliographic data and processing information for a wide variety of library data-processing operations. Among these libraries are those of the University of Chicago, Stanford University, and Columbia University. In these cases both on-line and batch processing are commonly used, depending upon the specific processing requirements. And, finally, there are many libraries that have developed essentially separate or independent computer-aided systems for specific tasks, e.g., book ordering, the preparation of serial title and holdings lists, book fund accounting, book circulation operations, etc.

At the present time—and I describe it simply for illustrative purposes because it is the system with which I am most familiar—the University of Chicago Library has in current operation a computer-based book-processing system with the following kinds of features. The system provides for:

1. Batch and on-line computer data input for machine record creation, record update, and error correction
2. Batch and on-line machine file update and logical error check reporting
3. On-line machine record retrieval and print-out by control number
4. Batch and on-line programs for processing, formatting, and high-speed product printing from a single "processing" record of the following kinds of products
   a. Catalog cards for each title processed with all required headings and each

card individually formatted for a particular catalog use and printed out in filing order for a particular catalog location, whether dictionary, main entry, or call number order

b. Book order forms printed out by the dealer to whom the order will be sent

c. Processing slips for all subsequent manual processing of books

d. Listing of daily fund commitment totals, and

e. Book cards and pocket labels for each physical volume processed.

The intention, of course, is to extend these functions as rapidly as possible to provide other services and products, including multi-key subject, author, or title searches of the machine-stored file. In the meantime, the functions described are carrying a heavy daily production load for the library with, in general, the capability of much faster response and a requirement for substantially less skilled labor. Other libraries are engaged in developing somewhat similar systems, though many are not relying upon the utilization of a central, common data base.

What can be said about the experience with these systems thus far? First of all, it seems fair to say that most of these systems, unless the application is a very simple one, present very difficult design, technical, and economic problems. The files required are large and complex, and the methods for efficient file maintenance and for sophisticated searches of these files, together with the required displays or print-outs, are still largely to be developed. Such developmental work will be costly, and so will the ongoing computer operating costs. These systems will, of course, be most beneficial when there has been a substantial conversion and computer input of retrospective file records and all current bibliographic data are readily available in machine-readable form. Such current data and conversions must clearly follow some national or international standards, which, thus far, have not been available. The Library of Congress MARC II format may now offer such a standard for some parts of the data

required in these systems. There are obvious economic and other advantages if retrospective data conversion could be undertaken once only to meet the needs of all libraries. Some attention is now being given to this difficult problem.

The *initial* unit costs of the more complex outputs from computer-based library data processing systems seem likely to be significantly higher than the manual processes they supersede. There are at least three compensatory factors, however. (1) Well-designed, computer-based systems have demonstrated their ability to provide faster responses, the possibility of a wide variety of services or outputs, at small incremental costs, and other performance benefits that would not have been possible with manually based systems and that may justify part or all of the higher costs. (2) The trends in the development of computer equipment have clearly been in the direction of substantial increases in speed and capability and closely related reductions in unit processing or storage costs. (Unfortunately these benefits of new generations of computers may often be offset to at least some degree by the high, one-time costs of the reprogramming required to transfer complex systems from one computer to another.) (3) Since a high proportion of the total costs for existing library operations must be allocated for salaries, and since salary costs are expected to continue to increase with increases in gross national productivity, it is evident that the present manual processes will tend to increase in unit costs. Since the machine costs are tending to decline, it is evident that sooner or later the unit cost curves for at least many of the manual and the computer-based systems are likely to cross, subject to increases in costs because of improved performance in new systems. The superficial economic questions, of course, are: "How far apart are the present manual and initial machine costs?" and "At what speed are manual and machine costs changing relatively to each other?" The underlying economic issues are more complex, for they relate to the quality of library and information access that should or can be offered; the intellectual or economic impact of improvements in such services; the extent to which the costs should be borne by an individual or by his institution, or by society, etc.

There are, of course, many other problems. In general, the computer equipment available has been designed for science, business, or industry. It has been difficult to get specialized terminal and other computer equipment designed or built to meet some of the specialized needs of libraries. There are very difficult character-font problems. Scholarly libraries need to handle data in roman alphabets as well as in Japanese, Hebrew, Greek, Arabic, Chinese, Sanskrit, and many other alphabets or characters. The capability for handling such materials is at present most unsatisfactory. Transliteration or romanization does not seem, to most scholars, to be the happiest answer. Finally, there are, as one might expect, shortages of library and computer personnel properly experienced and qualified for the design and implementation of such systems. Unfortunately, it is generally not now possible to take a computer system developed for one university library and use it without substantial modification —requiring major experience and technical knowledge—for another university. Some work is being undertaken by one or more commercial organizations to try to develop computer-based "general-purpose" library or data-processing systems, but whether this approach is functionally, economically, or technically feasible is still to be determined. There are some fears that such systems may be quite inefficient in computer usage and may be difficult to modify for new or extended applications.

While the very limited systems can be operated with relatively small, dedicated computers, the majority of the large systems require relatively large and, consequently, costly computers. This has meant that most university libraries that have undertaken such work have worked out appropriate procedures to share general university computer facilities. These arrangements, while sometimes difficult to work out, may at present be a very efficient way for the library to use what would otherwise be quite costly computer and

peripheral equipment, such as high-speed printers. In time it is possible that a number of libraries might share a common computer. Alternatively, highly specialized computers may become available, at relatively low costs, that would be capable of handling the great bulk of a library's data processing on a dedicated basis, switching to a large central computer only when required.

Future Developments

There are at least seven major areas in which we may probably anticipate important changes or developments in libraries and library services:

1. It seems likely that university and research libraries within the United States and other large countries will need to re-examine some of their basic premises and objectives to ascertain the extent to which reasonable objectives are being met and the alternative means by which these objectives might better be achieved.
2. A significant increase in interdependence among libraries and other information-related institutions on regional, national, and international bases would seem to be a probable consequence of such a re-examination. The critical determination of the objectives or functions to be sought through such interdependence and the designs for such interdependent systems will, in the United States and in many other countries, present difficult organizational, fiscal, and other problems. The general objectives of such interdependent relationships should be to enhance both resource and bibliographic access, but quite different arrangements and solutions will be required for these two broad objectives.
3. It is likely that basic bibliographic control will increasingly be a major national or international responsibility, with the product becoming increasingly sophisticated and responsive to readers' specialized requirements.
4. There will almost certainly be a substantially greater use of modern technology in the operation of libraries and in other information access processes. The effective transition to significantly greater utilization of technology will itself produce difficulties and strains. Technology is relevant

to all three of our general objectives: physical access, bibliographic access, and library service and operation.

5. It will be highly desirable to develop and to utilize better tools and analyses to collect management and performance data. Only when we have better measurements of loads, responses, and operating efficiency can we wisely identify critical problems and plan improved services.

6. Funding and staff to carry out very much more extensive programs of research and experimentation, both applied and basic in nature, will be essential to the basic improvement of library operations and information access.

7. In the United States, and perhaps in other countries, there may be quite substantial modifications in the sources of fiscal support and in the internal distribution of library costs.

With greater research efforts, with clearer understandings of our objectives and the requirements of libraries, with greater experience in the wise application of technology, when appropriate, to library and information access processes, it is reasonable to anticipate substantial improvements and changes in our libraries. Such changes and improvements should greatly assist in pushing back the frontiers of knowledge and in improving human understanding.

NOTES

[1]Verner W. Clapp, *The Future of the Research Library* (Urbana: Univ. of Illinois Pr., 1964).

[2]*Automation and the Library of Congress* (Washington, D.C.: Library of Congress, 1963).

Biomedical Communications: Developing a Mechanized Library Network

Martin M. Cummings and Mary E. Corning
U.S. National Library of Medicine

When I say "Our Medical Literature," it is not with reference to that of any particular country or nation, but to that which is the common property of the educated physicians of the world . . . the literature which forms the intra- and international bond of the medical profession of all civilized countries; and by virtue of which we . . . do not now meet, for the first time, as strangers, but as friends . . . whose thoughts are perhaps better known to each other than to some of our nearest neighbors.[1]

A zeal for scholarship and a keen appreciation of scientific achievement, wherever performed, characterize the spirit of scientific cooperation between the United States and Japan. It is not new. The United States in its early history looked to progress made in other countries as it developed its own medical and health programs. The first medical journal published in the United States in 1790 was actually a selection and translation from the *Journal de Médicine Militaire*. The first American medical journal *The Medical Repository* appeared seven years later. During this same period in Japan, translations were being made of Dutch texts on anatomy, surgery, and internal medicine.[2]

Learning may require a tremendous personal effort, but one which a scholar always makes. This was magnificently illustrated by Yukichi Fukuzawa, the founder of Keiō University. As a student in Ogata School in Osaka in 1856–57, he had available from Lord Kuroda, for two days only, a new Dutch translation of an English text on physical science. In his autobiography, Fukuzawa said:

All that we knew about electricity then had been gleaned from fragmentary mention of it in the Dutch readers. But here in this new book from Europe was a full explanation based on the recent discoveries of the great English physicist, Faraday, even with the diagram of an electric cell. My heart was carried away with it at first sight. . . . But, then, to copy a volume of a thousand pages! We decided to do just the final chapter, the one on electricity. If we could have broken the book up and divided the copying among the thirty or fifty "ready-quill men," the entire contents might have been kept. But of course injuring the nobleman's possession was out of the question. . . . One read aloud; another took down the dictation; when one grew tired and slowed down, another was waiting with his quill, and the exhausted one would go to sleep regardless of time, morning, noon or night. Thus, working day and night, through meal hours and all, we finished the whole chapter in the time allotted, and thus the section on electricity, about three hundred pages including its diagrams, remained with us in manuscript. We finished reading it against the text for correction and regretted that we had no more time for the other parts. But to have retained so much we counted fortunate, and when the evening of Lord Kuroda's departure came, we all handled the book affectionately in turn and gave it a sad leave-taking as if we were parting with a parent.[3]

Fukuzawa's respect for books and the scientific record and his effort to conquer distance and language were paralleled by the efforts of Dr. John Shaw Billings, the principal figure in the history of the U.S. National Library of Medicine (NLM). In 1879 Dr. Billings began the *Index Medicus*, the first comprehensive recurring bibliography of the world's biomedical literature. This publication was directed toward the individual medical practitioner, teacher, or scientist. The practitioner would find parallel and new remedies for his anomalous cases; the teacher could relate to what was taught elsewhere; and the scientist could either find data to be incorporated in his work or data which anticipated his work. Dr. Billings' basic philosophy of providing a subject access to the medical literature as an information service to the individual is valid today; only the size of the task and the technique of preparation and processing of bibliographic information differ.

Nature of Scientific Communication

Our current scientific literature consists of over 100,000 journals and 500 abstracting and indexing publications.[4] A library has always been considered the storehouse of knowledge. However, access to and use of this knowledge have stimulated the development of new information tools and packaging of specialized information, a process in which the library today has a dynamic role, whether it functions at a local, regional, national, or international level or within a network of libraries.

An individual need not rely solely on his own personal resources and initiative. There are translation services; photocopying machines which substitute for "ready-quill men"; abstracting and indexing journals; information analysis centers; and the selective dissemination of information. Thus there begins a new kind of relationship between an individual, the library, and a network of librarians. The prime and ultimate objective of effective scientific communication is to serve the professional user by identifying him, understanding his need, and tailoring a modality to meet his requirements. Communication underscores the advancement of scientific research, education, and application; it is dependent upon people, the scientific record, equipment, facilities, and technology.

To illustrate the new dynamic role of the library, the application of electronic and computer technology, and the "network" approach, we shall discuss the field of medicine and in particular the experiences of the U.S. National Library of Medicine with holdings of more than 1.35 million items. This report demonstrates the unanticipated rate at which electronic and computer technology precipitate action and progress. It also emphasizes the unique cooperation which is necessary between a library and the professional and scientific community it serves.

Computers and Libraries

Computer applications in a library may be for (1) management and administration; (2) library operations and procedures, and (3) storage and retrieval of scientific information for the professional user.[5] Management (budget-accounting-personnel) applications are out of scope for this discussion. Applications to library operations and procedures may be concerned with acquisitions; cataloging, serials control, circulation, interlibrary loan, and catalog production.

In a 1966 survey the characteristics of a mechanized library were identified as:

1. University or special research library
2. Holdings of 50,000 books and more than 1,000 periodical titles
3. Staff of 10–20, evenly divided between professionals and nonprofessionals
4. Serial control performed by electrical accounting machines (EAM)
5. Accounting performed by computer, and
6. Equipment usually belonging to the parent or host organization and serving many other purposes.[6]

The libraries leading in computer applications to operations and processing were mainly industrial or university-based.

To date NLM has used computer technology primarily for the storage and retrieval of scientific augmented references for the professional user: MEDLARS (Medical Literature Analysis and Retrieval System).

MEDLARS

In 1961 NLM began its planning and systems development for a computer-based information storage and retrieval system (MEDLARS) which became operational within three years (1964) and will be replaced this year (1969) after five years of successful operation.[7]

MEDLARS is a reference retrieval system beginning with the literature of 1963. The world's biomedical literature is analyzed and indexed according to subject by subject experts with various language capabilities. Some of this important intellectual effort is performed in Japan, the United Kingdom, Sweden, and Israel under special arrangement with NLM. *Medical Subject Headings (MeSH)* is the authority list for the indexing, for search formulation and computer retrieval, and for book cataloging in the library. This reference storage and retrieval system, MEDLARS, is effective for our library because the documents identified by the system can be made available from our library's holdings.

MEDLARS I has two primary purposes: preparation of bibliographic publications and provision of subject-oriented demand searches. The principal NLM publication, *Index Medicus*, is a monthly bibliography of the world's biomedical literature. In addition, the library cooperates with scientific and professional societies who have specialized information needs by providing recurring bibliographies in such fields as medical education, nursing, dentistry, rheumatology, cancer chemotherapy, nutrition, endocrinology, cerebrovascular diseases, and toxicity of drugs. These computer-produced bibliographies now number fifteen. Demand searches are performed in response to requests from individuals who identify their specific interests and needs (see figure 1). The current number of demand searches performed is about 10,000, with about two-thirds of these formulated at seven university-based MEDLARS centers, four of which also have computer facilities for processing.

An extension of MEDLARS that had not been originally planned is the computer-aided catalog processing system. The products of this cataloging system are the NLM *Current Catalog* (figure 2), and the production of catalog cards for not only NLM but also the Upstate Medical Center Library of the State University of New York and the Harvard Countway Library of Boston, Mass. (figure 3). The latter two libraries are participating with NLM in cooperative cataloging.

The NLM *Current Catalog* is published biweekly and is an acquisitions and cataloging tool for other libraries. This is an example of how experienced data-processing and library personnel may use available

```
                                                    191322
    PATINO JF

    PLANNING NEW PROGRAMS IN MEDICAL
    EDUCATION. EDUCATION IN THE HEALTH
    PROFESSIONS TO MEET THE NEEDS OF THE
    NATIONS.

    J MED EDUC, 43,221-31, FEB 68

    *EDUCATION, MEDICAL, GOVERNMENT AGENCIES,
    *HEALTH OCCUPATIONS/EDUCATION, HUMAN,
    ORGANIZATIONS, PROFESSIONAL PRACTICE,
    PUBLIC HEALTH ADMINISTRATION, SCHOOLS,
    MEDICAL, SOCIETIES, MEDICAL,
    UNIVERSITIES

                        NATIONAL LIBRARY OF MEDICINE (MEDLARS)
```

Fig. 1. Bibliographical citation on demand search computer-produced card

equipment to design and implement a new system to meet a demonstrated need. This service is now provided as a dividend from the original purpose of MEDLARS because it represents work performed at little additional cost.

MEDLARS I had been operational four years when it became clear that the system would have to be enlarged. Therefore, planning began in 1967 for MEDLARS II. The major improvements planned for MEDLARS II include:

1. Increased amount and speed of bibliographic services
2. Automated acquisition and cataloging system
3. Improved indexing and searching aid (on-line MeSH)
4. Ability to provide chemical compound searches, and
5. Graphic image storage and retrieval system.

A number of elements in MEDLARS II relate to assisting the intellectual aspects of preparing input for the system and application to library processes. The first level is scheduled to be operational in the fall of 1969.

Evaluation of Information Retrieval Systems

Evaluation of an information system is an extremely arduous and complex task. Unfortunately, few major operational systems have undergone a rigorous examination. NLM decided that MEDLARS should be evaluated objectively, and the MEDLARS Evaluation Study was conducted by F. W. Lancaster under the guidance of an external board of advisors.[8]

A 300-search sample of the 5,000 yearly computer searches gave results which indicate that over 55 percent of the citations in the file relevant to the request were retrieved. Of these retrieved citations, between 50 and 65 percent were judged relevant to the requester's needs. Considering the enormous size of the file (800,000 articles), we believe this represents satisfactory performance. However, this study has highlighted the need for more careful indexing, improved interface between the user and the system, further vocabulary development, and general quality control. Because this evaluation is unique, we believe that both its methodology and its results are noteworthy, not only for the development of MEDLARS II but also for other information retrieval systems.

ABNORMALITIES

Teratology. v. 1- May 1968.
Philadelphia. v. illus. ports. Official organ
of the Teratology Society. Published jointly by
the Teratology Society and the Wistar Institute
of Anatomy and Biology.
DNLM: W1 TE57G   Cit. No. 121233

ABNORMALITIES, DRUG-INDUCED

Teratology. v. 1- May 1968.
Philadelphia. v. illus. ports. Official organ
of the Teratology Society. Published jointly by
the Teratology Society and the Wistar Institute
of Anatomy and Biology.
DNLM: W1 TE57G   Cit. No. 121233

ABSENTEEISM

Robles Córdova, Jacinto Rubén. Ausentismo y
deserción escolares en el altiplano occidental de
Guatemala. Quezaltenango. 1966. 162 p.
Tesis - Univ. de San Carlos. Guatemala.
DNLM: LC 145.G9 R666a 1966   Cit. No. 122732

ACCIDENT PREVENTION

Svenska Institutet for kulturellt utbyte med
utlandet. Prevention of childhood accidents in
Sweden. [Stockholm, 1968] 40 p. illus.
Published by the Swedish Institute and the Joint
Committee for the Prevention of Childhood
Accidents.
DNLM: W6 P3   Cit. No. 122737

ACCIDENTS, INDUSTRIAL

Bergman, Lars G., 1908-   Personlig
sykddsutrustning i arbetet. [Stockholm] Bok
och bild... 1968. 111 p. illus.
DNLM: ...   Cit. No. 123310

ADRENAL GLAND DISEASES

O'Neal, Lawrence W., 1923-   Surgery of the
adrenal glands. St. Louis. Mosby. 1968. x, 295
p. illus.
SUNY: WK 790 O58s 1968   Cit. No. 123345

AGAMMAGLOBULINEMIA

Distrofia del lactante; contribución a su estudio y
tratamiento [por] Oscar R. Turró [et al.]
Buenos Aires. Librería Huemul [1967?] 223
p. illus.
DNLM: QY 455 D614 1967   Cit. No. 122245

AGGRESSION

Conference on Brain Function. 5th. Pacific
Palisades. 1965. Aggression and defense; neural
mechanisms and social patterns. proceedings of
the fifth Conference on Brain Function.
November. 1965. Sponsored by the Brain
Research Institute. University of California Los
Angeles. with the support of the U. S. Air Force
Office of Scientific Research. Editors: Carmine
D. Clemente and Donald B. Lindsley. Berkeley.
Univ. of California Press. 1967. xv, 361 p.
illus. (UCLA forum in medical sciences. no. 7)
Brain function. v. 5
DNLM: W3 U17 no 7 1965   Cit. No. 123751

AGRICULTURE

Food and Agriculture Organization of the United
Nations. Documentation Center. Animals -
Index. Animales - Indice: 1945-1966. [Rome]
1967. iii. 28, 183. 9, 174 p (PI: DC-Sp 6)
Covers publication and documents of the FAO
Animal Production and Health Division.
Introduction in English. French. and Spanish.
DNLM: Z 5074.L7 F689a 1945-66 Cit. No. 123325

ALCOHOLISM

Meza, César. Mimo. dependencia. depresión
alcoholismo. [1. ed.] Guatemala, 1967.
p. (Universidad de San Carlos de Guatemala.
Estudios universitarios. v. 3)
DNLM: WM 274 M617m 1967   Cit. No. 123445

Schmidt, Wolfgang. Social class and the
treatment of alcoholism; an investigation o
class as a determinant of diagnosis, prognos
and therapy [by] Wolfgang Schmidt. Redm
Smart [and] Marcia K. Moss. [Toronto]
Published for the Addiction Research Foun
by Univ. of Toronto Press [c1968] x. 11
(Brookside monograph. no. 7)
DNLM: W1 BR887 no 7 1968
MBCO: WM 274 S24s 1968   Cit. No

ALGAE

Mackenthun, Kenneth M. Algal grow
factors other than nitrogen and phosp
selected biological references [by] Ke
Mackenthun [and] William Marcus Ing
[Washington] 1966. vi. 41 p (Fede
Pollution Control Administration
DNLM: Z 5356 A6 M155a 1966   Cit

AMINO ACIDS

Myers, Terrell C. Chemistry of amino
peptides and proteins; a programmed
Terrell C. Myers [and] Jerome S. Alle
Contributing programers: J Walter Gl
New York. Hoeber [c1968] viii. 384
MBCO: QU 55 M996c 1968   Cit

ANATOMY

Arnold. Maurice. Reconstruc
method for hu...

Fig. 2. Sample of *Current Catalog* page

```
WI        Ashizawa, Shinroku.
17            I-naishikyo atorasu. [Gastroendoscope atlas, by
A825i         Shinroku Ashizawa and Tsutomu Kidokoro]  Tokyo,
1968          Bunkodo [Showa 43 nen, 1968]
                  116 p.   illus., plates
              .. ...  Bessatsu shiema shu [Supplemental collection of
              schema]  Tokyo, Bunkodo [1968]  115 p.   illus.
                                      WI 17 A825i 1968 Supp.
                  1. Gastroscopy · atlases  2. Stomach Diseases ·
              atlases  3. Stomach Neoplasms · atlases  I. Kidokoro,
              Tsutomu.  II. Title


DNLM                                      68-130657
                        12/16/68
```

Fig. 3. Computer-produced catalog card

Fundamental Role of NLM

Because MEDLARS revolutionized the technique of preparing publications and providing specialized bibliographic services to the individual user, it is very easy to equate NLM to MEDLARS and to de-emphasize all other NLM functions and responsibilities. However, the computer-based system represents only one functioning element of NLM's overall role in improving biomedical communications.

NLM has a national mandate from the U.S. Congress "to assist the advancement of medical and related sciences and to aid the dissemination and exchange of scientific and other information important to the progress of medicine and to the public health." The programs of the library are directed at both the individual and the institution, at the local, regional, and national levels. Through NLM programs medical libraries are receiving financial assistance to improve library resources and the provision of services, to increase the number of specialized staff, to apply electronic technology to library processes and information services, and to develop interlibrary network relationships.

NLM has a National Medical Audiovisual Center for production and distribution of audiovisual resources and related specialized services. The newly established (1968) Lister Hill National Center for

Biomedical Communications of NLM is a recognition that scientific communications must have the benefit of the latest technological advances and the continuing attention of research and development.

Thus the functions of the library have not remained static but have expanded as the communications needs of the health community have become more urgent. However, manpower and fiscal resources have not increased proportionately to meet these professional requirements. The sharp increase in requests for professional services is illustrated by the 900-percent increase in requests for demand searches over five years. This was accompanied by attendant increases in reference and interlibrary loan services. Accordingly, we began to examine centralization versus decentralization of operations, the indentification of existing regional and local resources, and essentially the question of how NLM should function as a national resource in its relationship to both the medical and library communities.

As a first step, NLM began to establish decentralized MEDLARS search centers and a network of regional medical libraries. There are presently seven U.S. universities and two foreign institutions operating as MEDLARS search centers where demand searches are formulated. Existing U.S. libraries which have a capability for expanding services to medical libraries within a broad geographic area are being selected for support and designation as regional medical libraries. To date, six of these have been selected on a competitive basis, and ultimately there may be twenty-five to thirty (figure 4).

The principle underlying the concept of a regional medical library is "service." In the United States there are all kinds of medical libraries. They may be located within a university, a medical center, or a local hospital. These libraries may differ in organizational setting but not in the service they should perform for the physician, and many are too ill-equipped and poorly staffed to provide this service. To reach these institutions in a systematic and constructive manner, we believe national, regional, and local institutional interrelationships are necessary (figure 5).

This hierarchical system consists of:

1. NLM as the national resource that can assist other medical libraries in terms of material not in their collection and in services to the user
2. Regional libraries that will improve and expand their reference and interlibrary loan services to medical and hospital libraries in a broad geographic area, and
3. The local libraries, which must serve many individual health professionals.

Our first regional medical library, the Harvard Countway Library, has been in existence for about a year and a half. Its

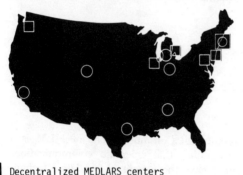

◉ Decentralized MEDLARS centers
▣ Regional medical libraries

Fig. 4. Decentralized MEDLARS centers and regional medical libraries

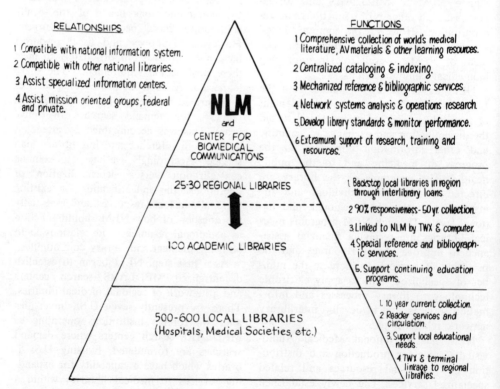

RELATIONSHIPS

1 Compatible with national information system.
2 Compatible with other national libraries.
3 Assist specialized information centers.
4 Assist mission oriented groups, federal and private.

NLM
and
CENTER FOR
BIOMEDICAL
COMMUNICATIONS

FUNCTIONS

1 Comprehensive collection of world's medical literature, AV materials & other learning resources.
2 Centralized cataloging & indexing.
3 Mechanized reference & bibliographic services.
4 Network systems analysis & operations research.
5 Develop library standards & monitor performance.
6 Extramural support of research, training and resources.

25-30 REGIONAL LIBRARIES

100 ACADEMIC LIBRARIES

1 Backstop local libraries in region through interlibrary loans
2 90% responsiveness - 50 yr. collection.
3 Linked to NLM by TWX & computer.
4 Special reference and bibliographic services.
5 Support continuing education programs.

500-600 LOCAL LIBRARIES
(Hospitals, Medical Societies, etc.)

1 10 year current collection.
2 Reader services and circulation.
3 Support local educational needs.
4 TWX & terminal linkage to regional libraries.

Fig. 5. Medical library network plan

experiences confirm both the validity of the basic concept and the benefits derived from local, regional, and national relationships of this kind.

The regional medical libraries and the MEDLARS search centers represent the beginning of a national biomedical communications network, the latest responsibility assigned to the National Library of Medicine. This biomedical communications network will interrelate the medical, scientific, and library communities, and the governmental and academic sectors, all aimed at providing informational services to individual physicians, scientists, educators, and students.

Networks

As NLM assumed its responsibility to develop a Biomedical Communications Network (BCN), it clearly identified the objective as improved and increased information transfer consistent with the demonstrated needs of both the individual physician and the medical community. The "network" does not connote a rigid unchanging snare of interconnections; it does signify a sharing of resources systematically and constructively so that improved services can be provided with maximum efficient utilization of available resources— manpower, fiscal, and technological.

Networking interest and activity are evident within the academic, professional, and federal communities. This activity may take different forms. American universities through the Interuniversity Communications Council (EDUCOM) are examining networks of universities; large universities with scattered campuses are developing computer linkages; the State University of New York (SUNY) has used the computer to prepare and publish a union list of serials for its 58 libraries scattered geographically throughout the state; professional societies in chemistry and physics are examining the totality of their communications efforts—publications (primary, abstracting, and indexing publications) with conferences—in an overall look at their responsibilities to their scientists. Thus this concept of networking represents one of the

most important new principles of delivery of library and information services. NLM's Biomedical Communications Network will have five components: library; specialized information services; specialized educational services; audio and audiovisual services; and data processing and data transmission.

To develop network capability and to explore techniques for making information immediately and easily available to physicians, scientists, and educators, NLM has established a Remote Information Systems Center (RISC). In one small room at the library with electronic equipment, the library has expanded its resources by terminal links to data bases geographically at a distance. The RISC Center provides four basic capabilities:

1. Access to remote data banks
2. Demonstration of computer techniques and applications
3. Experimentation in research and development in bibliographic apparatus, and
4. Networking.

Numerous examples in the literature cite the reluctance of librarians to adopt new techniques and sophisticated equipment; one article is specifically entitled "Librarians against Machines" (Shera).[9] One very rewarding aspect of the RISC project has been the receptivity to it on the part of our librarians and their use of the equipment.

Figure 6 shows the nature of the data banks with which RISC now operates. Essentially the linkages may be (1) to substantive information resources, or (2) for increased capability for manipulating data. RISC is currently linked to MEDLARS, MeSH, 100,000 citations of articles

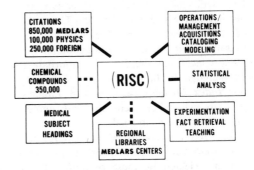

Fig. 6. Data bank connections of RISC

derived from 38 physics journals at Massachusetts Institute of Technology, and 220,000 citations to the foreign scientific literature in California. Linkages also exist for data on operational management activities, statistical analysis, cooperative cataloging with the State University of New York, and an experimental system for fact retrieval. RISC will be linked to information on 350,000 chemical compounds in Philadelphia. In the future all MEDLARS centers will be tied in to RISC for both substantive and operational purposes.

U.S. and Japan Cooperation

Japanese literature was included in the earliest collections of NLM as reflected in the initial issues of the Index Catalog, dating from the 1880s. We currently have an extensive program for the acquisition of contemporary and historical Japanese biomedical literature by purchase, exchange, and gifts. We have 102 exchange partners in Japan for journals and monographs. We purchase 1,348 Japanese serials and 600 monographs annually. We provide about 900 interlibrary loans each year to our Japanese colleagues through the Japanese Medical Library Association and send 50 copies of Index Medicus to Japanese libraries on subscription.

The Directory of Japanese Scientific Periodicals (1967) lists 928 journals in the medical sciences, almost a twofold increase over its listing of 491 in this category in 1962.[10] In view of the size, nature, and importance of the Japanese biomedical literature,[11] we decided a special effort must be made to improve our scope, quality, and speed of coverage. Mr. Tsuda of Keiō University, Mr. Urata of Tokyo University, and Mr. Fujii of Osaka University carefully reviewed the Japanese medical literature and made recommendations in 1965 concerning the Japanese journals to be included in Index Medicus. Currently, our Index Medicus includes 128 Japanese journals, which represent almost 6 percent of the total 2,300 journals.

In 1966 we established an arrangement with Keiō University to assist us in indexing the selected Japanese periodical literature and in the acquisition and cataloging of Japanese medical monographs. Staff from Keiō University have been trained at our library in indexing, searching, and cataloging operations. In the course of almost three years of this relationship, seven people have been trained at NLM (two physicians, one veterinarian, and four librarians). Upon their return to Tokyo they have indexed 15,000 articles from the 128 serial titles, and during the past six months they have cataloged 175 monographs for inclusion in our computer system.

We have been very pleased with these activities, which enable us to continue to make available to the U.S. biomedical community the results of Japanese research. In return, we appreciate the interest which has been demonstrated by our Japanese colleagues in all aspects of the functioning of our library. Considerable space and effort has been given to describing it in the Medical Library, the publication of the Japanese Medical Library Association.[12]

A Look to the Future

The role of the library in higher education should really not be interpreted as that of a library functioning solely in an academic setting. Education is a lifelong process, changing from a formal structured academic environment to the scene of the career of the professional scientist and physician. A physician's locale may be geographically far distant from a source of information, but his need is just as vital as that of the physician located within a medical center.

A first real advance has been made by trying to equalize man's access to information by the regional approach and the network concept of library information services. The modern biomedical library will have an increasingly active part in the continuing education of the medical and health professionals. This simply means that cooperation must exist between the library and its professional user community. In the United States the medical community is not only interested in, but is active in its support and use of, NLM's products and services. Only this interaction can provide and maintain a high professional role for NLM. This blend of scientific and library interests dates back to the turn of the century when the U.S. Medical Library Association was established by four librarians and four physicians, and this close collaboration continues today.

In the days ahead new advances in technology will affect the mode and speed of communication. Whereas present preoccupation is with computer technology and its application, the technique of satellite communications will be receiving attention and study for its applicability. In 1967 Washington and Tokyo exchanged messages and ceremonial telephone calls via INTELSAT II satellite. We are convinced that in the near future international library cooperation will be advanced by the use of this mode of scientific communication. This is the essence of the communications problem today: to provide in an appropriate modality the information when and where it is needed.

President Richard Nixon wrote in a statement on libraries on 22 October 1968, "In a world where knowledge is the key to leadership, a modern, progressive library system is a vital national asset."[13] We share his views and particularly stress the importance of the word *system*, since it connotes order and efficiency rather than disarray and inefficiency, which characterize so many of the world's libraries today. Modern communications technology is adequate for library systems and network development. Where we are lacking is in management and financial support, and thus in performance.

NOTES

[1]John Shaw Billings, "Address before the International Medical Congress, August 5, 1881," *Trans. Int. Med. Congress* (7th; London, 1881), vol.1, p.54–70.

[2]John Z. Bowers, *Medical Education in Japan: From Chinese Medicine to Western Medicine* (New York and London: Harper, 1965); W. Norton Whitney, *Notes on the History of Medical Progress in Japan* (Yokohama: R. Meiklejohn, 1885).

[3]Yukichi Fukuzawa, *The Autobiography of Yukichi Fukuzawa*; revised tr. by Eichi Kiyooka (New York: Columbia Univ. Pr., 1966).

[4]B. C. Vickery and D. J. Simpson, "Future of Scientific Communication," *Science Journal* 2, no.7:80–85 (July 1966).

[5]Martin M. Cummings and Ralph A. Simmons, "Automation in Medical Libraries," *Proceedings, Conference on the Use of Computers in Medical Education* (Oklahoma City: Univ. of Oklahoma Medical Center, 1968), p.74.

[6]Creative Research Services, Inc., *The Use of Data Processing Equipment by Librarians and Information Centers* (Chicago: ALA, 1966); "Information Centers: The Significant Results of the SLA-LTP Survey," *Special Libraries* 58:317, (1967).

[7]Charles J. Austin, *MEDLARS 1963–1967*; Dept. of Health, Education and Welfare, Public Health Service, National Institutes of Health, National Library of Medicine (Washington, D.C.: Govt. Print. Off., 1968). 0—308–816.

[8]F. W. Lancaster, *Evaluation of the MEDLARS Demand Search Service*; Dept. of Health, Education and Welfare (Washington, D.C.: Govt. Print. Off., 1968). 0—307–006.

[9]Jesse H. Shera, "Librarians against Machines," *Science* 156:746 (1967).

[10]*Directory of Japanese Scientific Periodicals* (Tokyo: National Diet Library, 1967).

[11]Shunji Onodera, "Past and Present of Japanese Medical Journals," *Medical Library Association Bulletin* 46:73 (1958) (Part I); 46:320 (1958) (Part II); Yoshinari Tsuda, Takeo Urata, Atsuko Kawabe, and Kimi Kondo, "Japanese Journals Indexed in Index Medicus, and the JMLA Survey of Important Japanese Medical Periodicals," *Medical Library* 12, no.4:231 (1965).

[12]Yoshinari Tsuda, "MEDLARS Activities and Its Limitation," *Medical Library* 12, no.3: 131 (1965); "About Index Medicus," *Medical Library* 13, no.4:239 (1966); Takao Fukudome, "Trends in Medical Libraries Activities in U.S.A.," *Medical Library* 13, no.4:233 (1966); Koichi Marutani and Yukio Hanabusa, "Improvements in Research Libraries," *Medical Library* 14, no.2:153 (1967); Yoshio Shibuya, "U.S. Medical Library Assistance Act of 1965," *Medical Library* 15, no.1:51 (1968).

[13]*Library Journal* 93:4461 (1 Dec. 1968); 94:247 (15 Jan. 1969).

Information Science and the Era of Cybernetics

Tosio Kitagawa
Professor, Kyūshū University
Director, Institute of
Fundamental Information
Science

Societies in the technologically advanced countries began changing from agricultural to industrial modes of production a few centuries ago. We are now in the process of technological innovations in "computation, control, and communication"—the so-called 3-C Revolution. Some contemporary scholars and thinkers, as well as many serious scientists and technologists, claim that we are now moving from the industrial age to the cybernetics era as the 3-C Revolution continues, and that this will exert an increasingly profound influence on all human activities in the future.[1]

Nothing can exist in reality without matter and energy, and there can be no production without materials and energy. Indeed, the main application of science and technology to production has been considered mostly from the point of view of material transformation and energy conversion during the centuries since the beginning of the Industrial Revolution. It is clear, however, that no production can occur if matter and energy are not controlled by human intelligence.

Moreover, with the incorporation of the 3-C Revolution into our technology, it has been increasingly recognized that automated production can be understood as a matrixing process where information is carried by information processors through control processes to matter and energy. Many contemporary thinkers now recognize that information should be regarded as one of the indispensable elements of pro-

duction, i.e., as one of the basic components of production together with matter and energy.

Furthermore, this recognition has profound implications for the coming new industrial revolution as well as for structural changes in science and technology. It has been observed that the information industry has undergone significant growth in the past five years. Some scientists and technologists have been working with the hypothesis that all the engineering sciences can be developed through combinations of scientific and technological principles derived from the three basic technologies, namely, those relating to material, energy, and information. It has now become an urgent problem for managers, engineers, and scientists to investigate the implications of this hypothesis and to accept the consequences in order to develop an adequate strategy for future research and development.

Still further, we may predict an entirely new scheme for classifying and cataloging all industries based on the technologies of materials, energy, and information. Such a classification scheme will provide a framework for coordinating existing industries and identifying revolutionary new industries to be created in the future.

The role of the engineering sciences was discussed by G. S. Brown as early as 1961.[2] Along with revolutionary changes in all industries, it is anticipated that the cybernetics era will be characterized by the predominance of the information industries as they assume their role of interconnecting all other kinds of industries. It seems to us to be crucially important that all scientists today have a penetrating understanding of the role of information science, since this new discipline promises to open up new channels of communication between the physical, biological, and social sciences as well as with the humanities.

Human Beings and Their Societies in the Cybernetics Era

Every member of society will be required to engage in a continuous sequence of education throughout his whole life, so that he may always be qualified to work with and to manage the machines and systems of the cybernetics era. There will be a vast diffusion and popularization of higher education through schools and universities, as well as through postgraduate instruction. There will also be a remarkable increase in the percentage of scientists and technologists in comparison to the number of individuals in other occupations. These effects have all been anticipated by many authors, such as Nigel Calder,[3] J. D. Bernal,[4] and others, and they should be taken into consideration as the principal factor in designing information systems in human learning societies if such societies are to be made adaptive to the progress anticipated.

While, on the one hand, we can expect to have many new possibilities opened up by information science and technology in the cybernetics era, on the other, there will be new social needs created by the introduction of multifarious information systems combined with control and/or communications systems. It is not unrealistic to imagine that such current functions as administration, regulation, and planning—all of which are performed by parliaments, central and/or local government agencies, and the like—will be replaced by appropriate sets of information systems. The present distribution pattern of the human population within a country will also be changed, so that the sole function of urban areas will be to act as centers of social information.

Another crucial aspect of human societies is the fact that nations have played a predominant role in shaping the social lives of human beings. It may be said that the appearance of towns, cities, and urban areas generally was closely related to the production and distribution systems of the agricultural age. Following this line of thought, we may present the hypothesis that the appearance of modern nations and large countries with sufficient political power to protect raw materials sources from seizure by enemies was, at least partly, due to characteristic features of the industrial age—an age characterized by the monopolistic acquisition, possession, and utilization of material and energy. Now when we consider a cybernetics era where information is one of the predominant factors in production and in society, the question of whether nations and countries need to exist and whether they are worth maintaining might well become an important subject to be thoroughly investigated by scientists. In particular, there remain unsolved such important research problems as how information scientists will initiate an evaluation system for information and how the rights of information ownership will be determined. These two problems may prove to be the subject of the deepest debate in attempting to organize international cooperation among scientists and technologists and in establishing any scientific information system.

We have so far restricted our discussion to anticipated technological feasibilities and their effects in the coming cybernetics era. It is, however, absolutely fantastic and excessively naive to imagine such an era solely on the basis of technical feasibilities or possible scientific achievements which might be expected in the future. Indeed, there exist numerous difficulties which may prove obdurate enough to extinguish our hopes and expectations, as Bernal has emphasized. We want to make it absolutely clear that we are not saying that a cybernetics era will definitely arrive, nor are we claiming that the age, if it arrives, will make human beings happier than they have been. We have based our discussion on the assumption that the era will arrive. But we should point out that our keenest concern in the coming years will be whether and how solutions to certain critical problems can be achieved, so that large-scale catastrophes can be avoided. Some of the critical problems facing us may be enumerated as follows:

1. *Food shortages.* The world's scientists and technologists must be aware of the relationship between food shortages and the increase in population in the underdeveloped "south" half of the world. There is an absolute need to increase the productivity of agriculture and industry in such a way that the problem of food shortages can be solved all over the world.

2. *International conflicts.* We have already referred to a new aspect of international affairs which may be realized in the cybernetics era. That is, we can expect that some of the functions of nations and countries will be transferred to other social organizations through the invention of new information and control systems. In view of the present situation where atomic bombs and nuclear forces can destroy human civilization with one mistaken message, however, we have no alternative but to argue that effective worldwide cooperation of scientists and technologists is urgently required to guard against any occurrence of mistaken messages.

We scientists and technologists should also cooperate in scientific and technical approaches to questions of imbalances between the "south" and the "north," particularly in their rates of economic development; to questions of contradictions between urban and rural areas; and to the dangers of world war. It is a consciousness of these responsibilities that should lead us to movements for establishing a world scientific information network.

3. *Conflicts between man and machine.* Conflicts between man and machine are far more dangerous to mankind as a whole than the two problems discussed above. This is so because we can anticipate that machines will be developed on a heroic scale. Functioning as general information processors, they will have enormous memory capacities and the capability to learn and to adapt on the basis of accumulated experience. On the one hand, the use of these information processors cannot be avoided, but on the other, we will always have to be conscious of the warning of the late Norbert Wiener,[5] father of cybernetics, that machines can replace any specific work done by human beings. In the future man will have to learn on a deeper and broader scale than he has hitherto, to enable him to adapt with a minimum of sacrifice to the coming revolutionary changes in human society. This is why a scientific information system is so urgently desired today, and this also suggests a set of criteria by which to measure the adequacy and efficiency of any scientific information system.

We have thus far analyzed some aspects of the world in the coming decades and have indicated some of the implications of the cybernetics era as well as some of the challenging problems facing mankind before and during the new age. We have pointed out that the critical reason for establishing scientific information systems is precisely to solve these problems of the most urgent concern, and our principal task now is to try to uncover an approach which will lead to their solution. Before doing this, however, we shall analyze these problems from three aspects: functions, systems, and coordination.

Functional Aspects of Information Problems

It is convenient to analyze the functional aspects in terms of three constituents: information organizations, information transmission, and information services:

Information organizations

In organizing for information storage and retrieval, the following four procedures are of critical importance:

1. *Deduction procedures to augment storage of information.* It is well known that simulation techniques have been used pragmatically to replace experimental investigations. In this technique, simulation models serve to simulate, in sufficient approximation, real phenomena under study. Such use of simulation techniques requires that descriptions be made in language appropriate to the subject concerned. What we wish to suggest now is the formulation of simulation techniques which can be used as indispensable instruments to augment information storage by deducing information from information previously stored. Simulation techniques are applicable through model constructions of subject matter.

There is a marked tendency for simulations to be performed nowadays by computers, and we can and should expect a vast expansion in the use of computers which will increasingly replace experimental work in laboratories as well as in field investigations, to say nothing about theoretical studies based for the most part on deductive reasoning.

2. *Reduction procedures in information organizations.* In view of the tremendous quantity of information which we may expect to receive from activities in research, development, surveys, investigations, etc., we believe that the invention of reduction procedures is an urgent necessity. Such procedures can be applied to organize information so that only the essentially new is extracted from incoming information and only the essence is added to existing stores. Indeed, it can be imagined that otherwise our stores of information will become an uncoordinated mass of accumulated data and knowledge from which no really efficient retrieval is possible.

To establish any reduction procedure, we must understand both the theoretical and practical implications and we must formulate a clear notion of essential new information with respect to a specified domain of scientific information. So far as we know, no systematic investigation of this problem has been undertaken. In fact, we rather think that there is an urgent need for experimental approaches in each of the fields of science, as well as for systematic researches based on theories of information science. In the meantime, we should like to comment briefly on this extremely sophisticated and delicate concept.

Broadly speaking, there should be some sort of criterion for nontriviality of information as an approximate notion to be used in identifying essential new information. A set of necessary conditions for nontriviality may consist of two members. The first condition is that a nontrivial statement should be sufficiently well-formulated and expressed by an appropriately short sentence in the language of the subject science covered. The second condition is that it should not have a short deductive proof formed by information obtained from the existing store.

3. *Self-organizing procedures applied to storage of information.* We shall now turn to a discussion of the further need to provide self-organizing procedures for information stores, so that they can be reorganized as necessary as nontrivial new information is added.

Such reorganization may lead us to new criteria for nontriviality, because information previously regarded as nontrivial may be reduced to the trivial level and should therefore be excluded in view of the newly included information. This implies that our store of information is always subject to the possibility of reorganization, and that nontriviality and triviality can be interchanged in the process. In short, we are discussing a reorganizing procedure as applied to stored information—an idea which has been referred to by V. M. Glushkov.[6] We can expect that advances in computers will make possible an automated process of reorganizing procedures—a process which may be called a self-organizing procedure for stored information.

4. *Learning procedures in information storage.* The combined functions based on the three procedures discussed above—deduction, reduction, and reorganization—will create a new image for information storage that is drastically different from present notions of information storage embodied in libraries and documentation centers. What we want to emphasize here in connection with the functional aspects of information is that we should commence with a reconsideration of science methodologies in all branches of science—natural and social—and the humanities.

Science methodologies are understood to be based on elaborations and evolutions of deductive, inductive, and abductive logic, as indicated by Aristotle. Now the time has come when we should ask whether and how some of these methodologies can be translated into the roles played by information processors. The present author has discussed the roles of so-called automated statisticians in an earlier paper,[7] in which are also found references to J. W. Tukey,[8] M. G. Kendall and P. Wegner,[9] and B. E. Cooper.[10]

It is said that automated mathematicians proving geometric theorems, automated statisticians dealing with statistical data analysis, and automated laboratory researchers using on-line computers for gathering and analyzing observed data have already come into being to some extent through the use of computers. It is true that most of these researchers are concerned with science methodologies based on deduction and induction, and not so much on abduction, which is more deeply related to human creative thinking. We should add, however, that an investigation has already been started in computer applications to abductive method, and the present author has pointed out in a recent paper[11] the uses of abduction in information organization problems.

Transmission of information

In spite of apparent differences in technical organization and emphasis, school education, broadcasting, and other mass communications media share at least one common function of information processing, viz., transmission of information. In this paper we shall not be concerned with the system aspects of these institutions, but with the functional aspect of the transmission of information in social activities.

Now it is our basic notion that people in the cybernetics era should be provided with a social system of continuous education throughout their lives, irrespective of their occupation and social position. From this point of view it is worthwhile investigating the present situation with respect to information transmission in our society. Today schools and universities provide students with pattern recognitions based on well-organized information, but for the most part only during the time they are students. At the same time, the mass communications media provide a tremendous flow of rather fragmented sequences of information throughout the entire life span of individuals, mostly, if not entirely, without systematic education effect on pattern recognition. We are conscious that we exaggerate our views by overlooking the educational roles played by current broadcasting and mass communications systems. It cannot be denied, however, that the educational functions currently being performed by social institutions will be inadequate in meeting in both depth and breadth the systematic, social, and professional educa-

tional needs of individuals living in the cybernetics era.

Turning to the technical feasibility of using extended social education systems as transmission systems for both organized and unorganized information, we find that the two central aspects to be considered relate to hardware and software, and here we can be optimistic because of some very promising developments. In particular, various kinds of plans and proposals, especially for the transmission of what we designate as unorganized information, have already been presented to the public by information technologists, thus demonstrating the feasibility of supplying information through information lines sponsored by an Information Service Authority—analogous to public services currently being provided by electrical and telephone utilities. With respect to organized information, however, the story is quite different, and so far as we know no systematic investigation has been published on this question. This should be taken into account in predictions of any future information transmission system. All scientific information must be closely coordinated with other systems of information transmission.

In the cybernetics era there will be clear recognition of the fact that education should not and cannot be restricted to the campuses of schools and universities, and that teachers and professors will not necessarily come from educational institutions. One of the crucial requirements of the cybernetics era is that social information transmission systems should be so established that the people can be educated and be ever ready to adapt to revolutionary changes in social patterns. In this era "education" will be synonymous with the social system of transmitting organized information which will serve to aid the people in establishing or reformulating their recognition patterns at any stage of their lives.

Utilization of information

In the cybernetics era there will be some social changes in the information utilization pattern. Specifically we shall observe the following remarkable tendencies:

Tremendous increase in the number of users and in the volume of demand for uses of information

More extensive utilization of various sources of information: research, development, surveys, investigations, etc.

More intensive utilization of organized information ranging over broad fields of the different sciences and technologies, and

Increase in the demand for information services satisfying the social trends alluded to in the three items above.

These trends should lead us to the conclusion that an adequate information service system should be designed and established to satisfy coming demands. An examination of existing information service systems convinces us that all our needs are not being satisfied. Moreover, we must conclude that, in the absence of a definite progressive move toward reconstructing current notions and introducing revolutionary change, we cannot be so optimistic as to believe that these needs will be satisfied by existing libraries and documentation centers. Nor should we be so unrealistic as to claim that drastic changes should be introduced into the functions of these institutions at the possible sacrifice of the traditional and characteristic services which human societies have succeeded in establishing through more than ten centuries of accumulated experience. We should rather set up a coordination plan under which existing institutions of science information service will be included as components of the total system in such a way that their traditional merits will be retained. This by no means implies that we should be conservative in introducing new subsystems to satisfy our information service requirements.

Systems Aspects of Information Problems

We shall now consider the systems aspects of information institutions in the light of the functions just discussed. By information institutions we mean such existing bodies as research institutes, academic societies, libraries, universities, schools, pro-duction plants, etc. We refer to them as information institutions simply because each is concerned with at least one of the following aspects of information function:

Production of original source information which is a candidate for categorization as essentially new information (abbreviated as "source production")

Formation of essentially new information within the framework of a specified store of information (abbreviated as "new formation")

Publication of essentially new information in the form of documents (abbreviated as "new publication")

Storage of information

Information organization processes which may lead to recognition formulation of deductive theory and/or a systematic framework of subject description (abbreviated as "recognition formation and organization")

Transmission of recognition

Utilization of recognition and information for rational purposes (abbreviated as "uses of recognition").

Even though this sevenfold classification may not be completely satisfactory—it does not provide mutually exclusive categories—it is at least convenient for the present purpose of analyzing existing institutions. Table 1 shows a breakdown of the functional aspects of information shared by these institutions. Although this table yields no more than an approximation of reality, it is worth observing that each of these institutions shares, through the division of labor process, a very restricted functional domain in information handling and that coordination does not seem to be great enough for these institutions to carry on cooperative work.[12]

Let us now turn to two recent examples of information systems, viz., a medical information system and a management information system. The idea of a medical information system has been proposed by many biological and medical scientists and physicians in advanced countries in the East and in the West. In some respects the success of the MEDLARS project has led

TABLE 1. Institutions and Systems with Reference to Information

INSTITUTION	NEW INFORMATION PRODUCTION			STORAGE OF INFORMATION	RECOGNITION FORMATION AND ORGANIZATION	TRANSMISSION OF RECOGNITION	USES OF RECOGNITION
	SOURCE PRODUCTION	NEW FORMATION	NEW PUBLICATION				
Research institute	●	●					
Academic society		●	●				
Library				●			
University (research)					●		
University (education)						●	
University (service)							●
School						●	
Plant							●

some of these experts to this idea. We may conclude that a medical information system can be recognized as a consolidated, total system covering all functional aspects of information (see table 2).

A management information system (MIS) is even more explicitly and clearly a total system. The very concept and the objectives of MIS led management people and computer makers to the idea explicitly described as a total system possessing all the seven information functions mentioned above (see table 3).

Coordination Aspects of Information Problems

Coordination refers to the need to produce either one large system or an aggregation of subsystems which can satisfy, as a whole, the requirements for information functions discussed above.

To illustrate our problem, let us consider a university with many faculties and research institutes and several libraries. Harvard University, for instance, is said to have adopted decentralized coordination of the many libraries on its campus. Similar information-coordination problems have already become of pressing concern not only within and beyond the confines of a given campus, but also within and beyond a specific area of the natural and social sciences. Moreover, information-coordination problems are now being raised by many scientific organizations throughout the world, and the solution to these problems would require coordination not only within a nation but also on an international scale. In this latter connection we shall now present two important points which must be taken into serious consideration, especially in the coming cybernetics era:

International cooperation for information coordination. International cooperation will be possible because we shall be equipped with the products of innovations in information technology in the coming cybernetics era. Cooperation will be required because we shall be faced with a variety of serious social problems, and without the establishment of international cooperation for information coordination, mankind will not be able to solve the many conflicting problems which beset it. We can perceive that, on the one hand, the establishment of

TABLE 2. Medical Information System

INSTITUTION	NEW INFORMATION PRODUCTION			STORAGE OF INFORMATION	RECOGNITION FORMATION AND ORGANIZATION	TRANSMISSION OF RECOGNITION	USES OF RECOGNITION
	SOURCE PRODUCTION	NEW FORMATION	NEW PUBLICATION				
Clinic	●						●
Hospital	●			●			
Medical research institute	●	●			●		
Medical society		●	●				
Medical library				●			
Medical department in university	●	●		●	●	●	●
Medical school						●	●

international cooperation for information coordination will result from international cooperation in solving these crucial problems, and that, on the other hand, it will serve to stimulate the coperative solving of social problems.

Interdisciplinary cooperation. Recent developments in information science and tech-

TABLE 3. Management Information System

INSTITUTION	NEW INFORMATION PRODUCTION			STORAGE OF INFORMATION	RECOGNITION FORMATION AND ORGANIZATION	TRANSMISSION OF RECOGNITION	USES OF RECOGNITION
	SOURCE PRODUCTION	NEW FORMATION	NEW PUBLICATION				
Laboratory	●	●					
Pilot plant	●	●					
Library				●			
Technical section				●	●		
Production section				●	●		●
Management school and training						●	
Marketing	●						

nology have been introducing revolutionary changes in research and development methodologies, as we can observe in laboratory automation, design automation, hospital automation, and simulation language techniques.

It must be said that today in any large-scale scientific research or broad technological development we can hardly rely on only one isolated discipline in the sense of the traditional classification of science and technology. This implies that there is an urgent need to establish coordination among individual specialized information centers so that they may be useful in research and development. The essential features of interdisciplinary cooperation in the cybernetics era, however, may be uncovered at a deeper level than we have indicated, because one of the characteristic features of the era may well be that classifications in science and technology will differ from those that have gained currency during the past two centuries. That is to say, we can no longer adhere to traditional classification schemes for science and technology, and we may say that we are now taking a pragmatic step forward as one approach to this problem by establishing interdisciplinary cooperation among the various divisions of science and technology. And we are taking that step before we can formulate an adequate and new revolutionary classification, and without knowing whether or not the traditional classification will be valid in the future.

Two Proposed Approaches

So far we have presented an analysis of scientific information problems in the cybernetics era; we shall now provide a general outline of possible approaches to the problems facing us. First of all, we should emphasize the need to adopt a systematic methodology to solve these problems. Among the systematic methodologies now available to us, we can recommend one which bears some similarities to the operations research method. Its four essential conditions may be described as follows:

1. *A set of conditions for our goal should be clearly defined.* It is required that we establish a clear set of conditions for our goal in designing scientific information systems. First of all, we should enumerate sets of all possible kinds of users of our systems and then investigate what service they require from the systems. In some cases a user's requirements for service may be shared in common with other members of the set and coincide with the requirements of members of other sets; in other cases user requirements may conflict with one another. This complicated situation reveals the need to lay out, before starting our task, an objective description of the conditions for our goal, and this is neither so trivial nor so easy as one might think.

2. *Our present state should be objectively described.* Once we have succeeded in an objective description of a set of conditions for our goal, it will be possible to describe our present state by means of descriptors which will have proved useful in describing the set of goal conditions. These descriptors may turn out to be a set of parameters, $x = (x_1, x_2, \ldots, x_n)$. Thus, in such cases our goal can be denoted by a particular vector $a = (a_1, a_2, \ldots, a_n)$ belonging to a certain set of parameter values $A : A \epsilon A$, while the present state can be denoted by another vector $p = (p_1, p_2, \ldots, p_n)$, presumably belonging to a certain set $B : p \epsilon B$.

3. *A set of strategies by which to transform our present state into the state satisfying the conditions of our goal must be definitely given.* It is not difficult to understand the notion of a set of strategies. For instance, when descriptors are given by parametric representations, as in the preceding paragraph, the set of our strategies may be denoted by $S = [s]$, where s is one of our strategies. Here strategies are understood in the broadest sense. For instance, with reference to a dynamic programming approach or to an adaptive control approach, each strategy s may actually be a sequence of sequential operations $s = (s_1, s_2, \ldots, s_n)$ in which the nth stage operation s_n may be determined in the light of information obtained by previous applications of operations $(p, s_1 p, s_2 s_1 p, s_3 s_2 s_1 p, \ldots, s_{n-1} s_{n-2}, \ldots, s_1 p)$. This is merely one example. There are quite a few other possibilities.

4. *A set of conditions restricting the set of strategies in such a way as to assure feasibility should be assigned.* A set of strategies as given by point 3 is concerned with technical possibilities. Therefore, to derive a set of feasible solutions to our problem, it is necessary to have a set of conditions restricting the set of strategies.

When we consider any combination of the four conditions, our task becomes something like the problem of a traveler whose destination area *A* and departure area *p* are assigned and whose feasible travel route is circumscribed within the area *D*. He can travel by any combination *S* of allowable transportation facilities. The problem then is twofold: (1) whether or not he can reach the destination area *A* and (2) how efficiently he can reach the destination area *A*. It is to be noted that some criteria should be given to answer problem 2, as we can see in any mathematical programming and control theory approach. We are not entering into the mathematical details of such a formulation, but we are concerned rather with our learning approach attitude.

Information science approach

The formulation of a scientific information system and its development will have to be done during a period in the cybernetics revolution when information science, information technology, and the information industry are in a stage of accelerated development and innovation. This fact makes our job similar to project controls rather than to an ordinary job of operations research because our strategies themselves are subject to revolutionary change during the course of transition from departure area to destination area.

We cannot overemphasize the need to be in a state of readiness and to be adaptable, so that any revolutionary information technology which becomes available can be put to use in our scientific information system. But this attitude is not enough. In formulating a scientific information system and promoting its realization, we should be sufficiently progressive and positive in our thinking to analyze the set of conditions for our goal in such a way that the requirements

for and demands on information science and technology can be deduced from the set of goal conditions. This is quite important, because without an adequate description of the goals we seek in a scientific information system in terms of information technology, there would always be the underlying danger of a lack of definite objectives for research and development in specific areas of information science and technology. Hence we would be trying to attain aims which are too idealistic and which have no practical implication for the conditions of our goal.

Information science will have revolutionary effects on almost all branches of the natural and social sciences, as well as on the humanities. It is expected that these effects will be brought about by various scientific information systems. In this connection, a systematic description of the information science approach in designing a scientific information system will be of the utmost importance.[13]

Strategy approach

Another indispensable aspect of our approach to the design, formulation, and realization of a scientific information system is that of strategy. We should pay due attention to the real state of affairs throughout the world today in scientific research activity and scientific information cooperation. To select an appropriate course in the development of our scientific information system, the International Council of Scientific Unions (ICSU) should prepare a systematic survey of the present state of scientific research activities with special reference to the possibility of automation of laboratory work, observation, and data acquisition.

Technical innovations will involve revolutionary changes in scientific methodology, and these in turn will produce a new set of requirements for a scientific information system. In these circumstances it is crucially important to establish our strategic approach so that we may be sensitive to such innovations and able to adapt to them. By being sensitive we shall be able to learn about useful developments in information science and technology, and we should be able to learn from experience. We should at the same time avoid any rigid concepts in the design of an information system originating at any given stage in the development of information science and technology.

In this context we wish to assert that the most urgent problem for us in considering a world scientific information system lies not so much in the formulation of a definite plan but rather in discovering how to organize a systematic learning process. Through such a process we can, first, accumulate varied experience in each country and in each branch of science and technology, and, second, we can deduce suitable conclusions in the formulation and realization of a scientific information system. In the final section we wish to summarize our proposals and viewpoints in more specific form.

In concluding this paper it may be appropriate to enumerate four specific proposals along the lines which we have been discussing:

Proposal 1. ICSU should organize a series of systematic annual surveys covering all science and technology and outlining the progress of automation in various fields: laboratory, statistics, documentation, library, and hospital. These surveys should be conducted with the cooperation of various international scientific organizations as well as with national bodies.

Proposal 2. ICSU should organize with the cooperation of appropriate international scientific societies a series of symposia and seminars on information science and technology to be held at regular intervals and with particular emphasis on such topics as functions of information processing, information systems, and coordination of information systems both from the hardware and the software points of view.

Proposal 3. ICSU should devise a plan for simulation experiments in scientific information systems to test crucial issues which will arise in the symposia and seminars suggested in Proposal 2, as well as to study the problems raised through observation from the series of surveys suggested in Proposal 1.

Proposal 4. ICSU should commence with the establishment of a committee and a series of special symposia to review the activities of science and technology and to discuss the possible introduction of a new classification for all the natural and social sciences and technology, as well as for the humanities, in the era of the cybernetics revolution.

NOTES

[1] Daniel Bell, *The End of Ideology: On the Exhaustion of Political Ideas in the Fifties* (Glencoe, Ill.: Free Pr., 1960); C. R. Dechert, ed., *The Social Impact of Cybernetics* (Notre Dame, Ind.: Univ. of Notre Dame Pr., 1966).
[2] G. S. Brown, *Some Problems of Engineering Education in the U.S. and Some Proposals for Their Solution* (1961).
[3] Nigel Calder, ed., *The World in 1984* (Baltimore: Penguin Books, 1964). 2v.
[4] J. D. Bernal, *World without War* (London: Routledge and Kegan Paul, 1958).
[5] Norbert Wiener, *God and Golem, Inc.: A Comment on Certain Points Where Cybernetics Impinges on Religion* (Cambridge, Mass.: MIT Pr., 1964).
[6] V. M. Glushkov, *Introduction to Cybernetics*; tr. by Scripta Technica (New York: Academic Pr., 1966).

[7] Tosio Kitagawa, "Automatically Controlled Sequence of Statistical Procedures," in Jerzy Neyman and Lucien M. Le Cam, eds., *Bernoulli, 1713; Bayer, 1763; Laplace, 1813. Anniversary Volume* (Proceedings of an International Research Seminar, Statistical Laboratory, University of California, Berkeley, 1963 [Berlin and New York: Springer-Verlag, 1965]), p.146–78.
[8] J. W. Tukey, "The Future of Data Analysis," in *Annals of Mathematical Statistics* 33 (1962).
[9] M. G. Kendall and P. Wegner, "An Introduction to Statistical Programming." 34th Session of the International Statistical Institute at Ottawa, August 1963.
[10] B. E. Cooper, "Designing the Data Presentation of Statistical Program for the Experimentalists." 34th Session of the Interna-

tional Statistical Institute at Ottawa, August 1963.

[11]Tosio Kitagawa, "Abduction Process in Statistics" (in Japanese). Annual Meeting of Japanese Society of Mathematics at Kyoto University, October 1967.

[12]James A. Perkins, *The University in Transition* (Princeton, N.J.: Princeton Univ. Pr., 1966).

[13]Tosio Kitagawa, "Information Science and Its Connections with Statistics," in Lucien M. Le Cam and Jerzy Neyman, eds., *Proceedings of the 5th Berkeley Symposium on Mathematical Statistics and Probability . . . Statistical Laboratory, University of California . . . 1965 . . . and . . . 1966* (Berkeley: Univ. of California Pr., 1967), vol.1, p.491–530.

Japan Information Center of Science and Technology

Chikashi Sasaki
Member, Board of Directors

The Japan Information Center of Science and Technology* (JICST) is not a library, and since its activities may not be well known to academic librarians, I shall start my presentation with a brief description. JICST was created in 1957 in accordance with the provisions of the JICST Act as a semigovernmental organization with emphasis on the public nature of the institution. Therefore, substantial governmental subsidies are extended each year. Its scope of activity includes:

1. Collection, worldwide, of science information
2. Efficient processing of the material, preferably with a mechanized system, and
3. Dissemination of organized informa-

*In Japanese: Nihon Kagaku Gijutsu Jōhō Sentā.

tion regularly and efficiently, and on request.

It is in this last point that our institution differs widely from traditional libraries. Though our services are being supplied mainly to domestic users, we do not neglect overseas clients, and orders are received constantly from abroad. As regards secondary information, the largest part of our effort is directed to the preparation of a series of abstracting journals bearing the general title *Kagaku Gijutsu Bunken Sokuhō* (*Current Bibliography on Science and Technology*). These journals are published irregularly, monthly, semimonthly, or every 10 days. The number of abstracts published annually now amounts to nearly 400,000, and there is a 10-percent yearly rate of increase.

As the first stage of our overall service, we subscribe to 4,500 foreign and 2,500 Japanese journals relating to the physical sciences and technology, as well as to 35,000 technical reports and 40,000 foreign chemical patent specifications. Due attention is also given to acquisition of conference papers and proceedings.

I should like to touch upon the need to introduce a large-scale electronic computer system for the entire work of JICST. As we all know, the annual production of documents and information in the physical sciences and engineering all over the world amounts to 2 million articles scattered among, say, 20,000 journals. It is also said that in ten to fifteen years the production of information will double. JICST handles 400,000 articles from only 7,000 journals. Therefore, there is a pressing need for us to speed up our work and to expand our processing capacity; otherwise conventional manual processing systems will no longer be serviceable.

The direct objective of the system is to expedite manual procedures and to integrate various interconnected operations in view of the future advancement of computer and telecommunications technology. At present the entire system is divided into six projects:

1. Automatic editing and photocomposition of the *Current Bibliography* (CB)

2. Editing of indexes to the CB
3. Selective dissemination of information (SDI)
4. Information retrieval
5. Vocabulary control
6. Source document control.

The new system was made practicable for our purposes by the application of *kanji* (Chinese-character) teletypewriters and the development of the *kanji* line printer. In the new system initial input is made with the teletypewriter in machine-readable form, and the line printer produces an abstract readable for correction and proofreading. When corrections are completed, the final output is recorded on film as an offset master plate. Among the processes, arrangement, cross-referencing, and page-formatting operations are automated.

Since we do our work primarily in the Japanese language and script, the greatest obstacle at the outset was the written language. Japanese texts are written today utilizing a mixture of Chinese characters (*kanji*) and Japanese syllabary letters (*kana*),* to which are added in scientific texts mathematical equations, chemical notations, and other symbols in other alpha-

bets and scripts. A prerequisite to automation, therefore, was the development of hardware capable of handling Chinese characters, i.e., a line printer. Cooperating with the Japan Electronics Manufacturing Company (Nihon Denshi Sangyō Kabushiki Kaisha), we developed, for the first time in the world, a dependable *kanji* line printer named JEM 3800. This was then coupled with *kanji* teletypewriters already used in telecommunications, and thus the obstacle was overcome. Consequently the system can handle about 2,000 *kanji, hiragana,*,* *katakana,** Roman-, Greek-, and Cyrillic-alphabet letters in upper and lower cases, numerals, and other symbols, totaling over 3,000. Characters, letters, signs, and symbols used in the system are shown in table 1. To secure more legibility, *kana* and alphabetic letters and numerals are also printable in boldface and italic, and all the characters are printable in superimposed, super-, or subscript form. Characters are coded in *kanji* code, composed of a pair of six-bit codes together with a four-bit functional

*Japanese syllabary letters (*kana* or -*gana*) are written and printed in two forms: the cursive (*hiragana*) and the block (*katakana*).

TABLE 1. System Characters and Letters

	INPUT			OUTPUT	TYPE FACE
	KANJI TELE-TYPEWRITER	FLEXOWRITER ALPHA-NUMERIC	RUSSIAN		
CHARACTERS					
Kanji	1,861			1,861	Regular
Katakana	81			162	Regular, boldface
Hiragana	77			154	Regular, boldface
Roman alphabet	65	52		195	Regular, italic, boldface
Russian alphabet	66		63	193	Regular, italic, boldface
Greek alphabet	33			99	Regular, italic, boldface
Arabic numerals	10	10	10	30	Regular, italic, boldface
Roman numerals	20			40	Regular, italic
Symbols	199	31	17	248	Regular, partly italic, boldface
Space	6	1	1	6	
Reserve	78			78	
Total	2,496	94	91	3,071	

code. The major drawback of this *kanji* code, or of the *kanji* script itself, is that it cannot be self-arranging; that is, though each *kanji* in Japanese has on the average two pronunciations, these cannot be differentiated by the code. This is compensated for by adding *furigana*,* or pronunciation in *kana*, to *kanji* keywords for arrangement and by conversion to the binary coded decimal (BCD) system.

Whereas the *kanji* typewriter-printer system is for the moment absolutely unique in our country, the *kanji* code system is converted to the BCD system to meet the needs of a wider market where the eight-bit BCD system, including *katakana*, is generally used in office automation. This will eventually lead to on-line, real-time access to the central data bank.

Now let me mention the work load we are planning at present. When we have to process 300,000 abstracts a year, the total number of characters to be punched will amount to 180 million, on the basis of 600 characters per abstract. Of the 600 characters per abstract, 400 are keyboarded with the *kanji* teletypewriter and 200 with the Flexowriter, for the sake of economy of equipment and personnel cost and speed. On the other hand, each *kanji* teletypist is scheduled to punch 10,000 characters per day, and each Flexowriter typist 20,000 characters. Therefore we need about 20 *kanji* keypunchers and 10 Flexowriter typists. At present about 60 persons are in our keypunching unit, including proofreaders and some administrative staff.

As I mentioned earlier, the system is a total system with the dual purpose of photocomposing journals and constructing a data bank for retrieval. The system for the preparation of abstracting journals in the new system in *kanji* code is based on the "segmentation" principle, in which every item has its own segment in magnetic tape format, as shown in table 2.

Since bibliographic work requires a high degree of accuracy for textual presentation, our software entity puts extreme emphasis

Furigana are signs of the Japanese syllabary written parallel to Chinese characters to indicate the pronunciation of the latter.

on correction of equipment- and human-originated errors. On the other hand, in the hardware system a verifying device is lacking, such as is usually provided in PCS and alphanumeric paper tape systems. As a result, all data, once punched, must be printed out with the fairly complicated *kanji* line printer, and correction tape must be punched anew, segment by segment or record by record. These procedures require much time and labor. Further technological development is actively under way as a joint effort of JICST and Japan Electronics Manufacturing Company.

On the operational side, the first computer-generated issue of *Kagaku Gijutsu Bunken Sokuhō: Denki Kōgaku Hen (Current Bibliography on Science and Technology: Electrical Engineering Section)** was put on the market in January 1969. A new feature of this issue is a keyword index. The second group, comprising the Chemistry and Construction sections, will begin with the June issue. At that time about half of the monthly production, in terms of number of abstracts, will be processed by the new system. By this fall (1969), the remaining sections will be computerized, and Phase I of the system, i.e., automatic editing and photocomposing, will be completed.

Frankly speaking, as regards printing quality, there are some minor insufficiencies inherent in this system. For instance, headlines for class or subclass headings, usually printed in large type or in boldface, cannot be produced. However, our computer-generated journal has been accepted generally without much objection.

Phase II is computer production of annual indexes to the *Current Bibliography*, scheduled in the April–June period of next year. At this stage the advantages of an automated system will clearly show up, because publication of author and subject

*As mentioned previously, JICST publishes a series of abstract journals bearing the general title *Kagaku Gijutsu Bunken Sokuhō* (English title: *Current Bibliography on Science and Technology*). Each journal bears a subtitle in Japanese only indicating its coverage, in this case, *Denki Kōgaku Hen,* here translated as "Electrical Engineering Section."

248 – Applications of Computers

TABLE 2. List of Segments and Data Elements

SEGMENT	DATA ELEMENTS	NUMBER OF CHARACTERS	NOTES
A	Subject discipline code	2 × 1	Codes for
	Information officer's code	3 × 1	working group
	Abstract number	8 × 1	
B	Abstracter's code	5 × 1	
	Document type indicator	2 × 1	
	Code number of source document*	5 × 1	
	Number of photographs	3 × 1	
	Number of illustrations, tables	3 × 1	
	Number of references	3 × 1	Type of
	Year of publication	2 × 1	documents
	Language	3 × 3	
	Code for reserving space for illustrations	4	
	Volume number	Variable	
	Issue number	Variable	
C	Classification code	10 × max. 10	
D	Pagination	Variable × 1	
E	Author(s)	40 × variable	
F	Original title	Variable	
G	Translated title	Variable	
H	Keywords	Max. 40 × max. 15	
I	Text of abstracts	Variable	

*Journal title and abbreviation code of issuing country are automatically added to the master tape from code number of source documents, and similarly the UDC numbers, from classification code.

indexes will otherwise require tremendous manual labor and mental stress, and if all indexes are to be prepared in parallel, a large labor force is needed during a relatively short time period. To level off our concentrated efforts, we have had to carry out our work in series, so that our most recent index was published well over two years after the completion of the volume it indexed. This critical time lag can be practically reduced to the minimum by designing the system properly and preparing and testing programs beforehand. Moreover, bibliographies, either in the form of indexes or abstracts, on special topics can be compiled quite easily and within a brief period of time. These last two phrases surely characterize Phase II.

Phase III will have a twofold purpose. The first will be to diversify publications, and the second will be to supply processed magnetic tapes and customer searches. In addition to regular abstracting journals, we are now experimenting with a KWIC index journal in physics. A second product is specialized bibliographies on topics of current interest. In this category we already have two examples relating to aluminum and metal surface treatment, both having been prepared manually by selecting and rearranging pertinent abstracts in readily accessible form. The supply of processed tapes (in BCD code) faces rewriting of programs appropriate for each equipment make. In this regard we are to start experimenting with conversion of FACOM (a Japanese computer) programs to the IBM 360 series. Customer tape searches will be carried out by both BCD and *kanji* codes. Programming has been nearly completed, and test runs have started. The tape search involves two objectives, one for current-awareness purpose and the other for retrospective search, after completing the data bank for several years.

Though the system was originally developed for the preparation of abstracting journals and retrieval of journal articles, it is also applicable to library catalogs, so I do hope my presentation will be of some usefulness to our American colleagues, particularly those who work with Oriental collections.

Finally, I should like to mention the meaning of our system in the coming age of exchange of information in machine-readable form. It goes without saying that our system was planned to meet the recent trends in computer-based international cooperation in scientific information work. On the domestic scene we have to set up our own national information system involving national libraries, university libraries, and information centers. Similarly, the national network must be compatible with the international network. In this connection cooperation between the United States and Japan will be most desirable, and it is in this sense that bilateral talks are now taking place, for instance, between MEDLARS, Chemical Abstracts Service, and their Japanese counterparts.

Part 10

ASSOCIATIONS, CENTERS, AND SERVICES

Association of Research Libraries

Stephen A. McCarthy
Executive Director

The Association of Research Libraries (ARL) is an organization of the large, general research libraries of the United States and Canada whose objective is to improve and strengthen the collections and services of its members in support of learning and research. Membership in the association is institutional, with each institution represented by its director or chief librarian. By limiting membership to institutions, this association is differentiated from other American library associations which have personal, or personal and institutional, members. Moreover, membership is by invitation only after a vote of the members. In this respect also ARL differs from other library associations.

The reasons for a library association of institutions rather than of individual librarians are twofold: (1) The American Library Association and other personal-membership library associations offer ample opportunity to engage in professional activity on an individual basis. (2) There are many serious library problems which confront research libraries particularly or in a special way, and these tend to be problems that can be dealt with best on an institutional basis. The directors and chief librarians who represent their institutions in ARL are members of the American Library Association and many of them participate in ALA activities, serving on committees, as members of the ALA Council, and as ALA officers.

At present ARL has seventy-nine members, consisting of seventy-two major university libraries of the United States and Canada; the three national libraries of the United States—the Library of Congress, the National Agricultural Library, and the National Library of Medicine; two large public libraries with research collections; two special research libraries; and the Center for Research Libraries.

The asociation is made up of libraries that maintain large, general research collections to support advanced study and investigation as a matter of policy. Membership is by invitation because the association is committed to the policy of including as members only those libraries that have common problems and that may be expected to contribute toward the solution of these problems. Because of this policy, the association does not, for example, consider it appropriate to include new university libraries until they have achieved a degree of maturity comparable to that of at least some of the present members.

The procedure used in selecting libraries to be invited to become members is to ask the Membership Committee to review the status of libraries that are believed to have, or to approach, the desirable qualifications. In its analysis the committee uses four criteria for academic libraries: (1) size of collection; (2) amount spent for books, periodicals, and binding; (3) number of fields in which the doctor's degree is offered; and (4) number of doctoral degrees awarded. For 2, 3, and 4, the averages for the last three years are used. For libraries other than university libraries, the purposes and characteristics of the collections and services are evaluated. The Membership Committee presents its findings to the Board of Directors. The Board then reviews this material and decides what its recommendations to the membership will be. The vote of the membership is determining, and invitations to become members are issued by the president.

The association is governed by a board of directors of nine members, three of whom are elected each year at the January meeting for a term of three years. The board elects the officers of the association from its own membership. There are three elected officers: the president, the vice-president, and the immediate past president. The vote in the board is on the vice-presidency, with the member elected serving successively in the three offices. The professional staff consists of the executive director and the associate executive director, both of whom are appointed by the president for an indefinite term.

History

ARL was founded in 1932 with forty-three members. The charter membership consisted of those university libraries whose institutions were members of the American Association of Universities, the Library of Congress, the New York and Boston public libraries, and several specialized research libraries. It should be noted that at that time the Association of American Universities included all universities that had significant graduate degree programs and research programs. At present, over 80 percent of the graduate doctoral degrees awarded are conferred by universities whose libraries are members of ARL.

The association was formed by this group of libraries because they had common problems that were largely peculiar to the group. These problems could best be attacked cooperatively, i.e., through an association or organization, and since there was no suitable library organization available, they created one.

For many years ARL continued at approximately the same size and with a simple governing device of an elected, voluntary executive secretary chosen from its membership, assisted by an advisory committee of five. The office of the association moved from library to library as new executive secretaries were elected. This practice continued until 1962, when ARL became a corporation, appointed a full-time, salaried executive secretary, and established a permanent office in Washington. Shortly after this reorganization the membership was increased substantially, to seventy-two members.

These changes were made because the work of the association could no longer be satisfactorily performed by a part-time man; it was evident that the membership should be increased; and there was reason to believe that closer involvement of research libraries and government agencies would develop. The National Science Foundation made a small grant to ARL to assist in establishing the permanent office. This was a terminal grant, and ARL is now supported by membership dues and income derived from studies and projects.

Activities of the Association

The association maintains liaison and cooperates with other library associations, organizations in the field of higher education, and learned societies, as well as with the three national libraries and other agencies of government, in working toward its objectives of improved research library services and collections. The work of the association is carried on chiefly through committees of its members and other interested persons co-opted for special services.

Because ARL was established to deal with the common problems of research libraries, much of its work has been concerned with resources for research and bibliographic access. The best known of these programs is the Farmington Plan, whose objective is to assure that at least one copy of all publications of value for research is available in the United States. The Farmington Plan began in 1949 and is still in operation. Under this program over fifty participating libraries agreed to acquire all current publications in various subject fields or from various geographic areas, to catalog them, and to make them available on interlibrary loan. The Farmington Plan is thus a decentralized cooperative acquisitions program.

The PL-480 program of the Library of Congress is in some respects similar to the Farmington Plan. It is operated in developing countries in which counterpart funds are available for the purchase of multiple copies of current publications which are deposited in sets in selected research libraries. The American Council of Learned Societies and ARL cooperated with LC in initiating this program.

The National Program for Acquisitions and Cataloging (NPAC) began as an effort of the Shared Cataloging Committee of ARL. This committee set out to eliminate duplication in cataloging by research libraries. As the effort progressed, it seemed that the objective might best be attained by centralizing and speeding up cataloging at the Library of Congress. To do this cataloging, it was necessary that LC acquire the books to be cataloged. At this time the Higher Education Act of 1965, with a section providing support for selected library activities, was under consideration by Congress. The committee recommended an amendment which authorized LC to acquire and catalog promptly foreign pub-

lications of scholarly and research value and provided special funds for this purpose. The amendment was adopted, and the program has been in operation for the past three years. What began as a cataloging effort has become the major foreign acquisitions and cataloging program of LC. As it has developed, this program has involved bibliographic centers in foreign countries, and thus "Shared Cataloging" has come to have a new international meaning.

These three programs, Farmington, PL-480, and NPAC, are all concerned with the acquisition of current publications, and two of them, Farmington and NPAC, are largely directed toward the acquisition of monographs. In time and with increased funding, PL-480 and NPAC may supercede the Farmington Plan. At present, however, since both of these programs are relatively new, and since they are dependent on legislation and funding that require periodic extension as well as annual congressional action, it is considered desirable to maintain the Farmington Plan. At a later date, if these programs are developed, expanded, and strengthened in their coverage of current publications and their continuation is considered assured, the Farmington Plan may be reshaped to concentrate on older publications which were not acquired at the time of publication. To a limited extent this effort to build up retrospective resources has already begun.

The Foreign Newspaper Microfilm project affords an example of another type of cooperative program. It stems from recognition of the importance for research of files of current newspapers from all parts of the world coupled with the fact that it is not necessary to duplicate these files in library after library, provided any library that needs a particular file can borrow or purchase a copy when the need for it arises. Thus this project, administered for ARL by the Center for Research Libraries, acquires and makes available through loan or sale microfilm copies of over 200 current foreign newspapers. Participation in the project is by subscription. The committee responsible for this project is now considering a plan for its expansion.

Doctoral dissertations presented problems to many ARL libraries because there was a continuing demand for them from faculty and graduate students and they were difficult to locate and to acquire. The first effort of ARL was to provide an annual listing of dissertations in the volume *American Doctoral Dissertations*, published annually from 1934 to 1952. Since 1952, under a plan worked out with University Microfilms, dissertations are published on microfilm and positive film copies may be purchased. Abstracts of these theses are published in *Dissertation Abstracts*.

ARL initiated and sponsored the publication of the *Catalog of Books Represented by Library of Congress Cards*, the first comprehensive book catalog of the Library of Congress collections published in modern times. This has been followed by supplements and since 1956 by the *National Union Catalog*, a continuing publication. This series of catalogs has become an indispensable bibliographic tool for American and other libraries.

Within the past year ARL, with the assistance of grants from the Ford Foundation, has established two centers intended to make research materials more accessible to libraries. One of these, the Center for Chinese Research Materials, is focused on materials dealing with contemporary China. It is engaged in a reprinting and microfilming program which enables libraries to acquire copies of materials not available on the book market. As it progresses, the Center expects to compile and publish bibliographies which will assist libraries in identifying significant materials for addition to their collections. ARL is assisted in directing and guiding the program of the Center by an advisory committee made up of three professors, recommended by the Joint Committee on Contemporary China, and three librarians, with a librarian serving as chairman. This type of joint committee has proved valuable in ARL work.

The second center is devoted to Slavic bibliography and documentation. Its efforts at the outset will be directed toward the evaluation of publications for library acquisition and to the acquisition of scarce and fugitive materials. Somewhat later the Center is expected to develop a reprinting and publication program. There is an advisory committee for the Slavic Center also, made up of Slavic scholars and librarians.

ARL was actively involved in the legislation which authorized the Shared Cataloging program. It has supported the extension of this act and has assisted in efforts to have adequate funds appropriated for the program. It maintains a continuing interest in legislation of particular relevance to research libraries and attempts to make the views of its members known to legislative authorities. In this work it cooperates with the Washington office of the American Library Association, which is responsible for all library-related legislation. In addition, ARL is concerned with the implementation of legislation that affects research libraries. In its work in this area, ARL is prepared to assist government agencies in determining administrative regulations and procedures as may be appropriate.

At the present time ARL is conducting a study of microforms with special attention to user needs, a study of the economics of book storage for large libraries, and a study of library lighting. The association has been concerned over a period of years with the problem of deteriorating paper, and its Committee on Preservation has studied means of coping with this problem and has promoted the use of permanent/durable paper. The potential contributions of modern scientific management to the operation of research libraries, as well as the efficient and economical adaption of new technological developments to library activities, are of continuing interest to the association.

ARL normally holds two one-day meetings a year, with one session devoted to discussion of a topic of current professional interest and the other concerned with committee reports and business matters. The *Minutes* of these meetings constitute the principal publication of the association. In addition, a newsletter is issued occasionally; *Academic Library Statistics* is compiled and published annually; and the *Farmington Plan Newsletter* appears semiannually. The Center for Chinese Research Materials issues a newsletter, and a similar publication is planned by the Slavic Center.

The Future

It seems certain that ARL will grow steadily but modestly in size. The recent development of studies and projects seems appropriate to ARL and promises to continue. The future of research libraries is closely related to that of higher education. Projections indicate that numbers of students and institutions will increase, with inevitable problems of financing and the provision of required collections, facilities, and staff. Attempts to forecast the future of research libraries envisage greater use of computers and other electronic equipment. To the extent that its resources permit, ARL will endeavor to make useful contributions in working toward solutions of the problems that confront its member libraries.

American Library Association in 1969

David H. Clift
Executive Director

There are fourteen national library associations in the United States. The purpose of each is, in most instances, to develop and advance a particular segment of librarianship.

Ten of the national library associations are affiliates of ALA. These are: American Association of Law Libraries, American Society for Information Sciences, American Merchant Marine Library Association, American Theological Library Association, Association of American Library Schools, Association of Research Libraries, Catholic Library Association, Medical Library Association, Music Library Association, and Theatre Library Association.

There are two national library associations not affiliated with ALA: Association of Jewish Libraries and Special Libraries Association. Each of these national associations has its own membership and operates independently. Many of their members are also members of ALA. Finally, there is the Council of National Library Associations, whose members include most of the national library associations.

The American Library Association, oldest and largest of the national library associations in the United States, is interested and active in matters affecting all types of libraries and library activities. Its wide interests, its activities, its age, and its large membership combine to give it an influential voice in the nation's library affairs. It undertakes to speak for and represent the library profession in matters of national interest and concern.

The association was founded in 1876. It will thus be 100 years old in a few years. One hundred and three persons gathered in Philadelphia on 4–6 October 1876 to found the association. This number had grown to 39,397 by 31 January 1969.

The objectives of ALA as stated in its charter, which was granted on 10 December 1879, are:

Commonwealth of Massachusetts

Be it known, that whereas Justin Winsor, C. A. Cutter, Samuel S. Green, James L. Whitney, Melvil Dui, Fred B. Perkins and Thomas W. Bicknell, have associated themselves with the intention of forming a corporation under the name of the American Library Association for the purpose of promoting the library interests of the country by exchanging views, reaching conclusions, and inducing cooperation in all departments of bibliothecal science and economy; by disposing the public mind to the founding and improving of libraries; and by cultivating good will among its own members, and have complied with the provisions of the statutes of this Commonwealth in such case made and provided, as appears from the certificate of the President, Treasurer and Executive Board of said corporation, duly approved by the Commissioner of Corporations, and recorded in this office.

Now, therefore, I, Henry B. Peirce, Secretary of the Commonwealth of Massachusetts, do hereby certify that said Justin Winsor, C. A. Cutter, Samuel S. Green, James L. Whitney, Melvil Dui, Fred B. Perkins and Thomas W. Bicknell, their associates and successors, are legally organized and established as, and are hereby made an existing corporation under the name of the American Library Association, with the powers, rights, and privileges, and subject to the limitations, duties, and restrictions, which by law appertain thereto.

Witness my official signature hereunto subscribed, and the seal of the Commonwealth of Massachusetts hereunto affixed this tenth day of December in the year of Our Lord one thousand eight hundred and seventy-nine.

HENRY B. PEIRCE

Secretary of the Commonwealth

One significant change has been made in the objectives. The charter was amended in 1942 to include the promotion of library interests throughout the world.

In 1969 the objectives are the same, although expressed in different words to reflect needs and opportunities at this point in the twentieth century. Today, the association states in less formal language that it seeks to make books and ideas vital forces in American life, to make libraries easily accessible to all persons, to improve professional standards of library service and librarianship, and to create and publish professional literature.

Structure and Government

Any person who is interested in the promotion of libraries and librarianship may join the association. The membership is made up of people who work in libraries, whether or not they have library science degrees; people who work in related fields (writing and publishing, government as it relates to libraries, education, and other such areas); library trustees; and students of library science. Some of these members, called "special members," voluntarily pay extra dues for the support of the association's program.

ALA also has organization members. This category consists of libraries, library organizations, and businesses, such as publishers or library supply houses. Organization members do not vote or hold office.

A president-elect and first vice-president, a second vice-president, and the treasurer are elected by the voting members of the association. The membership also elects the ALA Council, the policy-making body of the association and its highest authority. There are 246 members of the Council in 1969, 37 of whom serve as nonvoting members by virtue of their office or committee assignment. The Council meets twice each year, at the Midwinter Meeting and the Annual Conference.

The management arm of the association is the Executive Board of fourteen members. The Board includes the president, first and second vice-presidents, the treasurer, and eight members elected by and from the Council. The executive director (a nonvoting member of the Board) is appointed by the Board and serves at its pleasure. "At the pleasure of" means precisely that, and the executive director can be removed without further reason.

The members of the association have organized themselves into units of membership called divisions. Each of the fourteen divisions has a field of responsibility and authority distinct from those of the others. The five type-of-library divisions are: American Association of School Librarians, American Association of State Libraries, Association of College and Research Libraries, Association of Hospital and Institution Libraries, and Public Library Association. The nine type-of-activity divisions are: Adult Services Division, American Library Trustee Association, Children's Services Division, Information Science and Automation Division, Library Administration Division, Library Education Division, Reference Services Division, Resources and Technical Services Division, and Young Adult Services Division.

Any member, personal, special, or organization, becomes a member of any two divisions as a perquisite of payment of the basic dues and may join additional divisions by paying additional dues. The divisions are organized with boards of directors and committees and engage in many activities. Some divisions also have sections and subsections.

Each of the overall committees of ALA also has a field of definite responsibility which cuts across divisional lines. Some committees have organizational functions, such as the Nominating, Election, and Constitution and Bylaws committees and the Committee on Organization. Others are concerned with substantive matters, such as the Committee on Legislation, the International Relations Committee, and the Intellectual Freedom Committee. ALA, in addition, has joint committees with other organizations.

Round Tables are composed of not less than fifty members of the association who are interested in the same field of librarianship not within the scope of any divisions. They serve as forums for their members but do not speak for ALA on matters of policy as do the divisions. The Round Tables are: American Library History Round Table, Exhibits Round Table, International Relations Round Table, Junior Members Round Table, Library Research Round Table, Round Table on Library Service to the Blind, Staff Organizations Round Table, and Round Table on Social Responsibilities of Libraries.

The policies of the association are determined by the elected officials—councilors and the executive boards of the association and of its divisions—and can be amended or set aside by the membership. The activities of the association are planned by the membership, working in ALA committees or division committees or in Round Tables. About 4,500, or 1 in 7 members, take an active part in the association's work. The activities are carried out by the membership units, assisted by a paid staff, under the leadership of the executive director. Two meetings of the association are held each year. The Midwinter Meeting in January of Council, boards, and committees on the business of the association is attended by 1,600 to 2,000. The Annual Conference, usually held in June and at-

tended by 7,000 to 10,000, is open to all members and includes program and business meetings.

The chapters of ALA are the state, provincial (from Canada), and territorial library associations, each of which has a representative on the Council, and the regional library associations. Although the chapters are completely autonomous, admitting to membership persons who are not members of ALA, determining and collecting their own dues, and setting up their own policies and programs, they have strong ties with ALA. A chapter is the final authority within the American Library Association in respect to all programs and policies which concern only the area for which the chapter is responsible, provided they are not inconsistent with programs and policies established by the ALA Council.

Of the headquarters staff of 245 persons, about 15 percent work directly with the membership in the development of program activity; 25 percent are engaged in the publication of materials, both journals and monographs; and the remainder maintain the clerical and business functions of the association. Roughly 23 percent are engaged in professional (library, editing, accounting) activities and 77 percent in work of a supporting nature.

The structure of ALA has always been subject to change to meet the changing needs of society and the libraries that serve it. Special committees have studied the organization structure and management and have recommended changes that were subsequently made. Twelve years ago a major reorganization took place on the recommendation of a firm of management consultants employed to study the association. Today the Committee on Organization is charged with continuing review of the organization of ALA.

Financial Support

Membership organizations, professional organizations, educational organizations— and ALA is a little of each—have many problems, but none looms larger to the administration than the search for sufficient funds to support the many activities that are proposed by an active membership.

ALA is a nonprofit educational organization under the provisions of Section 501 (C) (3) of the Internal Revenue Code. It enjoys federal tax exemption under that section. This classification gives certain financial advantages to ALA; it also places certain restrictions upon the association in the conduct of its affairs. ALA does not pay certain types of taxes. Foundations may make grants to us. Gifts to ALA are deductible for income tax purposes.

The American Library Association obtains its funds from several sources. It has an endowment fund, created in 1926 and 1931 through gifts of $2 million from the Carnegie Corporation of New York. That endowment now totals at market value $2.8 million, after withdrawal of approximately $1 million to finance a new building in the early 1960s. From this endowment we received an income of $94,930 in 1967–68. Income from other endowment funds totaled $27,948.

Income from membership dues amounted to $917,597. Publishing income was $1,301,313. Of $1,715,537 received in grants, $1,633,502 came from foundations and $82,035 from the federal government. Other sources of income produced $418,012, including $241,891 from annual meetings. All figures are for 1967–68.

The uses to which income from grants and publishing may be put are fixed; grant income must be used for the purposes of the grant, while publishing income must be used for publishing and, to some extent, for printing. The amount available in 1968–69 for general purposes is $1,417,220.

To summarize, ALA's income in 1967–68 came principally from membership dues, publishing, and grants.

Foundation Support

Funding assistance from foundations merits special attention in discussing the income of the American Library Association. Foundations in the United States have the financial capability to aid very substantially in the programs of libraries and li-

brary associations. The foundations have constantly, throughout ALA's history, displayed an interest in aiding the association and libraries.

The third edition of the *Foundation Directory*, published in 1967 by the Foundation Library Center, lists 6,803 foundations in the United States. (The information on foundations which follows is taken largely from the introduction to this edition of the *Directory*.) The number of foundations included in the *Directory* is growing because the Internal Revenue Service now requires that the foundations provide not only the usual financial data involved in a balance sheet, but a history of every grant with name and address of recipient; a statement of market value of assets; a schedule of officers, directors, and trustees; and other related information.

There are approximately 18,000 active American foundations; the 6,803 mentioned are those having assets of $200,000 or making grants totaling at least $10,000 in the year of record. The remaining, numbering more than 10,000, are small. The assets at market value, for 6,799 foundations reporting this item, totaled $19,927 million for 1964 or 1965 (the year covered varies somewhat). The approximately 10,500 foundations too small for directory inclusion indicated assets of about $387 million, less than any one of the five largest foundations. Thirteen American foundations, less than 0.1 percent of American foundations by number, hold assets of $7,750 million, or more than a third of the assets of all foundations. A total of 6,802 foundations (all but one in the *Directory*) reported expenditures which amounted to $1,293.5 million. Of this amount grants totaled $1,212 million.

With this and other background information from the *Directory*, it ought to be possible to make a fairly correct estimate of the amount of grants made during any year to libraries and library associations. Such is not wholly the case because some grants affecting libraries are included under nonlibrary categories such as scholarships and loans, educational associations, international relations, and fellowships. Under libraries, however, 84 foundations in the third edition of the *Directory* report 131 grants amounting to $20,139 million.

Another statistic, from the *Bowker Annual of Library and Book Trade Information* for 1968, lists 138 grants for library purposes, totaling $11,847.5 million. The *Annual* for 1967 lists 170 grants totaling $24,366.5 million. Grants for foreign and domestic purposes are included.

Foundations all have their programs and these, over a period in time, vary in emphasis. One large foundation states, for instance, that it has no "library program." Nevertheless, it does make grants for education and often finds it must then support the library as an integral part of the institution it is aiding. Therefore, with few exceptions, a library or library association cannot turn to a foundation in the sure knowledge that libraries are of interest to that foundation. As the *Directory* observes, "Foundations are highly individualistic, and the projects they support are almost infinite in variety."

Programs and Activities

The ALA Goals for Action statement (1967) helps determine the activities and programs of the association. The emphasis varies from year to year because conditions and needs vary. Although broad goals remain constant, the priority given to each changes in relation to the times.

The Program Memorandum, issued each January, details ALA activities and programs at one point in time—the year in which it is published. I should like now to call attention to some of the programs and activities which most concern the members of ALA in 1969. In doing so, I shall necessarily be selective, and I refer the reader, for much that is not included in this paper, to the Program Memorandum for 1969 describing programs for the period 1 September 1968–31 August 1969. In discussing the programs of ALA, I must ask you to remember that I am discussing the programs of only one association. There are other associations and other agencies in the United States that carry out important ac-

tivities, but my topic is the work of the American Library Association.

Legislation

The American Library Association assumes the responsibility for promoting federal legislation advantageous to the development of library service in the United States and protesting against federal legislation that will be harmful to such development. The chapters of ALA, in cooperation with the state library agencies, assume responsibility for state legislation and look to ALA for background and assistance in devising and promoting effective legislation.

The specific responsibility for federal legislation activities lies with the ALA Committee on Legislation and its division and other subcommittees. Aided by an associate executive director and supporting staff, the committee determines legislative needs and formulates goals, policies, and programs of action to meet these needs. Such goals and policies must be approved by the ALA Council.

The committee concerns itself with many areas of federal legislation, such as financial support of libraries, copyright, intellectual freedom, and postal and customs rates and regulations. Through staff it arranges for the introduction to Congress of appropriate legislation and for testimony before legislative committees in support of the legislation. In cooperation with ALA divisions and chapters, it maintains a network of members across the country to explain library legislation to their national representatives and to urge their support of the legislation.

Since general legislation, such as economic opportunity for urban development, can be of importance to libraries, the committee is also concerned with interpretation of such legislation to the library world. The librarians of the country and citizens interested in the advancement of library service have worked closely together in the national legislative program. Other national library associations have cooperated, and some have been very active in their efforts.

ALA, after debate in Council, declared itself in favor of federal aid to libraries in

1936. The membership contributed a sum which made possible the establishment of the ALA National Relations Office in Washington in 1945, now called the ALA Washington Office. In 1956 the Library Services Act was enacted into law. This act authorized $37.5 million for library development in rural areas over a five-year period, and this amount was to be matched by the states. Federal aid to libraries has grown since 1956 to an authorization of approximately $500 million for fiscal 1970. This sum has provided federal assistance and encouragement in the development of services, buildings, cooperation, networks of libraries, training of librarians, research, and books and other library materials.

The Report of the National Advisory Commission on Libraries was delivered to the President of the United States on 3 October 1968. This report has been widely disseminated and discussed. Its several recommendations include two which are the subject of legislation introduced into Congress this spring. The two recommendations are: (1) "That it be declared National Policy, enunciated by the President and enacted into law by the Congress, that the American people should be provided with library and information services adequate to their needs, and that the federal government, in collaboration with state and local governments, and private agencies, should exercise leadership in assuring the provision of such services," and (2) that there be established a National Commission on Libraries and Information Science as a continuing federal planning agency.

Standards

Standards for the different types of libraries, dealing with quarters, staff, support, and coordination of services, are developed by the unit of ALA having responsibility for the type of library for which the standards are developed. Guidelines, or extensions of certain parts of the standards, are developed by the type-of-activity divisions. All standards and guidelines are revised periodically.

The *Standards for School Media Programs*, prepared jointly by the American Association of School Librarians and the Department of Audiovisual Instruction of the National Education Association, was published in the spring of 1969. *Standards for Library Functions at the State Level*, published first in 1963, is being revised by the American Association of State Libraries for approval at the 1969 Annual Conference. *Standards of Library Service for Health Care Facilities* is in preparation by the Association of Hospital and Institution Libraries in cooperation with other interested national bodies. *Costs of Public Library Service, 1963* was revised and published in 1968 by the Public Library Association. Containing three model budgets for library systems of various sizes, this supplement, to be done annually, updates *Minimum Standards for Public Library Systems. Junior College Library Standards* is under revision by the Association of College and Research Libraries. Guidelines are in preparation, especially for library service to adults and audiovisual services in public libraries.

Intellectual Freedom

The concept of intellectual freedom, especially the freedom to read, has long been a concern of ALA. The Library Bill of Rights was adopted by the Council in 1948 and amended in 1961 and 1967. This landmark document was followed in 1953 by the Freedom to Read Statement. Currently, the Intellectual Freedom Committee and the Office for Intellectual Freedom are engaged in a program of education in the concept of intellectual freedom. The target audience at present is practicing and student librarians.

Library Technology Program

The Library Technology Program is organized to search for ways by which modern technology and scientific management can improve library operations and services. To this end it evaluates library equipment, supplies, and systems, and conducts systems studies; works on the development of new or improved items of library equipment and promotes improvements in existing equipment; develops performance standards for library equipment and supplies; and continues with its information service to the library profession.

Under way now are the following activities: a test program of audiovisual equipment; promotion of wider acceptance and approval of three provisional binding standards: for durability, easy opening, and workmanship; the development of standards for microfiche, for permanence of photocopies, and for photocopying equipment; the development of a test target to test the capabilities of photocopying machines; the establishment of performance standards for wooden library furniture; the testing of bracket-type steel shelving; and a testing program for fifty plastic and wood chairs of the type used for general seating in libraries.

Publications of the Library Technology Program include: *Study of Circulation Control Systems*; *Development of Performance Standards for Library Binding*; *Photocopying from Bound Volumes: A Study of Machines, Methods, and Materials*; *Protecting the Library and Its Resources: A Guide to Physical Protection and Insurance*; *Catalog Card Reproduction*; *Copying Methods Manual*; *Floors: Selection and Maintenance*; and *Compact Library Shelving*. The program issues *Library Technology Reports,* a bimonthly subscription service for the library administrator.

The Library Technology Program owes its origin and most of its support to the Council on Library Resources, Inc., which has contributed around $2 million for operations and projects since May 1959. A study entitled *Evaluation and Planning Study for the Library Technology Program* by a management firm was completed in January 1969.

International Relations

The International Relations Committee and the International Relations Office are concerned with the improvement and maintenance of the quality of library resources, services, and personnel in countries beyond the borders of the United States and Canada. The Office serves as a source of advice and assistance to universities, foundations,

library schools, librarians, and others concerned with library development abroad. It assists foundations and other agencies to identify well-qualified American librarians for overseas service, furnishes information to librarians abroad, and at the request of American and foreign officials, reviews library development programs and provides professional counsel on such plans.

The growing attention paid by the United States government to the role of books and libraries in economic development has led to new opportunities for ALA to participate in government activities where association and government objectives and goals are compatible. Most significantly, a contract between ALA and the U.S. Agency for International Development led to the establishment of a project office within the International Relations Office in Washington, D.C. to provide advice and assistance to AID. The director of IRO and the ALA project officer have made survey trips to Asia and Latin America to identify the library and book needs of selected countries and to assist institutions in developing appropriate programs of action.

The Office is prepared to administer projects that are funded by grants or contractual arrangements. For example, a foundation may decide to support an effort to strengthen a library school in Asia. The International Relations Office will select the necessary consultants and faculty; it will aid in the selection of persons from abroad for training in the United States and will make arrangements for their travel and study; and it will find the right persons to prepare manuals and textbooks when necessary and will supervise their production.

The Office presently administers several grants for private foundations in their programs of institutional development overseas. A Ford Foundation grant for assistance in rehabilitating the library of the University of Algiers began in January 1967 and is scheduled to continue until July 1969. A Ford Foundation program of assistance to Haile Selassie I University in Addis Ababa was initiated in 1965 and will continue through 1971. A Rockefeller Foundation program to support the Department of Library Science at the University of Delhi, begun in 1961, will continue until May 1971. A Ford Foundation grant to assist the library of the University of Brasilia is near completion.

The International Relations Office administers the annual Multi-National Librarian Project of the Department of State. Last year's program included a special seminar on librarianship in the United States, a six-week internship in an appropriate library, and a study tour of selected libraries. The program for the current year will be similar, with the special seminar scheduled at the University of Pittsburgh's Graduate School of Library and Information Science.

Library Education

Since the preparation of personnel to staff libraries is basic to the development of library service, ALA has three units principally concerned with library education. The Office for Library Education conducts studies concerned with manpower and curriculum development. The Library Education Division is a membership unit in which library school faculty members and practicing librarians come together to identify the educational needs of the library world, including equivalencies and reciprocity between schools of various countries, and to plan ways to meet those needs. The Committee on Accreditation evaluates and accredits the programs of graduate library schools offering the master's degree in library science. The committee is studying the possibility of extending its scope to include the accreditation of undergraduate and postgraduate programs of library education.

A paper, "Education and Manpower for Librarianship," prepared by the director of the Office for Library Education following discussion with many representatives of the library profession, was published in the October 1968 issue of the *ALA Bulletin* and is serving as the basis for consideration by concerned groups all over the country. Out of the thinking generated by the problems facing library education and the content of the paper, a major revision in library education in the United States is expected to take place.

Publishing

Monographic publications, such as brochures, pamphlets, and books, may originate in a number of ways. Many of them are the products of other activities. Thus the proceedings of a conference on library buildings and equipment are published. A five-year project on the development of school libraries is completed with a published report.

Divisions or other units of ALA may instigate publications. Standards are a good example of division publications. The Library Technology Program has produced a number of publications. Almost every unit of ALA, at one time or another, is engaged in preparing material to be published. The editors of ALA publications may plan publications to serve the needs of the profession and seek authors to write the manuscripts. On occasion, authors submit unsolicited manuscripts.

Serial publications are of several kinds. The *ALA Bulletin* [now *American Libraries*], which goes to all of the nearly 40,000 ALA members, is the official voice of the association, carrying news of ALA and articles on significant developments within the profession.

Each division (except the Library Administration Division) publishes a newsletter or a journal. Newsletters are designed to keep members informed on the activities of the division. Journals add to this function the presentation of scholarly papers on subjects of concern to the division's membership. Some sections, Round Tables, offices, and projects also publish newsletters.

Two reviewing journals are published by ALA. *The Booklist and Subscription Books Bulletin* recommends books for all ages for general library collections and films for adult use. Beginning this year (1969) it will carry review of nonbook materials suitable for use with elementary and secondary school students. *Choice*, published by the Association of College and Research Libraries, reviews books suitable for college libraries but is used also as a guide to selection by high school and public libraries. Some of the division serial publications also include reviews of books of special interest to their members.

Some of ALA's publications, such as newsletters and journals, are perquisites of membership, although some of the journals are obtainable on a subscription basis. Almost all the monographic publications are sold. The association issues thirty serial publications and has two hundred monographs and three hundred pamphlets and brochures in print. The members of ALA value its publications highly and regard its publishing services as a major function of the association.

Most ALA publications are used as texts in library education as well as guides to practice in the field. Titles published in 1968 and 1969 include: *Guide to Reference Books,* Eighth Edition, First Supplement; *ALA Rules for Filing Catalog Cards,* Second Edition; *Standards for School Media Programs*; *Historical Sets, Collected Editions, and Monuments of Music*; *Subject Guide to Major United States Government Publications*; *MARC Manuals*; *Personnel Organization and Procedure*; *Use of the Library of Congress Classification*; *Career of the Academic Librarian*; *Carnegie Libraries: Their History and Impact on American Public Library Development*; *Junior College Libraries: Development, Needs, and Perspectives*; *Public Library Systems in the United States*; and *Realization: The Final Report of the Knapp School Libraries Project.*

The other two major library publishers in the United States are the H. W. Wilson Company and the R. R. Bowker Company, both located in New York. Their publishing is so important to American librarianship that each is referred to here briefly.

The H. W. Wilson Company was founded in 1898 by Halsey W. Wilson. Its first publication was the *Cumulative Book Index.* This has been the essential and definitive index of published books in the English language. The company also publishes the *Union List of Serials in Libraries of the United States and Canada.* It has developed and publishes a series of periodical and book indexes. Examples are: *Readers' Guide to Periodical Literature*; *Art Index*; *Biological and Agricultural Index*; *Education Index*; *Library Literature*; and *Book Review Digest.* Wilson also publishes the standard catalog series, including the *Children's Catalog, Junior High School Library Catalog, Senior High School Library Catalog, Fiction Catalog,* and *Standard Catalog for Public Libraries.*

In addition, it issues *Current Bibliography,* which is useful for its articles on important contemporary personalities throughout the world. Of interest to librarians is the *Wilson Library Bulletin,* which goes to 37,500 subscribers.

The R. R. Bowker Company is the oldest of the publishers directly serving the library profession and the book trade in the United States, having been in operation since the early 1870s. Bowker has published *Library Journal* since 1876. This is the oldest continuing library periodical in the world. The three men who were instrumental in its founding—Frederick Leypoldt, Richard R. Bowker, and Melvil Dewey, who was the magazine's first editor —also played an important part in the establishment of the American Library Association in 1876. For a short while, *Library Journal* was the official journal for ALA, as well as for the (British) Library Association. *Library Journal,* together with its offspring, *School Library Journal,* reaches nearly 64,000 subscribers.

School Library Journal, which appears both as a section of *Library Journal* and as a separate magazine, made its first appearance as a separate journal in September 1954; it was then called *Junior Libraries.* Aimed at children's, young adult, and school librarians, it has a separate circulation of nearly 27,000.

Bowker publishes many books for librarians and other bookmen, and a substantial number of standard library reference books, such as the *American Library Directory* and the *Bowker Annual of Library and Book Trade Information.* Among its bibliographic services, the best known are *Books in Print* and its *Subject Guide, Paperbound*

Books in Print, and, in the serials field, *Ulrich's International Periodicals Directory.*

Other Programs

Although legislation, standards, intellectual freedom, library technology, international relations, library education, and publishing are of major importance to every segment of library policy, development, and practice, they do not constitute the whole of ALA activities. Every unit of ALA is engaged in activities that are designed to improve and extend library services.

At this point in U.S. history, a principal concern of all is the necessity of relieving the poverty of a large number of our citizens and of upgrading the education and employment possibilities of those who have been discriminated against because of their race, color, or religious beliefs. ALA has accepted by action of its Council the development of library services to the disadvantaged as a major goal for as long as it shall be necessary. A Coordinating Committee on Library Services to the Disadvantaged is working with divisions and committees to bring their many activities in this field into a unified program of genuine impact. Thus the work of the divisions in evaluating materials for use with the newly literate, in providing guidance in using materials with underprivileged children, in identifying materials that speak to the condition of the young people who do not finish secondary school, and in defining effective library service to the inmates of correctional institutions will be supported and integrated by the committee.

The need for cooperation among all types of libraries grows greater as the awareness of the need for library service grows faster than do funds, staff, and other resources. The five type-of-library divisions, joined by the American Library Trustee Association, have conducted a study of the barriers to cooperation through conferences with librarians and trustees across the country. A six-division joint program, based on the study, "Mobilizing Resources for Library Services," will be held at the 1969 Annual Conference.

Implicit in the efficient use of resources is the employment of modern technological devices. The Information Science and Automation Division has cooperated with the Library of Congress in holding a series of conferences to explain the MARC II Project (Machine-Readable Cataloging) to librarians all over the country and in publishing a manual of practice. MARC II has established a standard way of identifying bibliographic entries and their constituent parts to make computer tape exchange among libraries effective. The method has been approved by the appropriate divisions of ALA.

Several divisions of ALA are pursuing the possibilities for holding an invitational conference on the establishment of a national network of information. The conference will be based on a series of scholarly papers, prepared in advance and studied by the conference participants.

The advent of automation has not overcome ALA's interest in traditional methods that have proved useful. The Reference Services Division has revised the Interlibrary Loan Code and prepared new manuals for its use. The Public Library Association has conducted a research project to determine the effectiveness of public library systems and to identify the elements that make for effectiveness. Revisions of such works as *Serial Publications* and *Simple Library Cataloging* are under way.

ALA maintains constant concern about the welfare of staff members in libraries, the basic resource for library service. The Library Administration Division is working on projects concerned with libraries, unions, and collective bargaining; salary scales; fringe benefits; and personnel practices. The work of the Office for Recruitment and of the Library Education Division, extending as they do from the education of library workers to their appropriate employment, is closely allied to these projects.

The American Library Association is constantly faced with the need for doing more than its resources in funds and manpower will permit. It must make choices dependent on the needs of the nation. Now almost one hundred years old, with almost

40,000 members, a reasonably flexible structure, and a distinguished history of contributions to society, the American Library Association looks forward to a useful future. It does not expect freedom from problems, but hopes to garner from among its members the wisdom, the patience, and the energy to overcome obstacles, and plans to continue vigorously the pursuit of its objective—the promotion of libraries and librarianship all over the world.

Center for Research Libraries: Its Origins, Policies, and Programs

Gordon Williams
Director

The Center for Research Libraries in Chicago, Illinois, is a unique institution. There is no other in the world exactly like it, though there are several that share one or more of its characteristics. Most simply, the Center can be described as a libraries' library. As individuals turn to a library to borrow those publications they cannot justify purchasing for themselves, in exactly the same way libraries turn to the Center for those publications they need but do not have in their collections. The problems that the Center was established to help solve are not unique to the United States, nor are the factors that make this particular solution practical. Both the problems and the factors are universal, and therefore a description of the Center's programs and policies and some account of its experience may be useful to others. And, if I may be forgiven for speaking selfishly, I hope that it may also lead to an international extension that will in turn benefit the scholars and universities served by the Center.

The origins of the Center go back to the mid-1930s, when the Harvard University Library, concerned about its constantly increasing need for more and still more space, proposed to some of its neighbors in New England that they cooperate to build a storage library in which each of them could rent space to store the less frequently used materials from their collections. This proposal was accepted and the New England Depository Library, as it was called, was built. Since this proposal at least slowed the rate of demand for more expensive library space in the heart of the campus and was therefore useful, in 1939 it was proposed that a group of Midwestern universities establish a similar facility to serve them. For a number of reasons this proposal was not accepted by the universities concerned, the most important reason being the conviction of a few that a storage library was at best only a partial solution to their problems. The whole matter lay in abeyance until 1948, when the question was revived and a committee of Midwestern librarians was formed to look into the whole question of library needs and to propose solutions. A number of librarians were involved, but most active were Errett McDiarmid, then Director of Libraries at the University of Minnesota; Ralph Ellsworth, then Director of Libraries at the University of Iowa, and Herman Fussler, Director of Libraries at the University of Chicago.

The report of this committee stated so well the problem and the general solution needed that it deserves quoting:

The library development of the past 50 years quite properly emphasized acquisition by each institution of the research materials it needed and would require in the future. True, libraries went beyond immediate needs and acquired materials against possible future demands; but in the early stages of development this was desirable, even necessary. Until basic collections of materials were built up in many areas, libraries could not at all underwrite the success of the extensive research programs which their institutions were undertaking. They had to grow and they had to grow fast—each individual one of them.

But now the time has come when a change must be made. Even the largest library of the country, the Library of Congress, has realized that it can no longer hope to be individually self-sufficient. It must now take into account the research resources of other institutions and limit itself to subjects which it can hope to fill out with some reasonable degree of success. Midwestern libraries have also come to realize that they can no longer hope to acquire everything that their people will need—now and in the future.

The reasons for this are simple. First, libraries are now approaching the point where there are not enough copies of research materials to be in every library where research in that subject is being carried on. As a result, libraries are placed in the position of having to bid against each other for scarce materials with unfortunate results for the limited budgets under which they operate. Second, the amount of materials being published in all fields of knowledge is too vast to lie within the financial resources of any one institution. To put it another way, there is entirely too much material available on every subject for one library to hope to acquire. Third, libraries are more than ever aware that space, and staff for assembling and organizing material cannot be expanded indefinitely.

It is clear that the time has come for a re-examination of library policies. Unconditional acceptance of traditional practices can lead only to duplication, confusion and fragmentary service. Libraries must now think and plan for the needs of scholarship in the nation and in their region as well as in their own communities. Any other way leads to chaos.

It seems clear, therefore, that what is needed for the Midwest is a long term plan for library development which would, first, make better provision for the total research needs of the area, and second, provide for economical and efficient utilization of existing and future resources to avoid duplication and needless expense. Stated in another way, the research resources of the Middle West must be increased and the means for doing so must be realistically planned and manageably financed.

To attain the fundamental objectives of improvement of resources and economy of operations four cooperative activities need to be organized:

1. Coordination of collecting policies for the region as a whole
2. Improvement and simplification of technical and bibliographic processes to avoid duplication and provide greater service
3. Provision of accessible and economical housing of little-used material for the good of the region as a whole
4. Acquisition for the region of materials needed for a forward-looking research program, but not now available.

It is proposed that to carry on these activities and-to direct them to the attainment of the goals listed, there be created the *Midwest Inter-Library Corporation.* The corporation would engage in three major activities with the end in mind of achieving improvement and economy for the library resources of the Midwest:

1. Cooperative collection and housing of little-used material for the use of the region as a whole
2. Developing a program for filling out and enriching the resources of the region
3. Development of cooperative bibliographic projects.

This committee's statement was doubly important because it confronted the really basic problem of libraries—their inability individually to be wholly self-sufficient for the needs of their patrons—and not merely the various minor symptoms of this problem, and then made a specific recommendation for action toward a solution. Fortunately, this recommendation was accepted, and in 1949 the Midwest Inter-Library Center was incorporated as a not-for-profit organization, with ten supporting universities, to undertake the suggested programs.

It is clear from the above statement that, from the beginning, the Center was conceived of as far more than a library to house infrequently used materials deposited by the member libraries. It was to be an organization that would act to increase the availability to scholarship of publications needed to advance research. True, it did have a deposit program, but this was quite different in conception from that, for example, of the New England Depository Library, which was merely a warehouse and nothing more. Libraries rented space in it to store their less frequently used publications, and paid in accordance with the amount of space used. No attempt was made to integrate the collections or to avoid storage of multiple copies of the same title. Libraries could have achieved the same end by renting space in a commercial warehouse, the only difference being that since the New England Depository Library was owned by a nonprofit corporation created for the purpose, presumably the rent was cheaper.

The deposit program developed by the Midwest Inter-Library Center is quite different. First of all, the material deposited is given to the Center, either as an outright gift, as in most cases, or in a few cases as a permanent loan. Practically, these amounted to almost the same thing since, as a permanent loan, the material could not be withdrawn by the depositing library. The library would get the material back only if the Center were ever to cease operation. Second, the material deposited is integrated into a single collection, with only one copy being kept of each title. Obviously there is no point in keeping two, or five or ten, copies of the same title when it is, by selection, infrequently used, and one copy would be sufficient to satisfy the demand for it. Not only does this program provide much cheaper housing cost per volume (costs that amount to about 13 cents per volume per year in the average American library as compared with about 3 cents per volume per year in the Center, with its simpler and more efficient building), but it significantly reduces the number of volumes that need to be housed to meet research needs adequately. More important than the space saving, or even the economy in housing, is the fact that the collection resulting from thus combining the deposits from many libraries of a given class of publications, for example, foreign doctoral dissertations, is far more extensive and complete than any one library had before, since, of course, all the libraries did not have identical collections. Still more important is the fact that the resulting collection is commonly owned and any title in it is available by right, not merely by courtesy,

to every participant. Each one is thus assured that he can have access to it when needed, and for as long as he needs it, and that he can get it more quickly than he could when it was in the original library.

This latter point is significant and justifies a brief digression. Libraries, such as university and other research libraries, are organized to serve most efficiently the patrons who come to the library. Interlibrary loans are a service they provide as a courtesy to others, and the procedures are of necessity different from those for service to a patron appearing in person. The result, inevitably, is that interlibrary-loan requests are processed more slowly. I do not know how it may be in Japan, but in the United States, at least on the average, it is five to ten days before a library receiving an interlibrary-loan request gets the book in the mail to the library wanting it. The Center, on the other hand, is organized primarily to service interlibrary-loan requests and gives these priority. The result is that publications requested from the Center are put in the mail the same day the request is received, and the user gets them much more quickly than if they had been requested from a regular library. This difference in service characteristics seems to be inherent in the two kinds of libraries, and while it is true that any library *could* give same-day service on interlibrary-loan requests, it could do so only at additional expense that it would find difficult to justify.

The second major program of the Center is its direct acquisition and housing, for the joint use of the members, of those publications whose use could be anticipated to be so infrequent that the members would not need to buy a copy for their own collections if one were available from the Center. These acquisitions are many and varied and include both older publications that the libraries either were unable to justify buying in view of the low frequency with which they would be used, or that were of a kind not then within their fields of research interest, and newly published works that can be anticipated to be infrequently used. I will return in a moment to a more detailed description of these acquisitions programs, but first two other things should be mentioned.

You will remember that four programs were originally outlined for the Center—a deposit program, an acquisitions program, a program to improve and simplify technical and bibliographic processes in the member libraries, and the coordination of collecting policies for the region as a whole. The Center has done nothing about these last two, and the reasons for this are of interest. In simplest terms, the bibliographic problem was really one of providing prompt and uniform cataloging for all publications so that every library would not have to catalog for itself every publication it acquired, needlessly duplicating the work of every other library that was also acquiring a copy. After more consideration of this problem, it was concluded that it would be far preferable to try for a solution based on the Library of Congress rather than on the Center, and this was done.

The question of coordinating collecting policies for the region as a whole turned out to be impractical. Basically, the idea was to have a division of collecting responsibilities based on individual library interests, one library taking responsibility for collecting materials in one area or subject, another library for another area, and so on. The other libraries would then borrow from the one with the collecting responsibility for a field when they needed materials within its scope. In essence, what was proposed was a kind of miniature Farmington Plan.

This program was not started for two reasons. One was that subject interests of universities are not predictable enough. Such a program is of value only so far as it permits a library to avoid collecting a particular class of material. A library can avoid this only when the institution it serves does not do teaching or research in that field, but as soon as its parent body, university or other organization, begins a program or department in that field, then it must acquire for itself at least the basic publications in that field. At this point, it can satisfy its needs by interlibrary loan only for those publications that are infrequently used in the field, and the library

from which the loan is requested may find itself unable to acquire these because it has itself been faced with acquiring publications in a new area of interest to its faculty and must give these needs priority. In addition, as mentioned above, interlibrary loan between libraries with primary responsibility for service to their local patrons is not wholly satisfactory because it is not fast enough.

For these reasons, it began to be recognized that such a division of responsibilities among libraries was not the best solution. A far better solution was to focus attention on those materials infrequently used, regardless of field, and to assign responsibility for these publications to the Center, where the burden of supporting their acquisition, cataloging, and housing could be divided among all the participating libraries, and from which they could be borrowed more readily. It is perhaps worth noting that these faults have been found in the Farmington Plan itself, and that, notable and important as this plan was when it was begun, more recently it has been proposed that it be abandoned in favor of central acquisition of the materials by an institution such as the Center for Research Libraries.

To this point I have used the phrase "infrequently used library materials" freely, as if everyone knew exactly what it meant. In a way we all do know what this phrase means, and we all know that some library materials are infrequently used. Until the last few years, though, we had little exact information about the frequency of use of library materials. The first and still the best and most comprehensive study is that by Herman H. Fussler and Julian L. Simon, *Patterns in the Use of Books in Large Research Libraries.* Originally published by the University of Chicago Library in 1961 for limited circulation, this study is now being published for general circulation by the University of Chicago Press. The authors discovered that in some subject fields as much as 25 percent of the collections are used no oftener than once in a hundred years.

In a study of the Northwestern University Library conducted by Richard Trueswell ("A Quantitative Measure of User Circulation Requirements . . . ," *American Documentation,* vol.16, no.1, Jan. 1965), it was discovered that over 99 percent of all use made of the collection in the Science and Technology Library was limited to only 25 percent of the collection. To put it another way, the Science and Technology Library is maintaining 75 percent of its collection to satisfy less than 1 percent of the requests from its patrons. In the general collection the pattern is similar but not quite as extreme, as one might guess from the fact that in the humanities and social sciences proportionately more use is made of older materials than in the fields of science and technology. Nonetheless, in the general collection over 99 percent of all use is confined to only 40 percent of the collection, with 60 percent of the collection accounting for less than 1 percent of the use.

The John Crerar Library, one of the greatest scientific and technical libraries in the United States, and a member of the Center for Research Libraries almost from its beginning, has deposited in the Center tens of thousands of older scientific and technical publications from its collections. It has kept a careful record of all the publications thus deposited that it has had to borrow back from the Center for the use of a patron and discovered that it thus uses each year about one volume for every 200 it has deposited. This is an average frequency of use of these publications of only once in 200 years. The John Crerar Library has also discovered from records of use that about 70 percent of the approximately 13,000 serial titles it is currently receiving are used less often than once a year.

Data from other libraries, such as the National Library of Medicine in the United States, and the National Lending Library for Science and Technology in Great Britain, confirm this general pattern, and there is no need to review all the studies here. Those with particular interest in this kind of information can pursue it readily enough in the literature. The point to be made here is that the evidence is clear that whether one chooses to call a publication "frequently used" in a particular library if it is used on the average oftener than once in five years, or to be more generous and say it is frequently used if used oftener than once in fifty years, or even once in a hundred years, there remain a great many publications that are infrequently used, and that this characteristic can serve as a basis for vastly improving library service.

When one stops to think about it, what makes any library a feasible operation is the fact that there are relatively few publications that an individual uses so frequently that it is more economical for him to have his own copy than to spend the time of going to the library to use its copy. When one begins to think about those books that an individual uses so frequently that he needs his own copy, one thinks of dictionaries, handbooks, encyclopedias perhaps, and a few others. In mentally compiling such a list, one begins to be aware that there are relatively few publications that a given individual uses more than once. Except for a very small portion of the library's collection—primarily that portion known as the reference collection—a frequently used library book therefore means one that is used by a number of different people, and the frequency with which it is used is a function of the number of different people who use it. A corollary of this is that when the frequency of use of a particular title rises above some critical number dependent upon the way it is consulted and the circulation period allowed for it, the book is less and less likely to be in and available for a patron's use when he requests it. The only solution to this problem is to duplicate—to provide more copies of it—and this is, in fact, what every library does to some extent. In most libraries, though, there is a real effort made to hold duplication to the absolute minimum that the patrons will tolerate. Since libraries do not have enough money both to provide all the duplicate copies required to avoid unduly long delays in access and to buy at least one copy of every title that some patron might sometime need, they have been forced to choose between these alternatives, and have in most cases in the past thought it better to add a new title to the collection than to add a second copy of a title. Clearly this was the best decision at a time when, if the library did not have a copy of the publication needed, in practical effect it was not available to the patron. But with the possibility of assured access through interlibrary loan, the situation becomes quite different. Such publications are in fact available, though not as quickly as if locally owned, and the library should now look at the alternatives of buying a copy of an infrequently used title or a duplicate copy of a frequently used one in terms of the effect on average speed of access to all publications the patron needs.

Several studies of research libraries in the United States show that, because of lack of enough duplication, access to publications actually owned by the library is now much delayed. These studies show that when a patron requests a book actually owned by the library, only about half the time is it on the shelf and available for his use. In such cases the delay until it is available can range from a few hours to weeks. Of course, the reason for this delay is not always that the book is in use by another patron; sometimes it is because the book is lost or misshelved, and sometimes because it is at the bindery. Nevertheless, the reason is frequently that it is in use by another patron, and when it is, duplication will reduce or prevent such delay. And since delay for this reason will occur most often with books that are most frequently used, it is obvious that when there is a choice, money spent for buying duplicate copies of frequently used publications will reduce the delay in access more than the same money spent for adding to the collection a title that is infrequently used. But such a choice is possible to the library only when it has both assured and ready access to publications not in its own collection, and the primary purpose and a major justification for a program such as that of the Center for Research Libraries is that it makes such a choice possible.

To illustrate with some imaginary figures, if each of ten libraries were to take $5,000 of its acquisitions funds that would otherwise be used for purchasing copies of new titles that could reasonably be anticipated to be infrequently used, and were to allocate half of this to the purchase of duplicate copies of frequently used titles for its own collection and the other half to a cooperative center for the acquisition of infrequently used titles to be shared by all ten, the following benefits would result. First, the library ensures the ready availability to its patrons, not of just $5,000 worth of additional titles, but $25,000 worth—five times as many. Second, the patron's average access time to the publications he needs is significantly reduced: he gets faster access to titles in the library's own collection by not having to wait so long for other patrons to finish using them; he gets faster access to those publications his library could only make available to him through interlibrary borrowing in any case; and he gets access to more such publications than would otherwise be available to him through interlibrary loan.

In 1949, when the Midwest Inter-Library Center was founded, such detailed information on frequency of use as has just been cited was not known. As it became known, at first in a general way through the Center's making its collections available for loan to any library in the United States and not merely to those in the Midwest region who were members of the Center, and then specifically through careful research studies, two things became clear. First, both in terms of use without conflict and in terms of access time, it was not necessary to duplicate the Center's collection in several different regions of the country; the one collection in its central location was sufficient to serve the entire continent at least—and some of its collections were probably capable of serving even a wider area than the North American continent. Second, the very large number of publications that needed to be readily available to scholars—a number that was growing exponentially—meant that the broadest practicable base of support was required to ensure adequate access to all of them.

Therefore in 1964 the Center undertook a careful re-examination of its programs and policies. The result of this study, which involved experts from outside the Center, a broad representation of nonmember research libraries, and, finally, a conference of the head librarians and academic representatives from every member library, reconfirmed the basic programs of the Center but made a few significant changes in its policies. The most important of these was the dropping of all geographic restrictions on membership. No longer was membership limited to institutions located in the ten Midwestern states, but was now open to any institution that supported research and maintained a library judged to be at least minimally adequate to support its program. As a rough guide, the Center defined this as one containing at least 500,000 volumes and spending an average of at least $200,000 per year on acquisitions and binding, but the final decision on the eligibility of each applicant is made by the Board of Directors of the Center, which makes its judgment using these figures only as a guide. In fact, the libraries of all members substantially exceed at least one of these minima, and most substantially exceed both. It was to reflect this change in membership policy that the name of the organization was changed from the Midwest Inter-Library Center, with its regional connotation, to the broader and nonrestrictive one of the Center for Research Libraries.

A few words need to be inserted here about the restriction on membership to institutions maintaining large research libraries. In fact, this policy had been followed by the Center from its foundation, though it had not been formally stated. The reason for it was simply to ensure that the member institutions had the maximum possible commonality of interest and of dedication to the basic purpose for which the Center had been founded. This basic purpose, it will be recalled, was to increase the availability of library materials for *research*. A library smaller in size than the minimum specified by the Center cannot be regarded as adequate to support research in a variety of subject fields (though, of course, a smaller size can be very adequate if it is intended to support research in only one or two fields, particularly if these are not historically oriented), and in general

is not intended to support research at all. Usually such libraries are public libraries intended primarily for nonspecialist use, or college libraries intended primarily to support education only to the baccalaureate level. While such libraries have very real needs for access to more library materials than they can usually afford to buy and maintain, in general the publications they need but do not already have are not the highly specialized publications needed for advanced research, but a more general type that the major research libraries already have or a more elementary type that they have little interest in. Real as the needs of this kind of library are, and much as these can also be met through proper cooperation, what is required to satisfy these needs is a collection different in significant ways from that the Center was founded to develop. To combine these in the same institution might be feasible under some circumstances, but there is also danger of conflict developing when libraries with such disparate primary needs try to cooperate on an exactly equal basis, and it was thought wiser not to risk any chance of subverting the Center's basic purpose.

But since these institutions with smaller libraries also have some need for access to the kind of research publications needed by their larger colleagues, the Center has made it possible for them to participate as associate members. As such they pay a substantially smaller membership fee but have no vote in determining the Center's policies. This solution is very fair to both groups, since it permits the smaller libraries to benefit without having to pay more than their interest justifies, while assuring the integrity of the Center's purpose and programs.

It will perhaps have been noted that the members have been spoken of not as libraries, but as institutions operating libraries. The distinction is intentional. Except for a very few independent and privately endowed libraries, libraries are supported and operated by some institution to serve the purposes of the institution. In the case of major research libraries this is most usually a university. Such libraries do not exist for themselves alone but are an integral and necessary part of the university, whose functioning is vitally affected by how well the library provides access to the information its faculty and students require. But at the same time library needs compete with the needs of other parts of the university, always for too little money. Since, then, it is the institution served that is primarily affected by the adequacy of its library, and not the library itself, the Center insists that it is the university, or other institution that operates the library, that must apply for membership.

In the Midwest Inter-Library Center, every member institution was represented on the Board of Directors by one person. By policy, these representatives were divided about equally between librarians and senior administrative officers of the university: vice-presidents, deans, and the like. This representation of different viewpoints had proven to be very effective, both in providing guidance for the Center itself and in helping to keep the university's administrators informed about library problems, not only in general but even sometimes specifically on their own campus. This arrangement, though effective, also had its disadvantage in that, for some institutions, the director of libraries was not represented, and for others the university administration was not directly involved. At least for the directors of libraries, this was solved by creating an Advisory Committee consisting of the director of libraries of every institution. This committee was advisory to the director of the Center on questions relating to acquisitions and various service programs.

When the Center dropped all geographic restrictions on membership and had to look forward to accommodating 75–100 members, it was clear that a new organizational structure would have to be devised to assure full representation of all members while holding the governing body to a small enough size for it to be efficient. The solution that the Center adopted, which has worked very satisfactorily, was to establish a Council consisting of two representatives from every member institution. One of these representatives is the head librarian of the institution and the other is any non-librarian appointed by the president of the institution. Usually this is the academic vice-president, the dean of the graduate school, the dean of the college of letters and sciences, or some similar administrative officer, though it may be anyone the president chooses and sometimes is the business manager of the university and sometimes a professor, such as the chairman of the library committee. This Council in turn elects from among its members a Board of Directors consisting of fifteen persons, no fewer than six or more than nine of whom are to be librarians. The director of the Center serves as a member of the Board of Directors ex officio, but has no vote. The elected members of the Board serve for terms of three years each.

Although the general management of the affairs of the Center is the responsibility of the Board of Directors, final authority for certain crucial matters lies with the Council. This body has the authority to change the bylaws of the Center; to approve the total of the Center's budget and of the membership fees; to determine the formula by which membership fees are computed; and to fix the criteria of eligibility for membership. The Council normally meets only once a year, though it may meet oftener if necessary, while the Board of Directors meets three or four times a year.

As already emphasized, the basic purpose of the Center is to be a library from which other libraries can borrow a needed publication that they do not have in their own collections, and that they anticipate will be needed so infrequently they cannot justify buying a copy for themselves if one can be borrowed from the Center. To accomplish this purpose perfectly, the Center would have to have a copy of every publication not in every one of its member libraries. This is virtually as impossible for the Center as it is impossible for every library itself to have everything it needs. Quite obviously the Center does not have such a collection now, nor is it likely that it ever will. It has, however, begun an imaginative program for five classes of publications that enables it to give almost the same service as if its collections of these classes were complete.

This program began with the recognition that library purchases are, in large part, made in anticipation of need. That is, the library buys many publications that no patron wants right then, but that it can reasonably be anticipated a patron will want. This is a rational thing to do and is what enables libraries in such a high proportion of cases to produce from their stacks the publication the patron wants. However, since a library cannot buy every publication, it can select for purchase each year only a small portion of those titles that it does not yet possess, and this selection is based on its guess of what will be needed. Such guesses about what will be needed at some time can be quite accurate, but guesses as to which title will be requested tomorrow, or next month, or next year, are much less accurate, particularly when made about infrequently used titles. The library therefore frequently finds itself in the position of having spent its available money for titles that are not needed this year and having no money left to buy what is needed.

Like all libraries, the Center bought many titles in anticipation of need and then found that it had guessed wrong, so that it did not have the money to buy what it was asked for. At this point the library that wanted to borrow the title from the Center either had to tell the patron that it was unavailable then, at the least slowing down his research and at the worse halting it completely, or it had to buy the work for the patron itself. This latter was obviously the preferable solution from the point of view of library service, but such a solution frequently forced the library to buy a publication that would be infrequently used by its patrons, and one that it would not have bought if it had been available from the Center—in other words, the least desirable kind of publication for it to buy for itself, and the kind that the Center was specifically created to acquire for the joint use of many libraries.

Once the problem had been seen in this way, the solution was obvious: for the Center to hold back a portion of its budget each year, instead of using this to buy what it guessed might be needed, so that

money would be available to buy those publications appropriate to its collecting policies that were actually needed. The Center is now doing this in five classes: foreign doctoral dissertations; back files of U.S. newspapers on microfilm; back files of foreign newspapers on microfilm; microfilm copies of U.S. archives; and microfilm copies of foreign archives. In all these classes the Center has fairly extensive collections already, and adds to them each year. Examples of some of the collections are:

Archives. One of the major classes of material the Center can collect most usefully for its members is microfilms of archives, since these are very expensive to acquire, individual sections are infrequently used in any one library, their use can readily be shared, and the microform can be easily and quickly shipped. The Center has only recently begun to collect microfilms of archives on a large scale, but it now has, or has ordered, such things as the British Foreign Office records relating to China; American Federation of Labor Letter Books; District Record Books from Tanzania; *Dajō Ruiten and Kōbun Ruijū* (compilation of the Cabinet Archives of Japan, 1867–1885); *Chōya Kyūbun Hōkō* (documents on the foundation of the Tokugawa Shogunate); etc.

Children's books. The Center has a nearly complete collection of children's books published in the United States from about 1950 to the present.

Current scientific journals. About 3,600 current scientific journals rarely held in U.S. libraries are received currently. Most are in foreign languages. The basis for selection is that the journal be important enough to be abstracted by *Chemical Abstracts* or *Biological Abstracts*, but not held by any member library.

Foreign doctoral dissertations. This is a collection of about 600,000 titles, mostly European and mostly written between 1890 and the present. The majority of the collection was deposited by the member libraries from their own collections or given to the Center as a gift by nonmember libraries such as the Library of Congress (which gave the Center nearly 250,000 titles). Since 1952 the Center has been acquiring most *printed* doctoral dissertations from Europe directly from the university granting the degree, or, in the case of France, from the Ministry of Education. As noted above, the Center will acquire and lend to a member any foreign doctoral dissertation it does not already have. The Center does not collect masters' theses or any American doctoral dissertations.

Foreign government documents. The Center now collects currently but selectively some publications of some foreign governments. Those documents collected are primarily statistical, or they are the journals, proceedings, or debates of parliamentary bodies. Many thousands of other foreign government documents have been given to the Center by its member libraries. This is a class of publication that the Center plans to collect much more completely as soon as more funds are available.

Foreign newspapers on microfilm. The Center administers the ARL Foreign Newspaper Microfilm Project, which is microfilming on a current basis about 150 foreign newspapers and has done so since 1952. The Center is acquiring older back files of foreign newspapers on microfilm for its own collection, is currently spending about $50,000 per year on such acquisition, and will acquire or request any file needed for a patron's immediate research.

General collection. The Center's general collection of older and now infrequently used books and periodicals deposited by the member libraries contains several hundred thousand volumes. Almost all subjects and languages are represented, but the collection is particularly rich in early science and technology, in medicine, and in the social sciences. It is less strong in the humanities.

Miscellaneous publications in microform. The Center is buying or has bought most major collections of publications offered for sale in microcopies. It is thus acquiring some forty major collections, for example:

Early music books and periodicals, mostly before 1850
All books in English printed before 1640
All books printed in the United States before 1800

Important U.S. periodicals printed before 1850
English literary periodicals printed before 1900
China Coast newspapers in European languages
English and American plays of the nineteenth century.

Newspapers in original format. The Center has nearly 2,000 newspapers in original format that have not yet been microfilmed. Both U.S. and foreign titles are represented. For many titles the files are quite long.

Textbooks. The Center has a very large collection of primary and secondary school textbooks. Most of these date from about 1900, but many are of earlier date.

U.S. newspapers in microfilm. The Center is now acquiring currently about 70 U.S. newspapers in microfilm. It plans to extend this list to about 200 titles as quickly as funds allow. It is also acquiring the complete back files of these and other U.S. newspapers as funds permit. It is currently spending about $50,000 to $100,000 annually on such back files, and will acquire on request any file needed for a patron's immediate research.

U.S. state documents. Since 1952 the Center has collected comprehensively all documents published by all states. Hundreds of thousands of pre-1952 state documents have been given the Center by member libraries.

In addition, the Center will buy, when needed for actually present research, any publication in any of these classes that it does not already have. In terms of service this policy has almost the same effect as if the Center's collections in these classes were actually complete, since the member libraries can now promise their patrons access, within reason, to *any* publication in these classes, not just those the Center has already acquired. It is true that the patron will have to wait longer if the Center has not yet acquired the publication than if it already had it, but at least he is assured of access as soon as the publication can be procured.

The Center now has forty members in the United States and Canada. For some special programs, such as the ARL Foreign

Newspaper Program and the Cooperative African Microfilm Project, it has subscribers in Great Britain, France, and Africa. It is anticipated that within the quite near future all the major research libraries in the United States will be members of the Center and that there will also be increasing international participation in the Center's programs. Hopefully, there will also develop similar institutions in other countries in which the Center can in turn participate, and by this means greatly improve the access to information internationally. Whatever troubles the world, the best hope for solution lies in increased understanding by everyone, everywhere. As librarians it is our function to help in this by improving the access to publications regardless of national boundaries.

Activities of the Japan Library Association

Seisuke Kanōzawa
Secretary General

The Japan Library Association (JLA) (Nihon Toshokan Kyōkai), which was founded in 1892 as the Nihon Bunko Kyōkai,* will celebrate its 80th anniversary in 1971. The membership, which at the time of founding was 30, has swelled to approximately 3,850. Of these, about 2,900 are individual regular members, and about 950 are institutions and organizations holding special membership.

In 1898 the Library Employees Joint Deliberation Conference (Toshokan Jūjisha Gōdō Konwa Taikai), predecessor of the All-Japan Library Conference, was held in Tokyo. In 1907 the first issue of *Toshokan Zasshi* (*Library Journal*) was published, and in the following year the association assumed its present name.

*"Bunko" and "Toshokan" are synonymous and mean "library."

The association took the form of a corporate, juridical person in 1930 (fifth year of Shōwa), when research, cataloging, and terminology committees became active and type-of-library divisions began their work. With the advent of the war, a change was wrought in the character of JLA, which lasted during the dark period until the reconstruction of libraries after the war. Parallel with the rehabilitation of library service, efforts were made to reconstruct JLA, which was reorganized and emerged once again as a corporate juridical person in 1947.

Among the accomplishments to be noted in the postreconstruction period we may cite particularly the revision and publication of the *Nippon Jisshin Bunrui Hō* (*Nippon Decimal Classification*) and the *Nippon Mokuroku Kisoku* (*Nippon Cataloging Rules*) under JLA auspices, and coordination of national efforts throughout the library world in pushing deliberations on and passage of the Library Law of 1950.

Organization and Activities

Only individuals are eligible for regular membership; special membership is available for institutions. The supreme decision-making organ is the General Assembly, which is followed in importance by the Board of Trustees, elected nationally through democratic procedures. The executive power is vested in the Board of Directors elected by the Trustees.

JLA carries out its activities through divisional meetings and committees. The divisions are as follows:

Public Library Division
University Library Division
School Library Division
Special and Professional Libraries
    Division
Education Division.

Committees are divided into standing and special committees. Standing committees are:

Toshokan Zasshi (*Library Journal*)
    Editorial Committee
Publications Committee

Library Research Committee
Building and Equipment Committee
Election Management Committee
Book Selection Committee
Information Management Committee
Processing Techniques Committee
Classification Committee
Subject Headings Committee
International Relations Committee
Nihon no Sankō Tosho (*Guide to
 Japanese Reference Books*) Editorial
 Committee
NDC (Nippon Decimal Classification)
 Award Committee.

Special committees are:

Terminology Committee
Future Planning Committee
Women Librarians Research Committee.

The routine work of the association is carried out continuously by the above divisions and committees, as well as by the secretariat (twenty-eight persons). Mentioned below are five noteworthy routine tasks:

1. Active efforts are directed toward publication of *Toshokan Zasshi* (*Library Journal*), the monthly organ of the association, and various reference books and research reports on library work. In 1968 the publications, not including periodicals, numbered thirty-four.

2. The association engages in book-selection activities primarily on behalf of public libraries. This is an attempt to facilitate book selection for librarians by designating current publications deemed appropriate for acquisition by public libraries. This activity, which has its roots in prewar projects, has been continued during the past twenty years.

3. Special emphasis has been placed by JLA, as a professional organization, on the education and training of library personnel. Various programs are planned every year to upgrade the level of education in library studies and to promote the training of library personnel.

4. For the past ten years special attention has been paid to the development of public libraries. Continuous research was first carried on in libraries in cities with

populations of 50,000–200,000 to study the actual state of their activities. The next step was to study problems in libraries of cities and towns with smaller populations, to suggest the direction in which future efforts should be made.

These studies have been extremely influential in the current development by public libraries in Japan of activities tied to the needs of the people served. Similar reports are to be presented on the activities of prefectural libraries, and we may therefore expect that action guidelines for all types of public libraries will eventually be developed.

5. JLA also conducts library surveys, extends assistance to improve reference service and the acquisition of books and equipment, encourages and fosters research and studies, and engages in interchange with foreign libraries.

All-Japan Library Conference

The All-Japan Library Conference, held every autumn, is one of the most important activities of the association. The convention in 1969 will be the fifty-fifth meeting. It is attended by librarians and library users from all over the country. Total attendance has amounted to some 2,000 people in recent years. At the convention library activities of the past year are reviewed, and immediate problems for future development are studied and discussed. The convention is based on the themes, "Let Us Establish Ties between the Library and the Community" and "Let Us Establish a System of Interlibrary Cooperation."

Specialized problems are discussed in divisional meetings. Typical divisional meetings have been as follows in recent years:

Public Libraries
Functions of Public Libraries and
 Building Design
Reading by Children
Reading Movements
Local Documents
Library Councils
University Libraries
Junior College Libraries
School Libraries

Special Libraries
Library Education
Processing Techniques
Reference Services
Research on Problems of Librarians.

Future Problems

The Japan Library Association, a professional organization of librarians, should endeavor to expand and strengthen its organization as the solid foundation of the Japanese library movement. The Committee on Future Planning (Shōrai Keikaku Iinkai) has been working for three years to analyze the present state of the organization, its activities, and its finances. It has suggested future plans on the basis of the analysis and identification of problems, and these plans will be implemented gradually in the order of their feasibility. International cooperation has gradually gained importance, and the association also plays a substantial role in this field.

Japan Library Association and University Libraries

Fujitsugu Okumura
Chief Librarian,
Meiji University Library

It was the fate of the universities of Japan to undergo fundamental reconstruction through the postwar reform of the educational system. All universities, whether public or private, experienced a period of confusion as institutions of higher learning were newly established or raised to university status, while other colleges were transformed into universities by the addition or creation of new departments. Every university of the time was so fully occupied with

adjustments and expansions that library improvement was shunted aside and delayed, and today the effects of that initial delay are quite evident in numerous ways. The handicapped start was due not only to intra-institutional confusion but also to a lack of understanding of the modern functions of libraries on the part of faculty members, as well as to a lack of recognition of the role of libraries during the transitional period by library specialists themselves. In an attempt to cope with this confused situation, the Council of National University Libraries prepared a document, issued in 1953, entitled *Kokuritsu Daigaku Toshokan Kaizen Yōkō* [*Principles for the Improvement of National University Libraries*], which specified in concrete detail ways in which the libraries of the new universities should be improved. In 1956 the Association of Private University Libraries drafted a similar document entitled *Shiritsu Daigaku Toshokan Kaizen Yōkō* [*Principles for the Improvement of Private University Libraries*], addressed to conditions peculiar to private universities. In 1961 the Council of Public University Libraries formulated its *Koritsu Daigaku Toshokan Kaizen Yoko* [*Principles for the Improvement of Public University Libraries*], addressed to public universities supported by local governments. These separate principles, followed as guidelines in efforts to improve national, public, and private university libraries, contributed in large measure to their advancement, not only during the initial period of confusion, but also during the intervening years to the present. It cannot be said, however, that all libraries in Japan have been improved, rationalized, and modernized in accord with the stated principles.

In the postwar period Japanese libraries have moved from the prewar emphasis on passive custody of materials as the prime function of libraries to a new stress on positive activities centering on reader services. Accordingly, emphasis has been placed on research and study aimed at improving processing techniques, restructuring library systems, and educating professional librarians. It was realized, however, that internal adjustments and expansions in themselves could not enable a university library to function fully and contribute to achieving the university's mission in the postwar period, characterized by rapid academic progress and an enormous flood of publications. That is, internal improvements are naturally limited, and in the absence of organized interlibrary cooperation, fulfilling effectively the essential functions of a library becomes a formidable task. This realization signifies that the Japanese university libraries have finally reached the stage of understanding the value of mutual cooperation.

Of course, discussions on interlibrary cooperation among Japanese libraries are not at all a new phenomenon, but the study of the actual implementation of schemes rather than theoretical study or research is relatively new and was brought about by immediate practical needs. Some libraries, such as those in the Japan Medical Library Association and other special libraries, have already harvested the fruits of interlibrary cooperation. However, in general, the study of cooperation as an essential and intrinsic part of library functions is only a recent development. Further in this direction, the holding of this Japan–U.S. Conference is an indication of the fact that academic progress in recent years has reached the stage where the systematization of international cooperation is inevitable.

There are three organizations of university libraries in Japan: Council of National University Libraries (Kokuritsu Daigaku Toshokan Kyōgikai), Council of Public University Libraries (Kōritsu Daigaku Toshokan Kyōgikai), and Association of Private University Libraries (Shiritsu Daigaku Toshokan Kyōkai).

Council of National University Libraries (Kokuritsu Daigaku Toshokan Kyōgikai)

1. *Objectives.* By maintaining close liaison and cooperation among members, and by furthering national university libraries, the council aims at the realization of the mission of universities, and simultaneously,

broadly at the advancement of library activities.

2. *Work.* This council, composed of libraries attached to the national universities, divides Japan into nine districts and elects one library to chairmanship, two to vice-chairmanships, twenty to directorships, and two to auditorships for one-year terms. To attain the aforementioned objectives, it conducts investigations and research necessary for the betterment of national university libraries, encourages mutual cooperation in the activities of national university libraries, and does other necessary work. The board of directors is divided into two subcommittees; one deals with items related to library administration and the other with interlibrary cooperation, library services, and those items not dealt with by the other subcommittee. Special committees are set up, when necessary, to discuss special problems.

3. *Finance.* Annual dues for member libraries are determined on the same basis as dues for other national university councils.

4. *Origin.* The Council of National University Libraries originated in the Council of Imperial University Attached Libraries (Teikoku Daigaku Fuzoku Toshokan Kyōgikai) established in 1924. As was true of public and private university libraries, the council had to undergo a radical reform of its organization in the reform of the educational system after the war, and in 1953, it took the lead in formulating *Kokuritsu Daigaku Toshokan Kaizen Yōkō* [*Principles for the Improvement of National University Libraries*], setting an example for public and private university libraries. Through the "Principles for Improvement," modernization has been advanced, and in recent years voluntary activities of the council have been of particular note. The results of investigations by two special committees, particularly one on librarianship and the other on standards for determining the minimum number of librarians to meet specified work loads, have contributed greatly to the modernization not only of national university libraries but also of Japanese university libraries as a whole.

Council of Public University Libraries (Kōritsu Daigaku Toshokan Kyōgikai)

1. *Objectives.* By developing public university libraries (including some public junior college libraries) through the maintenance of liaison and cooperation, the council aims at contributing to the realization of the mission of public universities.

2. *Work.* The council holds general meetings (once a year) for member libraries, holds committee meetings (special committees are established when particular study is needed), and carries out other activities necessary for the attainment of the above objective.

3. *Officials.* One library serves as chairman, eight as committeemen, and two as auditors. The council divides the country into five districts and elects officials from each district. The term of an official is two years. The committee members organize and form the executive committee of the council.

4. *Finance.* Finances are covered mainly by annual membership dues set at 3,000 yen ($8.33).

5. *Origin.* The council originated in the formation of the Liaison Committee of Public University Libraries (Kōritsu Daigaku Toshokan Renrakukai) in 1956. Before that, organizational activities were conducted by the Council of National and Public University Libraries (Kokkōritsu Daigaku Toshokan Kyōgikai). However, public universities supported by local governments differ from national universities financed by the national government, and various practical problems such as budgets, organization, staff, facilities, etc., cannot be discussed on the same level for the two types of universities. Thus, in 1956, a separate council was established. For the same reason, *Kōritsu Daigaku Toshokan Kaizen Yōkō [Principles for the Improvement of Public University Libraries]* was formulated in 1961. That is, it was formulated separately from documents compiled by national and private universities and indicates, from the standpoint of the public university, common improvements necessary for all public university libraries. The number of member libraries as of 1965 was forty-six, including fourteen junior college libraries.

Association of Private University Libraries (Shiritsu Daigaku Toshokan Kyōkai)

1. *Objectives.* Composed of private university libraries (excluding junior colleges), the association aims at their improvement and development.

2. *Work.* It carries out investigations and research on university libraries in order to attain the above objectives and to publish the results; holds meetings for study, lectures, etc., and publishes a bulletin; conducts liaison and other activities necessary to fulfill the purposes of this association; and holds a general meeting and a convention once a year to discuss and implement the above work.

3. *Officials.* This association is divided into two district committees. For directorships, four universities from the East District Committee and three from the West District Committee are elected; and one from each committee is elected auditor. All official terms are for two years. One director in charge (center university) is elected from each district by the director universities. One of the center universities becomes a standing director university and assumes the presidency of the association.

4. *Finance.* Finances are covered mainly by annual membership fees.

5. *Origin.* The association started in 1930 as an organization of 10 private universities in metropolitan Tokyo; in 1935 it expanded to become a nationwide organization, and today it includes the 165 major private universities throughout Japan. Besides a general meeting and a convention held once a year, committee activities are taken up at the district level to consolidate mutual ties. The secretariat for the above activities is located in the standing director university, which is the same as with the national and public universities. Research committees belonging to each district committee encourage free research by leading librarians of member libraries. Association awards are set up to offer prize money for

excellence of achievement. Through a system of granting research subsidies, library studies by professional librarians are assisted.

The fact that these three organizations have not always maintained close liaison with one another in their activities is noticeable from their separately drafted principles for improvement. Though each organization works in its own distinctive milieu, each has promoted library development for the same purpose, i.e., fulfilling the mission of the university. In their separateness lies one reason for the delay in cooperation among university libraries in Japan. Indeed, this Japan–U.S. Conference is the first occasion when the three organizations have acted as one body in pushing true cooperative activities in an organized fashion. Thus, from the viewpoint of organized cooperative activities among university libraries, too, this Conference is highly significant.

In addition to the above three organizations, we have the Japan Medical Library Association (Nihon Igaku Toshokan Kyōkai), the Council of Japanese Pharmaceutical Libraries (Nihon Yakugaku Toshokan Kyōgikai), and the recently established Council of Japanese Agricultural Libraries (Nihon Nōgaku Toshokan Kyōgikai). These bodies are active as special library associations, conducting their business across the board with national, public, and private university libraries alike.

Lastly, the oldest organization for university libraries, and one whose achievements are too numerous to count, is the University Library Division of JLA. The activities of this division can be traced back to as early as 1910 when the School Library Division was convened in the general meeting of the association in that year. The division included not only those concerned with university libraries but also those interested in all kinds of school libraries. The University Library Division developed out of this and is presently composed of university librarians from national, public, and private university libraries. The division is governed by a committee elected from among national, public, and private university librarians. It holds a general assembly and a general meeting once a year, where problems common to university libraries which have been investigated and studied are aired.

Since JLA is an incorporated association based on individual membership, some means must be devised to effect direct liaison with the three organizations previously mentioned. In addition to individual members, a considerable number of libraries join as special members to support the activities of the association, but these special members have neither voice nor vote. Therefore, while individual university librarians can assemble to study and investigate various problems as individuals, it is not possible for them to commit their university libraries to cooperative activities. Some measures looking toward linkage have, of course, been considered, but the time is not yet ripe for a solution. We hardly need repeat here that JLA, through its individual members, has contributed greatly to the university libraries as a whole, but the urgent questions before us are how to manage the affairs of the University Library Division and how to systematize efforts to strengthen its ties with the three other associations, so that cooperative activities will be further developed in the future.

In this connection, it may be significant to note the present situation of the Round Table Conference of the National Diet Library and University Library Directors, held regularly since 1960. In these Round Table Conferences JLA, in concert with representatives of the three associations, takes a leading part, and various practical problems of cooperation between the National Diet Library and the university libraries have been examined with constructive results. Although they have not fully developed on a nationwide scale, much is expected and noted of the Round Table Conferences' future activities, for, in a sense, they are suggestive of the ways in which cooperation among national, public, and private, university libraries should be carried on.

National universities and public universities as national and public institutions are confronted with special conditions; similarly, private universities, for the reason that they are private, operate in a special milieu and under special conditions. It is extremely important that while the three associations mentioned above are developing activities characteristic of each, they at the same time work toward the improvement of university libraries as a whole. In my opinion, moreover, it is of the utmost importance that these groups come together to organize a cooperative system, so that they can contribute to the advancement of learning.

In Japanese university libraries today there still remain a substantial quantity of transitional-period elements. Specific analysis of the residual elements reveals multifarious differences among the libraries. This situation is one of the major reasons why the implementation of cooperative activities has been so long delayed. It is imperative that while, on the one hand, we make every effort to perfect intralibrary organization, on the other we adopt measures which will promote as soon as possible a thoroughgoing system of cooperation among those organizations of university libraries qualified to take part in such activities. This was keenly realized anew during preparations for this Conference. At this juncture, serious study should be conducted on formalization of cooperation under the leadership of the University Library Division of JLA. With this division in a central and liaison position, ongoing activities can be developed and international cooperation advanced in a unified manner.

Activities of the Medical Library Association of Japan

Yoshinari Tsuda
Medical Librarian, Keiō University Medical Library

The Japan Medical Library Association (Nihon Igaku Toshokan Kyōkai) is an association consisting solely of institutional members. At present its central secretariat is set up within the medical library of Tokyo University. The objectives of the association include "contributing to the progress and development of medicine through the advancement of the activities of medical libraries," as stated in its by-laws. The eight categories of activities which the association should perform are given in the bylaws as follows:

1. Investigation and research relating to the administration and operation of medical libraries
2. Conciliation and mediation in the exchanging, supplying, interlibrary lending, and photocopying of medical literature
3. Promotion of interlibrary relationships, advancement of the functions of libraries, and cooperation with related groups
4. Training and qualitative improvement of medical library personnel
5. Publication of bulletins and other materials related to medical libraries
6. Sponsorship of research meetings, seminars, and exhibitions
7. Representation of Japan in communications with related overseas groups and in international conferences
8. Other activities related to the fulfillment of the objectives of the association.

At the general meeting held in October 1968 the institutional participants included fifty-one regular members (consisting of a core of forty-six medical libraries affiliated with universities throughout Japan, plus five dental college libraries), thirteen associate members (consisting of the larger libraries of medical associations and hospitals, as well as pharmacological libraries), and a small number of supporting members. To qualify as regular members of the association, libraries must possess a library of more than 15,000 volumes, 80 percent of which must consist of specialized medical literature; associate members must have more than 10,000 volumes.

The name Igaku Toshokan Kyōkai, or Japan Medical Library Association, was determined at the 1954 general meeting, but in fact the association was established in 1927 under the name Kanritsu Ika Daigaku Fuzoku Toshokan Kyōkai [Association of Medical Libraries Affiliated with Government Universities] by the five medical university libraries of Niigata, Okayama, Kanazawa, Chiba, and Nagasaki. The association has laid strong emphasis on interlibrary cooperation since its establishment, as is evidenced by the fact that interlibrary loans have been a topic for discussion ever since the initial meeting.

Because cooperation is the main objective of the association, it has long denied membership to the smaller medical and pharmacological libraries on the ground that "they will not only be incapable of fulfilling their responsibilities in the cooperative activities of the libraries, they will also be a burden to other libraries." Consequently, the number of member libraries has, until now, been very limited. However, the major medical libraries of Japan are all included as members. Recently there has been a movement to recognize as many libraries related to medicine as possible, and accordingly, the membership is gradually increasing. Because of the tremendous growth of the organization, the situation is such that when anyone consults it on the use of medical literature or requests a search for information, he is sure to obtain satisfactory results. On the other hand, if one does not consult the association, it is almost impossible to obtain satisfactory results.

According to the statistics of the association, as of March 1968, the fifty-one regular member libraries possessed a total of 3,978,684 volumes, including bound journals. This, together with the collections of the thirteen associate member libraries, made a total of approximately 4,250,000 volumes. The libraries subscribe to 60,000 journals, and the *Genkō Igaku Zasshi Shozai Mokuroku* (*List of Current Periodicals Acquired by the Medical, Dental, and Pharmaceutical Libraries*), published annually by the association, lists 3,458 overseas journals and 1,865 Japanese journals currently being received by member libraries. Included, however, are a limited number of journals which are not medical in nature.

The annual additions in volumes for all member libraries total approximately 170,000, and the total rises each year with the increase in the number of member libraries. However, the average number of volumes added to the collections in each of the individual regular member libraries has remained static for the past few years at 3,000.

The 4,250,000 volumes of medical literature, bound journals, and other reference materials in the collections of the member libraries of the association are utilized fully and smoothly within the tight national network of the interlibrary loan system. According to 1968 statistics, the number of library materials loaned totaled 663,341, the calculations being made from statistics provided by fifty of the fifty-one regular member libraries and ten of the thirteen associate member libraries. However, judging from the fact that increasingly library materials are being used outside libraries in the form of photocopies rather than in the original, it can be assumed that about the same number of items, or more, are being used in the form of photocopies. Also, since the library materials used freely inside a library far outnumber those used outside, it is evident that medical reference materials are extensively utilized.

Regarding types of outside uses, over 51,000 volumes were loaned through the interlibrary loan service to other libraries. Of these, loans of original material, by agreement between the libraries, were limited to only one-tenth of the total; the rest were all provided through microfilming or other photocopying means. To operate such an interlibrary loan service effectively, it is necessary to have a complete union catalog of books and journals. Many efforts have been made toward this end by the association since its establishment. The first complete union list of journals published by the association was issued in 1931 with the title *Ika Daigaku Kyōdō Gakujutsu Zasshi Mokuroku* [*Union List of Scientific Journals in Medical Colleges*]. This was followed by a second edition in 1934 and a third edition in 1942. With each edition the number of volumes listed increased, and finally, with the fourth edition, the work was renamed *Igaku Zasshi Sōgō Mokuroku* (*Union List of Medical Periodicals in the Medical Libraries of Japan*). This publication was divided into two separate volumes, covering Western-language and Japanese-language periodicals. The former was published in 1961 and the latter in 1963. At present the fifth edition is being prepared under the auspices of the member libraries of the Kansai (i.e., Kyoto-Osaka) area. In addition, the member libraries in 1957 began to publish *Ukeire Yotei Zasshi Mokuroku* [*List of Journals to Be Acquired*], which listed all the journals that were to be acquired the following year. This has become today the *Genkō Igaku Zasshi Shozai Mokuroku* (*List of Current Periodicals Acquired by the Japanese Medical, Dental, and Pharmaceutical Libraries*), which specifies the locations and the titles of the journals currently being subscribed to by the member libraries. It serves as a kind of supplement to *Igaku Zasshi Sōgō Mokuroku*.

In addition to the compilation of *Igaku Zasshi Sōgō Mokuroku*, there has been a move to standardize abbreviations for use in citing medical journals published in Japan. Thus, in 1955, *Nihon Igaku Zasshi Ryakumeihyō no Shian* [*Draft Table of Abbreviations of Japanese Medical Journals*] was published, and this was followed by *Nihon Igaku Zasshi Ryakumeihyō* [*Table of Abbreviations of Japanese Medical Journals*] in 1959. In 1969 the *Nihon Shi-*

zen Kagaku Zasshi Sōran (*Directory of Japanese Periodicals in Science and Technology*) was at long last published partly as a kind of revised edition of former publications and partly to serve as a catalog of Japanese journals in the natural sciences.

With respect to union catalogs of monographs, the *Union Catalogue of Foreign Books in the Libraries of Japanese Medical Schools* was published in eight volumes from 1949 to 1956 for the purpose of locating foreign medical publications. There have been no revised versions published since then. However, for foreign books acquired by the member libraries since that time, index cards are gathered at the Kitazato Memorial Medical Library at Keiō University, and an up-to-date union card catalog is maintained at that library.

Thus union catalogs and union lists have been developed and interlibrary loan agreements have been regularized, with the result that medical books and journals are used extensively in Japan. With respect to materials which are not present in Japanese libraries, after confirming the fact that such materials are not held by a member library by consulting union catalogs, the association asks for interlibrary loans, mainly through its central secretariat, from the U.S. National Library of Medicine, and obtains the required material in photocopy form. The number of such transactions during the year from March 1967 to March 1968 was 877. Furthermore, since April 1968, Telex facilities have been used experimentally in some of the member libraries as a means of facilitating interlibrary loan service.

According to an investigation made by the Ministry of Health and Welfare at the end of 1966, the number of registered physicians resident in Japan was 110,759. When we consider that there was a total of 3,711,801 volumes in the collections of the full member libraries, as stated in the association's statistics of March 1966, this means that there were approximately 34 volumes of books and bound journals per doctor available in the association libraries. Apart from serving approximately 15,000 to 16,000 medical students, the regular member libraries also serve 10,530 doctors in hospitals attached to medical-school institutes and 1,966 doctors engaged in education and research. Even if the two types are added together, the number is less than 10 percent of the total number of doctors. Therefore, considering the number of direct users of the medical libraries, the member libraries of the association possess fairly substantial collections and lending is very active. However, when it comes to literature search services, it is apparent that this service is still in an early stage of development. In a survey made in 1968, it was reported that thirty-five member libraries (54.7 percent) provide this type of service. Not all of these, however, have special personnel regularly assigned for this purpose. Some provide the service only when asked. On the other hand, one library has close to ten persons on its literature search staff engaging in over 500 searches a year. As yet, only a limited number of libraries provide such special services as translating, indexing, and abstracting. But most libraries provide limited current awareness service, e.g., providing copies of the tables of contents of the more frequently used foreign journals.

A recent trend has been a widening of the gap between member libraries in terms of volumes held, number of staff members, and service provided. Smaller libraries do not participate in the progress around them and face difficulty in maintaining the status quo, while, on the other hand, the larger libraries increase in strength. For example, in March 1957, the largest collection among regular member libraries was 141,351 volumes, and the smallest was 14,993 volumes. In March 1968, the largest was 166,546 volumes and the smallest was 35,838 volumes. The same trend is evident in personnel. In March 1957, the largest library had 18 staff members and the smallest had 3. In March 1968, the largest had 93 staff members and the smallest had 3. There are also wide discrepancies existing between libraries in the Tokyo and Osaka areas and those found in other localities.

With regard to personnel, the total number of staff members of the fifty-one regular member libraries is 662 persons. Adding a total of 44 persons reported by twelve of the associate member libraries, we have a grand total of 706. For the purpose of training and educating these staff members the association has, since the summer of 1956, cooperated with the Council of Pharmaceutical Libraries (Yakugaku Toshokan Kyōgikai) in holding an annual seminar lasting four to six days. In these seminars lectures on topics of current interest in the medical and pharmacological fields are given, related literature is discussed, and reference tools are presented and the practical use of these tools is explained. Other lectures and practical lessons in cataloging and computerization are also given. The lecture seminars are held in two places concurrently, one in eastern Japan and another in western Japan. Professors Estelle Brodman, Thomas P. Fleming, and J. R. Blanchard, who were at the Japan Library School at Keiō University for three years from 1962 to 1964 as visiting lecturers to give training courses for librarians in biology, have had a great influence on the modernization of the staffs of Japanese medical libraries. According to a 1967 survey, ten libraries out of a total of sixty-one regular and associate member libraries are conducting in-service training in the form of lectures or club activities to educate their staff members.

Igaku Toshokan (*Medical Library*), first published in 1954 as a bimonthly journal of the association, has now given up responsibility for transmitting association news to *JMLA News*, and has become a quarterly publication whose main purpose is to carry academic reports and case studies made by staff members of the member libraries.

There have been some very notable trends developing recently in the libraries. One relates to the seminars held to consider trends in libraries in the United States and their impact on Japan. This was stimulated by the medical literature search system of MEDLARS, using computers at the U.S. National Library of Medicine, and by the computerization of acquisition records of medical journals developed at the Washington University Medical Library and elsewhere. Another trend relates to the appearance of attempts to computerize the activities of libraries, as seen in the case of Tokyo University and Keiō University. At Tokyo University there is much enthusiasm about the installation of a computer in the medical library, and there are even hopes of extending its use to the activities of the association. The association was originally established to enhance interlibrary cooperation. The introduction of computers to library operations will now further contribute to strengthening the horizontal ties of libraries.

As the association through its activities develops a network to provide medical literature information in Japan, the need for closer cooperation with such large information and reference centers as the Japan Information Center of Science and Technology and the National Diet Library will become even more acute.

The National Diet Library as the Library Center of Japan

Yasumasa Oda
*Director of Automation Project,
National Diet Library*

Inheriting the collection of the Japanese Imperial Library (Teikoku Toshokan), which was founded as the sole national library at the beginning of the Meiji era (1867–1912), the National Diet Library (NDL) as the legal deposit library in Japan has made every effort since its founding in 1948 to develop a comprehensive collection of domestic publications. It is also the only library which is entrusted by the Ministry of Education with keeping, for public reading, all the doctoral dissertations submitted to the Ministry since 1923. Moreover, since 1953, in cooperation with the Japan Newspaper Association

(Nihon Shinbun Kyōkai), the library has reduced to microfilm all major national, regional, and local newspapers. As for foreign publications, in addition to those purchased and received as gifts, the library obtains government publications through exchange arrangements with 617 institutions in 87 countries. At the same time, it serves as a deposit library for sixteen organizations, including the United Nations, UNESCO, OECD, American Atomic Energy Commission, and RAND Corporation. The collection obtained through the above activities included, as of the end of March 1968, 2,366,920 monographic volumes, 21,714 current periodicals, 98,800 doctoral dissertations, 95,520 map sheets, 81,426 phonorecords, and 29,336 reels of microfilm, making it the largest collection in Japan open to the public.

NDL is engaged in the enterprise of publishing a weekly and annual national bibliography based on newly published works accessioned by the library,* and of producing and widely distributing at home and abroad printed cards representing these new publications. For newly arrived foreign publications, the library prepares for distribution among libraries and research institutes such lists as the *Yōsho Sokuhō* (*Accessions List: Foreign-Language Publications*) (semimonthly); *Gaikoku Seifu Kankōbutsu Ukeire Ichiran* (*Accessions List: Foreign Government Publications*) (semimonthly); *Chūgokugo Chōsengo Tosho Sokuhō* (*Accessions List: Chinese and Korean-Language Publications*) (bimonthly); *Ajia Afurika Shiryō Tsūhō* (*Materials on Asia and Africa: Accessions List and Review*) (monthly); *Kaigai Kagaku Gijutsu Shiryō Geppō* (*Monthly List of Foreign Scientific and Technical Publications*) (monthly); and *Genshiryoku Kankei Shiryō Mokuroku* (*Monthly List of Selected Atomic Energy Publications*) (monthly).

NDL compiles the *Shinshū Yōsho Sōgō Mokuroku* (*Union Catalog of Foreign Books*) in cooperation with sixteen univer-

*Nōhon Shūhō (Current Publications), weekly, and Zen Nihon Shuppanbutsu Sōmokuroku (Japanese National Bibliography), annually.

sity libraries, two public libraries, and its own thirty branches, located in various administrative and judicial agencies of the state. The library also publishes *Zasshi Kiji Sakuin (Japanese Periodicals Index)* monthly, *Nihon Hōrei Sakuin (Index to Japanese Laws and Ordinances)* annually, *Kokkai Kaigiroku Sosakuin (General Index to the Debates* [of the National Diet]) irregularly, and many other subject bibliographies.

Parallel with such activities, NDL extends interlibrary loan service, photocopy service, and reference service. Though there may be substantial differences in scope and intensity, NDL plays the same role as that played by the Library of Congress in the American library community.

The fact that its role in the Japanese library community is somewhat different from that of its American counterpart is a reflection of the different situations of the respective communities. Japanese university libraries and public libraries are much smaller in size and activity than are their American counterparts. Out of 370 university libraries, as few as 4 have collections of over 1 million volumes. Out of 739 public libraries, no more than 2 possess over 300,000 books. Moreover, in spite of well-known needs, cooperation and coordination among libraries, even within a university, have not been promoted to any substantial extent, nor have there been developed such cooperative ventures as the Farmington Plan or the Center for Research Libraries. In general, interlibrary loan service has not been adequately developed, although there are exceptions, such as the service promoted by the Japan Medical Library Association. In the public library sector there has been no movement toward the formation of networks like American library "systems." Prefectural libraries still do not function as regional "libraries for libraries," as do state and county libraries in the United States. There are no comprehensive catalogs compiled and maintained at the regional level by bibliographic centers—catalogs analogous to the California Union Catalog, the Pacific Northwest Bibliographic Center Catalog, and the Cleveland Regional Union Cata-

log. There is also no national library which specializes intensively in a specific discipline, such as the National Agricultural Library and the National Library of Medicine in the United States.

The poor state of individual libraries and of cooperation among them imposes a heavy burden on NDL as the sole national library in Japan. NDL has to answer reference questions which the Library of Congress might sometimes refuse by form letter or refer for consultation to local libraries. Its public reading room is occupied by Tokyo university students who cannot be served satisfactorily by the university libraries. In summer especially, students of those universities whose libraries are closed during vacation form a long queue in front of the public entrance to the library every morning. NDL has had the experience of being asked by a university professor from a metropolitan area to reproduce some well-known periodicals, whereupon it was found, upon investigation, that the library attached to another department at his university had most of the issues. There have been times when NDL has had to take upon itself, as an additional task, the publication of comprehensive catalogs of periodicals owned by local public libraries in the Kantō, Kinki,* and other areas.

To improve and strengthen, both in terms of scale and of quality, the services of the National Diet Library as the national library involves a variety of problems, and we often hear demands from librarians for improvement of services. For NDL to strengthen its functions and to discharge its responsibilities as the library center of Japan, however, the one indispensable condition is that it be utilized in ways appropriate to it as the national library, and that it not be used as a surrogate for university and public libraries. This means that university, public, and special libraries must do their utmost to improve their services so that they may discharge their responsibilities as libraries to their clientele. In this area the recent trend toward cooperation in the improve-

*Kantō: Tokyo area; Kinki: Osaka-Kyoto area.

ment and extensive use of NDL printed cards by university libraries promises a bright future.

NDL's distribution of printed cards is, of course, an attempt to centralize the cataloging of newly published books. The number of libraries using the cards is limited and was around 130 until 1968, in which year a remarkable increase of 37 was made in the number of libraries using the cards, swelling the total to over 160 libraries. Such an underdeveloped service as the above does not deserve the name of national centralized cataloging. The limited use of printed cards can be primarily ascribed (aside from some factors which NDL should improve) to insufficient understanding on the part of Japanese librarians of the significance of printed cards, and to lack of interest and willingness to use them. In the past few years, however, there has developed a favorable climate among university librarians for the positive use of printed cards. At the All-Japan Library Conference, held in 1968, a resolution was adopted requesting NDL to form a council to deliberate on the improvement and extension of the cards. It was suggested that the council be composed of representatives of university libraries, public libraries, the Japan Library Association, publishing circles, and NDL.

Even though small in real volume, the unprecedented 30-percent rate of increase in 1968 in the number of libraries using the printed cards is an encouraging sign. Through extending the use of printed cards to libraries throughout the country, NDL can fully implement national centralized cataloging, thus enhancing its function as the national library. University, public, professional, and school libraries, relieved of the burden of cataloging, can strengthen and expand their respective library services, consequently enhancing their capacities. Moreover, the integration of catalogs through the use of printed cards facilitates the compilation of integrated catalogs within a university, in a region, or among libraries of the same type, thus promoting that interlibrary cooperation through which respective libraries can augment their capabilities. Only when these libraries

work to improve their capabilities can the National Diet Library concentrate on its activities as the national library. The same holds true for the activities of the library as a bibliographic center, but this falls in the area of national bibliographic control and is treated elsewhere. My fellow Japanese librarians know the self-evident significance of the NDL printed cards, but the fact that they have not been fully used reveals the serious problems which we Japanese librarians should undertake to solve.

Council on Library Resources

Fred C. Cole
President

I should like to put one question to our Japanese associates: Is it possible and timely to establish means or institutions whereby a private fund may be made more adequately available for research and development in Japanese libraries? I do not know the laws of Japan, but is it feasible to establish a private organization or foundation whose goal it is to support the improvement of libraries and library services? If so, perhaps the Council on Library Resources can serve as something of an example. Copies of reports of the Council on Library Resources are available, and I will not attempt to review its activities. It may be helpful, however, to comment briefly on them.

All librarians know of the tremendous success the Carnegie Corporation had in regard to strengthening libraries all over the United States and in Great Britain. Many other foundations have had an important influence, both financially and otherwise, in regard to libraries in our country. The Council on Library Resources, however, was the first foundation in the

United States, I believe, that was established solely and wholly for the purpose of attempting to assist libraries in meeting their overwhelming problems and needs.

The council is an expression of interest in libraries by the Ford Foundation. We have no function other than that of providing funds and other services to libraries. As a former professor and president of a university, I say to you quite honestly that I take the greatest pride in being able to work with this organization which serves libraries, and to help forward its goals.

Although the council was established by and receives its funds from the Ford Foundation, it is an independently chartered organization which establishes its own programs and policies. In the recent past we have extended our area of interest to foreign libraries. We have shown our concern in this regard, particularly with the appointment of Sir Frank Francis to help us, and we consider it a great privilege to have Sir Frank as our associate and counselor.

International Federation of Library Associations

Sir Frank Francis
Consultant, Council on Library Resources

The International Federation of Library Associations (IFLA) was founded forty-two years ago, in 1927. To start with, it was an annual friendly gathering of eminent librarians. Such famous personalities in the world of librarianship as Isak Collijn of Sweden, Marcel Godet of Switzerland, William Warner Bishop of the United States of America, Arundell Esdaile of England, Wilhelm Munthe of Norway, and T. P. Sevensma of Holland met together

in friendly colloquy year after year. These gatherings of friends were the occasion for comparing notes about what was happening in libraries and librarianship in the various countries they came from. In recent years the circle of annual participants in the IFLA meetings has rapidly grown larger, but I am glad to say that the same easy relationships which were established when IFLA consisted of a handful of eminent librarians are still characteristic.

IFLA is basically a federation of library associations, with these associations as the constituent members; in recent times, however, a class of associate members has been created to meet the desire of libraries of many kinds, of bibliographic institutes, and the like to participate in the annual meetings. IFLA now has 86 members and a large number of associate members, and the annual meetings regularly bring together 300 or more participants. These participants are still drawn largely from Europe and the United States, but IFLA has always nourished the hope that it would ultimately be able to attract a worldwide membership. The word "international" does not necessarily mean worldwide, but nowadays there are so many matters calling for discussion which transcend national and regional boundaries that it is increasingly desirable to extend the range of IFLA's activities. The International Conference of Cataloging Principles, held in Paris in 1961, showed conclusively how great the gains are if it is possible to organize international meetings on a worldwide scale. The meeting in Paris, which was generously subsidized, attracted representatives from fifty-three countries in all parts of the world.

It is a truism that the distances between almost any two places on earth can now be measured in hours, instead of days or weeks or even months, as they once were; yet it is still a hard undeniable fact that the costs of long-distance travel continue to interpose barriers against the easy personal contacts we hope to be able to make, so that IFLA is still unable to speak with a world voice. IFLA still largely draws its strength from Europe (in which Eastern Europe is included), and, increasingly in recent years, from the United States of

America, where easy lines of communication have been maintained for many years. Although financial considerations make it really difficult to accomplish true world coverage, it has long seemed to the Executive Board of IFLA that it should be possible to provide a framework within which a world organization could function.

The ultimate future organizational pattern of IFLA to which we should bend our thoughts might well be a series of regional groupings, similar, perhaps, to the Latin America Regional Sections founded in 1962, each with its own organization and meetings. It might be possible for the regional sections to come together periodically, thus fulfilling the expectation laid down in the statutes of IFLA of holding a world congress of librarians every few years. In the intervening years the regional groupings might have their own meetings, which the president and the secretary of the main organization might be able from time to time to attend. It is the possibility of aiming at an organization of this kind that has prompted IFLA in the past to note, with great interest and satisfaction, attempts to set up regional groupings such as the Federation of Asian Library Associations, which was so ably and energetically discussed under the auspices of the Japan Library Association in November 1957. There has been widely felt disappointment that the excellent beginning made at that meeting did not apparently result in the permanent establishment of a regional group, though it is not hard to appreciate the difficulties which faced such an enterprise.

The question is bound to be asked, and should be asked: How far is it reasonable or useful to attempt to bring together librarians from widely separated parts of the world—librarians who, moreover, may have widely differing concepts of the purposes of libraries and the duties of librarians? Is there not a danger of creating a new organization just for the sake of creating one? This is a danger which must assuredly be guarded against. We must certainly not delude ourselves with illusions of grandeur.

There are many matters which can and should be dealt with on a local or regional basis. I mean such matters as interlibrary cooperation, interlibrary lending, exchanges, library techniques, and the like. These can be dealt with locally very satisfactorily. But libraries are now being thought of and are beginning to think of themselves as having new, wider, and more important tasks and responsibilities in the communities to which they belong. It now becomes desirable for them to examine what has been called the "undifferentiated mush" of speculation, assertion, and opinion which passes for a philosophy of librarianship. And it is almost certainly desirable for groups of us, just because we come from widely different backgrounds, to meet together, even if only occasionally, to compare our experiences and to see what solutions of contemporary problems have been arrived at in different places.

It is inevitable that, as so much of our thinking and writing about libraries and librarianship has originated in Western Europe, we tend to think of libraries as they grew up in Western Europe. The Bibliothèque Nationale, the British Museum, the Vatican, and national and university libraries throughout the European countries are indeed marvelous repositories of the handwritten and printed riches of the great thinkers, writers, and artists of the past. They represent a glorious human achievement for which we are, and for which posterity will be, continuously grateful. However, with the impact of the information explosion and the insistence of scientists, technologists, and businessmen on special services, we have learned the hard way that great libraries cannot be merely museums of books. They are living institutions, and they must replan their activities if they are to fit into the modern world.

It is time, then, that the view of libraries as they have grown up in Western Europe should be re-examined in the light of the needs of the day and the circumstances obtaining in other parts of the world. It is already impossible, and it is almost certainly inappropriate, to expect a proliferation of Westernized institutions of the traditional kind. The tendency nowadays is for libraries to be looked upon as tools in community development (and they are costly tools). They are no longer ivory towers segregated from the hurly-burly of life. They are now expected to earn their place in the society in which they have their being. Much is being made, for example, of the part that librarians can play in educational planning and the importance of information in every section of our daily lives, in personal recreation and instruction and in research.

It is important that experiences from widely different social backgrounds and social concepts should be contributed towards the creation of an expanded philosophy of library work. We have all of us contributions to make to the theory and philosophy of librarianship as it is and will be in the late twentieth and twenty-first centuries. Moreover, the internationalization of techniques and attainments, particularly in the realms of science and technology, demand the employment of methods of proved efficiency in the communication of knowledge about them. Western, Eastern, European, American, and Asiatic are terms that have no meaning where matters of this kind are in question.

IFLA provides the only international forum where discussion can regularly take place about the experience of librarians in all parts of the world and where ideas about the scope and aims of librarianship and the viability of new techniques can be compared. The tasks of librarians have intensified over the years, and it is certain that it will only be by cooperation, the sharing of burdens, profiting from collective experience, and discussion of practical ideals that we shall be able to meet them. Thus it remains the hope of the Executive Board of IFLA that it will be able, as time goes on, to maintain close contact with librarians from all parts of the world and from time to time to provide a world forum for informed discussion of matters of worldwide importance.

Final Communiqué

Toru Miyaji
Director, Osaka University Library

As the highly industrialized societies of Japan and the United States move into the postindustrial age, librarians in both countries are increasingly concerned with the problem of how best to serve researchers and students to whom a bewildering array of information sources is available, from traditional books to the latest in teaching machines. The so-called "information explosion" of recent years, resulting in a vast outpouring of publications, documents, research reports, and other forms of recorded knowledge, has led librarians and information scientists to seek new ways of storing and disseminating the flood of materials.

The First Japan–U.S. Conference on Libraries and Information Science in Higher Education, held in Tokyo on 15–19 May 1969, under the sponsorship in the United States of the American Library Association and in Japan of the Council on National University Libraries, the Public University Library Association, and the Private University Library Association, was attended by leading educators, librarians, and information specialists from both countries. The conferees, representing the diversity of universities and libraries in both countries, met to explore ways in which they could more effectively cooperate in developing programs of mutual benefit to education and research.

The American keynote speaker was Dr. Logan Wilson, President of the American Council on Education; his Japanese counterpart was Dr. Tatsuo Morito, President of the Japan Library Association. Dr. Morito linked student unrest in part to poor

Dr. Wilson wondered why more students did not "spend more time in the library freely pursuing their own intellectual interests, and less time milling about on the campus demanding pedagogical reforms." He also pointed to the growing emphasis on independent student learning and a corresponding decline in the significance of classroom lecturing and textbook memorization, concluding that "the modern college or university library is no less important than the classroom and the laboratory as a place where learning is disseminated and advanced."

The conference attracted over 350 participants, including 23 American representatives. Participants heard papers prepared by both American and Japanese specialists on such topics as the role of university libraries in higher education, the professional education of library personnel, the exchange of publications and personnel, and the application of computers to library management and information retrieval.

The conferees observed that they were meeting in a period of mounting unrest and changes in education in both countries, and that fresh and innovative approaches to the instructional and learning process were sorely needed. There was agreement that, because of the central importance of libraries in education, a qualitative improvement in library resources would lead to an improvement of the educational system. In the area of the automation of bibliographic controls, there was hope expressed for cooperative ventures seeking to solve common problems, for example, the handling of materials printed in a variety of scripts.

Resolutions

In its final session the conference resolved that:

1. Appropriate Japanese and U.S. committees be formed to provide continuity of leadership and to serve as channels of communication in the fields of library and information science between the two countries

2. A second conference in the United States be convened within three years

3. Interchange of personnel to provide opportunities for professional growth for librarians of both countries be promoted

4. Use of consultants and advisors in such areas as library automation, education, and the development of area studies collections be encouraged

5. Exchange of professional information, including the development of comprehensive collections of materials on bibliography and librarianship in each country, and close and effective collaboration between Japanese and American professional organizations be stimulated to the fullest extent possible

6. A central clearinghouse in each country be established, through which bibliographic information and requests for materials could be channeled

7. Cooperative bibliographic programs and the fostering of common bibliographic standards be stimulated, and

8. Library collections, especially in the field of government documents, be strengthened by providing improved bibliographic and acquisitions services.

Participants in the Conference met in an atmosphere of warm and friendly professional partnership in the analysis of problems of common concern. The stimulating papers and lively and candid exchanges led to extended discussions on questions of central concern in library and information science. The Conference succeeded in drawing Japanese and American librarians more closely together. It was agreed that further progress in librarianship might be accelerated on the firm foundation that has been established for the continuation of substantive binational talks. Thus the purposes of education and scholarship and the advancement of human understanding would be well served.

APPENDIXES

A / Research Design for a Study of the Political Modernization of Japan

Robert E. Ward
Professor of Political Science, University of Michigan

This project involves a five-year study of the political modernization of Japan. In a larger sense it is concerned with developments since 1868, but this particular part of it relates only to developments from August 1945 to 1961.

Political modernization is conceived of as an open-ended developmental process, the operational characteristics of which will be set forth in outline form below. The focus of the study is on political change, rather than on present or past political conditions viewed as static phenomena. The attempt is to identify trends and patterns of political change in postwar Japan.

My basic hypothesis is that the types of political change which have been occurring in Japan over the past century are broadly characteristic of a process of political change which, while it started and has proceeded farthest in the West, seems also to be taking place in many other parts of the world. This process I call "political modernization." It involves a gradual transition from a set of political characteristics described as "traditional" to another set described as "modern." Under appropriate circumstances this transition may occur in democratic, authoritarian, or totalitarian states. The form and philosophy of government in this sense is not a critical factor. Japan has experienced both authoritarian and democratic forms of government, and is today undoubtedly further advanced in this process of political modernization than is any other state in Asia. It is partially for this reason that the Japanese experience constitutes so ideal a case study.

I propose to study the postwar phase of this process in Japan in terms of the categories set forth below. Since the emphasis will be upon the identification and analysis of emerging trends and patterns, the time factor is of great importance in each case. A series of linked cross-sectional studies seems best calculated to meet this need. In general, therefore, it would seem desirable to study all the following categories at several different points in time. Tentatively I am considering doing this, using some such periods as 1947, 1950, 1955, and 1960. These are not to be rigidly construed, however. Different categories may demand different periodicities, and some will probably require continuous treatment for the entire 1945–60 period.

Within this time span, I am particularly interested in the impact upon Japanese political institutions, attitudes, and behavior of the Allied Occupation of Japan. The Occupation undoubtedly effectuated many political changes in Japan. Some have lasted in whole or substantial part, others have almost completely disappeared. If one views this experience in historical perspective, several questions arise. In both philosophical and operational terms, what specifically were the goals of the Occupation? Viewed from a social engineering standpoint, how did the Allies plan to accomplish and sustain these goals? To what extent were they successful in doing so, if one examines the total record from 1945 to 1961? What factors account for their relative success in some areas and their failure in others? To what extent was the Occupation itself responsible for the introduction of durable and important political changes into Japan, and to what extent did it merely serve as a catalyst for forces and movements already well established within Japanese society? And, finally, what light does Japan's experience during and after the Occupation cast upon the more general problem of directed or controlled social change? All of these are problems which relate intimately to this larger question of political modernization, and which may, to a considerable extent, be studied in conjunction with it.

For present purposes I am defining "political modernization" in terms of the following operational categories. These are also the subjects about which I am interested in collecting information for the period since August 1945.

I. The Social Foundations of a
Politically Modern Society

A politically modern society is characterized by relatively low birth, death, and morbidity rates; relatively high or improving standards of living; a high rate of consumption of mass media; a tendency towards the social emancipation of women; and a population which is in major part literate, urban, educated, socially mobile, and favorably oriented towards at least the concept of social change.

1. Demographic structure
   a. Birth rates and birth control
   b. Death rates
   c. Morbidity rates
   d. Age distribution patterns
2. Level of literacy
3. Level of educational attainment
   a. Compulsory education
   b. Secondary education
   c. Higher, specialized, and professional education
4. Urban-rural distribution patterns
5. Standards of living
6. Geographic, social, and economic mobility
7. Consumption of mass media
8. Social and economic role of women
9. Orientation toward social change.

II. Popular Interest and Involvement
in the Political Process

A politically modern society is characterized by widespread popular interest and involvement in the political system, though not necessarily in the decision-making aspects thereof.

1. Degrees of popular interest in and knowledge of politics at national, local, and international levels
2. Formal political participation
   a. Voting behavior in national, prefectural, and local elections
   b. Referenda and other forms of direct legislation
3. Informal political participation
   a. Development of political interest group activities—business, labor, agricultural, professional, religious, etc.
   b. Structure, support patterns, and political importance of interest groups
   c. Style of operations of interest groups
4. Popular attitudes and images with respect to:

a. The relationship of individuals, groups, or classes to government
b. The status and role of bureaucrats
c. The "perfectibility" of political society.

III. Structure and Role of Political Parties

A politically modern society is characterized by the prominence and importance of its political party system. This may be of the single or multiple type, and it need not be either representative or in actual control of the society's public decision-making system.

1. Nature of organization at national and local levels
2. Size and characteristics of membership and support patterns
3. Political roles and importance of parties
4. The role and importance of intraparty factionalism.

IV. Political Leadership

A politically modern society is characterized by the allocation of its political leadership roles in accordance with standards of achievement rather than ascription.

1. The problem of identification—who is properly regarded as a political leader in either the formal or informal sense?
2. Career profiles of both formal and informal political leaders at the several points in time indicated above:
   a. Birthplace
   b. Family's social, economic, and political circumstances
   c. Education
   d. Professional career outside of politics
   e. Political career
   f. Factional and personal affiliations
   g. Political program or views
3. Qualifications for political leaders— personal ability and achievement, subject-matter specialization, seniority, wealth or fund-raising ability, adroitness in tactics and interpersonal relationships, political connections, family lineage, others
4. Relationships between formal and informal political leaders, i.e., between

political leaders on the one hand and politically influential representatives of business, labor, agriculture, the professions, and such interest groups on the other.
5. Style and effectiveness of political leadership.

V. Administrative Leadership and Organization

A politically modern society is characterized by a predominance of functionally specific rather than functionally generalized administrative roles, allocated in accordance with standards of achievement, and organized in an elaborate and professionalized bureaucracy.

1. The problem of identification—who is properly regarded as an administrative leader?
2. Career profiles
   a. Birthplace
   b. Family's social, economic, and political circumstances
   c. Education
   d. Professional career
   e. Political career, if any
   f. Factional and personal affiliations
   g. Professional and political program or views
3. The bureaucracy as a career
   a. Prestige, power, pay, and satisfactions comparatively considered
   b. Entrance qualifications and tests, formal and informal
   c. Allocation to positions
   d. Promotional system—formal and informal aspects
   e. Responsibility and public accountability
   f. Interaction with party politicians
   g. Interaction with interest groups.

VI. Ambit of Governmental Activity

A politically modern society is characterized by a broad and increasing ambit of explicit governmental involvement in, responsibility for, and regulation of the economic and social aspects of individual and group life.

1. Size and functions of national and local bureaucracies
2. Size and allocation of national and

local governmental expenditures on both general and special accounts

3. Incidence of new laws and regulations tending to expand the functions of government.

VII. Centralization of Authority

A politically modern society is characterized by an increasing emphasis upon the centralization of political and administrative authority and responsibility for the performance of functions regarded as critical.

1. Centralizing tendencies at the sub-national level
   a. The amalgamation of cities, towns, and villages
   b. Increased authority or influence of prefectural governments and *chihō jimusho*
   c. Development of professional associations of mayors, assemblymen, heads of local assemblies, etc.
   d. Fiscal inadequacies and needs of cities, towns, villages, and prefectures
2. Centralizing tendencies at the national level
   a. Fiscal controls and influence
   b. Reconstruction of *Jichishō*
   c. Increased authority and ambit of action of other national ministries and offices
   d. Increased use of model or standard legislation.

VIII. The Role of Law

A politically modern society is characterized by judicial and regulatory techniques based upon a predominantly impersonal system of law.

1. Expansion of subject matter of laws and regulations
2. Increase in legal and judicial actions and decisions
3. Supplantation of informal means of settling disputes by formal ones, e.g., *chūnin* by conciliation commissioners.

IX. Political Decision-making

A politically modern society is characterized by a predominant emphasis upon rational, scientific, and secular techniques of political decision-making.

1. Increasing importance of action-oriented governmental research
2. Increasing importance of statistics in governmental decision-making
3. Proliferation of preparatory and review techniques and agencies in government
4. Growth of "impersonality" in administration.

Other attributes of importance to the process of political modernization can doubtless be adduced, but, for present and introductory purposes these may suffice as a tentative working definition of minimal characteristics possessed in common by all political groups generally regarded as either modern or well-advanced in the modernizing process, regardless of whether their particular forms of political organization are democratic, authoritarian, or totalitarian in nature.

In conclusion, it should be emphasized again that political modernization is a continuing process, not a fixed state. The above checklist of current characteristics is not considered to have any absolute or enduring validity. I view it rather as a working model useful in giving form and focus to this attempt to evaluate the process of political change in postwar Japan. It is tentative and subject to revision. All suggestions for its improvement and refinement will be gratefully and constructively received.

B / Sponsored Tours for Foreign Librarians in the United States

Lester Asheim
Director, International Relations Office, American Library Association

Programs of formal study for foreign librarians in the United States are outside the scope of this paper. This report will deal solely with tours for foreign librarians sponsored by some agency to provide either individuals or groups with the professional opportunity to visit the United States, to observe American libraries in operation, and to meet and speak with professional librarians about problems of mutual interest. Such educational and cultural exchanges provide direct experience of the American scene for the visitor and frequently include some informal orientation and instruction, and even a short-term work experience. The sponsors of such tours may be either the United States government itself through its State Department, or non-governmental organizations.

State Department Programs

The State Department programs of educational and cultural exchange are normally administered by the Bureau of Educational and Cultural Affairs. There are two major formal programs, specifically for librarians, which are sponsored by the State Department. One of these is called the Multi-National Group Librarian Program and is designed to bring librarians from a variety of countries together as a group for a four-month period of travel and observation in the United States. This project is designed to acquaint the participants with all phases of library work through seminar discussions with practicing and teaching librarians and through participation in the planning and execution of library activities. The International Relations Office of the American Library Association is now responsible for planning and directing the project for the Department. The American Library Association has the cooperation and support of the Library of Congress, public and private libraries throughout the United States, schools of library science, and the American book trade. For each program an outstanding library school in a major United States university is selected to conduct a seminar of up to four weeks as part of the total program. The time of year during which the project is scheduled depends upon the wishes of the particular library school selected for this purpose.

The program, which lasts 120 days, begins with a one-week orientation period in Washington, D.C., including attendance at lectures at the Washington International Center, visits to the Library of Congress and other libraries within the Washington area, and other activities designed to introduce the visitor to American institutions and procedures. A three-week library school seminar follows immediately upon this orientation. After the seminar, each member of the group is assigned on an individual basis to work for seven weeks in a library, which is carefully chosen to provide a situation similar to that of the grantee's own library. Following this "internship," five weeks of travel and observation throughout the United States are provided, and again the itinerary is planned on an individual basis to permit the grantee to visit institutions and agencies which will have some relevance to his own library problems and needs. The program ends with a one- or two-day final evaluation session to give the participants the opportunity to share their individual experiences and impressions and to clarify questions arising from their individual internships.

Last year's participants in the Multi-National Librarians Project began their visit to the United States on 25 November 1965 and departed from the United States on 16 January 1966. During this time the participants completed a seminar at the Library School of the University of Wisconsin, an internship in which each participant worked in a different library, and a period of travel and observation designed specifically for each individual. The participants met at Miami Beach, Florida, for the Midwinter Meeting of the American Library Association. There were a total of twelve: two from Germany, two from Jamaica, and one each from Argentina, Brazil, Uruguay, Poland, Czechoslovakia, Australia, Ghana, and Japan. The Japanese participant was Mr. Hiroshi Tanabe, Chief of Technical Processes, University of Tokyo General Library.

Usually the participants chosen for this program are young career men or women, preferably between the ages of 25 and 40, who are employed in libraries of genuine importance in the communities they serve. They may be public librarians, governmental librarians, or research librarians in university or technical libraries. They may be associated with publicly supported institutions or with libraries maintained by particular groups or organizations. The participants must have sufficient proficiency in English to benefit from the lectures, take part in discussions, and engage in fruitful technical conversation. As with all State Department programs, the recommendation of candidates for participation in programs comes from the Cultural Affairs Officer in the United States Embassy or Consulate in the foreign countries. This makes it possible for us to be assured that personal interviews have been had with the potential candidate, that his proficiency in English has been tested, and that the recommendations come from someone familiar with library needs of the country and with the particular candidate's qualifications and interests.

Similar in format to the Multi-National Group Program was a special program for Indian university librarians which the State Department supported on three occasions in the past. This program was made possible by money available under the India Wheat Loan Act, which explains its special attention to that subcontinent. It offered the same kind of seminar-internship-travel opportunity to selected university librarians from India, and was administered by the American Library Association. The last of these particular programs took place in 1961. Funds for this program are no longer available.

The second important group program for librarians sponsored by the State Department is known as the Jointly-Sponsored Librarian Project. This project is administered by the United States Library of Congress. Through this program the visiting librarian is afforded an opportunity to participate in library operations and to become acquainted with the philosophy, techniques, and administration of American library services. Under the sponsorship of a host library, he or she becomes temporarily a working member of an American community to observe American social, cultural, professional, economic, and political institutions. The host library is re-

sponsible for assigning the visitor to duties standard to the library profession with a view to giving him broad practical experience compatible with his background and training. The usual pattern of the program is for the participant to spend about ten days in Washington, D.C., in consultation with the State Department and the Library of Congress and to get a period of orientation at the Washington International Center. He then spends eleven months on the staff of the host library, followed by thirty days of travel in the United States to visit libraries in areas other than that to which he is assigned, to consult with colleagues, and to observe various aspects of American life.

Although this is called a group program, nominations for participation may be made whenever likely candidates become known, and each grantee's program is individually designed for him. Since the visitor is expected to participate fully in the activities of the host library and to be, to all intents and purposes, a member of the library staff, each candidate must have demonstrated professional ability, a substantial degree of experience, status as a librarian on the staff of a library in his own country, and fluency in spoken and written English.

The Jointly-Sponsored Program formerly brought from five to ten people to the United States in any single year, but the program is now slowing down. During 1966 a librarian from Thailand and a librarian from Guiana came to the United States under the Jointly-Sponsored Librarians Project. In 1967–68 Mr. Yoshitomi Okazaki of Hitotsubashi University, in the Tokyo area, was the only participant. (Mr. Okazaki came on a 1967 grant.) No funds were made available for this program in 1968. It seems doubtful that any funds will be allocated for this purpose in 1969.

Individual programs sponsored by the State Department are not selected for librarians, but librarians are eligible for them. One such program is called International Visitors Program, under which the Department attempts to select an outstanding leader or specialist in his profession for a short period of travel and observation in the United States. All visitors under this program are called "International Visitors," but a distinction is made in the administration of the program between a "leader" and a "specialist." A "leader" is someone with years of experience in librarianship, a position of considerable authority, and presumably with the full professional qualification in terms of education and experience. Such a person receives $30 per diem. A "specialist" is normally a person established in his field with capability for assuming top positions and influencing development in his home country. Here, too, it is assumed that he has had sufficient professional training and experience to understand American techniques. Because of his somewhat less exalted status in his position in his home country, the per diem for the "specialist" is $20.

The program is usually for two or three months of community placement for the visitor to study in depth activities in his specialized field and in addition to have some U.S. travel to relate to his own field of specialization. The number of foreign visitors who come to the United States either in the category of "leader" or "specialist" varies from year to year. Since they come under such a variety of programs for different lengths of time and to serve different individual purposes, they frequently do not travel through Chicago and may not be known to the American Library Association. Again, they are nominated for a grant by the U.S. Embassy or Consulate in their home countries.

Another familiar category of sponsored visitors in the United States under State Department auspices are the Fulbright fellows. This program was authorized in 1946 by the Fulbright Act, and was extended two years later by the Smith-Mundt Act to become fully operative in 1948. It, too, is administered by the Bureau of Educational and Cultural Affairs of the State Department and consists of a program of grants to individuals and institutions of learning. It is financed with dollar funds appropriated by the United States Congress. The program makes possible support for individuals who wish to study in the United States, to teach in the U.S. schools or study the U.S. educational system, to lecture in the United States, to do advanced research in the United States, or to get some practical training or experience in the professional field. Candidates for Fulbright support normally should be between the ages of 18 and 35, citizens of the country from which they are applying, and should have good academic background and command of English. Applications are made through the American Embassy or Consulate in the applicant's own country. Committees overseas composed of resident United States and local citizens review applications and nominate candidates for placement in colleges and universities in the United States. There is a Board of Foreign Scholarships which makes final selection of candidates.

Nongovernment Programs

Nongovernmental agencies, notably the private foundations, also frequently make study or travel grants to librarians or students of librarianship. Increasingly, however, the major foundations have tended to consider applications for such grants only when such a study or observation tour would contribute to a project in which they already have an interest. In other words, the foundations tend to support large-scale projects, of which the training of librarians or the development of library services is only a part. Where a foundation gives support to a university abroad, for example, it may very well make available some funds to support the study and travel of one or two persons who will contribute to the strengthening of the library services in that university. Individual study or travel grants to applicants who have no connection with an institution or agency which the foundation is supporting are seldom considered.

There are two exceptions to this general rule. One is a program of the Carnegie Corporation through which funds are provided to the African-American Institute, located in Washington and New York, to administer the travel of selected African nationals from Commonwealth countries. These individuals travel to the United

States, usually for observation, but may also come for academic study.

The other exception is the Organization of American States Program of Fellowships, which was created to provide advanced and specialized study and research abroad for those who have exhausted all sources in their own country of academic and professionalized or specialized study required by their profession, and is, of course, limited to citizens of the member states. Library science is one of the fields that is available under this program.

An example of a foundation supporting the travel of librarians closely associated with a project is the funding of a travel and observation program for four librarians of the Faculty of Exact and Natural Sciences at the University of Buenos Aires. Ford Foundation is supporting a program to strengthen this faculty. The American Library Association is administering a grant for the travel of four librarians from this faculty to the United States for a period of three months each. Two librarians have already visited the States, and two more will come during the next six months.

Many readers are familiar, I am sure, with the work of the Asia Foundation, which has done so much to assist libraries, library associations, and book programs in Asia. Smaller than some of the major foundations like Rockefeller and Ford, the Asia Foundation limits its attention to Asian countries, and tries to avoid duplicating work of other foreign and international assistance agencies, although it cooperates with such agencies on many occasions. It has placed its greatest stress on activity in Asia rather than in the United States. Thus travel grants make up a small part of its program, but it has occasionally given support to enable Asian delegates to attend international conferences concerned with educational and other fields within the range of its program interests. The Asia Foundation grants given to the American Library Association to make possible attendance at library meetings by Asian students studying in the United States are an example of this. They fall a bit outside the scope of this paper, but do

represent, in a limited way, an example of a sponsored tour for librarians to serve professional purposes.

The private foundations occasionally sponsor group as well as individual visits to the United States where such an arrangement will promote the objectives that the foundation wishes to support. An interesting example of this approach was the Rockefeller-supported project called the U.S. Field Seminar on Library References Services for Japanese Librarians. Under the sponsorship of the American Library Association's International Relations Office a group of nine young reference librarians from Japan spent three months in the United States in 1959 inspecting library services and facilities, talking with librarians, and participating in seven special seminars in seven different cities across the country.

Another interesting development is the recognition that the improvement of library services in any country needs the support and understanding of nonlibrarians as well as librarians. It is becoming increasingly clear that administrators of government departments and of universities are often the ones who will make the decisions affecting library services and that it may be desirable to expose such people to the philosophy and techniques of good library service. To that end, an occasional sponsored tour for nonlibrarians may be undertaken to promote a library program. As a case in point, in 1968 USAID sponsored a visit to the United States of the rectors and deans of the five major universities in Vietnam. These officials talked with educators and professional leaders. The Vietnamese visitors viewed library buildings and talked to librarians about library construction and the needs of Vietnam for trained librarians and library resources.

It seems probable that the attention paid to the value of sponsored tours will increase rather than diminish in the coming years. Many American librarians and administrators have testified to the value to American librarianship of such exchanges and have been urging increasing use of the talents and capabilities of professional people from other countries to enrich the practice and teaching of their subject matter in the United States. The comments and recommendations of the participants in this conference could have a constructive influence on the kind and extent of such programs that will be supported in the future.*

*Paper first published in a slightly different version in George S. Bonn, ed., *Library Education and Training in Developing Countries* (Honolulu: © East-West Center Pr., 1966).

Permission to reprint granted by the University Press of Hawaii.